CAMBRIDGE STUDIES IN
CRIMINOLOGY XLIV
General Editor: Sir Leon Radzinowicz

THE PHANTOM CAPITALISTS

*The Organisation and Control
of Long-Firm Fraud*

THE HEINEMANN LIBRARY OF CRIMINOLOGY
AND PENAL REFORM

CAMBRIDGE STUDIES IN CRIMINOLOGY

THE PHANTOM CAPITALISTS

The Organisation and Control
of Long-Firm Fraud

by

Michael Levi

 HEINEMANN   LONDON

Heinemann Educational Books Ltd
22 Bedford Square, London WC1B 3HH

LONDON EDINBURGH MELBOURNE AUCKLAND
HONG KONG SINGAPORE KUALA LUMPUR NEW DELHI
IBADAN NAIROBI JOHANNESBURG
EXETER (NH) KINGSTON PORT OF SPAIN

ISBN 0 435 82520 8

Publisher's note: This series is continuous with the
Cambridge Studies in Criminology, Volumes I to XIX,
published by Macmillan & Co., London

British Library Cataloguing in Publication Data

Levi, Michael
    The phantom capitalists. – (Cambridge studies in
    criminology; 44)
    1. Commercial crimes – England
    2. Fraud – England
    I. Title
    364.1'63'0942   HV6699.G7

    ISBN 0–435–82520–8

Photosetting by Thomson Press (India) Limited, New Delhi, India
Printed in England by Biddles Limited, Guildford, Surrey.

Contents

List of Tables

List of Figures

Statutes Cited (in chronological order)

Table of Cases Cited (name of defendant only)

(Full references are cited in the text.)

Acknowledgements

This research leaves in its wake a trail of irrecoverable debts as lengthy as that of a long-firm fraud. I am particularly grateful for the help and friendship of Laurie Harrop and Alf Kenyon of the Manchester Guardian Society for the Protection of Trade. Special thanks are due also to Richard Grobler, presently Deputy Circuit Administrator for courts in south-east England, for his general amiability and for providing me with such generous facilities to examine records and attend trials at the Old Bailey; to Detective Chief Superintendent Ray Connor and the Metropolitan and City Police Fraud Squad, who showed me how they worked although they knew that some uncomfortable conclusions about the policing of fraud might have to be drawn; to Marshall Palmer of the Court of Appeal (Criminal Division) and to the Lord Chancellor's Office, for permission to examine court records; to the Home Office Prison Department, for permitting me to interview prisoners; and last, but by no means least, to those members of the long-firm fraternity who, both inside and outside prison, gave of their time and, in some cases, of their friendship.

On the academic side, Roy King stimulated the development of some of the theoretical implications of this work, and Roger Hood and Terence Morris also made valuable critical contributions. I should like to thank my head of department here in Cardiff, Howard Jones, for his comments on my work and for not pointing out too often that this book has been 'forthcoming' ever since my appointment here in 1975. At least, unlike Billy Bunter's postal order, it finally has appeared! I gratefully received comments on the draft chapters I forced them to read from my colleagues Richard Jones, Dave Miers, Dave Reynolds, John Richardson, Lee Sheridan and Andy Willis. Much-needed thoughtful editorial advice was tendered by Sir Leon Radzinowicz. However, my prime debt of gratitude is to John P. Martin, without whose painstaking criticisms and attempts to keep me on the right research track this book might never have been completed.

I would also like to thank the following for kindly giving their permission to reproduce extracts from various publications quoted in this book:

The Accountant; Aldine Publishing Company; Basil Blackwell; The Free Press of Glencoe (Macmillan Publishing Company); Gee & Company; Penguin Books; Greenwood Press; Guardian Newspapers; Her Majesty's Stationery Office; Holt, Rinehart & Winston (Eastbourne and New York); Hutchinson General Books; John Clare; Little, Brown & Company; Michael Joseph; Oxford University Press; Pergamon Press; The Reprint Society (Macmillan); Stevens & Sons; Van Nostrand Reinhold Company.

Finally, my thanks to myself for the typing; to the College cleaning services for agreeing not to disturb my room over the past four and a half years; to the Heinemann editors, Robin Frampton and David Hill, for their work in preparing the manuscript; to my mother, for her continued encouragement and support; and to Penny, for her tolerance at home, her help with the proof-reading, and for designing and drawing all the diagrams in the book. I apologize to her and to all my friends for making them learn more about long-firm fraud than they ever wanted to know.

MICHAEL LEVI
UNIVERSITY COLLEGE, CARDIFF
JUNE 1981

Preface

Historically, the control of commercial fraud has been the Cinderella of the criminal justice system, attracting little police, prosecutorial, and media interest compared with other crimes, despite the fact that the losses involved in fraud are far greater than those arising from theft, burglary, and robbery. However, this situation has begun to change. In all advanced industrial nations, there are pressures upon governments and upon police forces to show that there is *not* 'one law for the rich and another for the poor'. Many Conservatives as well as socialists argue that the government should step in to remove, or at least to perform plastic surgery upon, 'the unacceptable face of capitalism'. Yet those who take commercial fraud seriously have found that its inaccessibility to normal crime intelligence networks, and the cumbersome quality of fraud investigations and trials, make it both difficult and expensive to 'bring fraudsters to justice'. And despite the growth of official interest in fraud control, its claims for increased resources have met with very limited success in societies such as Britain where the costs of dealing with crime are escalating continuously.

The regulation of commerce in capitalist countries is a major social issue, and already the 1980s have witnessed some important attempts to 'rationalise' the role of government and of the criminal law in this area. Since 1980, the Conservative government has sought to deregulate commerce by returning to the principles of the free market, of *caveat emptor* and of *caveat venditor*. Thus, its Companies (No. 2) Bill 1981 proposed to abolish the Registry of Business Names and to cease controls over the registration of company names that are similar to but not identical with existing company names, though the latter was modified after critical discussion in Parliament. The government has further proposed that bankruptcies should no longer be supervised by the State but should be left instead to individual creditors and to private liquidators. Debates upon these issues and upon non-government proposals to criminalise certain Stock Exchange practices have cut across simple class lines: deregulation has aroused greater opposition from major commercial interests than from the Left, for the former fear that *laissez-faire* may mean 'liberty to be "done"'. The heated clashes of opinion in the House of Lords over the Companies (No. 2) Bill 1981 indicate the wide divergences of view that exist over how much of the face of capitalism *is* unacceptable and over the role of the criminal law in the control of commercial activities.

The special difficulties posed by commercial frauds have led also to proposals to reform police powers and court procedures. Indeed, the absence of adequate powers to investigate fraud was one of the principal themes of the Association of Chief Police Officers Conference in June 1981, and the Royal Commission on Criminal Procedure[1] has recommended that under very limited circumstances, the police should be able to inspect evidence such as bank records *before* they commence criminal proceedings against an individual or a company. Conflicts between 'rationalists' and 'traditionalists' may be observed, for example in the accusation by the political head of the judiciary, Lord Hailsham, that the former Conservative Attorney-General, Lord Rawlinson, was 'too conservative with a small "c"' in his opposition to the abolition of the right to trial by jury in long and complicated *civil* cases such as those involving fraud and libel.[2] These limitations on the right to trial by jury were approved by the House of Lords but were rejected by the House of Commons. At present, then, there seems little prospect for proposals to abolish *criminal* fraud trials by jury (see Chapter XII of this book). However, their time may come.

The explosion of interest in crimes committed by and against businessmen may be fuelled too by the results of recent British and American research into public perceptions of the seriousness of different crimes. These studies indicate that commercial frauds are

---

[1]Royal Commission on Criminal Procedure, *Report* (London: H.M.S.O. 1981) para. 3.42. Para 3.43 states that

> the issuing authority should have to satisfy itself that the following conditions are met before making an order (for inspection):
>
> (a) other methods of investigation have been tried and failed, or must in the nature of things be bound to fail;
>
> (b) the nature of the items sought is specified with some precision;
>
> (c) reasonable grounds are shown for believing that the items will be found on the premises; and
>
> (d) reasonable grounds are shown for believing that the evidence will be of substantial value, and not merely incidental; that it will enable those responsible for a particular crime to be identified or the particulars of offences thought to have been committed by particular individuals to be determined.
>
> For the issue of a warrant, the following additional criteria should apply:
> either (a) a final order, after appeal, has been made and disobeyed,
> or (b) there is reason to believe that the evidence sought will be disposed of or disappear if there is delay or if the interest of the police in it becomes known.

[2]in the debate upon the Supreme Court Bill, 1981, *Parl. Debs.*, 2nd April 1981, et p. 323.

regarded more seriously than *any other non*-violent property crimes[3], and call into question our existing priorities in police and prosecution practices[4].

Although this book does not seek to encompass the entire spectrum of commercial fraud, it aims to illuminate in two principal ways. First, it is the only detailed criminological study in the English language of commercial credit fraudsters and of the agencies that attempt to control them. It thus makes a contribution to our understanding of the techniques, motivations, and of the social and criminal networks of a hitherto obscure set of criminals. And second, it relates the description and explanation of the world of commercial credit fraud to current and future debates about police powers, the criminal law, the system of trial, and sentencing policies. Although most of the original research was carried out in Britain, the experiences of other European countries and of the United States are incorporated into the analysis. The work thus addresses important issues of explanation and of policy that are of relevance to all commercial societies.

[3]For British studies, see the following:
  M. Levi, 'The seriousness of white-collar crimes: an empirical overview', (Unpublished research report, Cardiff, 1981);
  R. Sparks, H. Genn, and D. Dodd, *Surveying Victims*, (London: Wiley, 1977);
  M. Walker, 'Measuring the seriousness of crimes', *British Journal of Criminology*, 1978, **18**(4), pp. 348–364.
  For research in the United States, see the following:
  J. Conklin, *Illegal but not Criminal*, (Englewood Cliffs: Prentice-Hall, 1977);
  L. Schrager and J. Short, 'How serious a crime? Perceptions of organisational and common crimes', in G. Geis and E. Stotland (eds.) *White-Collar Crime* (Beverly Hills: Sage, 1980).
[4]K. Lidstone, R. Hogg, and F. Sutcliffe, *Prosecutions by Private Individuals and Non-Police Agencies*, (Royal Commission on Criminal Procedure Research Study No. 10, London: H.M.S.O., 1981).
  J. Conklin, op. cit., and *Criminology*, (New York: Macmillan, 1981).

I. Introduction

A merchant shall hardly keep himself from doing wrong, and a huckster shall not be freed from sin ... As a nail sticketh between the joinings of the stones, so doth sin stick close to buying and selling. (Ecclesiastes)

Criminology has been defined as the study of the 'processes of making laws, of breaking laws, and of reacting towards the breaking of laws' (Sutherland and Cressey, 1974, p. 3). This study represents an attempt to apply that conception of the task of criminology to a specific area of criminal behaviour, long-firm fraud. Although some criminals refer to *any* fraud in which they 'rob Peter to pay Paul' as a long-firm fraud, I shall restrict its use to the more conventional meaning of a business which orders substantial quantities of goods on credit at a time when the owners of the business either intend not to pay for them or suspect that, *as things stand at present*, they may not be *able* to pay for them. The restriction to frauds which obtain *goods* by fraud is analytically useful, because those who wish to obtain and dispose of large quantities of goods face rather different problems from those who wish to obtain and dispose of large sums of money.

Long-firm frauds are to be found in most western countries. They have been observed in the United States (Bequai, 1978, 1979; Cressey, 1969; De Franco, 1973; Edelhertz, 1970; Hoover, 1962; 1967; Kossack, 1964, 1965; Kossack and Davidson, 1966; and Teresa, 1973); in the United Kingdom (Lucas, 1969; Mack, 1975; and Payne, 1973); in Belgium (Kellens, 1974, 1977); in Germany (Mannheim, 1940; Tiedemann and Sasse, 1973); in France (Cosson, 1971); and in Sweden (Lithner, 1978). I have also been told of their existence in Switzerland and in some East and West African countries. Furthermore, it seems most unlikely that long-firm frauds are confined to those countries mentioned here. For wherever extensive use of credit is made in commercial transactions, long-firm frauds become feasible.

I have identified three principal sub-types of long-firm fraud:

(1) *pre-planned* frauds, which are businesses set up with the intention from the very beginning of defrauding suppliers;

(2) *intermediate* frauds, which occur when people decide to turn a

formerly legitimate business into one which defrauds its suppliers;

(3) *slippery-slope* frauds, which occur when businessmen continue to trade and obtain goods on credit although there is a high risk that unless their business situation improves greatly, they will be unable to pay for the goods. (The thought-processes entailed by this kind of situation are elaborated in Chapter V.)

The bulk of this book will be concerned with pre-planned frauds, but occasional reference will be made to the intermediate and slippery-slope types, since these illustrate interesting issues in the borderline between 'fraud' and 'legitimate' commercial conduct. As we shall see, it is often difficult to tell whether or not a long firm was planned as such from the outset since, as one expert practitioner expressed it to me, the art of the long-firm merchant is 'to go straight but with a twist'.

The volume of pre-planned long-firm fraud is very difficult to estimate, not least because it does not exist as a separate legal or official category. Informants in trade credit inquiry agencies state that during the past twelve years, the annual number of suspected long firms has ranged from 30 to 80, at an average cost to creditors of £12 million per annum at historic prices (that is, not taking into account price inflation). American estimates vary considerably: Glaser (1978, p. 466) observes that scams and bust-outs (the American terms for long-firm fraud) cost US creditors no less than $10 *billion* annually, while Bequai (1979, p. 87) gives the much lower estimate of $80 *million*. It is possible that Glaser's figure may include intermediate as well as pre-planned frauds, but in any event, I shall argue later that official figures are likely to understate both the number of such frauds and the losses sustained as a consequence of them. Data on the number of *convictions* in relation to long-firm frauds suffer even more from this 'hidden crime' factor. During the period 1962–72 inclusive, some 215 people were convicted at the London Central Criminal Court (the 'Old Bailey') for their involvement in long-firm frauds, and over the similar period of 1961–71, another 43 people were convicted for such frauds at Manchester Crown Court.

Long-firm fraudsters come from varied backgrounds. They include businessmen who have never before committed any substantial property crime (save perhaps tax evasion) as adults; business-men who have intermittently run legitimate businesses as well as frauds (whether simultaneously or consecutively); people who make their living principally from fraud; and people – from 'small-time thieves' to major 'gangsters' – who also participate in crimes other than fraud.

Since the 1950s, there has been a trend towards the involvement in long-firm fraud of people who are not purely business criminals, particularly in Britain, France and the United States. The Chief Constable of Northumbria sums up the situation nicely in his annual report for 1979, in which he observes that 'some members of the criminal fraternity have recognised the advantages of "white-collar crime"' and that convicted criminals with long records of a more conventional kind have moved into what for them is the less dangerous trade of long-firm fraud (*Guardian*, 18 April 1979).

Long-firm fraud offers us a crucible within which we can examine the social, moral and technical organization of commercial crime and of social reaction towards commercial crime. There are two main reasons why we should consider it to be of criminological as well as of social importance:

(1) because it provides a rare example of a crime committed by businessmen whose principal victims are large businesses rather than workers, consumers, small businessmen or investors;

(2) because the people who commit it possess far more heterogeneous backgrounds than do most convicted adult property criminals. This offers us an unusually wide range of motivations for and organizational techniques of crime, as well as guidance concerning the impact of social status upon the processing of those who commit the 'same type of crime'.

The fact that, unlike most types of commercial and 'white-collar' crime committed by businessmen (rather than by employees), long-firm fraud represents an offence by 'the little man' against larger corporations makes it particularly intriguing to examine the extent to which it is treated as 'real' crime. As we shall see, it appears that numerous psychological, legal and organizational obstacles have to be overcome in order for the label of 'criminal' to be attached to any businessman, even when that businessman is as unwelcome to capitalists as is a long-firm merchant. I use the word 'unwelcome' advisedly, because, although no modern economy could function without the extensive use of credit, the long-firm fraudster only benefits himself and those businessmen to whom he resells his goods: long-firm goods are seldom sold to final consumers at anything like the low prices generally asked for 'hidden economy' goods, for example, 'things that have fallen off the back of a lorry'. And whereas people generally replace (with the insurance money) the goods that are burgled from their homes, the goods obtained by long-firm fraudsters do not have any such stimulating effect on the output of producers. Furthermore, in so far as the fear of becoming the victim of a long-firm fraud induces caution in the granting of credit, long firms may depress the volume of trade generally. In brief, long-firm frauds lead neither to the benefit of capitalism nor to the 'socialist' redistribution of wealth to the poor in the shape of cheap stolen property.

This study is the first empirical application to the study of 'substantial property crime' in Britain of the ideas advocated by A. K. Cohen (1977) and McIntosh (1975, 1976, who argue that criminologists should focus their attention on the ways in which 'crime' is moulded by the contours of social organization in general and by the system of policing in particular. I will seek to emphasize throughout the interaction between the practical organization of 'the underworld', the commercial world and criminal justice agencies, in a way that is absent from the few existing British studies of major property crime. For example, the thorough work of McClintock and Gibson (1961) tells us little about the social or technical organization of robbery in London, nor does it map out its social control. (For two very different approaches to the filling of these gaps, see the excellent journalists' account of armed robbery by Ball *et al.* (1978), and the powerful Marxian analysis of social reaction to 'mugging' by Hall *et al.* (1978).) The otherwise illuminating work of Mack (1964, 1970, 1975, 1976) takes for granted existing frameworks of social control and tells us little about offenders as people or about the practical organization of the police and the courts, except in so far as they affect the acquittal rates of 'professional criminals'. Probably the closest parallels to this study are the penetrating analyses of pilfering by Ditton (1977) and of 'amateur fencing' by Henry (1976, 1978), although it should be noted that pre-planned long-firm frauds are generally regarded as unambiguously 'criminal', in contrast to crimes in the workplace, which tend to be viewed more as 'perks' than as 'crimes'. (More detailed comparisons are made in later chapters.)

This book can be read as if it were in three main parts. The first part – Chapters II–V inclusive – examines the history of long-firm fraud and the social, moral and technical aspects of the world inhabited by long-firm fraudsters. The second part – Chapters VI–X – examines the social control process, from credit control through law-making and law enforcement to the sentencing process. The third and final part offers a theory of the genesis, organization and control of long-firm fraud, and critically analyses some of the implications of the study for the social control of commercial crime. It might have been more *theoretically* coherent to place the second part before the first, on the grounds that one can only comprehend the conduct or even the existence of 'criminals' within the context set by law-makers and law-enforcers. However, it will be easier to understand the study of social reaction to long-firm fraud when one first knows something about the people who practise it and the techniques they employ. Hence, my ordering of the chapters in this particular way.

The organization of long-firm fraud: some preliminary analyses

Although this section will be elaborated in the next few chapters, readers may find it useful to orient themselves by the following synopsis of the organization of long-firm fraud, the underlying assumption of which is that we can only understand the organization of crime by examining the problems that intending criminals confront in any given society at any given moment in time. A would-be long-firm fraudster has two principal concerns and one important but slightly subsidiary one. He must be able to obtain goods on credit and he must be able to dispose of those goods before his creditors can get their money or their goods back. He must also seek to minimize the risk of being convicted for his activities. A number of ways exist by which these aims may be realized.

(1) In the case of slippery-slope fraud the individual already has access to goods on credit and to trade outlets for their resale. These are identical to his normal trading partners. From the point of view of personnel organization, the slippery-slope fraud is no different from any ordinary business in a similar field. A crucial difference between the long-firm fraud and 'ordinary' property crime is that as far as buyers are concerned, the 'fraudster' has a legitimate title to the goods he is seeking to resell. Hence, he does not need to find a buyer who is prepared to purchase goods that he knows to be stolen: the resale transactions can be negotiated 'as if' they were normal and lawful ones. The sale need not even be accomplished by the 'ambiguous presentation' which Henry (1978) observes to be the norm when pilfered goods are resold: genuine invoices can be given by the long-firm merchant. The only technical problem for the slippery-slope fraudster, then, is the avoidance of conviction, and this is dealt with in later chapters.

(2) Organizationally, there is no need for intermediate fraud to be any different from the slippery-slope fraud. In practice, however, intermediate frauds may be run with the assistance of others who are

better versed than the original owner of the business in the art of long-firm fraud. In such cases, extra cash may be injected from 'criminal sources' to provide a base for building up more credit, and the goods may be resold through outlets that know that the business is a long firm as well as through pre-existing trade outlets.

(3) In the case of pre-planned fraud, too, there is no need for any organizational differentiation when compared with legitimate business. *Any* person may set up a business, start purchasing goods on credit, and resell them. There may be no need to become involved with members of 'the underworld' in order to do this. When there is *no* such contact, I have used the descriptive term 'businessman-fraud'. On the other hand, many pre-planned frauds do enjoy a high degree of organizational differentiation, largely to reduce the risks of identification and conviction for the principal organizers. These long firms are referred to subsequently as 'villain-frauds', to distinguish their exponents from 'businessman-frauds' in terms of social status and prior criminal involvements.

In 'villain-frauds', the following functionally distinct roles exist, (even though the same individual may fill a number of them):

(a) the *backer*, who puts up the money to finance the fraud;
(b) the *organizer*, who selects the people to help him run the fraud and who generally directs operations from the background;
(c) the *minder*, who is put in by the backer (and/or the organizer) to protect his interests and to make sure that his instructions are carried out by the others;
(d) the *front man*, who nominally owns the business and who is expected to 'take the rap' if a criminal prosecution arises from the fraud;
(e) the *fence*, who purchases the goods from the long firm, though strictly speaking, those businessmen who believe that they are buying goods lawfully in the ordinary course of trade should not be called 'fences', since they lack the requisite 'guilty knowledge'.

This is not an exhaustive list of the organizational roles. On occasions, there may be further subdivisions. For example, there may be a *blower man*, whose specialism is to order goods on the telephone and to answer inquiries; a *placer*, whose job it is to find purchasers for the long firm's goods; or a *torch artist*, a professional arsonist hired to set fire to the long firm's business premises, thus allowing the fraudsters to claim that the goods had never been sold. The criminal organization of 'villain-frauds' is far more complex than that of 'businessman-frauds', where the organizers are their own 'front men' and hence do not need 'minders' to look after their own interests, and where the organizers are often able to resell their goods without telling the purchasers that they are running a fraud. It is clear, then, that the expression 'long-firm fraudster' can refer to any one of a number of very different 'sorts of person'.

Generally, long-firm frauds require some initial capital to get them off the ground, and the principal sources of such finance are the organizers themselves, 'bent' bank managers, shady businessmen with 'black money' that they have hidden from the tax authorities, retired or currently active 'big-time criminals' and the intending purchasers of the long firm's goods. One former leading American mobster (Teresa, 1973) claims that large numbers of doctors, dentists and businessmen with 'black money' are delighted to seize upon opportunities for further enrichment by unlawful means. (This may be even more true as inflation reduces the real purchasing power of money that cannot be invested legitimately.)

The goods obtained by long-firm fraudsters are resold through the following major routes:

(a) wholesale or retail businesses owned or controlled by the backer and/or organizer;
(b) independent wholesalers who run businesses that are part legitimate, part 'fencing' operation;
(c) 'placers', who receive a 'cut' or a fee in exchange for finding trade outlets for the goods;
(d) wholly legitimate businessmen, who purchase the goods direct from the long firm in the belief that they are buying legitimately obtained stock from a 'normal' business;
(e) a network of small businesses and street traders;
(f) any combination of the above.

A crude organizational typology of long-firm frauds from the perspective of an organizer is set out overleaf.

It is important to note, however, that in all types of long firm, the suppliers of goods on credit are the main financiers. The category of 'source of finance' in the table's typology refers to the capital required to get any business to the stage where it can build up a 'reasonable' amount of credit.

Finally, in this introduction to the organization of long-firm fraud, one may identify four principal *modus operandi* of pre-planned frauds. Three of these are variations on a similar theme, and are labelled accordingly.

(1a) Those in which one or more persons set up a new firm or

TABLE 1.1 A basic organizational typology of long-firm frauds

Roles filled and persons involved	*Type of long firm*			
	slippery-slope	intermediate	pre-planned businessman-fraud	pre-planned villain-fraud
Front man	self	self	self	other
Minder	none	usually none	none	usually
Organizer	self	self/criminal	self	self
Source of finance	self/bank	self/bank/criminal	self/bank	self/other
Purchaser of goods	other, often without guilty knowledge	other, either with or without guilty knowledge	as intermediate	self/other usually with, but sometimes without, guilty knowledge

limited company, gradually building up a good credit rating by paying debts reasonably promptly for a while, before extending considerably the amounts purchased on credit and making 'the kill'.

(1b) Those in which one or more persons set up a new firm or limited company, order small amounts of goods on credit, paying for the first few orders if necessary. They provide as their references non-existent firms which purport to trade but in fact are mere accommodation addresses. In other words, the long firmers write their own credit references, thereby inducing the credit required to operate the long firm.

(1c) Those in which a group of people set up a number of actual trading firms or companies, which build up good credit ratings by prompt payment of bills and which support each other with good trade credit references. Then, at the end of the planned life of the fraud, the whole group collapses, leaving behind a series of assetless shells.

(2)   Those in which one or more persons purchase an existing perfectly respectable firm or limited company, preferably on credit terms, and then, usually without informing suppliers of the change in ownership, obtain extensive credit on the basis of the former owner's reputation before finally absconding with the proceeds.

The matters mentioned in this introductory chapter will be expounded in detail in the next four chapters, and form the background against which the social control of long-firm fraud is organized. As we shall see in the remaining chapters, the social control of long-firm fraud modifies in turn the extent and the *modus operandi* of long-firm frauds themselves. The description and analysis of this feedback process is one of the principal themes of this book.

Sources of information used in this study

A more detailed account of the research methodology I adopted and some of the theoretical difficulties connected with it are contained in Appendix A. However, even those readers who are uninterested in issues of method should be aware of the evidence on which my findings are based, for they will doubtless want to know what credibility they can attach to them.

At the most general level, I have chosen to adopt an 'appreciative' stance towards *all* the subjects of my research, though I have tried to relate the views and perspectives of my subjects to broader considerations such as the borderline between 'fraud' and 'legitimate business'. I have followed Cohen and Taylor (1972), Henry (1978) and Weber himself in suggesting that there is no innate incompatibility between carrying out *verstehen* sociology (an approach which seeks to describe the world as seen by the subjects of the research) and discussing penal policy in the light of that analysis. Official agencies (or academic critics of various political persuasions) may seek to cast doubt upon the scientific quality of research and policy analysis which threaten their existing ways of dealing with 'deviant populations', but that is another matter. Readers are quite free to recast my penal policy discussions in Chapter XII within their own ideological framework. Indeed, I have no doubt that they will do so.

Unlike most contemporary criminologists and sociologists, I have sought to appreciate the perceived problems and working perspectives of both fraudsters and social control agencies such as the police and trade protection societies. Chapter II, which sets out the history of long-firm fraud, was culled from books, journals, law reports, newspaper articles, and from the examination of the transcripts of *all* cases tried at the Old Bailey in London between 1850 and 1872 and between 1898 and 1910 (when the transcripts ended). Chapters III, IV and V, which set out the techniques of fraud and the fraudster's moral, social and operational world, were based on interviews with a number of convicted fraudsters, a few unconvicted ones, dozens of businessmen, officers of the Metropolitan and some provincial police Fraud Squads, and commercial credit inquiry agencies.

The majority of the fraudsters to whom I spoke were in prison, where I was able to interview them in reasonable privacy. Clearly, this does not represent an ideal location – particularly for them – for research on professional crime, but I would justify my interviews there on two principal grounds (for more extensive discussion, see Appendix A).

First, I assured each person that I was not in a position to help him either financially or in terms of parole. This assurance was given greater credibility by my youth and lowly status! The six organizers and three 'front men' whom I originally selected were asked in advance if they wished to talk to me: only one refused, on the grounds that he was upset about his sentence. Of the remaining eight, only two were in a position where they were likely to be considered for parole in the near future.

Secondly, although – by definition – a sample drawn from prison will almost invariably contain a disproportionate number of incompetent criminals, at the time of my study, there were a number of highly skilled fraudsters in prison who had been caught out either by sudden improvements in police efficiency or by the clean-up within the Metropolitan Police which followed Sir Robert Mark's appointment as Commissioner.

I also interviewed three retired fraudsters *outside* prison, with one of whom I became particularly friendly and who gave me what I hope is reasonable insight into the world of fraud. I was also given information by friends of fraudsters about their friends, although they did not want me to approach them directly: I have explicitly mentioned in the text when I have quoted their indirect remarks.

It may be argued that my interviewees are a small and unrepresentative sample. However, I do not claim that I have uncovered a representative sample of motives for and routes to fraud, though I came across wide variations on both of these dimensions. My hope is that I have illuminated at least part of the setting within which fraud takes place, on the basis of a sample much larger than that of most studies of 'professional crime' in England or America.

Chapter VI, which deals with credit control, is based on extensive discussions with people in the two principal commercial credit inquiry agencies in the UK – the Manchester Guardian Society for the Protection of Trade, and Dun & Bradstreet Ltd – as well as a number of company credit controllers and smaller credit inquiry and debt collection agencies. Chapters VIII and IX are based on interviews with police officers, mainly those in the Metropolitan and City Police Fraud Squad; with officials from the Department of Trade and from the Office of the Director of Public Prosecutions; with solicitors and barristers; and on the observation of four trials at the Old Bailey – two in full and two in part – over a period of seven months. And Chapter X is based on an exhaustive documentary study of long-firm frauds tried at the Old Bailey between 1948 and 1972 and at Manchester Crown Court between 1961 and 1971, supplemented by interviews with two judges about the sentencing of long-firm fraudsters.

In a broad-ranging study of this kind, carried out by one researcher on a meagre grant, there are inevitably some issues that would repay study in greater depth. (Of what study is this not so?) However, I have taken all reasonable steps to check those data that are capable of being tested, and to obtain comments on drafts of these chapters both from the people I interviewed and from others in the 'same line of business'. For example, draft chapters on policing and the control of fraud were sent to senior provincial officers for their comments. A few people did not reply to the material I sent them: they have only themselves to blame if there is anything published here to which they take exception. In the comments of others were some minor criticisms which led me to modify the text when I considered them justified. I promised anonymity to those who wanted it, and I have sought to keep my faith with them, occasionally at the expense of the reader who might prefer me to 'name the names' and to maintain a consistent narrative. I have tried to build up and reproduce a picture of the organization and control of what, to me, is the fascinating world of long-firm fraud. I can only hope that it is as interesting to read about as it was to research.

II. History of Long-Firm Fraud in England until the Second World War

The etymological origin of the term 'long-firm fraud' is obscure. Dr Johnson (1773) observed that 'long' is an adverb meaning 'by the fault; by the failure. A word now out of use, but truly English'. *Gelang* was the old Saxon word for fraudulent, and this could be its source. It is possible that if one puts together this meaning of 'long' and the early usage of 'firm' as 'signature', this could account for 'long-firm fraud' as being a fraud based on false signatures for orders. However, it should be noted that 'firm' does not appear in Dr Johnson's dictionary as a noun meaning 'business'.

The first trace of the *term* 'long-firm fraud' that I have been able to find is on 2 January 1869, in a periodical called *The Orchestra*. The article refers to 'the doings of the "long-firm", a body of phantom capitalists who issue large orders to supply an infinite variety of goods'. Thereafter, the expression appears with some regularity. In *The Slang Dictionary* (1874), Hotten defines the long firm as 'A gang of swindlers who obtain goods by false pretences. They generally advertise or answer advertisements'. Fredur (1879), a writer for the *Pall Mall Gazette*, discusses the *modus operandi* of the long firms, their professionalism, and the fact that those of them who end up in court are but a small segment of the 'octopus-like' structure of the firm.

The *Oxford English Dictionary* quotes Ogilvie (1882) as having defined the long firm as 'that class of swindlers who obtain goods by pretending to be in business at a certain place and ordering goods to be sent to them, generally from persons at a distance, without any intention of payment'. The *Daily News* (20 September 1886) referred to one case as follows:

> This was the usual case of what is termed long-firm swindling. The prisoner pretended to carry on business in the city, and ordered goods of all descriptions, which were never used for legitimate purposes but which were immediately pawned or otherwise disposed of.

In the *Dictionary of Slang, Jargon, and Cant*, Barrere and Leland (1897) define a long firm as 'an association of swindlers who pretend to be a solvent firm of traders'. They add that the long firm is called *bande noire* by the French, although they do not state whether this refers to indigenous French fraudsmen or merely to British ones working abroad. Finally, in *The Encyclopaedic Dictionary* (1909), the long firm is defined as 'a party of swindlers who obtain goods on credit, which they immediately dispose of, moving from place to place to avoid detection. The epithet probably has reference to the number of persons engaged in such nefarious pursuits'.

It is clear, then, that the term 'long firm', was in fairly common use from the late 1860s onwards, though it was defined as a class of *individuals* rather than as a class of *activity*.

The activity of obtaining goods under the false pretence that one had a solvent and honest business may go back to the time of Henry VIII. For in 1543 an act was passed (34 & 35 Hen. VIII, c. 4) whose preamble referred as follows:

> For as much as many light-hearted and evil disposed persons not intending to get their living by truth according to the laws of this realm, but compassing and devising daily how they may unlawfully obtain and get into their hands and possession money, goods, cattels, and jewels of other persons for the maintenance of their unthrifty living, and also knowing that they being lawfully convicted thereof according to the laws of this realm, shall die therefore, have now of late falsely and deceitfully contrived devised and imagined privy tokens and counterfeit letters in other names unto divers persons, their special friends and acquaintances for the obtaining of goods, cattels and jewels into their hands and possession, contrary to right and conscience.

However, the first law case resembling a long-firm fraud that I have been able to find is that of *R. v. Hevey, Beatty and McCarthy* (1782), 168 ER 218. In this case, which appears to be a precursor of later forms of long-firm fraud, the defendants were indicted

> For that they...did fraudulently and unlawfully confederate, conspire, and agree that Richard Beatty should write his acceptance of a certain paper-writing purporting to be a Bill of Exchange...and thereby fraudulently to obtain from the King's subjects goods and monies: and that they, he the said Samuel Read the elder, of his goods and monies did deceive, cheat, and defraud, against the Peace of our Lord the King, his Crown and Dignity.

Beatty had been in business previously as a ballast-heaver; Hevey was an insolvent debtor who had been liberated from the King's Bench Prison during the riots of 1780; and McCarthy was a poor man who had absconded from St Giles. Their *modus operandi* was analogous to that of the American big confidence tricksters discussed by Maurer (1940) in its use of a phoney place of business.

They set up two business houses, one of which was a counting house (an early form of bank or discount house). They had 500 bills of exchange printed, and Hevey would offer them in payment for the goods he purchased, suggesting to vendors that they check the validity of his bills with the counting house. When vendors went to the counting house, they would observe Beatty hard at work there, apparently carrying out the duties of a clerk, and he would assure them of the bona fides of Hevey's bills. Then, before the bills of exchange matured, the parties would abscond. Lacking the corruption and the dishonesty for the original transactions characteristic of big cons, they were convicted, but only after they had obtained considerable quantities of rum, brandy, watches and other merchandise.

Similar frauds (although on a far larger scale) were operated by one Richard Coster (Pelham, 1841, vol. 2, pp. 370 ff.). Coster was a man of poor origins, who dealt in horses and apples as well as receiving stolen goods. In 1810, he started up business in Bristol as a general agent and discounter of bills of exchange, and in that same year he was acquitted on a charge of obtaining goods by false pretences. He later moved to London, where he worked as a job-broker and clerk. In 1825, by destroying all the evidence against him, he succeeded in obtaining another acquittal, this time on charges of conspiracy to defraud and obtaining bills of exchange by false pretences. (His partner was less fortunate, being sentenced to transportation.) He became a Freemason under a false name, and under different names in different premises, he owned a feather-bed factory, a wharf, and businesses dealing in bills of exchange, bullion and coral, all of which changed their addresses frequently.

Coster used the (naturally) excellent references from his other genuine trading firms to obtain goods on credit from home and abroad. In this way, he obtained the entire stock of a celebrated German wine-grower, a large quantity of Dublin stout (beer) and a large stock of timber, as well as general merchandise. The combination of physical distance and false names minimized the risks of detection and active prosecution, particularly in an age of poor and erratic communications. Furthermore, as Pelham (1841, p. 371) points out

> The number of his aliases and the impossibility of identifying his person, secured him from the consequences of arrest, for in no transaction did he ever appear personally to complete the terms of his contract, or to give any security for repayment. All this was done through the medium of agents, whom he had bound to himself by some ties of more than ordinary firmness, and who

acted either as principal or agent, as purchaser or referee, as the necessities of the case might require their employment. To these persons, who were mostly decayed tradesmen, he behaved with little generosity. They were retained at salaries ranging from ten to twenty shillings per week, according to the extent of their usefulness; and he scrupled not, whenever an opportunity presented itself, to cheat them out of their stipulated share of the plunder which he might procure.

Then as now! Not only did Coster specialize in long-firm frauds but he also sent forged notes in payment when this was required in advance of delivery. In the end, one of his men fell into a trap set for him and was arrested when picking up some goods sent to an alias. Coster was discovered to be the 'brains' of the scheme and, unfortunately for him, the letter ordering the goods was found to be in his handwriting. Two of his minions were induced to give evidence against him, and on 16 April 1833 he was sentenced to transportation for life.

The general pattern of long-firm swindling during the nineteenth century is well attested by the cases tried at the Old Bailey in London. Prior to 1850, almost all the cases prosecuted fell into two categories.

(1) The business would operate normally, except that the firm would go bankrupt – a large number of bills of exchange remaining unpaid – and the proceeds of the sale of goods would not be declared at the bankruptcy examination for the benefit of the creditors but would be secreted away by the bankrupt. In these cases, the trader would be indicted 'for that he, having been declared a bankrupt did conceal part of his personal estate to the value of £10 and upwards'. Although it is difficult to tell, it appears that these cases were not 'pre-planned' frauds from their inception, but rather they were the reactions of traders to the ruin which expected bankruptcy would bring in its wake.

(2) A trader would claim some renowned market for the goods he wished to purchase on credit, for example, in 1836 one man claimed that the goods were urgently required overseas by Sir John Byng. Depending on the commercial competence and contacts of the fraudster, the goods would then be sold off through normal channels or be pawned for cash, never to be collected. Indeed, 'villains' frequently were caught pledging the goods they had just bought or with the pawn tickets in their jackets. In the latter cases, though it is not stated specifically thus, one may presume that, having got rid of the goods to and having been paid by the pawnbroker, the fraudster would try to find a buyer for them and, if successful, would redeem

the pledges. If this were not the case, there seems no reason for the keeping of the pawn ticket, which would provide evidence of guilt.

The comparative rarity of prosecutions for long-firm fraud before 1850 is evidenced by the fact that out of 3475 cases tried at the Old Bailey during 1836, only two were long firms. One cannot deduce that long firms themselves were uncommon then, for many may have remained undetected or unprosecuted, but the examination of all the prosecuted cases reveals that the most common type of frauds in this period were 'short cons'. A servant would come into a shop or warehouse and take goods on the pretext that they were for his master. The goods would then be pawned immediately. Or a man would bring to a wholesaler or manufacturer customers of good repute, show them around, and subsequently would get goods on credit on the false pretence that they were for his clients, whereas in fact they were for himself. In many of these cases, reference is made to the person having been driven to crime by extreme poverty.

After 1850, prosecutions, for long-firm fraud became far more common than they had been hitherto, and they received some public comment. For example, Mayhew (1862, vol. IV, pp. 388–90) states

> Large quantities of goods are sent from the provinces to parties in London, who give orders and are entirely unknown to those who send them, and fictitious references are given, or references in town connected with them... A considerable traffic in commercial swindling in various forms is carried on in London. Sometimes fraudulently under the name of another well-known firm; at other times under the name of a fictitious firm.

These long firms were not confined to London, for Mayhew discusses in detail one carried out at Droylesden, near Manchester.

A study of the transcripts of *all* cases tried at the Old Bailey during the period 1850–1872 reveals that, during that period, 80 people were convicted of involvement in long-firm frauds. In addition, 19 were acquitted of such involvements: one of these was an accused conspirator, but the others were dismissed on the grounds that no criminal offence had been proved to have been committed. This is connected with the legal difficulties encountered by prosecutions under the False Pretences Act of 1757, discussed in Chapter VII (and, in greater depth, in Levi, 1979, ch. 5).

In some instances, long-firm frauds are carried out in the kind of abstract setting mentioned above by Mayhew. In others, however, they operate by means of the abuse of *personal* trust. For example, supposedly independent agents would 'set up' suppliers to sell goods to swindlers who – unknown to the suppliers – were their confederates. One of the earliest such cases prosecuted was tried in 1852.

(The cases discussed hereafter are taken from the transcripts generously made available to me by Richard Grobler, former Clerk at the Old Bailey.)

A man called Henry Keene, who had worked for a large corn firm, went to a corn-factor whom he knew and told him that he would recommend him to some good customers, who would buy his flour. In evidence, the factor said:

> I told him to bring no customers but those he knew; he said he would bring me none but the very best. I met him soon after in the corn-market, and he recommended Jerrard to me. I asked if he was a man of property and trustworthy; and he said 'yes' he had known him for many years and he had always paid uncommonly well.

Jerrard came along to see the factor later with a prosperous-looking man called Nicholls, who said that he would lend Jerrard £50* to pay for some goods. In fact, they both ran bakers' shops, which used the flour and oats that they obtained on credit. The business was transacted in the (appropriately named) Mark Lane. Jerrard said he would pay for the goods the next week and when he could not be found – he was in jail for civil debt – Nicholls said that payment had nothing to do with him. Keene was later arrested in Gloucester, doing a similar swindle under a different name. (Further evidence of the geographical mobility of commercial criminals.)

It was discovered later that the goods invoiced to Jerrard had been sent on to Nicholls, the driver having been given a substantial tip to keep his mouth shut, and that the oats had been sold to a dealer in the Old Kent Road for 80 per cent of their invoice value. Keene had at one time rented a shop at Maidstone for a week, installed an accomplice under the name 'O. Watkins & Co.', and ordered two chaff machines from a firm in Reading, asking them to be forwarded to Paddington for collection. The police stated in court that there was a team of 14 arrant swindlers working together on various projects, which more than rivals present-day teams of villains.

Of a slightly less sophisticated, but still professional nature, was the fraud carried out in the same year by Henry Gerhardt and Thomas Hogg. They used each other as referees, having rented premises and represented to the suppliers that they were going to improve them, and got ale, boots, flour and groceries on credit. They used false names, since as one supplier stated when asked if it was on Hogg's representation that he had given Gerhardt credit:

*All sums in this Chapter are at 19th Century prices.

> No, I would not have given credit unless I had had that character – I would not have given Gerhardt credit if I had known his name was Gerhardt – certainly not, because that name was well known to me, as having appeared frequently before me in the 'Trade Protection Circular', in the Swindler's List.

Gerhardt had previously been sentenced in 1847 to twelve months' imprisonment for fraud, and was well known in the trade. His practice was to pay for a small amount, and then to 'pay' for the larger order with a bill of exchange, which was valueless. By offering the hope that he would want still larger orders in the future, he induced suppliers to give him credit: 'He should want rather a large amount, but as he was going to alter and beautify the premises, he should want but a small quantity now'. This has always been a clever way of disarming people who might otherwise be suspicious, as the carrot of supplying large quantities in the future makes the supplier eager to open up a potentially profitable connection.

In some cases of this period more complex situations occurred, in which people who had traded – to all appearances legitimately – for some time were accused of fraud. In one case, a textiles merchant who had been trading for two years resold goods for 50–66 per cent within days of purchasing them. When a creditor who had known him for some years went to see him about a renewed bill, he said:

> You shall be made right tomorrow, but the fact is, I am going to make a *smash* of it – I said 'Indeed, and to what amount?' – he said 'It will be such a *smash* as has not occurred in London for some time, it will be at least £10 000; it is a bad job, and I shall start off for Australia, for I shall never face my friends again.'

Since the creditor in question was not in fact paid, one cannot necessarily believe this evidence, but his timing of goods purchased was certainly well thought out. Indeed, where extended credit by bills of exchange at three months is given, the losses can be easily compounded by placing large orders before the previous bill is due.

Some individuals sought to exploit apparent loopholes in international law to escape conviction. For example, for twenty years, Messrs. Braun and Kortoske acted as an intermediary purchaser of textiles for a Canadian firm, English businesses being unwilling to trade direct with foreigners. Then, in 1861, they suddenly set up their own Canadian business, and supplied it with £36 000 of goods that year, comprising large amounts from existing suppliers and £12 000 from 62 new suppliers. One man, who lost £1000 was more cautious than some:

> 1860 was the first time we dealt with them as commission agents, and the goods were all paid for – I had no more difficulty, when I

first went, in selling the goods than I have with anyone else – I found no greater readiness to buy goods until the end of August – I went one day and they gave me an order for 30 pieces of black cloth, which I never solicited – I then began to be cautious and never sold them any more because they were bought in a very loose manner, such as no man, who meant to pay for the goods, would have done.... I had gone to them for, I think, ten years, but I could never sell them any goods till 1861.

After lengthy wrangles in court, the prosecution was allowed to proceed on one count, the rest being bad in law, and the accused were convicted. Braun was recommended to mercy by the assignees, on the grounds that he was acting under Kortoske's influence and he was given two months imprisonment, Kortoske receiving twelve months. This *modus operandi* was common in the 1860s, reflecting the growth of international trade.

Changes in commercial structure between the mid-nineteenth century and today are also mirrored in the organisation of fraud. For example, the more personalised system of commercial contacts which existed in earlier periods was paralleled by a far greater degree of abuse of *personal* trust as a component of long-term fraud than one generally observes today. This was manifested in two main ways: in deliberate conspiracies between a supposedly impartial agent and a long-firm, the former recommending the latter to his contacts; and in the exploitation by a fraudster of an agent's or a supplier's personal trust in him. The latter sometimes had extremely tragic consequences, for agents were driven into bankruptcy or even to suicide when they used their good names to obtain goods for fraudsters whom they believed to be honest.

There were many other cases of international long-firm frauds in the latter half of the nineteenth century. One ingenious pair of fraudsters engaged (apparently) in trade between England and Australasia obtained goods from both countries on Bills of Exchange which were dishonoured, and also money from the shippers of goods from the discounting of invoices for goods which were never delivered.

In this selection of cases from amongst the many, I have attempted to characterise the major methods by which long-firm frauds were organised in the middle of the nineteenth century. Although this illustrates the organisation of crime, it is more difficult to assess the relationships between criminals at this time. Instances occur in which a man at his trial is stated by the police to be one of a gang of swindlers, but much of the background organisation does not appear in the trial transcripts. Then, as now, the shadowy figures who may instruct the 'front men' and 'fence' the goods remain unprosecuted or, if prosecuted, the evidence against them is often insufficiently strong to justify conviction. Fredur (1879) provides an intriguing guide to some aspects of this background organisation, but one does not know how far his description of long firms as organised by a centralised organisation – the Long Firm – is valid on a national basis. It appears more likely that there is a whole spectrum of organisational formats ranging from the loner who pawns the few goods he is able to get to the syndicated crime model that Fredur espouses.

Rollo Reuschel (1895), the London correspondent of the German *Koelnische Volkszeitung*, gives us a fascinating perspective on the ambience of long-firm fraud. (I should point out that 'sledge-driving', a synonym for long-firm fraud, is a literal translation of the German 'schlitten-fahrer', whose etymology is unknown to me.) Reuschel states that

> Twice a year, the London sledge-drivers hold their 'International Congress', and the worthy proprietors of the leading long firms decide upon their common action for the coming season. From time to time they visit Germany too in order to get connections. Their honest mien, their manners and appearance, their liberality in spending money on good dinners and champagne, dazzle their chosen victims, who do not wake from their trance until they are caught by a heavy loss, that their amiable visitor and customer, the proprietor of 'that leading London firm', was nothing more or less than – a German sledge-driver. [p. 25]

The implication here is that long-firm fraudsmen are fairly loosely organized into a federated body, in a crude parallel of the modern conception of American syndicates. There is no doubt as to which is the strongest link in the chain fraud:

> A most important person is the 'sharper', usually a 'respectable City firm', exporting goods to Australia, India, the Cape, and other British colonies. He is nothing better than a receiver of stolen property, who disposes of the goods obtained by fraud from the manufacturers by the sledge-drivers. The sharpers are very careful to conduct their shady business in such a manner as not to come into conflict with the law. Whatever they pay for the goods, and if it be the tenth part only of the real value, they always insist on getting a receipt for an amount representing the current market price of the commodity they buy, and they never make a payment in the presence of witnesses. They remain thus always on the safe side and, never being betrayed by the thieves, enjoy undisturbed the fame of most respectable firms. [p. 6]

The practice was for all the goods bought from any one long-firm fraud to go to one 'sharper'. This did not prevent the 'sharper' from beating down the price as far as he could. A great deal of effort was expended by the villains in trying to pull a fast one on each other, but the 'sharper' always has the whip hand, for the fraudsman cannot do without him whereas, without them, he would simply be less rich.

Rollo Reuschel writes of one rare case of female emancipation in long-firm fraud. In this case, a businessman in Germany was ruined by a long-firm fraud, and brought his wife to England to see if he could salvage anything. His wife ran off with the long-firm merchant and he died. When her new husband was forced to flee to Australia, the good lady did a long-firm fraud herself, and shipped the goods off to Australia. After that the firm closed down.

> Her sex rendered it difficult for her to secure another office, and she had to associate herself with former colleague of her husband. This man died 12 months later; but his wife, an Englishwoman, had also profited by his instruction... The two ladies went into partnership, and they engaged a disgraced clergyman as manager. [p. 57]

However, her husband did not like this situation, and returned to London, where he

> established the women as 'sharpers', and their firm is now highly respected, because no goods are any longer obtained by 'sledge-driving'. All goods are bought at 10% of their value. No goods are sold in London; all is forwarded to Australia, and thus the stolen property cannot be traced. The police has no cause to interfere, as the ladies are always able to produce receipts showing that the goods were bought from 'a firm' at the proper market price, and the firm remains highly respected in the City to this day. [p. 57]

The crucial and powerful role played by the 'sharper' makes his position both the most profitable and the safest in the long firm. Reuschel does not tell us whether the 'sharpers' originated the long-firm frauds, or merely took their goods, but it seems more likely from the tenor of his book that they confined their role to the purchase of goods after they had been obtained. I have studiously avoided using the term 'fence' in connection with these 'sharpers' because until the Theft Act, 1968 it was not a crime merely to buy goods from a long firm. Provided that the 'sharpers' did not conspire with long-firm fraudsmen to *obtain* the goods, or to commit a bankruptcy offence, they were safe from any form of criminal liability.

One particularly interesting feature of the organization of long-firm frauds at that time was the role played by two prominent firms of trade protection agents. These agencies were run by two

German swindlers called Lehnert and Opitz, and although they had
separate entrances in different streets, they were in fact connected by
doors to each other's rooms. The agents charged low fees and wrote
long florid reports, and they were well patronized as agents for
French, German and Swiss trade protection societies.

Lehnert would be paid for his protection by the organizer of a
long-firm fraud, and in exchange would give his firm good references
and would 'cool the marks out' (Goffman, 1952) when the firm
failed. His technique was very clever. For example, the following is
his reply to a credit inquiry:

> This firm exists since last year and is exporting goods of all kinds
> to East India. The proprietor, B. Arnold, is said to have been
> there with the following firms [named], who have sent him as their
> buyer to Europe. He is said to draw from each of the firms a salary
> of £400 per annum and $2\frac{1}{2}\%$ commission. The person enquired of
> is a capable man who understands his business. He had his bank
> account at the City Bank, Fore Street. B. Arnold have paid until
> now. Payments are made according to the terms usual in the East,
> that is cash against shipping documents, and as regards any
> eventual credit, it is strongly advised to insist upon these terms.

This advice cleverly combines what is obviously an excellent
reference with a recommendation not to give credit which Lehnert
knew would be disregarded. By this method, he can later claim that
he was right all along. His custom was that just before the smash of a
'friendly' long firm, he would warn manufacturers that the firm was
totally rotten, and without funds. In this way he would gain the
reputation of being well-informed (as indeed he was). Very often he
would be given the task of pursuing the malefactors and, after a long
and (for the creditors) expensive search, would declare himself
frustrated, and suggest that there was no point in throwing good
money after bad. In his capacity as London agent for 23 credit
bureaux in Germany and Austria, he was able to supply a
'sucker-list' to the long firms, since he knew the customers of those
agencies to whom he supplied reports.

Lehnert's techniques of doing business were highly profitable for
him and for his associates. For example, one Martin Zucher
swindled merchants in Russia, Germany, France and Hungary out
of eggs, and even the Russian Consul-General could not get them to
pay up. He also got vegetables from Croatia, hams and sausages
from Germany, wine from Italy, salad oil and bicycle bells. He had
paid Lehnert, so when creditors employed him to look for the villain,
he told them that the man had gone to the south of France with

terminal galloping consumption. (In reality, the only consumption was that of the foodstuffs and their proceeds.)

However, Lehnert did not pay Zucher his share of the proceeds from the sale of bicycle bells, and Zucher did not arrange 'protection' for his next long firm. Consequently, this did not prosper, because Lehnert gave him bad references. They then made friends again and he was given good references. A similar thing happened with another long-firm merchant. Lehnert further distinguished himself in villainy by giving evidence in Dresden that a German was a swindler in exchange for £75. As a consequence, the man was sentenced to twelve years' penal servitude.

The success of this brilliant scheme was naturally threatened by Reuschel's exposures so, with characteristic verve, Lehnert first used a rival German newspaper to try to discredit him and, when that failed, got Opitz to prosecute Reuschel for libel. The libel action was dismissed, however, and the *Koelnische Volkszeitung* took out a private prosecution against the pair for conspiracy to defraud. Lehnert jumped bail and fled, but Opitz was sentenced to eight months' hard labour.

A variety of goods were obtained by the long firms. As Reuschel (p. 30) states, 'The sledge-drivers do not disdain anything, be it trousers, buttons, glass eyes, liver-sausage, whole flocks of sheep, ship-loads of timber, organs, or violins – all is fish what comes to their net. They obtain anything, and they find buyers for everything.' He tells the amusing story of how one long firm got a gross of artificial eyes from Germany, but no-one wanted them, and they eventually had to sell them to a 'sharper' for the cost of the postage. In another case a firm was left with a homeopathic medicine chest.

A man called Arnstein, having organized a successful long firm in cigars, set himself up as a Professor of Music at a fictitious college. He advertised for violins in German newspapers, saying that he would pay good prices, but when violins were forwarded, he would not pay up. Many of the hapless creditors complained to the Consulate, but in order to prosecute, the plaintiff had to come to England personally, and this meant more cost, which they were loath to undertake. In Germany, the Public Prosecutor would have taken over the case and the expense would have been borne by the general body of taxpayers. Most German creditors found it difficult to understand why this was not the case in England.

This is a classic illustration of the problem of something being in the interest of all collectively, but being against the interest of any one individual. As Reuschel stated:

The chief of the London police is quite willing to help, but one of the victims must appear personally as plaintiff. Characteristic are the words of the Commissioner of Police; he knew, he said, Arnstein a long time, and the police knew Arnstein to be everything else, but not 'a clean potatoe'.

The instruments he obtained from these long-firm frauds were used in the legitimate Colleges of Music which he and his associates ran. In general, the method used by most long-firm frauds was simply to write to firms abroad on smart headed notepaper, preferably with the backing of the good Lehnert, asking for goods. Since trade was bad in Germany, and the manufacturers there believed that London was paved with gold, they victimized themselves. On occasions, however, the long-firm merchant would do the buying abroad, or set up a mark for some confederates in England, whom he would recommend as people in a large way of business. Reuschel propounded his own lay theory about why people went into long firming:

> It is sad that the greatest part of these long firm swindlers are Germans... To a certain extent the cause might be found, perhaps, in the abundance of educated men in Germany, who are unable to find a suitable occupation; to do a common labourer's job they are too lazy, and thus they turn to sledge-driving. (p. 120)

This pre-Mertonian hypothesis has much to commend it, but one must leave it at the level of speculation. In the main, the actual *process* by which they got into long-firm fraud varied considerably. First, there were those who arrived penniless, gravitated to the beer-houses in the City Road which the German community, and especially the long-firm community, frequented. They would thus join the guild of the Knights of Industry, as Reuschel ironically calls them. Then, there is a further group:

> The greatest pleasure to the heart of a veteran sledge-driver is to receive into the heart of the guild a clerk who fled in the company of his master's cash box and who trembles at the sight of his own shadow. They are the genuine material from which sledge-drivers are made, and they form the aristocracy of the German vagabonds in London. (p. 20)

These are either seasoned villains already or else soon become so after they have been parted from their cash.

The last group of recruits arrive as a consequence of what he terms 'the Export Swindlers of the German Empire' (p. 74). German manufacturers want to sell abroad. However, rather than test the market at their own expense: 'Their scheme is to look for, and to find an agent possessed of a few thousand marks, and offer a commission of 2–3%, that he, at his own expense, may lay the foundations for a future "world-renowned firm"' (p. 74). They mark up the prices by 15 per cent, which they think the English can afford, and all they pay him until his half-yearly commission is due is postage expenses. They then offer him goods in lieu of his commission, and he finally has to accept this, even though he may have worked hard to build up a connection. In order to live, the agent has to sell goods quickly, at a loss, and does so again to survive, until he cannot extricate himself. At that point, the greedy manufacturers find out their mistake, but the long-firm guild has another member.

When someone did a successful long-firm fraud, his cover was 'blown', and he would thenceforth have to employ 'front men' to clerk for him, if he wanted to stay in the same line of business. What more often happened, however, was that the villains would open up one company after another, using different names and often dealing in different goods, so that they would not be recognized. The picture one builds up is that the long-firm scene consisted of a large number of people in a group characterized by an often justified mutual distrust, who band together in 'teams' for an unspecified period to carry out a fraud or a series of frauds. Just like today, much of the villains' time was spent looking over their own shoulders to see if their partners were swindling them. The only people whom they could not afford to 'turn over' were the 'sharpers' for, otherwise, they might not be able to sell their goods from the next long firm. Reuschel writes of one old sledge-driver who robs his confederates and then betrays them for a consideration (p. 84). 'Those "in the swim" despise him; but the "sharpers" are constantly at his heels, because they know that he can help them very often to extremely cheap lots.' The valuable role of the 'swag man' in commercial life, especially in textiles, has continued up till the present. The greater part of the goods ordered by long firms came from abroad, since the English firms were too fly for the villains, and also because the risk of prosecution was so small, the victims being loath to lose still more money by coming to England. Reuschel states:

> In England, credit is not so easily given and obtained as in other countries. But here, as elsewhere, the small manufacturers and the beginners are far more disposed to open a credit to customers than old-established firms in a large way of business, who have greater experience, and who may dare to demand from new customers cash at the first, second, and third transaction. (p. 113)

Thus far, the actual frauds themselves that I have mentioned have been fairly crude affairs, although the background organization which protects them and which buys their 'gear' is very well organized. However, some of the frauds were highly sophisticated, and I should like to describe one in some detail, for it demonstrates a degree of international criminal co-operation which would be the envy of many latter-day villains.

A German fraudsman called Listmann came to Naples in 1885, and set up in business as a commission agent. He employed as his travellers two other Germans called Ernest and Arfest Schreck; with excellent genuine references from two very well-accredited German manufacturers, they began to order large quantities of goods. The first orders were paid for in cash, without trouble, and then came the 'ramp'. Listmann wished to start credit transactions, and this is done on the Continent by means of bills of exchange. He did not have the organization in Italy to generate fraudulent bills of exchange, so he utilized a London connection for this purpose.

In London every long-firm swindler had with him all the time rubber stamps and indian ink, and he would endorse or accept any bill of exchange, for any amount, for a commission of two shillings and six pence per £100 accepted. With the aid of these worthless bills of exchange, Listmann bought at least £32 000 of goods from Germany and France in the space of some forty days. He claimed, when ordering the goods, that they were for the most renowned firms in Naples, and gave their genuine names and addresses. However, he also bribed postal officials in Italy to intercept the mail of those firms, and when the 'letters of advice' from forwarding agents were sent, they were instead given to Listmann, and with the assistance of bribed customs officials and railway clerks, the goods never reached their destination. The Neapolitan firms did not even know that the goods had been ordered until the fraud 'broke'.

By mid-May 1886, the bills were soon to become due, and the villains arranged through a Hamburg solicitor to notify creditors that a creditors' meeting would be held on 23 May. This was in fact a delaying tactic and, when the day came, neither they nor their solicitor was there. By the time the Public Prosecutor issued a warrant, all three had long since left the country.

The fraudsmen did, however, have one problem. Cash transactions are the exception in the Italian trade, and although they had sold a lot of their goods at 60 per cent below cost, Listmann had in general to sell to his customers at the same 3–6 months bills that he had given himself. Not wanting to lose the benefit of this extra cash, he hit upon a scheme. While he went to Buenos Aires and Ernest Schreck went to London, Arfest was sent to Germany, where he obtained a job as a bank clerk on a small salary. With the help of a third person, Arfest got the bills discounted through a leading firm in Altona. At the last moment before he was to join Listmann in South America, Arfest Schreck was arrested in Germany. On him were four savings books with £3000 in credit, £700 in sovereigns and bank notes, and many boxes of goods. He was imprisoned for this, but after two years he was released, because he had become 'mentally diseased', whereat he joined his brother in England.

Meanwhile, the legal tangles over the bankruptcy were so drawn out that the creditors eventually accepted an agreement with the Schrecks that they would keep only 7000 marks of the money seized, and would withdraw their action against them. At this point there is a tie-in with the London long-firm scene, for Ernest set up in London, but not under Lehnert's protection, so in a reference given in 1889 Lehnert described him as an 'arch-swindler'. Having learned better, Schreck paid his percentage to Lehnert, so by 1891 he had suddenly become 'an excellent man of business... respectable and diligent'. Lehnert had doubtless transcended labelling theory!

One of the respectable German firms which had given references for the Neapolitan fraud suggested to a German manufacturer that he appoint Schreck's firm as his London agent. After he had been swindled he met, apparently by chance, none other than Opitz who had been sent to Germany by Lehnert for that purpose, since he had heard that the manufacturer was going to prosecute Schreck. Opitz offered his help in tracing and prosecuting the swindler so, needless to say, no prosecution was ever instituted. The German finally accepted Lehnert's advice to accept £100 in full and final settlement of his claim for £380.

By the late nineteenth century international long-firm frauds had become so advanced that they were becoming a source of diplomatic concern. An article in *The Standard* (date unknown) commented that

> The Austrian Consul-General in London having informed the Vienna Chamber of Commerce that Austrian merchants have repeatedly incurred heavy loss by giving credit to long firms in England, the Chamber has issued a notice warning traders of the risk of opening accounts with foreign customers, without first obtaining satisfactory information respecting their position.

However, it is clear that given Lehnert's strategy, reasonable diligence in obtaining credit references was not a sufficient condition for the prevention of fraud.

During the nineteenth century there developed a clearly identifiable 'long-firm subculture', bound together in part by common national origin (in the case of the Germans) but by no means exclusive to immigrants. As Reuschel (1895) showed, the German subculture possessed a very sophisticated support system for the granting of credit references and for 'cooling the marks out' (Goffman, 1952). The 'sharpers' were well-organized and could dispose of all manner of goods with reasonable ease and, perhaps more importantly, safety. If Reuschel is to be believed (and I see no cause for doubt), their apparent respectability in the eyes of the outside world was founded upon an edifice of systematic fraud. In these respects, long-firm fraud was more 'organized' than it has been at any time since, even in the supposed heyday of English 'syndicated crime' during the 1960s. For all this, however, there is no evidence that Lehnert exercised any centralized financing, organization and 'fencing' functions in the manner of the great thief-taker Jonathan Wild (Howson, 1970). His continued existence depended upon his ability to make money for others rather than on any physical muscle he had to back up his situation: he was more a cunning Peachum than a dangerous MacHeath.

Unfortunately, I have been unable to unearth any information of a comparably detailed nature about the long-firm underworld between the late nineteenth century and the 1960s. One must be content, therefore, with the somewhat more limited perspective that one can glean from the literature and from trials at the Old Bailey.

During the period 1898–1910, 21 people were convicted and 6 acquitted in long-firm fraud trials at the Old Bailey. The cases appeared to fall into two main categories:

(1) 'intermediate' frauds, occurring mainly in the context of the bad business conditions which existed at the turn of the century;

(2) 'professional swindlers', who traded for very brief periods before going bankrupt.

The case of Lewis Solomons, who went bankrupt for £5000 in 1904, provides a good example of intermediate fraud. He had traded honestly for twenty years, and had always paid promptly until his bankruptcy. He was a book manufacturer, and sold all the leather he bought on credit to a convicted fraudster and bankrupt, whose wife traded as a boot manufacturer in the East End of London.

An example of the second category, that is, of the professional swindler, is described below. In 1901 Charles Frederick Matusch and Richard Harvey were accused of conspiring with others in a series of long-firm frauds. They had six companies, all of which were properly registered. However, some of them traded from the same address and supplied each other with good trade references. On occasions, they used false names and accommodation addresses (such as lodging houses). Once, they even traded in the name of a respectable firm, but used their own address. The trial proved that they had obtained at least £2500 in goods comprising pianos, paper, typewriters, cigars, wine, spirits, bicycles and furniture.

When the police arrested Matusch, they found upon him a letter addressed to 'Mr Anderson, GPO, Poste Restante, Stoke', in which 'Anderson' was asked to come up to London immediately and tell him what had happened, that they were all in danger, but he should try to get the warrants against them withdrawn. They sent off the letter, but informed the Staffordshire police, who arrested Harvey when he picked up the letter. They found upon him a loaded six-shooter, indicating a preparedness to use violence. However, by the time the police got to the others, they had escaped already and were never captured.

After their conviction, the police stated that Matusch had been engaged in frauds since 1893, and that Harvey had been similarly occupied since 1897. Matusch was sentenced to five years penal servitude, and Harvey to 18 months hard labour.

In 1909, there was a similar instance of systematic swindling, which led to sentences of eight, six, five and three *months* respectively for four brothers who had run different long firms from different addresses over a period of at least six years. Before the Pallash brothers were sentenced, a police inspector observed the

Information was laid against them at Highgate Police Court on two occasions, but there was difficulty about getting the witnesses up from the country, and the evidence was not sufficiently strong to succeed.... In another case, we laid the facts before counsel, but were advised to take no action in consequence of the loose way in which the (supplier) did their business.

Here, too, there are themes which are familiar to those who seek to prosecute international frauds today. This case also draws our attention to the social reaction component in fraud which has remained implicit hitherto. The invocation of the criminal justice process depends on decisions that are made by victims, police, and prosecutors about what action should be taken. It also depends on the perception that what has happened is a criminal offence: in this case, a *fraud* rather than an 'ordinary' trading loss. I came across a few cases in which tradesmen have taken action against long-firm fraudsters on the apparent grounds of general public interests rather than direct personal offence. For example, in the case of *R. v. Sheen and Keeling*, tried at the Old Bailey in 1862, a witness stated that he had known the accused to have been trading under different names since May 1860. At his suit, Keeling had been imprisoned by the Insolvent Court in 1860 for a debt of £40, and had served seven months' imprisonment. In the instant case, he had told a detective that they were engaged in swindles:

> and he stopped numbers of goods that had been delivered there, and some hams – I did not do that on my own responsibility, but upon information – I am an upholsterer, but I considered it my duty as a tradesman to interfere with hams or anything else I saw them getting – I have made it my business to check these people wherever I could, because they sold the goods three days after they got them – I have thought it my duty when they were trading under a fictitious name to give information to the police, to prevent the public being defrauded.

However, one may hypothesize that this degree of public spiritedness is fairly uncommon, and that there must have been many cases where no similar action was taken.

One element that one must take into account when assessing the cases discussed here relates to the provisions for civil incarceration of debtors (see Hadden, 1967a; Rock, 1973b; and Levi, 1979). In so far as the availability of such imprisonment may have affected the decision to prosecute, the Old Bailey cases may not be representative of long-firm frauds as a whole.

Another factor of importance is the cost of prosecution. Until 1869, when the Debtors Act (32 and 33 Vic., c. 62) was passed, long-firm fraud prosecutions were private matters, paid for by the victims. Thereafter, the state took on the burdens of prosecution in cases where it appeared to the Bankruptcy Court that conviction was probable.

In 1879, the Prosecution of Offences Acts (42 and 43 Vic., c. 22) brought into existence the role of the Director of Public Prosecutions, and this extended further the 'public interest' aspect of the decision to prosecute. It seems likely that the cost of prosecution may influence the decision to prosecute and that, *ceteris paribus*, state-financed prosecutions may have led to an increase in the rate at which long-firm frauds were prosecuted. However, it is impossible to validate this hypothesis, since there is no way of knowing how many long firms there 'really' were at different times during the nineteenth century.

Although the Old Bailey transcripts cease in 1910, there is clear evidence that long-firm frauds were a 'significant social problem' during the 1920s. For example, at the end of a trial at the Old Bailey in 1929, Sir Henry Dickens pronounced that

I have given fair warning that anyone convicted of long-firm fraud will go to penal servitude. I have tried a good many of these cases, and I am getting tired of them. Statistics show that losses to traders through long-firm frauds amounted to £28 million, and generally the largest sufferers were people in the textiles trade. The judges are determined to put down that class of offence. (From the archives of Dun & Bradstreet Ltd; source unknown.)

There is extensive discussion of long-firm frauds by Moore (1933). He states (p. 85) that

> By far the heaviest losses incurred by supply houses have been in respect of long firms ... The swindling firm itself is 'long'. That is, there are confederates dotted about the place who name each other as referees when seeking credit, and thus weave a web in which wholesalers and manufacturers have been caught and 'bled white' times without number.

Moore distinguishes the 'long firm' from the 'bogus retailer' on the grounds that the latter forges his references. Long-firm merchants, on the other hand, operate as follows: 'A good account is established by one of the gang to start with. Duly paying his bills, he becomes, in time, a "reference"' (p. 85). The 'reference' then is used by the other members of the gang in a concerted series of frauds. Moore (1933, p. 86) adds that

> There have been numerous exposures of heavy sentences passed on such rogues, immediately after the War especially. On the whole, successful big-scale long-firm swindles are not so numerous as they were. This is due no less to closer co-operation among supply firms themselves than to vigorous police action. Suppliers were compelled to realise that their own independent action in taking up references could never give them more than inadequate protection, owing to the subtlety of the long-firmer's methods. It was seen that counter-methods of equal subtlety would have to be employed, for these swindlers know how to play their cards to get a 'good mark' with the very best houses in the trade and even with the most vigilant status-enquiry offices. The long-firmers, it was argued, presumably did not suddenly blossom forth as swindlers, but in all likelihood would have an antecedent somewhat dubious history. They were probably hardened tricksters, experienced in this field, and the need, therefore, was to build up a record of such individuals, a register in which would be entered every black mark recorded against any such person, together with details as to aliases and the like; a valuable record which any supply house which 'had its doubts' might consult. The textiles trades have been perhaps the worst sufferers, and after the War, the preliminary move came from them ... As a result, the would-be long-firmer now finds the road, in the textile trade at any rate,

much thornier than it was a decade back ... It is not uncommon for a wholesaler or manufacturer to consult the [Textile Trades] Association, and to learn out of hand that the individual about whom information is sought is known to the officials under half a dozen aliases, as having operated in perhaps as many different branches of trade and parts of the country, and as one, possibly, who has served several terms of imprisonment. One comment needing to be made is that this excellent preventive system is, as yet, far from complete. The fuller co-operation of other branches of the trade, besides drapery and the like, is needed. When this has been secured, the long-firm swindle should become very difficult ... except in cases where individuals make absolutely their first appearance as cheats from a respectable environment, so that nothing is known against them.

However, Moore makes no mention of long firms in the second edition of his book, so one may presume that they were no longer perceived as a major commercial problem by the end of the 1930s.

In the preceding pages, I have sought to set out some of the most salient features of the organization and techniques of long-firm fraud from the early nineteenth century to the Second World War. The cases that I have quoted reveal that there have been long-firm frauds both of considerable sophistication and of considerable crudity during all the periods concerned. Similarly, in every period, there has been a wide spectrum of modes of organization, from the sole trader who carries out a 'one-off' long firm to the groups of 'professional swindlers' who act in concert to carry out a series of systematic frauds. There is no evidence that long-firm frauds have ever been integrated within a single organizational format: 'villainy' may come from anywhere. It is noteworthy, however, that there is very little indication of overlap between long-firm fraudsters and 'traditional' property or violent criminals. In so far as the long firmers were 'professional criminals', they tended to be 'professional *commercial* criminals', eschewing other forms of predatory crime, unless they turned to the latter subsequently. The exclusive concentration on commercial crime distinguishes these persons from many of those who turned to long-firm fraud during the 1960s: the developments in the organization of long firms after the Second World War are discussed in Chapter IV.

Finally, however, some caveats on the interpretation of these data. Cases tried at the Old Bailey may not be representative of those in the country as a whole: different patterns of organization and of technique may have been observable elsewhere. Furthermore, these cases represent only those about which enforcement decisions have been taken: we do not know how many or what kind of long-firm frauds remained unprosecuted during these periods. Consequently, it would be most unwise to extrapolate observations about officially defined fraud and to apply them to 'actual', but not officially defined, long-firm frauds. As we shall see, inferences about the latter category are difficult enough to make when examining contemporary commercial conduct: the problem is greater still when we try to separate out the 'real fraud' component from the 'social definition and reaction' component in historical essays.

III. Craft of the Long-Firm Fraudster

The craft of the long-firm fraudster may be divided into two categories: the obtaining of goods on credit; and the avoidance of conviction and imprisonment. The top-class fraudster is able to succeed on both of these counts; the middle-range fraudster succeeds on the first but not the second count; and the incompetent fraudster fails on both counts.

Success at obtaining goods on credit may be attained in a number of ways, to be discussed later in this chapter, but there are two essential components to this process: first, the provision of a confidence-inspiring front for the fraud; and second, the negotiation of credit within the framework provided by this front.

The ideal long-firm fraud is one that does not require the manufacture of a 'front'. In other words, a company with a good established credit rating. For if this is the case, then the fraudster can allow the reputation of the company to provide him with credit without his having to do anything further in the way of specific confidence trickery. Thus, the dream of many long-firm merchants is to be able to induce the owner of such a business to stay on to 'front' the firm himself while obtaining, say, £50 000 at low interest rates from the bank to back the operation, and 'fencing' the goods thus obtained through his own trade outlets. If, in addition, he can blackmail the owner into co-operation and silence, he will have defrauded the bank, the trade creditors and the owner, at the same time as seeing the latter take the blame for the fraud. This, however, is a dream that is seldom realized. In practice, the fraudster must attempt to generate as convincing a front as possible with the means at his disposal. Some long-firm fraudsters are fortunate enough to be generously financed: others must work on shoe-string budgets.

During the early and mid-1960s, the most common technique of long-firm fraud was the setting up of a number of apparently independent, but actually linked, companies. These companies might all be trading companies, or some might exist solely on paper: for the price of £25 (£100 in 1979), any number of companies could be bought 'off the shelf' – 'no questions asked' – from agencies specializing in company formation. In the simpler type of operation, the 'front man' would be installed in rented or leased accommodation and would order goods from lists of suppliers who advertise in trade directories or from those mentioned by other fraudsters as a 'good touch'. If asked for a reference regarding his creditworthiness, he would refer a supplier to his own 'paper' companies.

These 'paper' companies would operate from accommodation addresses: these might be newsagents or other shops willing to act in the capacity of poste restante; or they might be rooms rented by fraudsters solely for this purpose. The mail would be collected and brought to the main premises, and the trader would write out the references himself, sometimes even using the same typewriter that he used for his trading firm, which some times proved to be his undoing. The crudest operators would cage their references in such glowing terms that they aroused suspicion. For example, one small firm with a paid-up capital of £2 at the beginning of the 1960s was provided with the following 'in-house' reference: 'Have dealt with this firm for five years, and have always found them very prompt payers and very reliable. I would consider them good for credit up to £5000.' This very crude effort was often successful at that time, because few firms had any sophisticated form of credit control or were sensitized to the possibility of their being defrauded. However, a credit inquiry agency might well pick up the similarity in the typeface used in the references, check the dates of registration of the companies involved, and check the places of work of the referees. In these circumstances, the 'front' would prove inadequate to withstand the most superficial checks, and there would be clear evidence of deception if the fraudsters were caught. However, they would generally use false names, and fingerprinting was not at that time standard in police investigations of fraud. Consequently, unless the police were alerted during the operation of the fraud, the chances of escaping unidentified were quite high.

The more subtle operator, again within this basic technique, would use different typewriters, have headed notepaper printed for each firm by a different printer, and give a more sensible estimate of the creditworthiness of his trading firm than the one quoted above. In this way he would hope to pass the superficial scrutiny of investigators, and since he often obtained the typewriters and printing on credit, he would have to pay out little more than the crude fraudster.

If the fraudster was part of, or had access to, a wider circle of 'villains', he might extend this technique of self-reference-writing to a number of *actual* trading firms. The organizer or organizers would buy anything up to six 'off the peg' companies (or, if the price was right, existing trading companies). Each company would write to or telephone creditors, giving the other companies as referees, and in this way, a chain of long-firm frauds could be created. Although this method had the advantage over the cruder ones that the integrity of the would-be debtor could not be falsified simply by physical examination of the business premises of the referees, it had the disadvantage that it provided clear evidence of conspiracy to defraud if the police were able to detect the perpetrators (and if the crime was perceived and reported as such).

In order to surmount these 'little legal difficulties', the more subtle operators adopted two refinements. First, they would carry out 'dummy' transactions between the companies, so that there would be a record of trading to which they could refer the police for 'authentication' of the references. This might be done in two ways:

(a) a cheque could be paid into the account of company A by company B and, to maintain cash-flow, company A would draw out the equivalent sum in cash which would be returned to company B;

(b) a cheque would be paid into the account of company A by company B. At the same time, a cheque for the same amount would be paid into the account of company B by company C, and into the account of company C by company A. By this method, one sum would suffice for all three transactions.

All of these transactions would be purely paper ones: they would not relate to any actual transfer of goods which such payments would normally represent.

Secondly, operators would give slightly more ambiguous references, such as 'I have done business with the owner of this firm for a number of years, and I feel sure that he would not enter into any transaction which he would be unable to fulfil.' References such as this might make it difficult to prove a substantive deception, particularly in regard to the crime of 'false pretences' as it existed before the passage of the Theft Act, 1968.

In the early 1960s, a large number of such cross-referenced frauds were operated by people connected with the Kray and Richardson gangs, both inside and outside London. Their normal practice was to set up the companies in mid or late summer, pay the first few bills in cash, and gradually to increase orders 'for the Christmas trade', thus mirroring the patterns of trading of legitimate businesses. Then, as Christmas approached, there would be a large increase in orders, the goods would be sold virtually overnight, and the premises closed down. The timing of the frauds was done in this way because it provided a 'normal' context in which large orders could be justified and goods could easily be resold as part of the pre-Christmas spending spree. This technique was equally popular in the United States during that period (compare Edelhertz, 1970; Hoover, 1962, 1967; Kossack, 1964, 1965; Teresa, 1973).

The cross-referencing technique is normally used for relatively small operations, but is sometimes used in the larger ones. In 1967 a fraud was organized which involved six companies and some twenty fraudsters in an interlocking series of long-firm frauds in England. In this conspiracy the principal organizers even had the nerve to issue a fictitious debenture by one company to another. They knew that company A was about to fold, so its nominal owner signed a minute stating that he had received £2000 from company B. The aim was to make company B a preferential creditor in the liquidation of company A, so that it would receive the full £2000 from the assets that remained in that company. Eventually the chain of frauds folded, leaving debts of some £200 000 (at historic prices). However, the main difficulty in attempting cross-referenced long-firm frauds within a time-span longer than two or three months is that the chain is only as strong as its weakest link. As one organizer stated to me,

> cross-referencing by l.f.s is not a good idea, because if one of them crashes for some reason, and another has used it as a reference, that other may find that the suppliers are wary of delivering. In that way, you can lose very large orders. It is also very difficult to get the timing of the fraud right, and there is a much greater risk of police observation. So I would never try it unless I was so short of cash that I could not finance the payment of the first few orders to suppliers.

These types of fraud tend to be the largest long firms, those which obtain over £250 000. They may be operated in two basic forms: first, the owner of the business builds it up and then extends his credit in the classic long-firm manner; and second, the organizer of the fraud builds up his business 'as if' it were legitimate, resigns as director in favour of his 'front man', and gets the long firm to 'take off' under his *covert* control.

An example of the former technique is the defunct company Fraudwear Limited. This company was incorporated in 1959 with an issued share capital of £100. It traded normally as a wholesale textiles company and, in January 1963, increased its paid-up capital to £10 000 while still under the ownership of its founder, who was the sole director. After this date, the owner began to order from a number of suppliers in England and Europe, paying his debts in the normal manner. In September 1963, he began to make very substantial orders to those same suppliers, paying them by post-dated cheque or by bill of exchange, as is the custom on the Continent. When these cheques and bills became due, they were dishonoured and, finally, in March 1964, a creditor petitioned for the company to be compulsorily wound up. At this time, the owner of the business entered a nursing home for treatment for his 'mental illness'. (This was probably a ruse to turn away the wrath of his creditors and to escape prosecution, for the police are generally held to be reluctant to prosecute 'nutters'.) The company had amassed a deficit of some £240 000 (at 1964 prices), and the cloth had been sold to 'job buyers' for between 60 and 85 per cent of its cost price. The creditors included firms from England, France, Germany, Italy, Portugal and Sweden, and the *modus operandi* was fairly typical of the large-scale 'independent' long-firm fraud.

The technique favoured by the most expert fraudsters is the use of a well-established business as the vehicle for a long-firm fraud. By doing this, there is no need to use false references or even to pay cash for the first few orders. The company already has a good credit rating and is ready for the 'milking' (for American examples, see De Franco, 1973, and Teresa, 1973). The organizers usually attempt to conceal from the suppliers the fact that there has been a change in control. Sometimes they are able to persuade the vendor to stay on in an advisory capacity, 'to help them find their way around the business'. Sometimes they put in their own 'front man' with the same name as the vendor, who claims to be a relative. In most cases, to give the impression of continuity, they keep on existing staff in all departments save that of accounts. The following is a good example of this technique.

In 1963 a well-known firm of Manchester grocers decided to sell their business and advertised for offers in the national press. Among the replies they received was one from New York, to which they replied, giving details of their business. Some time later they received an inquiry from London, from someone who – unknown to them – was a 'front man' for the American respondent, and who agreed to purchase the company for £10 000 and was given a list of existing suppliers and customers. The new owners rented a mill, stating that it was required for a 'Cash and Carry' business: in fact, it was so that they could order and store goods without the knowledge of the former owners.

On completion of the sale, the former company secretary wished to notify the Registrar of Companies of the change of directors, but was unable to get the new owners to hold a meeting of the company or to provide him with the necessary details. In consequence, an inquiring creditor or credit agency which examined the records at Companies House would find nothing there to confirm any suspicions. The new owners then ordered vast quantities of goods from both new and existing suppliers. The latter unquestioningly sent the goods requested; new suppliers checked on the standing of the firm and received glowing reports. The company secretary was wholly ignorant of these orders, since the goods were delivered to the mill and did not pass through the company accounts over which he had control.

Unfortunately for the conspirators, however, an error was made. The 'backer' promised to pay £10 000 into the company account, and cheques for this amount were made out to some of the creditors who were pressing hard for payment. The aim of this was to enable the long firm to 'snowball' the credit in the next round of orders. However, one of the fraudsters sent out the cheques before the backer's money was paid in, and the bank 'bounced' the cheques. This ruined the good standing of the company and stopped the fraud in its tracks, albeit that a loss of £28 000 had been generated within ten weeks. In its concept, though not in its operation, this was a perfect example of the 'take-over' type of long-firm fraud.

Where it is not possible to deceive the creditors into believing that there has been no change in ownership at all, the 'front man' using the same surname will often claim that he is a nephew or a cousin of the original owner. However, this can lead to exposure, if the supplier meets the latter and makes some comment about his 'relative'.

If the fraudsters are sufficiently skilled, they may be able to induce the original owner to sell them the business 'by instalment'. The advantages of this are twofold: first, the initial outlay on the part of the fraudsters is reduced; and second, the fact that he is owed money gives the original owner an incentive to help the new proprietors obtain credit and make a success of the company. (Indeed, it is conceivable that such a 'mug' may be mis-defined as a conspirator in an 'intermediate' fraud.) If he becomes suspicious of the purchasers of the company, he may remain silent, nonetheless, in the hope of retrieving his money.

One man has made a speciality out of the purchase of more or less insolvent companies which are advertised for sale in trade newspapers. Generally, the business is sold to him in exchange for his promise to pay off its liabilities, but since he has no intention of doing so, he obtains control of it for nothing. He then utilizes the 'goodwill' of the company and runs it as a long firm as described earlier.

In those cases in which the fraudsters feel that they must inform suppliers about the change in ownership, they invent a reason for their seeking to expand their orders. This may involve the creation of a fictitious army of door-to-door salesmen, a 'Cash and Carry' warehouse, or a mail-order business. The cruder operator will merely assert the existence of these sales staff: the sophisticate will generate some back-up documentation, such as placing some advertisements in the media or making 'mock-up' mail-order catalogues to show his suppliers. In this sense the fraudster is a conjuror, a manufacturer of reality. He is literally a 'phantom capitalist' for his capital is wholly illusory, an entity woven into the imagination of his suppliers.

The final category of 'fronts' comprises firms which are run for a period of time in an apparently respectable fashion before their owners turn them into long firms. These may have been wholly straight firms, part-time 'fences' of long-firm goods, or may have been built up *ab initio* with the intention of being turned into long firms. Whatever the case, the credit rating will have been generated by earlier trading experiences with the long firm itself in its legitimate or pseudo-legitimate phase, and the fraudster makes use of the unwillingness of creditors to suspect people whom they know. For example, when businessmen seek to delay payment, their creditors will question them about their reasons for delay in such a manner that one feels that they seek reassurance rather than conflict.

A similar type of operation was carried out in the early 1970s by the owners of a business which had featured in many earlier frauds as the *purchaser* of long-firm goods. The proprietors were ageing and presumably wanted to make their exit from the long-firm scene. They utilized their knowledge of that profession and increased their orders to existing suppliers as well as new ones. Finally, before going into liquidation, they sold part of their premises – 'cut price' – to another team of fraudsters.

Although this particular firm had traded in a superficially respectable fashion for almost a decade before it went 'bent', this length of time is not necessary for this particular technique. For example, again in the early 1970s, an enterprising organizer set up two 'front men' in a wholesale fruit, vegetable and grocery business in Covent Garden, London. They were given substantial financial backing, and they gradually built up the level of their orders over a year, paying well and inducing confidence. Then, at the planned end of the firm, orders were given for approximately £750 000 worth of goods, including £250 000 of fresh fruit and vegetables which were obtained on the normal trade terms of seven days' credit. Virtually overnight these goods were disposed of, and the 'front men' disappeared.

The confidence game works slightly differently in the case of those firms which are built up originally by their long-firm organizers before being sold to 'front men'. In order to give credence to the sale of the business, the organizer has printed impressive-looking headed notepaper from a company with, say, worldwide subsidiaries based in Luxembourg. The 'British directors' of this company will hand over the money for the completion of the 'sale' in front of respectable lawyers and bankers, and the connection of the organizer with the firm will thus be severed. Or will it? For in reality, the organizer will have given the money beforehand to the illustrious purchasers, who will then go through the charade of taking over the company. This technique creates a good 'front' for the company, gives it a good rationale for expansion, and in most cases serves to protect the organizer from prosecution, since he can claim that he severed all connection with the business long before it went 'bent'.

Within this outline of the basic forms of 'fronting' for long-firm frauds, there are a number of variants which enable individual fraudsters to display their ingenuity. One of these is the careful cultivation of a respectable supplier by paying him promptly, so that his firm may be used as a solid reference to induce the confidence of other suppliers. The larger the amounts bought from this supplier, the larger the amounts of credit for which he will be able to give his recommendation. However, the money for the payment has to come from somewhere, so unless the long-firm merchant has substantial financial backing, he may have to 'rob Peter to pay Paul', which can overstretch his resources.

Another aspect of the fraudster's technique lies in his use of banks. A bank can make a very useful referee, or can stop the fraud in its tracks by commenting neutrally upon the business's potential. Moreover, bank managers can be helpful, for example, by allowing a firm to pay out money against uncleared cheques that have been paid in, or unhelpful, by forbidding this and 'bouncing' cheques. For this reason, most fraudsters attempt to keep their banks 'sweet'. This may involve actual corruption, as a number of fraudsters have stated, or merely a clever 'snow job', that is, the production of a 'whiter than white' image in the eyes of a bank manager. One way in which sophisticates attempt to generate a good image of their business turnover is by the use of 'accommodation cheques' on a large scale: this is sometimes called 'cheque kiting' and is used by many small businessmen to create a good impression for less nefarious purposes. One such operation is described thus by a great 'cheque artist':

> What you need is at least three people, and you get number 1 to give a cheque to number 2, who gives another one to number 3, and so on, in a circle, with, say, number 3 giving a cheque to number 1. You know how long cheques take to be processed and you time it so that each cheque can be fed in at the time when the debit is coming through the account. In this way, you can build up a large turnover of money going through your account without needing to have a great deal of money in the first place. The object is to impress your bank with what a lot of business you are doing, because he gives you an overdraft on the basis of your turnover. Naturally, the more people you have giving you cheques, the better it looks, because the manager might be a little suspicious ... Also you would be amazed at the number of people who will exchange cheques for you for a small percentage. My friends and some of the people I used to meet at the Club would exchange cheques for me at between one and five percent of their face value, and I had four drivers and four cars permanently stationed at my command, all the time running around to pay in the cash to meet the cheques as they fell due. If you exchange your cheques for cash in this way, you don't run the risk of being caught by a manager refusing to pay out against uncleared effects. But the strain of doing this is terrible ...
> Not many people could do this with the accommodation cheques, for few people had the connections and could be trusted, and few people had the knowledge of the banking system that I had. For example, at that time, cheques drawn on and paid into Barclays Bank took one day less than the other banks. Sometimes, I would ask the bank manager to hold up the payment of a cheque until 11.30 the following morning, which I was quite entitled to do.

In another case:

> I was introduced to this bank manager as a man of ability by a big client of his. I didn't pay him anything – he was just trying to help me. He couldn't give me an overdraft of more than £1500, because that was his limit from his Head Office. But every day, I would arrive at the Bank before it opened, and we would spread out all the cheques that the company had to pay on the table, and sort them into groups. Some went for immediate payment, others were less urgent and were sent back 'effects not cleared', some with 'words and figures don't match', and still others we would tear slightly and send back 'cheque mutilated'. However, we always made sure that the cheques were paid the next time that they were presented, and in this way, we were never technically in default.

In still more sophisticated instances, stolen shares and bonds are used as collateral on bank loans, since the banks seldom check the standing of such certificates. The general aim is to create an impression of affluence. The need for such accommodation cheque operations arises because banks operate on the principle of 'to him that hath shall be given', and any would-be borrower therefore has to create the impression that he is already wealthy and successful. For the less one appears to need money, the more likely one is to be given some. The 'props' for this impression-management exercise are smart clothes, discreetly expensive car and address, and an active bank account. Although bank managers today are attuned to this *modus operandi* because of the losses they have sustained through the 'kiting' process, informants state that it is still a common practice among small businessmen, both licit and illicit.

The use of a foreign bank or a 'dodgy' bank provides still further scope for manoeuvre. Several perfectly respectable foreign banks, such as the Bank of Bilbao, the Allied Irish Bank and the Bank of Cyprus, have been unwittingly used by English fraudsters in relation to long firms. They have the great advantage that it takes about ten days for them to clear cheques, as they are not members of the Clearing House scheme set up by the major banks in Great Britain to expedite transfers. A bank run by 'villains' is even more useful, as it can be counted upon to provide good references for fraudulent concerns, for a fee, of course. In the past, a number of banks of non-British origin have been employed for this purpose, although the power of the Secretary of State for Trade to prevent a non-authorized bank from calling itself a bank *in England* may inhibit this in the future.

Part of the fraudster's craft is the ability to tell a good story, and this is done both to banks and to trade victims. A good example of this craft is a long firm which was carried out in South Wales in the 1960s. A man with an American accent arrived at a South Wales coastal resort and announced that he represented an American syndicate (*sic*!) which wished to purchase a leisure and amusement arcade in the town. He offered a generous price, which was accepted gratefully by the owners. Unfortunately, however, there was a small snag preventing immediate completion: the money was temporarily tied up. However, he asked the owners if, pending completion of the sale, they would allow him to order goods for the coming season; this request was acceded to, the owners even going so far as to give him their headed notepaper to use in ordering. He wrote off to a number of suppliers as if he already owned the arcades and obtained some £350000 worth of fancy goods, toiletries and groceries on credit. One night all of these goods were covertly taken away, and the man disappeared for good. His identity remains unknown to this day.

Less audacious long firms, however, require a little more subtlety:

I used to do this really good double act with Blank. I would be the baddie and he would be the goodie. A rep would come in from one of the suppliers and Blank would say that his stuff was fantastic, but I would say it was rubbish and I didn't want any of it. Blank would pretend to try to persuade me to take it, but I would storm out of the office, saying 'I don't want it, but if you do, *you* buy it. As far as I'm concerned, it's your responsibility'. I would switch on the intercom in the other room to hear what went on after I left, and on many occasions, the rep would actually bribe Blank to take the stuff.

Another organizer, who used to front his own frauds, made the following observations:

The psychology of l.f.s is very important. I know that credit controllers and these trade protection societies are wise to the straight l.f. pattern of ever-increasing orders. So what I would do was to gradually increase orders at first, paying promptly, make one large order, pay, and then order little or nothing for a couple of visits by the rep. This would get him nice and worried, because he would think that maybe I'd found a better and cheaper line from a competitor ... Then, after a few gaps in my orders, I would put in a really big one coupled with a good excuse, like a half-page advert in the local paper, which I would show to the reps and tell them that my business was going like a bomb. Which it was, only they didn't realize that it was them who were going to be blown up! ... You have to be a good judge of the right tactics to adopt with suppliers. Things don't always work out though. There was one case where I owed Schweppes £11000, paid them, and put in an order for £25000, but they stopped my credit. I could have screamed. Things have changed a lot, though, and gone are the days when you could set up your own grocery store, print letter headings, and coin the money. The suppliers have got too cute.

In order to be successful, the fraudster has to adapt his technique to the methods of control: he has to simulate the style of the sharp businessman and yet obtain large quantities of goods. Some trade representatives, however commission-hungry they may be, will not sell goods to people who appear to them to order recklessly: others are not so particular. In many cases, representatives do not seem to question why a firm should want such large quantities of their products, and believe that they have 'pulled a fast one' over on the purchasers. This 'kidology' is part of the long-firm fraudster's tradecraft.

A further crucial aspect of his skill is the way the long-firm merchant organizes the 'fronting' of his fraud. In some cases people prefer their 'front men' to use their own names, because this gives a better impression if the business is investigated and court proceedings ensue. In other cases, however, particularly when the 'front man' has a criminal record, elaborate measures are taken to build up a false identity which will withstand all but the most thorough scrutiny by the police and by credit inquiry agencies. The aim here is twofold: to generate a respectable image for the 'front man' and to make it difficult for him to be traced after the fraud has been carried. out.

Examples of the production of a false identity may be found in some of the larger frauds. The organizer obtains a copy birth certificate from Somerset House, for preference selecting a child born to an unmarried domestic servant or barmaid from a high-mobility area. Thus, it will be very difficult for anyone to prove that the 'front man' is not the person he purports to be. The 'front man' then obtains accommodation in his false name near to the proposed area of business, and writes from that address to obtain a provisional driving licence. He (or a skilled driver using his name) then takes a driving test, thereby obtaining a driving licence in his new name and address. He may then buy a car, which will also have his new name and address on it. Consequently, anyone checking up on his background is likely to believe that everything is as it appears to be: everything about him fits together.

If the 'front man' does not possess previous business experience, he requires some training before he can 'pass'. Sophisticated long firms require 'front men' to be highly disciplined individuals who do exactly what they are told but who are able to deal astutely with trade representatives and with 'screamers', as angry creditors are called. To do this entails careful tutelage. In one case, in preparation for a vast *coup* of over one million pounds (at current prices), the 'front man' was given simulated situations in which he had to learn what to say to 'reps', when to say it, how to haggle with them so that it would appear that he was a sharp businessman, thereby allaying any suspicions that they might have. All this was done before he was introduced into the business, which had been built up in preparation for the fraud.

Another organizer would find people who were prepared to front a fraud in their own names, start up a business and train them *in situ*. He would place a tape recorder in the office and get them to record every single conversation that they had, whether on the telephone or in person. At the end of the day the 'front man', making sure that he was not followed, would bring over the tapes and they would go over them in detail, pointing out mistakes and making suggestions for improvements in technique. The length of these evening classes depended upon the ability and experience of the 'front man'. In general, however, there is some coaching with regard to the market for the goods, trade jargon and other allied matters: the 'front man' has to appear to be a principal.

Banks, tradesmen and credit inquiry agents may ask the 'front man' about his previous business experience, so he may have to put on a very convincing cover story. Where such cover is not readily available, there may have to be a false explanation for his taking up business, such as 'I have just come back from Rhodesia: there's no future there any more for us whites.' However well he builds up a false identity though, he cannot be proof against chance contingencies which may penetrate his cover. In one very substantial fraud, tremendous care was taken to generate a front capable of withstanding any amount of investigation. Everything was proceeding according to plan when, as the man concerned said to me:

> I had settled into the l.f. quite nicely when one day, out of the blue, in came my old RSM [Regimental Sergeant Major] from the army – right bastard he was too! He was a rep from one of the companies we were buying gear from, and I must say, it was nice to see someone you thought of as God Almighty crawling to you for orders. Anyway, I nearly choked when he came in, because I was sure that he was bound to recognize me, and he would know I wasn't Mr Blank. But thank heavens he didn't do so, and I quickly made an excuse to go out into the warehouse and got somebody else to deal with him. I nearly fainted when he left, but I must say that I especially enjoyed 'doing' his firm.

It is the ability to withstand tests of cool and of character such as this which distinguishes classes of long-firm fraudster. It is a major element in their status system, as well as a source of considerable personal satisfaction.

Strategies to avoid arrest and conviction

To be a successful long-firm organizer, one must be able to set up a business, obtain large quantities of goods on credit, and dispose of them rapidly through one's own business outlets or through other businessmen. However, these abilities are possessed by many businessmen. The ultimate test of the fraudster's craft is his ability to evade the clutches of the law and to this end, organizers have devised a number of strategies.

(1) They provide inducements to 'front men' to deter them from 'grassing' to the police if arrested. As discussed in greater detail next chapter, 'heavies' are often involved in the background organization of long-firm frauds, and where this is so (or is believed to be so), the threat of violence is generally an effective deterrent to the potential

'grass'. It should not, however, be thought that fear of underworld retribution is the only reason why 'front men' do not inform upon their organizers. As one of the latter said:

> I have never found it necessary to threaten violence against a front man. Right at the outset, I would tell him that he stood a very good chance of going to prison but if he wanted in, there would be, say, £10 000 in the bank for him. That way, if he did get nicked, he wouldn't feel that I had let him down. The only people who feel the need to threaten their front men are those who don't have any idea of how to handle people, or those who want to do the front man out of his share. To my mind, that is stupid as well as greedy. It is in your own interest to treat the front man right. If you do that, you're safe.

It should be added that the low sentences imposed upon 'front men' and the fact that there are no insurance rewards available for the recovery of long-firm goods or for the arrest of the principals help to reduce the likelihood of 'grassing' in long-firm fraud cases. In these respects, there are major differences between long firms and armed robberies or major hijackings.

(2) The long-firm organizers may get out of trouble by giving information about or evidence against higher-level criminals, such as the backers of frauds or gangsters in whom the police have an interest. At least one professional long-firm fraudster is reputed to have survived unconvicted by systematically 'grassing up' other criminals who ranked higher in the police conception of dangerousness. Most long-firm organizers are sufficiently opportunistic to sacrifice others in order to save their own skins, especially if they themselves have been mistreated, as they were by the Richardson, Kray and Dixon gangs in London during the 1960s. Some of these 'deals' between police and fraudsters go on at a formal level, with the approval of the Director of Public Prosecutions and the courts, but I have been given to understand that some of them also occur at an informal, low-visibility level without any formal sanction from above. Long-firm organizers are in a better position to 'grass' than most other types of criminal, for they are often multilingual, highly mobile and practised in the arts of disappearance and identity change, as well as skilled in talking their way out of danger. Moreover, the long-firm merchant can operate independent of a criminal underworld, so he has more room for manoeuvre than do many more traditional criminals.

(3) The 'front men' or organizers may flee the area of their crime, perhaps leaving the country altogether. Eire, Canada, Australasia,

Zimbabwe and South Africa are the most popular places for 'front men', mainly because they are English-speaking and, with the exception of Australasia and Canada, ill-disposed towards extradition. Indians, Pakistanis, and Bangladeshis often return to their ancestral homes. As one informant stated: 'Can you imagine trying to find a bloke called Singh once he's gone back to the Far East: or even in bloody Bradford, for that matter. It's a joke, isn't it? Especially when they all look alike to the reps.'

In one case, according to a long-firm organizer, some fraudsters took a meths drinker from the street, bathed him, dried him out, bought him suits, drilled him with instructions and got him to act as their 'front man'. When they finished with the long firm, they put him back on the streets and he returned to drinking meths. As the organizer put it:

> The whole thing was absolutely perfect. For him, it was like a dream – it was like every day was Christmas. Flash gear, a bit of money, birds – it was fantastic. The only thing was he wasn't allowed any booze while the l.f. was still running. And once it was all over, he was back in Noddyland again. Could you imagine the Fraud Squad trying to interview a wino?

Amusing and attractive though this story is, I find it difficult to believe, but it clearly represents one of the ultimate strategies to minimize the risk of 'grassing' by taking the 'front man' out of the effective jurisdiction of the courts.

Organizers tend to favour Europe, the Bahamas, Eire, South Africa and Israel as hiding places, although some find the Israeli police too co-operative towards extradition for their taste. Where organizers have stable family lives, however, they may be unwilling to disappear, and in any event, they may be identified and convicted years afterwards if they choose to return. One organizer was convicted some five years after fleeing the country; another after three years 'on the run'; and a third was convicted some six years after the conviction of his co-conspirators, when he was deported from Zimbabwe.

(4) Police corruption, generally in advance of the fraud, is another important technique for reducing the risk of conviction. As we shall see in Chapter IV, it does not always work as a long-term strategy, but it has proved successful in the short term in some cases.

(5) Organizers may generate bogus transactions which are difficult to prove fraudulent. For example, the organizer may get a long firm going by operating 'upfront' for a while before appearing to sell the business, in the manner described earlier in this chapter. Even if he is seen on the premises *after* the transfer of ownership, he

can claim that he was conned by the 'diabolical villains' into quite innocently helping them out in the running of his former business.

Other bogus transactions are designed to protect those who 'fence' the long firm's goods. In some cases the purchasers are genuinely innocent of the fraudulent nature of the vendor of the goods. Henry (1978, p. 57) points out in his study of the resale of goods stolen from work that

> Typically, then, goods are sold by ambiguous presentation; that is, the sale is accomplished by a gloss which relies in the fact that the purchaser will supply his own explanation of their origin... With goods presented in this way, a person may feel morally free to go ahead and make a purchase.

This ambiguous presentation is far easier to carry out in the case of long-firm frauds than in more traditional types of property crime because the vendor has an apparently genuine trading concern and has a genuine title to the goods that he is selling. Even if goods are offered at below cost price, there are many circumstances in which traders do this quite lawfully, for example, to get rid of unwanted stock when their cash-flow is tight. In many cases, however, the goods are sold to people who *do* know that they are buying from a long firm. Here there are two principal ways of protecting the 'fence' from subsequent prosecution.

(a) The fraudster may issue the 'fence' with an invoice marked up to the full market value of the goods. However, this is not the price actually paid, for the fraudster is paid a sum in cash that is agreed between him and the 'fence'. When the goods have been delivered and resold by the 'fence', the invoice is destroyed and there is nothing to link the fraudster to the 'fence', unless the police have been carrying out covert observational work.

(b) The fraudster may issue the 'fence', with an invoice marked up to the full value of the goods. In this case, however, instead of paying cash, the 'fence' pays the full amount by cheque, thus giving him hard evidence of bona fide purchase should an account be demanded of him subsequently by the police or the courts. In reality, the fraudster gives him a kick-back in cash to make up the difference between the agreed and the phoney price.

These techniques help to protect the 'fence' considerably. The second method tends to be preferred, since although it exposes the identity of the purchaser, at least until all documentation is destroyed before the fraudsters abscond, it provides the semblance of a normal trading relationship and is proof against undercover police surveillance of the long firm. Furthermore, by helping the 'fence', they also provide security to the organizers, by removing a major incentive for 'fences' to 'grass', that is, the fence's need to trade off the organizers in exchange for his own non-prosecution.

(6) A robbery or a fire is sometimes used as a means of hiding the true nature of the fraudulent enterprise. This is particularly common in 'businessman-frauds', as the frequent references in business humour to the good fortune of having a fire or robbery may imply. Typical of this humour is the following story related to me by a long-firm fraudster: 'These two l.f. men were sitting down having a brandy in the dining room when they heard a fire engine going past with its siren going. So one says to the other: "there they go, interfering again".'

Some informants have suggested that English gangsters were also involved in arson as an adjunct to long-firm fraud. Sometimes the business premises are left uninsured, so that the fraudsters can claim their fire loss as a reason for failure; at other times the premises are insured, and a fraud is perpetrated upon the insurance company. In his history of fire insurance, Cato Carter (1972, p. 204) states that during the 1920s and early 1930s, a gang of fire raisers was organized by a

> highly experienced loss assessor who nearly always acted for claimants, most of whom were persons or corporations of impeccable integrity... The conspiracy began in earnest with a fire in Deansgate, Manchester, in 1927. [The loss assessor] happened to be at the Midland Hotel, Manchester, when it occurred. The claim for £32 000 was agreed with the assessor at £29 000, and four members of the fire raisers' gang were later proved to have received £22 000 of this, which was the profit on the claim, the balance of £7000 being the real cost of the stock and contents plus expenses. The Company's assessor had failed in his duty. A man had been found who was willing to start fires. A salvage merchant, able to supply rewrapped defective or previously fire-damaged stock, was already in the gang. The object was to start bogus businesses with the intention of setting them on fire to make money from the insurance claims. Premises with the right physical characteristics had to be carefully selected, stock and account books constructed, and insurance cover obtained, for grossly inflated sums.

There is no evidence to link the assessor with frauds which obtained goods from creditors, but the basic principles are the same, whether the offence be 'pure' finance-oriented arson or arson-cum-long-firm.

Arson is also popular with American crime syndicates in connection with long firms, though it is not clear whether creditors are paid from the insurance money or whether both they and the insurance company are defrauded. Teresa (1973, pp. 83–4) states that

> Bust-outs are big business in New England. The mob makes millions off them every year and it's hard as hell for the law to get a handle on it. Everyone has his own technique, but the way we worked it was to first get a guy to front for us who had a good credit rating and no criminal record. That's not as hard as you might think. People are greedy, especially businessmen, and if they see a way to make a fast buck, they'll grab at it . . . [Describes the standard credit build-up of a long firm before Christmas.] We'd sell as much as we could before the Christmas rush, and then hire a torch artist, a good arsonist. But before he torched the place, we'd move all the toys and appliances out the back door and sell them to a fence. All we left in the place were some broken toys and crates or some refrigerators and stoves we took from a junk pile. Then when the place burned down, we'd collect the insurance and declare bankruptcy . . . When we were ready to bust the two places out, we called in Billy . . . Now Billy was an artist when it came to handling an arson. When he burned a building down, believe me, you could put what was left of that place in a tea cup . . . he had some special stuff that he'd never tell anyone about. He charged 5000 dollars for a job and when he was through the insurance company had to pay up because there was no way they could prove an arson.

In the English cases about which I have been told, care was taken to leave in the building goods similar to the normal trading goods of the business concerned. For modern forensic techniques can identify the alien matter, thus generating 'heat' from the police and insurance investigators. In one case a perfume factory was burned, and here there was little left to provide evidence of arson.

My informants have stated that to the best of their knowledge, full-scale arson in relation to 'villain-frauds' is relatively rare in England. What is far more common is the burning of documentation relevant to the fraud, for it is widely believed that the less information the police have about the fraud in their possession, the harder the fraud will be to investigate and the better the chances of the fraudsters escaping punishment. However, sometimes plans can misfire, and one unfortunate organizer took home all the company invoices and accounts for burning, only to find that heavy rain doused the fire. The next day, before he could re-light his bonfire, the police raided his home and recovered all the documents intact.

In other cases, long-firm fraudsters may arrange genuine burglaries or hijackings (or report non-existent ones to the police) as a way of accounting for the disappearance of stock from the warehouse. However, this may increase rather than reduce police interest, and requires considerable nerve on the fraudster's part. As with arson, it can be used as a money-maker in its own right or as an acceptable way of explaining away to creditors the 'losses' sustained by the business. In his classic study of crime in England between the wars, Mannheim (1940, p. 189) reports that as a Berlin magistrate, he frequently had to deal – shortly after the stabilization of the Deutschmark – with unsuccessful burglaries, 'staged at times when trade was particularly slack, and usually combined with fraudulent bankruptcy. They do not seem so prominent in this country, and the Commissioner of the Metropolitan Police testifies that they are "comparatively rare".' (This is Mannheim's only reference to long-firm fraud.)

Burglary and hijacking have the advantage over arson that they require no capital outlay on the goods to be burned, but they can generate greater police suspicion than arson, particularly if the police are unable to pick up any trace of the allegedly stolen goods. In any event, the police are better geared to dealing with burglaries than they are with arson.

(7) The final technique for avoiding conviction to be discussed here is the use of the voluntary liquidation to 'con' creditors. This is used only by the more sophisticated long-firm merchants, and was particularly popular during the 1950s and after the mid-1970s.

A businessman may obtain, say, £100 000 worth of goods on credit. He sells them for about £70 000 cash, pockets £50 000 and leaves the remaining £20 000 in the business in the form of cash and goods. For some £5000 he will buy approximately £30 000 of bankrupt stock from another trader, and get his accountant to write the value of these goods into his books of account as £50–60 000. With £15 000 in cash, and what appears to be £60 000 worth of goods, the businessman will try to get his creditors to agree to a voluntary liquidation. The deficiency will be explained by 'bad debts': he may arrange to receive cheques from a dummy company or even another long firm which conveniently bounce and remain unpaid. He may claim that a 'trusted employee' has disappeared with his funds or stock, or put the losses down to 'stock pilferage': 'You can't trust these blacks or Irish. You treat them right and all they do is thieve from you.' Finally, he may provide a rationale in the form of a fire or burglary, as mentioned in the previous section. Carried out with nerve and panache, and sometimes aided by corrupt accountants and provisional liquidators, this can be a highly profitable and risk-free technique. Much later the creditors will find out that the stock is not worth the book value, but after all, valuation is a difficult matter and values change! Mostly, creditors will 'put it down to experience', unless the police intervene on their own initiative on the basis of information received elsewhere. Even if the police try to do something about the suspected fraud, they may be unable to find a complainant. The voluntary liquidation long firm requires the ability to handle creditors and others 'upfront' and the acceptance of a lower *percentage* profit than the cruder 'bust-out' techniques. However, as the hypothetical example above demonstrates, it can combine profitability with relative safety to a degree that other *modus operandi* cannot.

This type of operation can be and is carried out in many areas of trade, but in the late 1970s it has been particularly popular in the record business, where companies going 'bust' may sell their perfect stock for a good price in cash and replace them with almost worthless 'deletions' which they have bought for a very low price. They then claim to the liquidator that these deleted records are their normal stock, if he takes the trouble to ask them.

In order to become a top-class long-firm fraudster, the skills described in this chapter have to be refined until they become almost 'second nature' to the person concerned. The top-class fraudster can judge within moments the strengths and weaknesses of the people with whom he is dealing, can sense when one of his partners is trying to 'con' him, can adjust his public *persona* to the environment in which he operates. He will have had to improvise schemes and stories for the benefit of creditors, backers, partners and 'front men': social skills for the human jungle. As one skilled professional explained:

I had developed a sixth sense of perfect timing to know what to say and when to say it. Even when I had to get some credit but I was skint [had no money], I had a way of dealing with it. I would go to a restaurant where I was well known and just as I was leaving, before I had to pay the bill, I would arrange with the waiter to call me to the phone. I would leave a note saying that I was sorry, but an emergency had called me away before I could pay, but I would always come back and pay within 24 hours. Or I would say to the waiter: 'book me a table for this evening, and I'll pay both bills then'. And the waiter, knowing he would get a good tip, would pay the bill out of his own pocket. You have to cultivate certain places where you can do this though, and they have to trust you.
In some people, like myself, this sixth sense is innate, but other people have to try to develop it. A lot of people are highly intelligent and competent, but they can never manage it: they are not intuitive enough. To be really skilful at l.f.s you need this intuition and also years of experience. You need to build upon this gift and learn from your mistakes. Then you can acquire real *finesse*.

IV. Social and Criminal Organization of Long-Firm Fraud

The description of the social and organizational settings in which crimes take place is a necessary prelude to the analysis of criminal careers, because although to some extent, individual criminal entrepreneurs can modify the organization of crime, they are nevertheless constrained by existing organizational structures. Consequently, it makes as little sense to discuss criminal careers without looking at patterns of criminal organization as it does to examine the latter independent of patterns of social control and policing.

At the most general level, it may be observed that social and criminal organization are inseparable, for it is the social contacts of criminals that determine the possible range of their organizational activities. Furthermore, the specific forms that social relationships take, for example, on the continuum between co-operation and competition, determine the relative advantages and disadvantages of different *modus operandi* and organizational forms.

I have already stressed the fact that large-scale long firms can be carried out by people who have no social or commercial contact with the underworld proper. For people such as these, the organizational and social setting of their frauds is identical with that of equivalent legitimate businesses, and provided that they are not caught, their crimes are in a sense 'private' crimes. Moreover, these types of fraud can be practised without the difficulties of property disposal and profit reduction experienced by the solo master-burglar Charles Peace (McIntosh, 1975, p. 24). Like many 'criminals of the upperworld', the 'businessman-fraudster' can make large amounts of money from crime without ever becoming a 'known criminal', still less a convicted one. In the former respect, he differs from the racketeer and the 'professional fence', whose clients must know about them in order for them to make a good living, in consequence of which they generally become 'known to the police'. (However, as I shall argue in Chapters VIII and IX, internally satisfying knowledge is one thing: proof in court is quite another.)

In this sense, the organization of long-firm fraud can be independent of a 'criminal network'. Although it is difficult to run a large number of long-firm frauds sequentially without employing 'front men' or without being seen as a 'fraudster', it is quite possible for someone to have long-firm fraud as his principal source of income while remaining completely unknown to the 'criminal fraternity'. To place this in an academic context, one can be what Mack (1964) has charmingly called a 'full-time miscreant' but not a 'professional criminal' by the criteria adopted in Sutherland (1937).

The series of people above – they cannot be called a group because they have no *collective* identity as 'fraudsters' – may be wholly secret deviants. More commonly, however, unlike Cressey's (1953) embezzlers with their non-shareable problems, their activities are known to a select circle of friends or, if there is no great stigma attached to 'bankruptcy fiddles' by the local community, more widely still. However, they are seldom known to the police, because the police do not mix socially with the people who are 'in the know'.

A similar type of long-firm fraudster is he who carries out frauds in collaboration with other shady businessmen but yet does not mix with 'the chaps', that is the underworld. The criminals in this category may restrict their criminal business activities to long-firm fraud, or they may branch out into value-added tax frauds or used-car hire purchase swindles, arson or the arranged robbery of business premises to defraud insurance companies, but they would not commit what to them are 'real' crimes such as armed robbery or burglary. Although they are well aware that what they are doing is an offence contrary to the criminal law, they do not see themselves as 'criminals' but as 'clever businessmen'. In many cases the activities of these people are known within their social circle, but the merchant community does not want to become involved with the police, so neither the police nor the Department of Trade are informed. Furthermore, unless the 'villains' become part of the pub-and-club circle from where the police derive most of their information, they will remain outside the police intelligence network. Consequently, their major risk is that they will be prosecuted by the Department of Trade for bankruptcy or liquidation offences: a somewhat less daunting prospect than prosecution by the police.

Under certain circumstances, however, businessman-fraudsters may become enmeshed into a more traditional 'underworld' structure. They may have weaknesses for the gaming tables, women, men, young boys or girls, and this may bring them into contact with members of the criminal fraternity as it is conventionally defined. Night clubs and casinos are the haunts of the respectable rich and the not-so-respectable rich alike. They may also become the setting in which the former are transmuted into the not-so-respectable *poor*.

A businessman may get into casual conversation with someone in a club and talk to him about his business which is going downhill. The other will sympathize with the unfairness of a world in which hard work brings so little reward and after careful probing to make sure that he is not being 'set up' by 'the law', may suggest that 'if you are going to go bust, you might as well get something out of it for yourself'. If his intuition tells him to continue, he may offer to help the businessman turn his firm into a long firm; or he may try to 'con' him into letting him take over the business with its liabilities, but request that he stay on for a while to maintain 'goodwill', the secret intention being to loot the business as described in the last chapter.

In the case of a businessman who knowingly co-operates in the fraudulent scheme, the organizer will promise him payment and assure him 'on my baby's life' that he will not be 'involved'. However, the first priority is to pay money into the businessman's account or to find some way of implicating him in the fraud, thereby making sure that the businessman will not 'grass him up'. Once the man is trapped into doing something overtly illegal, he is unable to renege upon the deal and should he attempt to do so, he may find that the threat of violence is a very real one.

The businessmen who become involved in long-firm fraud in this way are often surprisingly unaware of the deviousness of their new partners, perhaps because they are looking for a glimmer of light or perhaps because the world of small business deals is very far removed from the sharp hustling world of the professional fraudster. Whatever the reason, they can be persuaded to stay on at the business. At the end of the day, however, he may discover that the minutes of the board meeting which registered the change of ownership have been 'lost' and that there has been no such notification at Companies House. Consequently, in the jargon of the trade, the fraud is 'down to him'. If he threatens to tell the police or the Department of Trade the whole story, he will be reminded of his own part in the conspiracy and may find that the 'nice chaps' have become 'gangsters'. Informants have stated that 'they threatened to shoot my legs off' or that 'they asked me how my wife would feel with acid burns all over her face'. This kind of pressure can be expected to deter the average businessman from 'grassing'. (These examples were provided by lawyers whose clients had told them but had not wanted them raised in defences.)

One question that might be asked about this type of long-firm fraud is why does the businessman not carry it out without underworld help. After all, he has trade outlets to whom he can sell and has a reasonable amount of business acumen. The reasons are complex but relate mainly to the fear or timidity of the businessman and to the presumed ability of the 'professional villain' to make the operation easier. What is being planned is a major *coup* against creditors and, hopefully, the police: many businessmen do not have the nerve to carry out this type of operation alone. Furthermore, they may not have the finance required for a major long-firm fraud, nor may they have the outlets to take large quantities of goods for cash. Finally, they may feel that they do not have the expertise to pass off the failure as a legitimate one, whereas the 'villain' may reassure the businessman that his accountants will straighten out the matter for him (*sic*!). The desire for safety under the umbrella of a large criminal organization is not confined to those 'legitimates' who stray from the fold for the first time, however; as I shall demonstrate later, it also afflicts already active criminals.

So far, I have discussed the social organization of what by Sutherland's definition are 'non-professional' long-firm fraudsters. For Sutherland (1937, pp. 197–8) argues that one cannot become a 'professional' thief without receiving one's education through association with professional thieves. By contrast, I have argued that if a businessman has the necessary cunning and aptitudes, he has no need for the 'differential association of thieves'. Indeed, if he wishes to avoid police surveillance, he might do better to avoid 'the underworld' altogether. It may be that Sutherland's model applies well to skilled, particularly small-volume thefts, but one does not have to carry out many long-firm frauds to maintain a life-style that is reasonable by conventional standards.

There are some further points of interest here. Both Sutherland (1937) and Maurer (1940) state that professional criminals rely for their immunity from conviction (if not from arrest) upon 'the fix' who operates in major towns and cities in the United States: the criminals pay 'the fix' either in advance or when they get into trouble, and he in turn pays off the police, lawyers, and judges. However, the long-firm fraudsters discussed hitherto either remain so close to the margins of the law that the courts are unable to classify them as 'criminals' or else remain unperceived as criminals by any others at all. Consequently, even where corruption is possible, they have no need of 'the fix'.

Granted that the existence of a 'subculture of professional fraudsters' is not a *necessary* condition for the existence of profitable long-firm frauds, it is nevertheless the case that such subcultures have existed during some historical periods. The material presented in Chapter II provides ample testimony of this, and even where there is no positive evidence, one cannot infer that no long-firm underworld existed: the fraudsters may have been very skilful, or they may have been dealt with non-criminally, or the police may have been incompetent.

The Sutherland type of analysis is not particularly helpful in the way we classify the organization of long-firm fraud. As Mack (1975, p. 177) points out, it

> gives too simple a picture of the complex undercover activities and relationships sustained by full-time miscreants ... the concept [of professional crime] treats a fairly complicated system of relationships as though it were a primitively structured aggregate of individuals, a mass of petty criminality dominated by a high table of criminal eminences.

Far more useful, though it too neglects the background organization of crime, is the typology of criminal organization developed by McIntosh (1975). Four basic types of organization are distinguished, of which three are relevant here: *craft* organization, typical of routine thefts and confidence tricks in less developed societies, whose depredations do not involve losses sufficiently great to generate energetic attempts at control; *project* organization, for sophisticated operations involving large sums which require *ad hoc* teams of specialists; and *business* organization, which arises when police corruption enables monopolized extortion and the provision of illegal goods and services to take place. The main mention of long-firm fraud occurs in McIntosh's discussion of project crime (p. 42) and of business organization (p. 65). However, although the typology is not clearly enough differentiated to make categorization certain, there is some evidence to suggest that there have been times when it has been carried on as *craft* crime.

Support for this may be taken from the data on the activities of the Pallash family in Chapter II. Also relevant is the following quotation from one of my informants:

> Right at the beginning of the '60s, it was really incredible. All you had to do was to get hold of a lease on a little shop, get two accommodation addresses, a bird to do the typing, and you were away. If you had a few hundred quid [pounds] cash, you would pay for the first few orders on time, double them up, flog the gear through your mates on the markets, and fuck off fast. You'd make about 60–75 per cent of the value of the gear, and virtually no overheads, so it was a real doddle [very easy]. We used to do this time and time again, and they couldn't do fuck all about it.

For what one wag called a 'little quickie', no sophistication is necessary, since genuine small businessmen are often incompetent and inarticulate buyers, and commission-hungry reps will often take great pleasure in what they regard as 'pulling a fast one', that is, selling someone a large number of articles for which, were he legitimate, he would have no use. At times when credit is easily available and law-enforcement agencies are very busy or disorganized, long-firm fraud can be carried out on a craft basis: trade protection societies carry the main burden of crime prevention.

When credit becomes harder to get and the police become more efficient, long-firm frauds become project crimes. However, this does not mean that changes in personnel are *required*, as McIntosh (1975) appears to believe. It means that planning and organization have to be more careful, but unless goods are involved which are particularly difficult to resell or there is a large increase in the volume obtained or a need for large initial finance, there may be no change whatever in personnel. It depends how adaptable the fraudsters are.

Finally, for reasons to be discussed, long-firm frauds may become subsumed under the umbrella organization of 'syndicated crime'. Just as 'fences' have sought sometimes to control 'thieves', so too have 'gangsters' sought to impose their hegemony over long-firm fraudsters.

In connection with the supposed hegemony of syndicated crime, Albini (1971) has noted that the power of any one syndicate may be subject to severe geographical limitations. I would add to this and state that the range of the gang's intelligence network imposes a further crucial constraint upon its power to control criminal activities. In the case of long-firm fraud, in particular, the fact that businessmen can run successful frauds without recourse to the resources of the underworld makes syndicate control over them highly problematic. As I have argued earlier, this lack of underworld involvement also reduces the probability that the police will learn of the fraud, so in circumstances where the syndicates control the police, 'businessman-fraudsters' may still remain outside their criminal intelligence networks. Furthermore, even though 'villain-fraudsters' in London may all operate under the aegis of crime syndicates there, there is no *a priori* reason to believe that long-firm fraudsters in, say, Manchester will not continue to operate on a craft or project basis. The range of a gang's power is not necessarily constant over time and space: it has to be validated by empirical study, however difficult this may be in practice.

In London in the 1950s there were criminal gangs, but they were involved principally in prostitution, gaming and extortion. This is clear from the memoirs of prominent criminals of the period (Hill, 1955; Phelan, 1953) and from journalistic accounts such as that of Lucas (1969). The general impression gained is that during the

1950s members of what one might term the 'underworld proper' were too unsophisticated to move into business crime: the sole exceptions were their involvement in motor trade 'fiddles' and black marketeering (Hill, 1955; Payne, 1973).

It is not possible to assert definitively that there was no major 'gangster' involvement in long-firm fraud during this period, but none of my informants have given any indication that there was any centralized organization of long-firm frauds during the 1950s. This is consistent with the data on the previous criminal records of all those convicted at the London Central Criminal Court (Old Bailey) in connection with long-firm frauds, presented in Table 4.1.

TABLE 4.1 Criminal backgrounds of persons convicted for long-firm frauds at the Central Criminal Court, London, 1948–72

Prior convictions (type)	Number	1948–61 Percentage	Number	1962–72 Percentage
Business[1]	47	33·6	30	16·7
Mixed property and violence	8	5·7	25	13·9
Robbery	0	0·0	1	0·6
Non-property related violence	2	1·4	3	1·7
Theft	13	9·3	14	7·8
Mixed property and business	19	13·6	53	29·4
Other[2]	2	1·4	6	3·3
Total previously convicted	91	65·0	132	73·3
Total *without* previous convictions	49	35·0	48	26·7
Total overall	140	100·0	180	100·0

NOTES:
[1] includes receiving and handling stolen property.
[2] includes taking and driving away, motoring offences, bigamy and soliciting for the purpose of prostitution.

If we examine the data for the period 1948–61, we observe that offenders with no previous convictions or with those solely for business crime, that is, fraud and receiving, form 68·6 per cent of the total. This suggests that if there were any traditional underworld involvement in long-firm fraud, those 'villains' either must have operated at a background level or at least must have been more successful at evading prosecution and conviction than were those in the convicted sample. The first hypothesis is unfalsifiable, and I have found nothing to support it. The second hypothesis is unlikely, for the following reasons:

First, businessmen with no previous convictions are less likely than 'known villains' to enter the police intelligence network. Secondly, businessmen with no previous convictions (or with convictions only for motoring offences) are more likely than 'known villains' to be believed by the police when they seek to account for the failure of their businesses as if they were legitimate failures. Thirdly, related to the second point above, businessmen tend to use long-firm fraud techniques which are legally more ambiguous than those employed by underworld-connected people. For example, they use the 'voluntary liquidation' technique, or cover their tracks by falsifying their books of account rather than by running the business in a false name and then absconding. The consequence of this is that irrespective of whether or not the police *believe* their stories, 'businessman-fraudsters' are less likely than 'underworld-fraudsters' to be prosecuted, the reason being that it is harder to categorize their activities as 'crime'.

If *any* of these points is accepted, it will follow that the sample of convicted offenders significantly *under*-represents the proportion of sophisticated business criminals. The consequence is that the picture of the 'typical long-firm fraudster' of the 1950s becomes skewed still more strongly against the involvement of the 'thief subculture' in long-firm fraud. Using a conventional conception of 'the underworld', a fair summary of the criminal organization of long-firm fraud in the 1950s in England is that it was carried out as craft or project organization by fairly autonomous small groupings of 'professional fraudsters' or by individual businessmen acting outside mainstream underworld subcultures.

Long-firm fraud and 'organized crime' in England in the 1960s

The 1960s saw the emergence of criminal gangs in London on a scale not hitherto experienced. Long-firm frauds played a principal part in both the rise and fall of those gangs: the rise, because they provided the financial base on which the edifices of the Kray and Richardson 'criminal empires' were constructed; the fall, because the fraudsters eventually turned upon the 'monsters' who had grown fat upon their labours and became the crucial prosecution witnesses without whom the principals of both gangs might have remained unconvicted until much later.

The impact of long firms upon the Kray gang is described by their leading organizer as follows (Payne, 1973, p. 65):

> The goods bought on credit in Brixton were sold through another Kray long firm in the East End. The gang made a lot of money in Brixton, and the success of this fraud first pumped life into the organisation, and turned it from a loose collection of villains into a

continuing criminal creature that was larger and more powerful than its components.

This analysis has been confirmed by other independent sources. It applies equally to the development of the Richardson gang 'empire'.

As far as I have been able to ascertain, before the 1960s, the long-firm fraudsters connected with the underworld remained organizationally separate from their 'backers' and 'fences'. Because their activities were carried on *sub rosa*, the market relations between 'fence' and organizer and between 'backer' and organizer were more unequal than the equivalent relations in legitimate commerce, but there was no attempt on anyone's part to impose any *general* organizational rationality upon long-firm frauds. If an organizer had the ability to do so, he would improve his profitability by financing his own frauds and 'fencing' his own goods, but that was his individual business decision. The social network of each individual fraudster determined his possible sources of finance and trade outlets, and these in turn were often related to the area in which he lived and worked.

Within this context, the Krays and Richardsons began to develop an interest in long-firm fraud. They sought to replace this relatively unorganized system with a vertically-integrated hierarchical system headed by themselves. The Krays modelled themselves upon their media-derived portrait of Al Capone, while the Richardsons preferred the less brash business-executive type of gangster image, but their basic aims were the same: to use the profits from long-firm fraud to pay their underlings and gain a monopoly on extortion and on criminal activity generally. Moving from a somewhat narrow initial geographical base, they would extend their operations as far as they could into both the underworld and the upperworld.

Although Mack's (1964) conception of the criminal community as no longer a place but a system of social relationships and functions was valid in the early 1960s, geographical factors were still important then in the organization of crime. Indeed, they still are important, as the study of 'fencing' in the United States by Walsh (1977) indicates. This 'criminal area' aspect is expressed in the following observation about the 'long-firm scene' by one of my informants:

> L.f. men tend to group together, according to the areas in which they live, or at least they used to live. In London, the East End, the south-east London, and the west London mobs kept to themselves, and there were fences in each area who took the gear from that area. Sometimes, areas specialized in certain types of goods. For instance, the west London mob specialized in

radios... Even though X was rich and Jewish, he was accepted by the south-east London mob because he had grown up with them. Y, on the other hand, was an immigrant and an outsider. In each area, all the villains knew each other, because they were at school and grew up together. The point was that you would only deal with people you knew, and each l.f. man guarded his finance sources and his customers from the others. I would think that newcomers would not be able to find any of the big 'fences' for their gear, because they would not trust them.

It was upon this rather localized world of little coteries that the London gangsters sought to impose order. The Krays initially heard about long-firm frauds through their superb system of criminal intelligence. They would receive information that John Doe was 'running an l.f.' in the East End, go down to his premises and simply demand money from him. The proprietor knew that if he refused to pay them, he would be very severely beaten and/or the Fraud Squad would be given an anonymous tip-off that he was operating a long-firm fraud. This tactic was pure extortion, and led one organizer to describe them as 'nothing more than glorified ponces [pimps]. They had no idea whatever of business. All they would do was to grab whatever they saw and nick it.' Consequently, they often ruined the long firms from which they extorted money before the latter had come to fruition, thereby killing the goose that laid the golden eggs: a characteristic that continued throughout their careers in crime.

The early activities of the Krays are described fully and excellently in the books of Pearson (1972) and Payne (1973), and there is no point in my repeating them here. They followed the classic 'hard man' route of the 'heavies' who are to be found in many large cities. In 1960, however, they met a sophisticated fraudster who suggested that they go into the running of long-firm frauds themselves rather than simply extort funds from independent long-firm merchants. The techniques they used were fairly routine but highly effective. They selected 'front men' from the available pool of thieves and aristocratic layabouts, and put them into large numbers of companies. These companies either cross-referenced one another or else used phoney references from phoney companies based at accommodation addresses. The 'front men' were promised a 'cut' of the proceeds and were told that, if they were convicted, their families would be looked after. They often were caught and convicted, with the consequences for the pattern of 'criminal backgrounds' seen in Table 4.1. One observes a great increase in the proportion of those convicted who had previous convictions for a number of different crimes in the period 1962–1972 compared with the period 1948–1961. This reflects the increase in the number of 'villains' involved in long-firm fraud during the later period.

In fact, the 'front men' were very badly treated by the Krays. Their families might get a few pounds and a card at Christmas, but little more, and the only advantage of working for the Krays was that one would derive some prestige and privilege in prison from being one of 'the Kray Firm'. Their long firms were run by a mixture of intimidation and casualness, with a continual interchange of people between one long firm and another, and threats or actual beatings from their 'minders' to those who appeared to be stepping out of line. The Krays not only had their own 'heavies' to support them but also the occasional lawyer to whom they could turn for assistance in advance of or during a fraud. Sometimes, this assistance involved 'cooling out' potential 'grasses'. The following quotation from a statement to the police – the names have been changed – serves to illustrate nicely the flavour of these operations:

> Jimmy and I went to see a West End solicitor. Jimmy told him that I wanted to sell my business. Mr Lawsoc (the solicitor) asked what type of business it was and I said 'wholesale electrical'. He asked how much I was in debt. I said '£5000 or £6000' and Mr Lawsoc said 'It's an l.f., isn't it?' I knew he meant fraud and I didn't answer. Jimmy didn't answer. Then Mr Lawsoc said, 'You can tell me, I know all about these things'. Mr Lawsoc then said to me 'How did you get involved in it?' I didn't answer. He then asked Jim his name and he told him it was Mr Smith. Mr Lawsoc laughed and said 'You must tell me your proper name'. Jimmy then told him it was Jimmy Jameson. Mr Lawsoc asked my name, but not our address. Jim asked him how he stood getting goods on cash on delivery and paying with cheques although we had no cash in the bank to meet them. The solicitor said that the only way round it was to get a letter from someone to the effect that we were expecting to have £5000 paid into our bank. He said that even then it might not work. Jimmy asked him if he would defend him if he was charged with this offence. Mr Lawsoc said that he would but that he could not be sure of getting him off. Jimmy then asked if I could sell the business, and Mr Lawsoc said that I could but as I was the only principal, I could not sell the debts owing to the fact that it was not a limited company.
> Jimmy then asked him if there was any way we could get out of trouble and Mr Lawsoc said, 'Why don't you arrange a burglary and make out that there are thousands of pounds worth of goods stolen?' He asked me if we were insured and I said 'no'. He said, 'That's good, it won't make you any money but it will get you out of trouble.' Jimmy then gave him £10, or I should say placed it on a cabinet in the room and we left...
> [Later on] I went to see Mr Lawsoc in the West End. I told him I

intended to give myself up to the police. He said, 'How much money have you put aside?' I said 'nothing'. He said 'You must be joking.' I said 'I have no money'. He said 'I will defend you but it will cost you a great deal of money. Where do you intend getting it?' I did not answer and he suggested that I contact Jimmy. I said I would. Then I asked him what he thought I would get, and he said 'I won't flannel you, 3 to 5 years.' He said 'If I were you I would tell the boys before you go to the police as they might not like it.' He suggested that I should not put any of the boys in it as I would be cutting my own throat. He said I should make out that I was having an affair with an Italian who took all the money out of the business and then left me. I should take all the blame on my own and he would get me off as lightly as he could. He said to me that if you are seen by the police you can tell them anything you want, but don't sign anything. He then said, 'Maybe it is better to say nothing to them at all.'

Given this kind of advice, it is not surprising that the Krays were not charged with long-firm frauds until they were arrested for murder. Payne, with the Krays in tandem, did succeed for a time in imposing some kind of order upon the organization of long-firm fraud in the East End of London. They discovered that most businessmen and long-firm fraudsters were not accustomed to coping with threats of violence, and that they were easy pickings for people with violent reputations. As one long-firm organizer said:

The twins used to rely on the fact that most businessmen were just ordinary blokes who didn't want to know about violence. They found that they could do the same thing with straight business-men: they wouldn't dare tell the police because they knew all about the Krays' reputation. Besides, they thought that the police were all bent. So by and large, they just got away with it.

However, their control even over those long firms in East London that they knew about was not total, and their power outside the metropolis was extremely tentative. The same long-firm merchant:

I had met the Krays through Brown, who had sold me some stuff, cheap... I did this l.f. from which I supplied all the furnishings for the Krays' clubs and for some of their other little rackets. They tried to muscle in, but I made sure that I got my share. That l.f. closed down and I moved up to Manchester to open up a couple of other l.f.s which were supposed to be mail-order firms... Anyway, even though I thought I had seen them off the previous time, they still went up to Manchester when they found out I was doing an l.f. there. Fortunately, though, the police heard about their visit, met them at the Station, and escorted them back again. But that was the way they did things. I knew that once I let them take liberties with me, they would be back again every time.

The Krays' involvement in long-firm fraud, though substantial, was lacking in any real sophistication. Charles Kray, who was older than the twins, comprehended the potential of the frauds, but the twins themselves really regarded them as an easy source of 'readies' (cash). Instead of waiting for the frauds to mature and build up their credit ratings, they would grab the takings and spend them immediately. Their general lack of understanding of business procedures is nicely expressed by Payne (1973, p. 41):

> Reggie was always split between two images of himself: the big gangster, and the smooth business executive. Every month or two the executive would come to the top and he would get the urge to keep books. 'You have to keep books to see how the finance is going', he would say. At first his idea was to accumulate a mass of bits of paper on which he had written, in his appalling hand, 'Long firm in the City, £40', 'Pension from club in Walthamstow, £30'. After a while, he sent out for expensive ledgers and used to write it in all of them. I tried to tell him books were rather too incriminating for gangsters to keep, but he wouldn't listen. He would say that no-one understood them but him, and when I pointed out that 'long firm' meant long firm, and 'pension' meant pension, whatever way you looked at it, he just walked away.

Why, then, did a sophisticate like Payne go into partership with them? He states (p. 47) that

> They were an advantage to me because they had promoted a lot of hero-worship throughout the East End. If you wanted faces for a long firm, they would produce a couple of idiots who would do as they were told. You didn't have to worry too much. The Krays had control of the situation... There were advantages in the club world, too, because everybody knew their association and no-one came in demanding pensions... They kept employees in line, stopped them taking too much out of the till, made sure no-one in the firm was talking in the pubs, kept the opposition under control, kept order in the clubs. These are all things that the real police do for legitimate businesses.

Eventually, however, their inability to deliver their promises and the resentment that their haphazard behaviour generated in their 'front men' led to Payne's disillusionment with their long-term prospects. In particular – although Payne appears to play down the importance of this – their denial of what he considered to be his proper remuneration, coupled with their attempts to kill him, made him decide to make a statement about their activities to the police. Payne comments, somewhat disingenuously, on this:

> This is not to say that deals with the police were not done, but that in this situation, deals were hardly necessary. For instance, I

put myself in considerable jeopardy with my first statement, but in my then situation it was worth it. I was at the time being tried for Carston Securities [a long firm] and I was amazed when no evidence was offered against me.

The reader may draw his own conclusions about the genuineness of Payne's claims to amazement.

Despite their brief but profitable venture into the world of fraud, the Krays remained above all racketeers and extortionists. Their principal ability was the fear they managed to instil into everyone around them, and this generated a perverse popularity in their area, as well as a glamorous mystique which attracted celebrities to them. As one man said of them, respectfully; 'They got together a tightly-knit group which had real loyalty towards them. In the East End, they respect animals, and they were the roughest animals in the pack. So, like any animals, the others followed their natural leader. They weren't terrorized so much as hypnotized.'

Although they had come from similar social class backgrounds, the Richardsons, particularly Charles Richardson, were more attuned to the business world than were the Krays. Whereas the very random unpredictability of the Krays' violence was an important part of their mystique, the Richardsons used violence in a much more instrumental way to maintain their control over south-east London. The essence of their activities was captured nicely in the opening speech for the prosecution at the Richardsons' 'torture trial' in 1966:

> The eight men in the dock are part of a gang of thugs under the leadership of Charles Richardson whose policy and practice over a number of years was to enforce his will and his intentions by violence and intimidation... The principal object of that policy was to secure for Charles Richardson the absolute domination of a somewhat disreputable business fraternity who were actively engaged in carrying on what I think can rightfully be called tinpot companies, dozens of them, who were busily occupied in buying large quantities and large amounts upon credit and in the end not paying for them, or certainly not paying for all of them... It will be impossible to avoid reference to these business transactions and dealings because they provide both the background and the motive for the offences charged... Charles Richardson grew in power and influence in that particular fraternity over which he presided, and the policy was so successful that no person who had become a victim of it dared complain lest worse, if worse were possible, befell him or the members of his family...

Counsel went on to describe the varied kinds of torture which were inflicted upon victims, from having a canteen of knives thrown at them at the 'mild' end to having their penises wired up to electric generators at the 'heavy' end. He added that many of the witnesses for the prosecution were 'carrying on companies which were not run on the strictest lines of honesty – and it would not be right to put those witnesses forward... as models of rectitude and propriety'.

A nice piece of understatement as a reference to professional long-firm fraudsters! How did this situation come about? The Richardson brothers ran a large, semi-legitimate scrap-metal company in south-east London, which served as a cover for their criminal activities as well as a source of lawful profits. They started off on robberies, fraudulent car deals, and protection rackets, and gradually moved into some more or less legitimate mining operations in South Africa as well as into fraud. The origin of their involvement in long-firm fraud was probably a large 'fence' who had grown up with them. Later on, an important long-firm organizer started to do some purchase-tax frauds for them, and he introduced them to the other long-firm merchants in his circle. The way they operated and the way they moved into the long-firm scene is illustrated in the following extracts from my interviews with a 'prince of the long-firm' (All names have been changed except those of the Krays, Richardsons, Dixons and Leslie Payne, all of whom are sufficiently public already not to suffer from this further exposure.)

I had been doing a few fiddles here and there, and after running clubs for a bit, I met Blank, who suggested that we do something in the motor trade. We found somewhere in Camberwell [south London] and we did all right... I was introduced there to Charlie and Eddie Richardson, who bought a couple of cars off me on hire purchase. They did not keep up with the payments, and the H. P. company repossessed them and gave me a lot of aggravation. I phoned the Richardsons up, and they immediately paid me the full amount in cash, which impressed me greatly. That was all I saw of them for some time... While I had been in France, one of the villains who had given me a dud cheque for the car came to see me and told me that there was a warrant out for my arrest in England. He offered me a grand to go to South America if I would sign a form saying they had not swindled me. I refused... After I came back, I no longer wanted to see Blank, who had given me the dud cheques for which I had been nicked in France – I don't blame him now, but that's a different matter – and I went to see Thomson, who had previously run a successful l.f. He introduced me to a friend of his, who set me up in a shop with £1500. The idea was to get goods from the Continent. I went to Italy to order goods in small quantities, which we could pay for, but Thomson had acquired a taste for big money from his l.f. and wanted loads of stuff immediately I disagreed and had to buy him out at a profit to him of £1000. I had met Green and he gave me the money to pay Thomson off, and promised me £8000 on condition that his brother ran the warehouse.

I found Jameson, an Old Harrovian [a famous English private school], who used to have a real lah-di-dah manner, and Smithson, who had been in the travel business before, and I made them directors. Smithson meanwhile met the managing director of Fraudways Travel, who was a playboy married to an heiress. His firm was doing very little business, but he had plenty of money and did not care. We had a spare room in the front of our firm's premises, and we set up a travel business and agreed to split the commission on tickets with the managing director of Fraudways. We got a fantastic connection through a Pakistani, and we sold him tickets at 10 per cent discount, although we got back 4 per cent in commission. We were losing money, but since we were paid in advance for the tickets, we used the money to finance the main business. We also got lots of liquor and cigarettes, which I sold to a fence I knew.

We decided that we would change the name of our company to something a bit flashier, and we did that. At that time, I had the idea of importing nylon stockings, which I was one of the first people to do on a big scale. Everybody in Italy – even the priests – wanted to sell stockings, and I thought we could get hold of them easily. So I moved into the *prima* hotel in Milano and got myself a flat in the hotel, and found myself a good shipper. By doing this, I knew that the shipper would give me a good reference, since he had a direct interest in the quantity of goods exported.

We also had £100 000 worth of bills of exchange printed, which on the Continent they use to pay for goods. I had them printed in denominations of £1500, because I knew that I could always get hold of that amount of money in an emergency, whereas if the bill was larger, I would not. You have to be very careful in Italy – like in France – because there, if you do not pay a bill, that is an offence, and they put you in jail and throw away the key...

What we used to do was to give, say, a bill of exchange worth £1500 on a £1200 transaction, and get £300 cash for the difference. People will do this if you look affluent and like you do not need the money: they want to get well in with you. We would keep this extra cash in my safe, and Jameson would take it back to England to pay our bills there. In this way, we paid off all our English creditors at that time.

Smithson suggested that we take over Fraudways Travel, which had these poncey offices in Mayfair, and a friend of his who ran a Building Society told him of a bank manager who might help us. He wasn't bent or anything: he just wanted to keep in well with the other fellow.

So far, everything was legitimate, and I thought I had a good business. I got paid £30 a week, and Green and Smithson got £20. Green seemed OK, and I felt that I could go back to Italy. I went back to the flat in the hotel, and I hired a secretary and got a butler-cum-chauffeur, so to the Italians, I was a wealthy man. I got all the stockings, because Green said he had all these contacts for selling them.

Unfortunately, he wasn't selling the stockings: his brother was busy nicking them from the warehouse. We had so many that the Customs people refused to take any more in bond, and we had to sell them cheap to a fellow who became a millionaire. He must have made at least a hundred grand out of us.

So we were losing £25–50 000 on the stockings, we had to pay the bills of exchange in Italy, I was flying three times a week to London, and I couldn't get the outlets in England. Green came over to Italy in his new 'E' type Jaguar, dressed like a playboy on what he had nicked from me. He knew nothing about stockings and he made a bad impression on the suppliers, so I decided that I had to get rid of him. I had exchanged one villain backer, Thomson, for an even bigger villain. I needed some money quick, so I did a little fiddle with some jewellery, and with that, I paid Green off and raised some money to pay the bills of exchange.

One big problem was that on the basis of the orders I had given, some of the Italian suppliers had ordered machinery. If I stopped their orders, they would be ruined. They were all small people, and I did not want to break them. Fortunately, Blank came to Italy, and he said that he wanted to buy stockings, so I gave him the names of my suppliers. Meanwhile, Jameson came to me and told me that a man called Leslie Payne was interested in doing business and buying stockings from me. Payne flew out, and I got him and his wife a suite in the hotel. We had a little chat, and Payne said he was short of a few bob in Italy and he gave me a cheque for £250.

I wanted to see what kind of fellow he was, so I had the cheque 'expressed' and needless to say, it bounced. So I thought to myself, he can't be much of an operator if he hasn't got 250 quid in his account. But anyway, I carried on with him. He said he would introduce me to his partners, and Reggie Kray came out with a couple of other people. I had tangled with one of them over the car business, but he apologized, and I bought him a St Christopher medallion as a present, and gave Payne a Rolex. They were all smartly dressed and had the appearance of businessmen. So I said I would go and see the Krays next time I was in London: I didn't realize that they were big gangsters then.

Meanwhile, my overheads were going up all the time, as all my employees wanted more money, so I went to London and got in touch with Les, who invited me to Esmeralda's Barn, which he was running. He sent a car to the flat in London where I was staying, and apart from the driver, there were two heavies who sat on either side of me. I thought to myself: 'This is like Chicago!' I went to Esmeralda's, and Les introduced me to Ronnie and Reggie and some heavies and their l.f. man, who was supposed to be their 'expert' on textiles. After talking to him for a short while, I realized that he knew very little about the trade. But the Krays suggested that I supply them with stockings, for which they would pay along with expenses. Realizing from the whole scene that it was not healthy to disagree, I agreed to do this...

At the end of the meal, the bill came, and Ronnie sent it back, saying that it was down to him. But I wanted to show that I was a class above them, and I insisted on paying my share. I said I had to get up early the next day, and I left in a taxi. I was very relieved to get away from them.

I had no expectation of being paid for the goods in advance, as we had agreed, but I sent Jameson around anyway. Surprisingly [*sic!*] they did not want to know about paying in advance, the whole thing was dropped, and apart from one time, I never saw the Krays again. While all this was going on, Blank was building up his stockings business... He always had good ideas, so I listened to him. One day, he mentioned some man who was in trouble but who had a bank which was insolvent, and which I could have for £20000, which was what it owed. This was a way round my financial problems, but I did not have the money straightaway. I had met another Pakistani, who wanted air tickets, and I sold him a lot at 10 per cent below cost price to raise the money. I had met a fellow some time previously called Blackman, and I gave him £10000 to buy Fraudways from the owners, and I made him Managing Director of Fraudways and of the Bank. Blackman said that he would find me some backers for the Bank, but I nearly died when I arrived there to find that the backers were going to be the three Krays and Les Payne. I had no idea that Blackman was in with them, and they wanted to muscle in, which I would have nothing to do with.

At that time, Blank introduced me again to Charlie Richardson and his fence. They wanted stockings and transistor radios from Italy. We became very pally. Charlie gave me £17000 in cash to buy stockings and radios, so I thought he was a reliable man: I knew nothing of the mob at that time, because I never used to mix with villains, only with businessmen and fraudsters. His fence had a terrific business, taking thousands of pounds a day – all cash – and he was a very flashy character. He had made a lot of money on the black market during the War, but in spite of that, he was very likeable. He was a big spender and would think nothing of spending a few hundred pounds in an evening, which in those days, was a lot of money. He and Charlie did a few transactions with me, and always paid cash on the nail.

One day, Charlie came to me and said he had heard that I was having trouble with the Krays at the Bank. He asked if I wanted them to go away, I said yes, and nothing more was heard of them. Later, I met Les Payne at the Club we used to go to, and Les made some remark about my working for Charlie. I asked him what he meant, and he said that Charlie had told them that I was working for him. I half-denied that, but I thought I was better off if Les thought that I was working for him.

Then, there was another incident. Alberto, my supplier in Italy, came to England to try to collect £1000 that Thomson owed him for some stockings. I introduced Alberto to Charlie, and when Charlie heard about the money, he phoned Thomson about it at eleven o'clock in the morning, told him to bring the money round by the time that the banks closed and bring it himself. The money arrived by one o'clock, and Charlie said to Alberto: 'here you are, £500 for you and £500 for me'. He then gave him a few hundred pounds' worth of presents for his family, which didn't cost him anything because it was all nicked. Alberto was very impressed, and he told me about the way Thomson came in shaking with the money. That pleased me because I had the dead needle with him over the travel business, when he had given me a right-hander.

I suppose I should have thought then about the sort of fellow who could see off the Krays and make Thomson shake, but it never occurred to me. You're right when you say that you repress what isn't convenient for you to remember or think about. To me, Charlie and his fence were very charming fellows. They had Walker there doing their purchase-tax fiddles, and all of them seemed to be very pleasant, wealthy people. They told me that we would make a lot of money together, that they would get me a lot of birds, anything I wanted.

I had all the problems with the stockings and the radios, the travel business and the Bank, and it was all too much for me on my own. I had to supervise all of them very closely because the only one I could trust was Jameson. Everybody I knew said what a fantastic guy Charlie was, so I decided to go in with them. That was the only way I could see that I wouldn't have to worry about being fucked by my workers. When I agreed to join them, Walker said to me: 'Welcome to the inner circle. We'll make you a rich man'.

The idea behind the Bank was not to run it like an ordinary bank. In fact, there was this very funny occasion when some old lady came in to open up an account and make a deposit. We didn't know what to do! She put the money in, and almost before she had left the room, the thieves had nicked the money from out of the till.

My idea was to send about ten men around the world to the Far East with a million pounds' worth of travellers' cheques drawn upon the bank. In those days, the cycle of payments took three to six months, because the cheques went to Japan, and then to America, and then to Europe. With the cheques they would buy precious stones, sell them in England, and invest the cash in properties, etc., which were going up like anything in those days. We would earn enough in the period before the travellers' cheques had to be paid to cover our expenses and pay off the airline tickets, for which we had six weeks' credit. The airline tickets, in turn, had been sold to pay off the debts of the textiles and radio business.

We would repeat this cycle every three months, in effect borrowing from the drawees of the travellers' cheques, and the assets we would have would give the Bank a good credit rating with the other banks. I thought it was a good idea then and I still think so now, but that villain Blackman started fiddling and so we had to close down. It was a legitimate bit of juggling, as I intended it in the beginning. It wasn't legal, but it wasn't fraud either.

At the same time, though, I had a lot of debts to pay off, and all the small stockings manufacturers in Italy were owed money, and I paid them from the tickets and from the little fiddle in jewellery that I had started up. I had met this jeweller in Milan who used to buy jewellery at one-third price from people who had lost more than they could afford in the casinos. I was to be his partner, but I needed 20 000 dollars, which I borrowed from a Mafia Don whom I had met. I was to give him 40 000 dollars back, but he demanded 40 000 dollars in cash, not in the nominal value of the jewellery we bought cheap. I didn't have that kind of money, and he installed two gangsters 24 hours a day in my flat until I paid him. So I phoned Alberto and got him to hire a car, and with two suitcases, I jumped out of the window in the middle of the night and drove straight to Switzerland, where I changed my passport, because I had heard that the jeweller had complained about me in Italy and in Switzerland. I told Smithson to take his wife and get away that night, but he was afraid of leaving his nice luggage! So when he got the train to Switzerland the next day, he was arrested: all due to his greed.

While I was in Italy, I had left unpaid debts for £60 000 of jewellery and 20 000 dollars of air tickets. To them, I was a big businessman, and they did not worry about credit. It is easy to do fiddles with bills of exchange, and if they ever become common in England, you will really see big l.f.s. I had paid the stocking suppliers, though.

Meanwhile, I started with the air tickets in earnest, and the firm eventually went bust for over £250 000. I thought to myself: if the Americans can spend all that money in Vietnam, why shouldn't I take a little bit of it for myself? I had this brilliant idea to exploit a loophole in the travel business: that travel vouchers for an unlimited amount could be issued by a travel agent. These vouchers were in principle aimed at payment for excess baggage in, say, pounds sterling rather than in foreign currency, so that people would not have to use up their foreign exchange allowance, which might be restricted, on paying for the extra weight. These vouchers could be used to get around exchange controls, by taking out a voucher for a large sum in pounds, taking it abroad, and cashing it in for foreign currency, since it was valid in every country. So the people I sold the vouchers to would pay me, say, £1000 for a voucher for £1200. Some of them were probably doing little immigration rackets as well – I don't know – but this way of buying tickets meant that they did not need to know the names of the people they were taking before they flew. In any case, the real profit came from the resale of the foreign currency they could get hold of from cashing in the vouchers, which they sold on the black market.

These vouchers were only supposed to have been for smallish amounts, and strictly speaking, they should not have been used to buy tickets. After my fraud, the IATA [International Air

Transport Association] changed the rules so that a travel agent could only issue a voucher for up to £20.

We had no trouble at all in getting credit for the tickets. The airlines were happy that we were doing such good business for them, and the situation was very competitive at that time. We had taken over the posh agency in Mayfair and as far as they knew, we were ordinary businessmen. Indeed, if everything had come up right, and the thieves hadn't plundered the business, we would have repaid them. Once you start, though, you have to go on till the bitter end. You cannot change a thief into a fraudster: his mentality is all wrong.

I decided that the best thing to do was to return to England, and a couple of people I knew who had been doing an l.f. suggested I come to Brighton, and run an l.f. there. We put Waters in as a front man. However, I soon got a phone call from Charlie, who had been tipped off by Thomson, and ordered me to London to see him. I could have gone away again, but I never liked to be a coward, so I went to see him. I got beaten up and told to see him the next morning.

Charlie suggested that I finish with Italy and start a firm here to get goods from Germany. I had heard that he had taken over my firm while I was in Italy and had nicked a lot of stuff from it, but by then, there was no way out. He would find you wherever you went. Charlie introduced me to Lennie, who was a wealthy man, and he put £10 000 in, because Charlie never liked to put his own money into things. I liked Lennie, but he was at that time on bail and was sent to prison. This left the problem of who should replace him. Charlie put in a couple of fellows and one of his heavies to learn how to do l.f.s. One of these was a half-caste with a double-barrelled name, who would turn up every day with a brief case, bowler hat, and an umbrella – it was a riot! I went to Germany, but I couldn't get any credit there straight away, so Charlie beat me up again.

I wanted to do as little as possible with Charlie at that time, and I did not try to get much stuff in Germany. After all, why should I get nicked for his profit? When I told Charlie I wanted out, he immediately apologized and gave me some money, but I had seen the writing on the wall, and started to take money out of the firm in dollars. Then I did a moonlight flit, but they found me and stabbed me. I then disappeared for a while, and when I came back I was nicked...

Even apart from the violence, I was very upset about Charlie. Before I met him, I was a skilled amateur, but with him, you couldn't survive on that basis. You had to become as big a villain as he was. Although at first, I had thought he was a fair businessman, underneath he was still a thief, and with a thief backing you, and thieves working for you, there was no way that you could do a big l.f., let alone become rich in a more or less straight way.

After the War, I got to know some Corsicans, who sold almost perfect counterfeit dollars for 20 per cent of their face value. The

Corsicans were gangsters, and if you cheated them you were dead. But if you played the game with them, they were 100 per cent straight with you. But in England, the gangsters have no self-discipline, which is why they always end up getting fucked themselves.

So the experience of long-firm fraudsters working with gangsters was far from happy. They discovered that whatever their level of expertise, there was no such thing as working *with* the Krays or Richardsons: you worked *for* them. This was not at all appealing to a group of fraudsters who were very 'wide' and accustomed to cheating each other with consummate artistry (and few hard feelings). As one of them stated to me:

> The trouble with Charlie is that he had no sense of proportion. He always expected 100 per cent return on capital invested and if you did not pay him 100 per cent he would regard it as money you owed him. So if you paid him £25 000 on £20 000 he put in, he would think that you owed him £15 000. It was ridiculous. Nobody expected that kind of return in three months... No matter how hard I tried, I could never persuade Charlie that firms must be started straight and end with a twist. He could never overcome his thief's mentality of grabbing whatever was at hand. Consequently, you could never do a big l.f. with him. He was sophisticated, but he never really understood what it was to be a businessman.

Some of the long-firm merchants had not previously realized the extent of the Richardsons' operations, which also included hijackings, car 'ringing', and protection rackets both in clubland and in already illegal operations such as the London Airport car park fraud – a swindle in which employees at a car park issued their own tickets to parkers, pocketing the proceeds for themselves. The latter operation alone netted the Richardsons £200 000. As one fraudster said:

> It was incredible what they could do. One night, a hijacked lorry arrived outside their warehouse at two o'clock, and by four o'clock, all the gear had been fenced out and the lorry was in pieces in the scrap-metal yard. Other times, gear was delivered from robberies in broad daylight, with police walking about up and down the road all the time. From that, we figured they had to have the law straightened [corrupted]. Once you were in with him [Charlie], you were in: there was no escape.

Not that Charles was without his genuine apologists, as the following statement by one prominent 'backer' suggests:

A lot of rubbish is talked about how terrible the Richardsons were, when in fact, they weren't a great deal worse than a lot of other big villains. No-one ever joined them who didn't want to, and the only reason that the l.f. men got done over was that they were always trying to fuck him for money that they had nicked from their l.f.s. If they hadn't done that, he would have left them alone. The trouble with the l.f. men was that they were too greedy, and violence was the only way he could keep people like that in line.

In this comment, we may see a curious parody of the classic conflict between the capitalists who finance business and the entrepreneurs who put that capital to profitable use. The rewards offered by the Richardsons for enterprise did not match the long-firm merchants' estimates of their own worth, and they attempted to make up the differential by stealing. Goods ordered would disappear from the warehouse on delivery, to be 'fenced' by the organizers, the invoices destroyed, and the profits not declared. The Richardsons would look at the weekly takings and suspect, rightly or wrongly, that they were being 'done'.

To the Richardsons, over and above any pathological enjoyment they may have obtained from it, torture represented the rational solution to their problem. In a legitimate operation, an employee *can* be dismissed and prosecuted for his crime, however unlikely this is in practice (Ditton, 1977; Henry, 1978; Martin, 1962). If a gangster has corrupt contacts in the police force, he also may be able to use the criminal justice system against his 'employees'. In this instance, however, Charles Richardson wished to enjoy the continued service of the fraudsters, and intimidation, plus the threat of being 'grassed up', secured this end, at least for a time. The fraudsters' belief that all the Metropolitan Police were in the pay of the Richardsons made them ill-disposed to complain, particularly when word of a conversation between one of them and an East End police officer got back to the Richardsons.

The fraudsters thus felt trapped. They were doing large-scale long firms all over the continent of Europe, getting vast amounts of nylons from Italy, transistor radios from Hong Kong, textiles and machinery from Germany, and helping to organize countless small frauds in England. Yet they felt that they were getting little out of it financially, were under constant threat of arbitrary torture and were at risk from the police. Finally, then, one of them decided to go to an officer he knew on the Regional Crime Squad, who set up a special investigatory squad. In exchange for the promise of non-prosecution or early release, they decided that it was in their best interests to reveal everything they knew, for it was only in that way that they could ensure that as many as possible of the 'Richardson gang' would be imprisoned. Only then would they be safe from reprisals, at least temporarily. As soon as it seemed likely that the Richardsons would be convicted, the flow of money from their 'pensions', that is, protection rackets, dried up, cutting off the gang's life-blood.

It is clear that under the Richardsons long-firm frauds were organized on the basis of a curious admixture of craft and business lines, to use McIntosh's (1975) typology. Although the frauds were syndicated, this owed less to the corruption of law enforcement than it did to the failure of commerce and the police to mobilize themselves against long-firm fraudsters at that time. The ease and crudity of long-firm organization is nicely expressed in the following observations:

> The nucleus of Charles' gang was a core of 30–40 old lags [recidivists] who worked for him in his scrap-metal yard. They were paid wages and were very loyal to him. Outside of that there was a loose grouping of people engaged in various frauds and other activities. These people did not necessarily have anything to do with one another. They may have been in the same line, but that was all. Fear and blackmail kept us under Charlie's thumb.

> With all the l.f. men working for them, the Richardsons must have organized around 100 frauds between 1963 and 1965. They had a list of between 1000 and 5000 suppliers, and as people came out of the nick, they would install them in a shop costing about £5 a week, with a phone whose bill they would not pay and an Olivetti electric and a manual which would be on 90-day credit. They would give these men, say, 50 firms from the list to order from, and tell them what to order. The firm would last about 1–2 months and would be closed down and all the papers burned as soon as the first writ came in. The front men would change their names and move to a different part of south London and start ordering gear from a new 50 firms...

> All these were little l.f.s for about £2–5000. At that time, the police were not organized to cope with small l.f.s and they didn't want to know about them. The mugs would only be paid about £20 a week, so there was a good profit. We all used to meet and discuss business in London clubs, because the coppers used to hang around in the pubs, and they wouldn't be able to overhear us there.

When the gang leaders were locked up for their long prison sentences – the Krays for life (specified by the trial judge to mean no less than thirty years), Charlie Richardson for twenty-five years and his brother Eddie for fifteen years – it was widely believed by the police and trade protection societies that the great era of long-firm fraud was at an end. They believed that the gangsters were the main impetus behind long firms, and that the long-firm merchants who had given evidence against them would have to disappear somehow from the criminal scene. This is analysed perceptively by Leslie Payne (1973, p. 149), who states that the taking of witness statements from gang members makes the other gang members suspect that they may have been implicated by them in uncharged crimes. Their fear that such evidence may be used against them if they misbehave again checks their future criminal careers. However, Payne's observations may have been somewhat tongue-in-cheek, since he was subsequently convicted and sent to prison for offences related to an international car-ringing racket.

In fact, none of the principal long-firm fraudsters who worked for the Richardsons retired from the scene for very long. There may not have been any great trust between them, but they worked together in fairly fluid cliques, supplemented by incomers from the quasi-legitimate business world who not only organized long firms but also 'fenced' the goods through their own trade outlets. Some of the major operators 'did a big one' and left the country; others carried on much as before, attempting to carry out the more sophisticated frauds that had been made impossible by the short-term approach of the Richardsons and Krays. The major change was the decline in the routine, small-scale long firms. For the police, trade protection societies, and credit controllers had become alert to the crude techniques they adopted.

Towards the end of the 1960s, another gang sought to occupy the ground lately vacated by the Krays and the Richardsons. They received heavy prison sentences for their pains. They too had moved into long-firm fraud, but their alleged expert adviser failed to emulate Payne's freedom from prosecution: he was sentenced to twelve years' imprisonment for blackmail. Basically, however, 'gangster' domination of the long-firm scene ended with the imprisonment of the Krays in 1968.

During the late 1960s and early 1970s, long-firm frauds were organized on a project basis, although there was a fairly continuous thread of background personnel. This continuity was achieved in two ways: first, by the exercise of great care on the part of the organizers to ensure that there was no hard evidence to link them to the fraudulent operations; and secondly, by the corruption of officers in the specialist long-firm section of the Metropolitan Police Fraud Squad.

The second aspect will be discussed in detail in Chapter VIII, but its operational consequence was that most of the corruptors became over-confident about their immunity from 'the law'. They came to act as if they were crime syndicates as popularized in America, albeit with operations restricted mainly to fraud and allied areas. Their confidence proved to be misplaced when they were eventually convicted. Their incarceration damaged the background organiza- tion of long-firm fraud, because each fraudster's circle of contacts is fairly small, and it takes time to establish a degree of trust or rapport with other operators. Some prominent organizers were not convicted until the late 1970s, but, at the time of writing, there is something of a lull in long-firm fraud in London and, as far as I know, its background organization has disintegrated there. There has been something of a boom in long firms in the north-east of England, as more conventional criminals there have turned to 'white-collar crime', but it remains to be seen how long this will last.

Whether this lull in pre-planned frauds is due to the difficulty of non-established businesses obtaining credit in a cost-of-credit- conscious world or to a temporary falling off in the popularity of long firms among the London underworld is a moot point. It seems clear, however, that the great expectations of syndicated organisation possessed by long-firm fraudsters in the early 1960s have been very far from fulfilled. The major trend of the future appears to be the 'intermediate' frauds run by formerly legitimate businessmen and the international long-firm frauds mentioned in my discussion of the law of venue in Chapter VII, organized on a project basis and involving a number of countries.

Relationships between members of the long-firm network

My discussion of the use of violence by syndicated criminals against long-firm fraudsters indicates that the former felt unable to trust the latter. Indeed, one organiser characterised the long-firmer's code as 'Make sure you "do" your partner before *he* "does" *you*'. However functional in principle it may be for all members of 'the underworld' to trust each other and to operate in the solidary and respectful man- ner of Sutherland's (1937) professional thieves, few fraudsters are willing to take the risk of being the first to establish such a principle. Consequently, a culture of systematic distrust tends to be perpetu- ated, in respect both of fair dealing while the fraud is still in progress and of 'grassing' to the police subsequently. (Here, too, they differ from Sutherland's thieves, who did not inform upon each other, though it is arguable that the difference arises because American professional criminals can corrupt law enforcement agencies and therefore have no need to 'grass'.)

Socially, long-firm fraudsters are often very generous with their colleagues. One organiser told me about another who had no friendship, kinship, or business connection with him but who with no ulterior motive paid for lavish accommodation and medical care for him when he fell ill abroad. If a long-firm merchant is down on his luck, whether in prison or on the outside, he will generally be able to count on some help from others. There does seem to be some kind of mutual helping ethic among the long firm fraternity, possibly related to the *Grand Seigneur* patron image with which many of them identify. (This is also true of some pilferers and amateur 'fences': see Henry, 1978.)

Commercial relationships, however, tend to be rather guarded, and unless there is any long-term reason for behaving well towards one's collaborators (or even if there *is*) the operational assumption is that no-one can be trusted. Wealthy businessmen who finance long firms but who do not have any underworld 'clout' are quite likely to end up as victims of the fraudsters. As one organizer stated:

> Very often, you might meet somebody who has some spare cash. Take Billy, for instance, whom I met at the home of a friend of mine. It turned out that he had a lot of *schwartz* ['black'] money which he did not know how to invest. He had earned it in the rag trade and, believe me, the Inland Revenue would have loved to learn about it! Anyway, Lennie took him for a few grand. Some of these people are so greedy, you wouldn't believe! They want the money, but they haven't the control or the guts to run an l.f.... So it ended up that he got fucked without even being kissed.

Some fraudsters have a reputation as good payers, but others seem to survive adequately even though they frequently renege upon their deals. The powerful patrons within the underworld who finance some long firms and/or 'fence' the goods tend to be treated with appropriate respect, not least because of their command of violence, but sometimes short-term expediency triumphs over long-term rationality. For example, in 1977 one organizer disappeared with the proceeds of the long firm at the expense of his underworld-connected backer. As one fraudster said:

> Brown was a brilliant fellow who used to dream up fantastic schemes, but he had no money and did not have the strength of character to be a good organizer. But in spite of his orginal brain, I used to hate working with him, because he would fuck you for a few quid. Nobody would lend him any money because he was such a thief, and so most of his schemes failed, because he had to bounce cheques right from the beginning.

Another man complained to me that things were not what they used to be in the underworld before the early 1960s, because the old trust had gone.

It is not possible to say how many l.f. backers there are. A lot of retired villains who have plenty of money but are still greedy for more do it. Some of them specialize in backing l.f.s. They put down, say, £10 000 and expect £25 000 in return, or a certain value in goods... In the old days, I might go along to Stevie [a more or less retired big-time criminal] and say to him: 'Stevie, I need five grand for an l.f. I'll pay you back six grand in 3 months.' That's all. He would give me the money, no questions asked, and I would go away and do my l.f. A couple of days before the 3 months were up, I would phone him to tell him that I had the money. He would invite me round for dinner with him and his wife. I would go and have dinner with them, pay him the money, and that was that. It was like a gentleman's agreement.

But Stevie would not trust many people like that. Others knew what they could expect if they welshed... My former backers, like I said, knew that if they were not repaid one time – perhaps the l.f. did not succeed as planned – then they would be repaid from the next one. If they really wanted the money right there and then, I would get it from somewhere... Now, though, they have either died or grown so wealthy that they are no longer interested in l.f.s... Although my credit is still good in the underworld, backers are not trusting any more. They [that is, the fence-cum-backers] will give you money only when you deliver the goods, not before, at least not until you have dealt with them for some time...

People generally use the same fence in all their l.f.s. This is because you need to build up confidence, so that they will do you little favours and maybe lend you a few bob when you need it. They don't generally give you a better price just because they know you, though. X, especially, was a real *chazayr* [swine]. He took diabolical liberties with people, in the sense that when he knew l.f. merchants were very short of cash and needed some, he would squeeze them down to 40 or 50 per cent instead of the 70 per cent he normally gave on l.f. gear. He would do this even to people he dealt with all the time. This would create a lot of resentment, and so the l.f. merchant would try and do him back. He would always pay, though, generally one-half before and one-half after delivery. You usually need to know more than one fence, for two reasons. One, if you don't, the fence knows that he can screw you, because you haven't got anyone else to turn to. And two, because you can rarely get one fence who can take all the gear that you can get: his business is not diversified enough. X was good because he could take quite a variety of gear, but then, he had a very big business. For this reason, it is always best to get different kinds of stock. In the provinces, the l.f.s. tend to specialize more, such as cloth in Yorkshire. If you do that, the fence has you over a barrel with the price, and the goods can be easily traced, and you may have trouble with the police...

When you talk about trust in the underworld, it varies a lot. With X, for example, although he was such a *chazayr*, you could trust him: if he said that he would pay N pounds for your gear, he would do. With Y and Z, [other fences], though, I would never let them have any goods without first seeing the money in my hand: they would fuck you rather than look at you. But sometimes you need these people: this is the basic problem. That is why I used to like to work with Black, because he was a good organizer who mixed freely everywhere in this country. I only knew a certain circle, which limited me...

For a lot of l.f.s, the fences are the backers. The backers and the fences get wealthy on the backs of the l.f. merchants and when you need them, they don't want to know you... The practice now is to give you a specific list of suppliers and the goods they want, and pay you on delivery. Anything not ordered or not wanted is not taken... The system is not so good as the old one, because you can't get the capital you need to get you off the ground. This is why you can't do the l.f.s. you used to. To make money, you need money, but today, everyone's too scared to take the risk. I think it was because in the old days, everybody had a code, but now, you can't trust nobody.

This general theme of the inability to trust led some backers and 'fences' to develop a system of vertical integration of the finance, organization and retail functions. As one man said:

In l.f.s, at any rate, the backers *are* the organizers *are* the buyers. Unless you have close supervision, you may find that the police have come and nicked the people and you have lost your money; or else the l.f. men have flown. You just can't afford to sit back on your arse and wait for the money to roll in... One of the biggest problems when you're running an l.f. is your own partners. You have to spend so much time protecting yourself from them that you can't concentrate on the l.f. or on the Law. For example, if a load came in that D had ordered, while the partner was out, by the time he came back, the goods would be out of the warehouse, the invoice destroyed, and the money from the sale in his pocket. So you couldn't afford to take your eyes off him for a moment. If you went for a piss, you didn't know what could have happened while you were away. If you could trust the people you worked with, you could get a fantastic organization going, but instead, you find that everyone's ripping off everyone else all the time.

It appears that far from being a solidary subculture, the world of long-firm fraudsters is a case of criminals parodying the rampant individualism of the legitimate commercial world: a *bellum omnium contra omnes* characterized by short-term tactical alliances rather than stable working friendships. This *anomie* is not restricted to relationships between the 'background operators': it extends to those between the organizers and the 'front men'. As one organizer put it, echoing with unintended irony the lamentations of more respectable employers:

The only trouble with l.f.s is that you have to employ thieves to front them. Some of them fancy themselves as real tearaways and they would sell their own grandmothers for a halfpenny. If you're not careful, they will nick all your gear and knock it out to their mates in the pubs or on the markets. All you need when you're trying to make a hundred grand is some bright spark going independent. Their main problem is that they have got the mentality of thieves, not of businessmen; the moment they see some money in the till, they put their fingers in. You can't afford to do that when you're running an l.f. Some of these front men are no better than gas meter bandits, but sometimes you can't get anything else.

The problem is that some of these front men go crazy when they work for you. You give them a nice company car and fifty quid a week expenses, you make them a director, but it's not enough. They think to themselves 'I'm a big businessman' and they go round to their friends like they're Charlie Clore [a prominent millionaire]. They're buying rounds of drinks and telling all their pals that they're running an l.f., and by the time they've finished, the *chappers* [police] are round and you've lost your *gelt* [money].

In the old days, people had a code: you shook hands on a deal and that was that. But now, there is no such thing as a code in the underworld: they are all *ganovim* [thieves].

Another organizer stated that

The only reason I get nicked is that I am a perfectionist. You wouldn't believe the number of schemes I have had that would have made me a millionaire if I had had the right reliable people working for me. But you can't get them! All these thieves want to do is grab, grab, grab. So I have to do things myself, and when you do that, you expose yourself.

A further problem arises from the failure of 'the workers' to display their staunch adherence to the protestant ethic:

When you recruit front men and give them a bit of money, they sometimes go mad, spending money like there was no tomorrow. They go to expensive clubs, putting their mouth about, and through that, the other mobs get to hear about the l.f. and they want in, knowing that you can't scream to the police. It's all a bit difficult, because they might grass you up if you tell them where to go... This happened with an l.f. called Bustout. B tried to muscle in on that one because he had the dead needle into S, but I was too involved to get out and I joined S's side. So I told B that if he came after us, he had better be well tooled up [armed], because we had a little fortress down there, and we would blow his head off.

So, far from respecting each other's territory, as Sutherland (1937, p. 12) claims for his 'professional thieves', long-firm fraudsters are happy to muscle in on somebody else's long firm if they think they can get away with it, particularly if they have a grudge against the other party. This observation is not restricted to times when gangs such as the Krays and Richardsons were trying to gain hegemony: it has been a not uncommon feature of long firms since at least the 1950s.

The consequence of all the factors discussed in this section is that backers, 'fences' and organizers felt that they had to become operationally involved in their long firms *on site*, in order to protect themselves from fellow criminal predators. Furthermore, vertical integration of the finance, organization and resale functions enabled the 'fences' to take for themselves the high profits formerly appropriated by others. However, the breakdown in organizational autonomy between these roles led to a much greater risk of conviction for the background operators, partly because it enabled clearer inferences to be made in court about their 'guilty knowledge' and partly because 'organized crime' attracts greater police interest than does a 'free market' between criminals.

In the absence of effective *long-term* corruption, the system of vertical integration resulted in the conviction of (as far as I know) most of those who adopted it in the late 1960s and early 1970s. This lends support to the critique of Cressey (1972) by McIntosh (1975), who disputes Cressey's claim that there is an inexorable trend towards business-type organization of crime, arguing that where conditions of policing do not favour business organization, it is positively disastrous for its practitioners.

Conclusion

While they operated either one-off project frauds or a series of low-profile frauds, the organizers found long firms highly profitable and risk-free. However, when long firms became associated with 'organized crime', they attracted substantial police interest, for the 'unholy alliance' of gangsters and fraudsters has been the subject of 'moral panic' both in this country and in the United States (see Kossack and Davidson, 1966; Edelhertz, 1970; Bequai, 1979). The great ambitions of some of the principal long-firm merchants led to their own downfall. Perhaps the most fitting epitaph for this chapter comes from one of the most subtle long-firm merchants of the great era of the 1960s:

> Charlie Richardson's real problem was that although he fancied himself as a businessman, he had the mentality of a thief. His way of dealing with a business problem was the method of the 'right-hander'. He never fully understood that the *really* clever people kill with the pen.

V. Motivations and Criminal Careers of Long-Firm Fraudsters

This chapter is an essay on the moral and criminal careers of long-firm fraudsters, along the lines suggested by Becker (1963, pp. 19–39). The principal questions I shall be attempting to answer are:

(1) Why do long-firm fraudsters come to undertake that form of activity?
(2) What factors influence them in their decisions either to continue or to stop committing long-firm frauds?
(3) How do their perceptions of the costs and benefits of long-firm fraud change: (a) as a result of their experiences while taking part in long-firm frauds; and (b) as a result of the reactions of 'society' towards their behaviour?

A major role in the existence of long-firm fraud is played by language. For it is language that we use to locate our actions in relation to social and criminal rules about what behaviour is or is not permitted. When we define for ourselves and for others 'what kind of behaviour our behaviour is', we may regard it in any one of four principal ways: (1) as both conventional *and* lawful; (2) as lawful but not conventional; (3) as conventional but not lawful; and (4) as neither conventional nor lawful. When I speak of defining our behaviour, I refer to the definitions imputed by 'respectable society'. If one troubles to break social audiences down into the gamut of subcultures, one may meet with considerable complications arising out of social dissensus (although to a far lesser extent than is often claimed, see Sparks *et al.*, 1977, pp. 183–5).

Long-firm fraudsters define their behaviour under categories (1), (3) and (4) above. Later in this chapter, I shall attempt to outline the conditions under which they allocate their behaviour to these respective categories. I shall also examine the consequences of the definitions made by the actors themselves and by 'significant others', that is, social control agencies such as the police and courts. First, I must discuss some of the problems surrounding the concept of motivation, among which are the role played by language in awareness, and the relationship between the way we look at the world, motivation, and social action.

The problem of 'the first mover' is one which has absorbed theologians, philosophers and scientists for millenia, and there is no space in a work of this nature for a full discussion of the ultimate causes of human action. What this chapter does aim to achieve is the somewhat less ambitious target of showing how those who take part in long-firm frauds – from financiers to 'fences' – depict their conduct to themselves and to others.

I have already dealt in Appendix A with some of the difficulties which surround the attribution of motives. However, if non-academic readers will bear with me for a short while, I will elaborate briefly on these themes, if only to caution readers against the uncritical acceptance of my interpretations.

The basis of the sociological conception of motive is to be found in the work of C. Wright Mills (1940) and Cressey (1962), who argue that motives are not biological drives which 'cause' us to act in certain ways but rather are the words and concepts with which people interpret the meaning of their desires and actions (see also Taylor, 1979, for a valuable contribution to this debate). The basic idea is that language is the means by which actors and their audiences are able to assess whether or not a given action is 'deviant', 'conforming', or 'ambiguous'. Other members of society may not honour one's account of one's motives, but that is a separate issue. The main point is that by depicting our actions to ourselves – whether self-consciously or not – in a favourable light, we are able to redefine 'what-might-be-considered-as-crime' as either 'no crime' or 'justifiable crime'. This is true irrespective of whether or not we would feel guilty about our actions if we *did* define them as 'crime'. By formulating the hypothesis in this way, we are able to divorce the discussion of vocabularies of motive from that of guilt neutralisation. We thus avoid – at least in part – the question of whether or not delinquents feel latent guilt: the problem that absorbs Sykes and Matza (1957) and, to a lesser extent, Cressey (1953). One might further argue that theories which relate the use of vocabularies of motive to the 'need' to neutralize guilt have to assume (i) that actors perceive that some of what Goffman (1971, p. 109) refers to as 'remedial work' is called for, that is, they perceive that they are rule-breaking, and (ii) that actors do in fact feel guilty about what they do, or would feel guilty if they described their acts differently. Both of these are empirically problematic.

Cressey (1953, 1965), Ditton (1977), Gerth and Mills (1954), Henry (1976, 1978) and Mills (1940) indicate that vocabularies of motive are related to general cultural themes which are regarded (at least by the actors themselves) as *justifying* criminal behaviour in certain contexts. They are not just the bizarre *post hoc* rationalizations of a few distorted intellects. As Cressey (1965, p. 113) puts it:

Vocabularies of motive are not something invented by embezzlers (or anyone else) on the spur of the moment. Before they can be taken over by an individual, these verbalizations exist as group definitions in which the behaviour in question, even crime, is in a sense *appropriate*. There are any number of popular ideologies that sanction crime in our culture: 'Honesty is the best policy, but business is business'; 'It is all right to steal a loaf of bread when you are starving'; 'all people steal when they get into a tight spot'. Once these verbalizations have been assimilated and internalized by individuals, they take a form such as: 'I'm only going to use the money temporarily, so I am borrowing, not stealing', or 'I have tried to live an honest life, but I've had nothing but troubles, so to hell with it'.

At a deeper level, Gerth and Mills (1954, p. 123) argue that people in American (and presumably all capitalist) societies *learn* to view their behaviour as motivated by the desire for monetary benefit and to regard other motives (such as the desire to help) as shams, facades, and 'rationalization'. Unfortunately, the type of analysis developed by Cressey makes it far from clear how it comes about that some people and not others define their situations in such a way that they turn to law-breaking; and, secondly, at what stage these verbalizations occur to the actor. On the latter point, as Ditton (1977, p. 164) has observed, people are quite capable of forming a genuine belief that they developed their 'technique of neutralization' *prior* to their criminal acts, although in fact they developed it afterwards. The implication of this is that we cannot take their statements about their motives as valid, even if they are honest with themselves.

Although the conceptual issues to which I have alluded appear to be beyond the present state of social scientific knowledge to resolve, most of the literature on 'vocabularies of motive' does illuminate criminal behaviour, not least by emphasising the moral and linguistic links between 'crime' and 'normal behaviour' and by demonstrating that verbalization is part of what we mean by 'behaviour'. One of the best illustrations of this is Cressey's (1953) absorbing study of the social psychology of embezzlement, which concludes (p. 30) that

Trusted persons become trust violators when they conceive of themselves as having a financial problem which is non-shareable, are aware that this problem can be secretly resolved by violation of the position of financial trust, and are able to apply to their own conduct in that situation verbalisations which enable them to adjust their conceptions of themselves as trusted persons with their conception of themselves as users of the entrusted funds or property.

This seems to provide an excellent way of visualizing the process through which embezzlers go, despite Nettler's (1974) demonstration that the formulation cannot account for all embezzlers. However, as Clinard (1954) has pointed out, the Cressey model is deficient in as much as we cannot predict trust violation until *after* someone has defined his situation as appropriate for embezzlement.

Clinard's observation does raise a major difficulty which bedevils theories based on 'definitions of the situation'. However, if one takes a non-deterministic model of human action, for example, man as 'self-monitoring agent' (Harré and Secord, 1972; see also Matza, 1969; and Beyleveld and Wiles, 1979), then prediction ceases to become anything more than probabilistic *in principle*. The solution lies in the vanishing of the problem! However, the inability to predict does leave us with a gap in what we might *like* to know about why people commit crime. In particular, we do not know what part 'reflexivity' or active self-awareness plays in the adoption of particular motivational accounts by social actors: somehow, these verbalizations 'just arrive' out of the stock of context-related motives which are on offer in the individual's subculture or in society as a whole at a given historical period. Unfortunately, as I have suggested in Appendix A, this matter does not appear to be amenable to 'valid' or even reliable investigation.

Bearing in mind these important theoretical difficulties entailed by the study of motives, let us turn our attention to the motivations and criminal careers of some long-firm fraudsters. Most of the people mentioned in this chapter have been defined as fraudsters before a crucial audience – the jury of a criminal court – though few of them have been so adjudged in respect of *all* the crimes they have committed. However, some of the people discussed here have never been so categorized. (Readers should recollect my statement that most of my information about unconvicted fraudsters is second-hand, though it is possible that statements made to me about the motives of close friends may be more valid than those made to me by the 'villains' themselves: there may be less incentive to perform 'remedial work' on behalf of friends than on one's own behalf.)

We shall see that from the point of view of vocabularies of motive, the most intriguing distinction is between the 'slippery-slope' fraudsters and the 'deliberate' ones. However, before examining the motives for participation in fraud, it may be useful to set out briefly the pre-long-firm fraud criminal records of those long-firm fraudsters convicted at the Old Bailey. These are clearly relevant to the consideration of why people engage in fraud and how they come to be thus involved.

(1) *'Slippery-slope' fraudsters.* Apart from motoring offences, none of these had any previous *convictions*. It may be that they had committed other offences in the field of business crime, such as income tax or value-added tax evasion, without being detected or prosecuted. This, however, illustrates the difficulties involved in the use of crime statistics which are peculiarly vulnerable to the policy decisions of 'white-collar crime control' agencies not to prosecute suspected offenders (compare Sutherland, 1961). The sample of convicted offenders in the 'slippery-slope' category is itself small because of the social and legal definitions of 'crime' made by the police, the Department of Trade and creditors.

(2) *'Intermediate' long-firm fraudsters.* Few people in this category have any previous convictions other than for motoring offences. There are some, however, who have a number of prior convictions for a range of crimes from handling stolen property to a mixture of theft and violent offences.

(3) *'Pre-planned' long-firm fraudsters.* This is an extremely hetero-geneous category of offenders. If we ignore the 'hidden crime' aspect, very broad generalizations about subcategories may be made as follows:

'Front men' vary between two main groups – those with no previous convictions and those with a considerable number of them. This corresponds to the distinction between 'front men' used because organizers prefer them without previous convictions and those simply plucked out from the group of available 'thieves', generally by syndicated organizers.

'Minders' generally have previous convictions for offences of violence, and some also have convictions for property offences.

'Second-level organizers' usually have a number of previous convictions, often including at least one business crime, but with no particularly common pattern of other offences.

'Top-level organizers' have either no previous convictions at all or have previous convictions only for business offences.

Entry into long-firm fraud
In the development of what he terms a sequential model of rule-breaking, Becker (1963, p. 23) argues that adequate explana-tions cannot assume that people are transformed into 'criminals' instantaneously: they may change their conduct and way of looking at the world gradually over a period of time. Thus, we must explain

.te stages how someone finds himself in a position to commit
., how and why he decides so to do, and why he decides either
continue or to stop committing crimes. This appears to me to be
the correct model to follow, though it is important to realize that
'slippery-slopers' may not define their business conduct as a break in
normal behaviour: thus, it is not as easily differentiated from lawful
behaviour as are most property crimes.

Let us therefore examine the routes through which people come to
know about the techniques of long-firm fraud. For 'long-firm fraud'
cannot become available if one has no conception of what it *is*. (The
naming of what one does as 'long-firm fraud' or even 'crime' is a
subsidiary aspect of this and will be discussed later.) There are three
principal routes to knowledge about long-firm fraud:

(a) via the transmission of information from people 'in the
underworld' who either have carried out a long-firm fraud
themselves or have learned the techniques from someone who
has done so;
(b) via businessmen who may or may not be 'shady' but who are
not part of 'the underworld' as that term is commonly
understood;
(c) via a process of introspection.

Route (a) is clearly subject to the usual social network constraints
which prevent access to 'criminals'. If one is not privy to intimate
discussions with people 'in the know', then route (a) is not open.
Consequently, the amount of long-firm fraud committed within the
milieu of 'the underworld' at time (t) may be an important factor
influencing the amount committed there at time (t + 1). The change
in the organization of long-firm fraud from project to syndicated
crime in the early 1960s led to the widespread dissemination of its
cruder techniques throughout the London underworld, and this
knowledge in turn was spread via the prison system as the fraudsters
were incarcerated.

Route (a) is illustrated in the following quotations from my
interviews with occasional and full-time fraudsters:

While I was in business – a straight business, you understand – I
met this fellow called Dave who sold me a lot of tables dirt cheap
for a while. After a bit, I got very curious, because I knew the stuff
was below cost, and I asked him where he got it from. Through
that, I learned about l.f.s, 'cos Dave was working for the Krays at
that time.

In the period you're talking about [the 1960s], everybody knew
about long-firm frauds – at least everybody I knew in the East

End [of London] did. You'd be there at the [gaming] tables or in the boozer [pub], and one of your pals would say: 'See that bloke over there. He's running that l.f. over in the Lea Bridge Road', and you'd think no more about it. Some people did l.f.s, like some people sold toiletries. Mind you, you made damn sure that you didn't get caught out giving him credit yourself. But if I ever wanted to do an l.f., all I had to do was to fix it up with a few of my mates, and that's all there was to it.

The basic idea was to give post-dated cheques, which count as payment, give the rep double the order we had just given the cheque for, and that way, get three times the value of the cheque in goods...We had some idea of what to do, 'cos my partner's brother had done a successful l.f. previous, and nobody had done anything to him about it.

Knowing *how* to do a long-firm fraud does not mean, of course, that one is *able* to do one: one has to have the necessary contacts for financing the business and disposing of the goods. As discussed earlier, this can act as an important constraint.

Route (b) to knowledge about long-firm fraud is in some respects similar to route (a). It too depends upon social networks. However, businessmen tend to be more careful than 'villains' about the preservation of a respectable 'front', and the range of people with whom they discuss their *own* 'real' crimes may be restricted to close family members or to people whom they know to be 'deviants'. Nevertheless, businesspeople often discuss frauds among themselves at a general level, without implying any involvement in actual frauds themselves. Although I did not carry out any *systematic* survey of businessmen's knowledge of long-firm techniques, informal discussions with many small- to medium-sized business owners indicate that such techniques are widely known. The difference between the businessman who has knowledge of these techniques and the 'villain' who has this knowledge is that the former is already in a position to carry out a long-firm fraud, by virtue of his established role. This distinction is important. For *any* businessman in manufacturing, wholesaling or retailing could carry out a long-firm if he was motivated so to do.

It should be noted that there may be no clear demarcation in practice between routes (a) and (b): semi-legitimate businessmen may have contact with 'real' fraudsters, possibly through 'fencing' their goods, and may then pass on information about their techniques to a third party. For example, I was told of one case in which a small-time businessman operated a kiosk in a municipal swimming pool and had access to council notepaper and to the pool's telephone, which was an extension connected to the general switchboard which covered all municipal offices. One day the man noticed that his order for ice-creams was invoiced to the council, and he mentioned this in casual conversation with a friend who had connections with long-firm fraudsters. The friend expressed interest in this happy accident and under his tutelage, the concessionaire began to order huge quantities of foodstuffs and toiletries, all of which were delivered to the pool and invoiced to the council. Firms which telephoned him were reassured by the fact that they were connected via the council switchboard, and apparently did not ask themselves why such huge quantities of goods were needed by a small swimming-pool kiosk. Eventually, the man 'quit while he was ahead' and, after running up debts of over £50 000, disappeared judiciously. He never learned whether or not the council paid for the goods but, as far as he knew, no attempt was ever made to trace him.

The people concerned were so exhilarated by this experience that they organized a similar operation at another council park. This had the disadvantage that the telephone was some distance from the kiosk, and the other council employees were kept busy rushing to and from it with messages. None the less, the fraudsters netted some £50 000 of hardware, foodstuffs and furnishings, such as patio tables and chairs. These examples, if true, illustrate the element of chance which may influence entry into long-firm fraud. People may stumble into it by serendipity rather than as a consequence of the active pursuit of crime.

Route (c) is particularly interesting because it demonstrates that contact, whether direct or indirect, with others who have performed long-firm frauds is neither a necessary nor a sufficient condition for the performance of a long-firm fraud oneself. This observation is also true of black marketeers (compare Clinard, 1952). In a sense, this should be self-evident, for all crime *originates* from creative introspection or serendipity or both: by definition, imitation cannot explain the *origin* of crime. In principle, long-firm fraud should be obvious to any businessman, just as embezzlement is to anyone in charge of accounts (compare Cressey, 1953). Indeed, there is no reason to suppose that a 'professional fraudster' would be able to carry out a long firm more successfully than a first-time formerly honest businessman could do. A major 'background operator' expressed the issue thus:

> What you must realize is that in order to be a 'bad' businessman you've got to be a good businessman. There is no way that anyone would figure that I was doing an l.f. until the very end, by which time it would be too late. The point is that I know what I'm doing. I know how to screw someone down when I'm buying, and I know

where to go for the best price when I'm selling. I'm not one of these gangsters who run an l.f. like it was a toy they had just learned to play with. I'm a businessman, not a thief.

Although he was involved in a large number of long firms as well as in legitimate businesses, his observations apply almost equally to the amateur fraudster, provided that he is a sharp businessman. The point is, however, that most sharp businessmen (or, for that matter, not-so-sharp businessmen) do not normally *think* of going 'bust' deliberately for profit until something goes wrong with their normal pattern of trading. As one man who later became a major fraudster said:

The first firm that I had which went *mechullah* [bankrupt] was a straight firm. I had done a few deals which did not work out, and I got caught out. As I was going through the liquidation process, I realized how easy it would be to get away with a 'bent' liquidation. I didn't need anybody to tell me about l.f.s. It was obvious.

Motives of first-time long-firm fraudsters

Throughout this work, I have stressed the variability of the criminal intentions of long-firm fraudsters when they entered business initially. This issue of initial intentions is important to the fraudsters themselves, partly because of their desire to preserve their self-image and partly because the intensity of societal reaction depends upon the imputations of culpability made upon 'the fraudster' by significant others. Societal reaction and 'criminal motivation' are interlinked, because the availability of justificatory and exculpatory accounts depends on what society, or specific subcultures within society, regards as 'deviant', 'conforming' or 'morally ambiguous' behaviour. The businessman's conception of the 'fit' between his behaviour and approved social *mores* may not be shared by those entrusted with law enforcement and adjudication, but this may be apparent only *ex post facto*.

Long-firm frauds are particularly vulnerable to linguistic rede-finition of the culpability of their participants. This is especially true of 'slippery-slope' and 'intermediate' fraudsters. As part of the acquittal-game, spurious accounts of motives may be offered by all types of fraudster, for as we shall see, the issue at trials is often whether or not a crime has been committed at all rather than the identification of a suspect as the person who committed the act recognized by everyone to be a crime. However, in this chapter what I am interested in is the ways in which 'people-potentially-definableas-fraudsters' genuinely maintain the belief that they are not 'defrauding' their creditors. What, in other words, do they construe as the social meaning of 'fraud'?

Slippery-slope fraudsters

If we apply this theoretical orientation to the area of business often regarded as the mildest form of fraudulent trading, if fraud it be labelled at all, we may observe in detail the vocabularies of motive that are used. In these 'mild' cases, a businessman orders goods on credit although he knows that *as things stand at that moment in time*, he will be unable to pay for them when his credit period elapses. However, the businessman genuinely believes and expects that in the interval between the ordering of the goods and the last possible moment for payment for them, his business cash-flow will have improved sufficiently for him to be able to pay all his bills and continue trading. He may make specific false statements to his creditors, such as 'I'll put the cheque in the post tonight', or he may leave a necessary signature off the cheque, put on it non-matching words and figures, in the knowledge that his bank will send back the cheque 'Refer to Drawer', thus giving him time. However, even during the period 1968–78, when these were criminal offences against Section 16 of the Theft Act, 1968, he was able to justify his behaviour easily as merely *mala prohibita* rather than *mala in se*.

The ease of his justification may be attributed to a number of factors. First, in his own mind he is able to make use of what Sykes and Matza (1957) call in their analysis of techniques of neutralization, 'denial of injury'. He believes that no *real* wrong will be caused by his actions: *'when'* his business recovers, he will repay his creditors, who will be better off than they would have been had he declared his insolvency right away. The significant point about this mental process is that this 'calling to account' rarely happens except when a businessman is over-sanguine about his prospects and consequently goes 'bust'. Although I have not carried out any systematic survey of business attitudes towards this behaviour, informal discussions indicate that it might well receive substantial support within the small business community. In other words, I would hypothesize 'common' business agreement with the proposition that 'faced with a choice between "telling a few white lies" and going "bust", the former path should be chosen'. The 'slippery-slope' fraudster, then, derives crucial symbolic support from the general *mores* of the business community. The fact that he has traded honestly for some time prior to his lie-telling means that dishonesty is not regarded as a 'master status' in his personality and character assessment. Indeed, the perception that his entry into the 'crime-prone' situation was not prompted by dishonest motives is crucial to the way his acts are labelled by others as well as by himself. In long-firm fraud, evidently, one *can* be 'a little bit pregnant'!

This is an important matter. Motivational accounts and techniques of neutralization generally have been examined within the context of acts that are relatively discrete and simple in nature: breaking windows, vandalism, sex offenders and violence (Sykes and Matza, 1957; S. Cohen, 1973; Taylor, 1970; and Toch, 1972). Even in these cases, it has been shown that the evaluation of the conduct is morally problematic. In circumstances where the criminality of an individual act can be legitimated by reference to an overall socially acceptable purpose, negative moral evaluation is easier still to avoid. Ditton (1977) and Henry (1978) have shown how this is accomplished by those who trade in goods stolen from work; and Cressey (1953) has shown how trust-violators do this by breaking up their defalcations into completely separate acts. 'Slippery-slope' fraudsters are able to do this with even less difficulty, because they are not necessarily dipping their fingers into the till when they 'con' their creditors: they benefit from the tacit expectation of creditors that they will be repaid by all normal debtors rather than indulge in *active* trickery.

The fact that the businessman has no desire or conscious expectation that his creditors should not be repaid raises serious problems for our description of his behaviour as 'fraudulent'. Austin (1979, pp. 200–201) expresses the issue with elegant clarity thus:

> It is in principle always open to us, along various lines, to describe or refer to 'what I did' in so many different ways... Apart from the more general and obvious problems of the use of 'tendentious' descriptive terms, there are many special problems in the particular case of 'actions'. Should we say, are we saying, that he took her money, or that he robbed her? That he knocked a ball into a hole, or that he sank a put? That he said 'Done', or that he accepted an offer? *How far, that is, are motives, intentions, and conventions to be part of the description of actions?* And more especially here, what is *an* or *one* or *the* action? For we can generally split up what might be named as one action in several distinct ways, into different *stretches* or *phases* or *stages*. Stages have already been mentioned: we can dismantle the machinery of the act, and describe (and excuse) separately the intelligence, the appreciation, the planning, the decision, the execution, and so forth. Phases are rather different: we can say that he painted a picture or fought a campaign, or we can say that first he laid on this stroke of paint and then that. Stretches are different again: *a single term descriptive of what he did may be made to cover either a smaller or a larger*

stretch of events, those excluded by the narrower description being then called 'consequences' or 'results' or 'effects' or the like of his act. [my italic]

The businessman in a tight corner may do small individual acts of a 'naughty' nature which together form what to an outsider may look like a fraudulent pattern of behaviour, but he does not see it as such. He is too immersed in the world of action, of juggling to stay afloat, to consider the matter as a whole. Furthermore, he may not even be doing anything unusual. For example, a man who has been used to taking out £300 per week from his business in 'normal' times may continue to do so as a matter of course, even when his business does not justify his doing so in the eyes of an 'objective' observer. However, the businessman himself thinks that he is behaving normally and not fraudulently, for it does not occur to him that he is now insolvent and should change his established pattern of withdrawals. Even if he becomes aware of his insolvency, he may justify his continuing to trade by referring to others around him who have been similarly placed without being labelled 'dishonest'. The following account by a man who was later convicted may illustrate this point, even though it is taken from the artificial setting of an interview with the police:

> It's quite true that I told all these fellows that I would put the money I owed them in the post that night. If someone is on the blower [telephone] or in your office screaming for their money, you tell them anything just to get them off your back. It may not be what *you* expect businessmen to do, but it's my way, and there are plenty of others who do the same.

The 'mere' fact of insolvency is regarded as an obstacle in the way of continued trading rather than as a 'crime'. As a wholly straight business friend of mine stated:

> The notion that trading whilst insolvent is a crime is totally absurd. I doubt if there is a businessman in the country who does substantial buying and selling on credit who could always rely on paying all his debts when they fell due on every occasion throughout his business life.

This analysis of the lie-telling behaviour of businessmen fits in nicely with Lemert's perceptive remarks concerning risk-taking and deviant behaviour. Lemert (1972, pp. 38–40) states that

> Persons who are caught in a network of conflicting claims or values choose not deviant alternatives but rather behavioural solutions which carry risks of deviation... risk-taking, rather than deviation, is perceived by the conflicting person as a 'way out'... it is fair to assume that a considerable amount of risk-taking is built into business culture.

Lemert states that this applies particularly to his study of cheque forgery by businessmen.

To the insolvent trader, then, his behaviour may appear completely justified, and he may be genuinely surprised if allegations of wrongdoing are made against him. The acceptability of his account, if such an account is demanded of him, depends upon the empathetic position of the questioner. (Many business failures, particularly those of limited companies, receive only very cursory investigation by the Department of Trade.) The questioner may also regard his account as deceitful or as so self-deceitful that it must be denied legitimacy. However, from a phenomenological perspective, if the businessman believes his own account, it cannot be said that he *intended* to defraud his creditors. He therefore cannot properly be convicted of fraudulent trading under Section 332 (3) of the Companies Act, 1948. Indeed, it is not even clear whether he can properly be said to have been trading 'recklessly', neither knowing nor caring what the consequences of his acts might be. For he *does* care: the problem for the attribution of blame is that he was in such a state of mind that he did not define what he was doing as putting his creditors 'at risk'. When people are in this sort of situation, they sometimes become so ego-absorbed that their perceptions of the consequences of their acts for others become distorted and their feelings blunted. If jurors in criminal trials take this phenomenological issue seriously, they may have great difficulties in convicting this type of defendant. However, as Carlen (1976) and Henry (1978) have pointed out, formal court proceedings are a very poor medium for the communication of the full *ambience* which surrounds crimes, particularly when jurors or judges have a background far removed from that of the defendant.

Looked at in this way, the search for early background predictors of commercial deviance seems unlikely to bear fruit. There is no clear break between the 'slippery-slope' fraudster and others whose businesses fail or succeed after 'similar' risk-taking behaviour. Rather, there is a continuum. Perhaps the most tricky problems of labelling occur when a businessman who has traded while insolvent is lucky or skilful enough to 'make it' back into solvency. Phenomenologically, has he not committed the same offence as has the 'slippery-slope fraudster'?

'Intermediate' long-firm fraudsters

So far, we have examined the case of the businessman who continues to order goods on credit when he believes that he will be able to pay for them but when he ought to realize that he will be unable so to do. Now let us look at the next category on our common-sense dimension of 'seriousness': that which comprises businessmen who run a business honestly for a time, but then decide to go 'bent'. They do this for two main reasons:

(1) they feel that they are not getting as much as they require from their business;

(2) they believe that they are going to go 'bust' anyway.

Neither of these situations are *sufficient* conditions for becoming a long-firm fraudster. There are, of course, many businessmen who feel that they are not getting enough money and/or who realize that they are about to go 'bust' who do not do anything fraudulent whatever. Even those businessmen who seek dishonest solutions to their problems may not turn to long-firm fraud: they may become occasional or professional 'fences' (to be discussed later); or they may siphon off large sums from their businesses – 'black' money – thereby cheating the taxman. It should be noted also that bankruptcy fraud is a matter of degree: someone may conceal assets from his creditors without necessarily committing a fully-fledged long-firm fraud.

As I have discussed in earlier chapters, the 'how' and the 'why' questions may merge when someone comes to transform his 'straight' business into a long-firm fraud. He may merely be dissatisfied with his lot in life, with no intention of grandiose crime, when he chances upon a 'wide boy' who induces him to go 'bent'. From the point of view of motivational accounts, however, it is clear that the statement that 'I was just trying to keep going till I got over the bad patch' is no longer tenable as a self-justification of behaviour. Instead, the businessman can appeal to higher loyalties: 'I was only trying to save a few pennies for my wife and children. After all, I had worked all my life in the business. Why should I have to lose everything?' This account is a justification rather than an excuse: the fraudster is asserting his right to have done what he did.

Another 'intermediate' fraudster put forward the following justification:

> My business was going through a hard time and I knew we were going into liquidation. So I thought to myself: well, those fucking creditors made enough fucking money out of me all those years. Why shouldn't I get some of it back now that I need it? After all [he names some large companies], can afford it.

Finally, there is a case in which someone's account of his motives straddles the line between a justification and an excuse. Although the person does not appear to feel any guilt about his behaviour, he realizes that it was not socially acceptable:

> You probably won't believe this, but we really did start out legitimate. My brother had worked his bollocks off all his life, and he couldn't even lay down one grand in cash. I didn't want to end up like that, and I teamed up with Bianco who also wanted out. We didn't want to be villains, but we also didn't want to be skint [very poor]. We fancied ourselves as businessmen, and in fact the firm was doing very nicely...
> Unfortunately, when we had reps [trade representatives] actually suggesting that we give post-dated cheques and we saw thousands of pounds rolling in, the temptation was simply too great. I had always wanted to graduate to white-collar crime, and so instead of just getting good wages, which we were, we wanted to live like kings. So the expensive parties to impress other villains, the free gifts to show them we had made it as affluent businessmen, and most of the money was spent as we went along...
> At one stage in the l.f., I had the choice between accepting or rejecting an offer for £2000 of cooking oil. At that stage, I could have said 'no' and there needn't have been any fraud. But I had my eyes on the money, and although I knew that there was no way we could ever pay for it, I ordered it. Once I had done that, I thought we might as well go the whole hog, and we did.

None of the accounts of motive offered here have indicated any guilt about the behaviour. The existence or non-existence of guilt is not something that is scientifically demonstrable, despite psycho-analytical claims to the contrary. If one assumes that guilt is related to the pervasiveness of the negative lebelling of any given action by 'society', however, then one may conclude that my hypothesis about the lack of guilt is a reasonable one. For there is no great stigma attached to the conduct of 'slippery-slope' or even 'intermediate' fraudsters and, consequently, there is little that requires neutraliza-tion. In brief, I suggest that these accounts take the form of 'radical', that is, guiltless, rather than 'apologetic' justifications, within the model expounded by Matza (1964, pp. 41–8).

In summary, the 'slippery-slope' fraudster holds a view of himself as 'respectable' before, during and after 'the offence' (if so it be deemed). While he is still in business, his continued trading may not present him with any explicit and conscious 'problem' requiring justification. If he does feel the need to neutralize moral or social anxieties, he may do this by arguing to himself that his behaviour really is in the best interests of his creditors as well as of himself, that 'everybody does it in a situation like this', and that, consequently, there is nothing wrong with it. If his business fails, he is able to justify his conduct by saying that he was only trying to keep going till he got over a bad patch: the problem was that he wasn't able to keep going for long enough! He may even blame his creditors (or the bank) for failing to grant him sufficient time to get back on his feet. When called upon to account for his conduct to official agencies such as the Official Receiver's department, the police and the courts, he will draw attention to the honesty of his intentions and to the reasonableness of his assumptions about the future when he deceived his creditors. Whether he realizes it or not, he will be making use of the same conception of 'fraud' employed by MAUGHAM J. in the following dictum: 'Fraud . . . should be taken to mean . . . actual dishonesty involving, according to current notions of fair trading among commercial men, real moral blame', in *Re Patrick and Lyon Ltd* (1933), 1 Ch. 786.

He can only hope that the agencies of social control will place a similar construction upon his behaviour to that which he himself places. For if they adopt the position that one can only blame someone for something he deliberately set out to do, then he will have got away with it: they will have concurred with his justification and the imputation of criminality (or deviance) will have been rebutted.

'Pre-planned' long-firm fraudsters

This category presents the smallest problems for negative societal labelling, at least in principle. For as discussed in earlier chapters, there may be considerable difficulty in the practical determination of whether or not any given long firm was a *planned* long firm, but if one *knew* that it had been so planned, a person in authority would not accept any explanation of why it was done as an adequate *justification*.

Most of the intentional long-firm frauds which reach the courts are of the 'conspiracy-by-villains' kind, for the deliberate business-man-fraudsters are too cunning to make themselves vulnerable to easy conviction. Many of these conspiracies are characterized by a high division of labour and the roles played are fairly constant, in the sense that there are few opportunities for graduation from, say, 'front man' to organizer, though there may be interchange between 'backer', 'fence' and organizer. For this reason, I shall consider the motivations of the different role-players separately, because they do tend to be 'different sorts of people'.

'*Front men*' For the small-time criminal in 'the underworld', long-firm fraud offers high status within his occupational subculture, a higher probability of getting money than is the case in 'normal' crime, and some degree of job satisfaction. This is revealed in the following quotations by two men:

> They'll never have any trouble getting mugs to front l.f.s. Every small-time villain aspires to running an l.f., or at least they used to in my day. Take the average villain: he sees a mate of his in a flash motor, wearing fancy suits and with a smart bird next to him, and he asks what he's up to. His mate tells him he's doing an l.f., and he thinks that's where it's at. He doesn't realize that you are Mr Big while it lasts, but once you're nicked, you're forgotten, you're nowhere . . . You see them in the nick, the front men, in their own private *clique*. They wear flash rings (usually *rolled* gold) and Swiss watches, and they order *The Times* or *The Financial Times*, which they display where everybody can see what they're reading. But if you ask them what's in the paper, they've got no idea. They never actually *read* their papers. The only reason they get them is that they know it will impress the other villains and make them believe that they are big-time financial whizz-kids. In fact, they're not. They're rubbish.

> I won't pretend that money wasn't part of it. But I genuinely think that the main reason I did the l.f. was for my own self-discipline and self-respect. I had just come out of prison and had begun to see myself as an old lag, gradually drifting from one prison sentence to another. Then, through one of the people I had met inside, came the prospect of fronting an l.f. I hardly dared hope that they would pick me, but they did. They tested me out, and it was a real privilege when they said they would trust me. It's a funny thing, I suppose, but when I found I could do it properly, it gave me back my self-respect.

The next quotation from a 'front man' applies equally to the attractions of long-firm fraud to 'background operators' coming to fraud from other types of property crime:

> L.f.s used to be better than other types of villainy because you got the money from the gear before you got nicked. In other types of crime, you can be caught in the act and end up inside without benefiting at all. The credit used to just come to you, and if you were nicked, well, at least you had something to show for it. Now, though, things have changed, because Old Bill [police] move in on you while the business is still running. So it's not really worth it any more.

All the 'front men' discussed to date were already committed to crime when they took on that job. Consequently, it may not surprise us that they discuss the pros and cons of long-firm fraud in a matter-of-fact way. For others, 'contingencies' may be important in guiding them into long-firm fraud. This is nicely expressed in the following quote from a struck-off barrister who become involved in running long firms for the Krays:

> One day I came out of my house. I didn't have a penny to my name. I was on the way to see a friend...who had a stall in Fulham Market and, to tell the truth, I was going to borrow money from him. While I was on the way there, a car drew up with Dave in it and that was the start of everything.

This man, then, had a non-criminal self-image, despite one previous conviction for making false statements to procure a passport. Many others have no previous convictions at all, yet belong to a subculture of hedonism. One prominent fraudster puts it as follows (Payne, 1973, p. 19):

> Aristocrats and successful criminals have a great deal in common: boredom and selfishness, ample money and free time and a complete lack of interest in conventional, cautious bourgeois morality. The fallen professional man, the struck-off barrister, the crooked accountant, falls naturally into company with them.

Other organizers have confirmed his statement that the spoiled children of aristocrats and rich parents are well disposed to participation in long-firm fraud, generally as 'front men'. It gives them excitement, or 'restores the mood of humanism', as Matza (1964) would doubtless have it. Although such 'spoiled little rich kids' may be difficult to control, they have more social graces and 'front' than do upwardly mobile petty thieves. This is particularly true where a modicum of commercial knowledge is required.

'Minders'   I did not interview anybody who had been a 'minder' in a long-firm fraud, so I have no first-hand or even second-hand accounts of their motives for involvement. As far as I know, those given the task of 'minding' long firms are recruited from the general pool of underworld 'heavies'. In the case of syndicated frauds, they are often employed already by their gangster boss, but in other cases, they are merely freelances who are known to one of the background operators in the fraud. In other words, there is no *special motivational* account required to explain involvement in long firms. The *explananda* are (i) how did you come to know long-firm merchant X? and (ii) why do you work as a 'minder' generally? If I can generalize from my knowledge of 'minders' in other spheres, the answer to the second question is that throwing one's weight around

is a more prestigious and remunerative activity than the only available alternative: manual labour.

'Fences'   Some of the major 'fences' of long-firm goods are also organizers and are discussed later. The motivation for 'fencing' long-firm goods is the desire for more money, supplemented occasionally by the 'kick' from doing something risky. The 'dark figure' of undetected 'fences' is likely to be very large. As one organizer said to me: 'I never had the slightest trouble in getting rid of my gear. Most businessmen will jump at the chance of getting something on the cheap. I always remember the old saying: "If you scratch at a rich man, you will always find an old villain."'

As I have noted earlier, buying goods from long-firm fraudsters is far less risky than buying them from 'real' criminals. Furthermore, the decision to buy goods from a long firm made less *morally* problematic by the relative absence of stigma attached to long firms compared with 'ordinary' theft. Equally important, however, is the availability of the 'everybody does it' mode of justification referred to in the analysis of amateur fences' accounts by Henry (1976, p. 93). The would-be long-firm 'fence' says to himself: 'If I don't buy this gear, somebody else will, probably one of my competitors. So if I don't take the profit, I might actually be *worse* off than before. Because the man who buys it off the l.f. can undercut *me*!' Indeed, there is some force in this argument, as some businessmen *have* been ruined by cut-price competition from long-firm goods.

Both Henry (1976, 1978) and Klockars (1975) state that 'fences' have little difficulty in reconciling their 'crimes' with their view of themselves as – on balance – 'good' or 'respectable' people. As Klockars's 'Vincent' puts it (p. 151):

> Sure I've done some bad things in my life. Who hasn't? Everybody's got a skeleton in his closet somewhere. But you gotta take into account all the good things I done too. You take all the things I done in my life and put'em together, no doubt about it, I gotta come out on the good side.

Some long-firm fraud 'fences' who also purchase goods from burglaries and hijackings take part in these 'moral ledger' balancing exercises too. However, as stated earlier, the 'fencing' market for long-firm goods extends far into the world of those with large legitimate businesses who would not 'fence' what *they* regard as 'stolen goods'. One long-firm organizer made the following comment about this issue:

> I don't really regard purchasing l.f. gear as fencing. I prefer to call
> my outlets 'wholesalers'. The people I sell to would happily buy
> gear from an l.f., but they wouldn't dream of buying stolen gear.
> For instance, they certainly would not go within a mile of hijacked
> stuff... I'll give you an example of what I mean. If there had been
> a hijack of, say, Oxo cubes, and I had some in an l.f., people
> would be very wary of me and I would not be able to get rid of
> them. The 'fences' didn't regard themselves as 'fences'. To them,
> there was the world of difference between l.f. gear and stolen gear.
> With stolen gear, they stood to lose their businesses, which were
> substantial, so it just wasn't worth the risk. Of course, all this was
> before the 1968 Theft Act, so it actually wasn't stolen gear. Now
> things may have changed a bit.

The Theft Act, 1968 incorporated the offence of obtaining goods by
false pretences within the crime of 'theft'. So purchasing goods from
long-firm frauds is not only *legally* safer than doing so from burglars
or hijackers, but it is also *morally* superior. To a businessman living
in a world of 'deals', the moral gap between purchasing from a long
firm and doing ordinary business is not very great. Furthermore,
and this is particularly important, when he buys from a long-firm
merchant he buys from a *businessman, not* from a 'thief'. This makes it
easy to 'normalize' the purchase as 'just another bargain'.

Although many long-firm 'fences' are greedy businessmen who
are already rich, some become involved in a desperate attempt to
maintain the solvency of their businesses. This is particularly true of
one owner of a chain of supermarkets, but it applies equally to other
smaller businessmen. Not all businessmen in this position would
'fence' long-firm goods, even if they were approached by a fraudster,
but the ability to refer to the 'need' to keep one's business going is a
useful salve to the conscience pangs of a 'respectable' businessman.

In brief, there is no need for any 'deep' explanation of why a
businessman engages in 'fencing' long-firm goods. Given contacts
with long-firm fraudsters – a necessary condition – the decision to
'fence' is facilitated by the verbalization of it as 'not *real* crime' but is
largely a matter of weighing up the practical consequences of
participation. Although the justification of 'need' here may take the
form of the subjective experience of 'relative deprivation', there are
cases in which there *is* an absolute need for below-cost goods to keep
the business afloat.

The model suggested here corresponds closely to that offered by
Walsh (1977, p. 42) who argues that for one group of US
'fences' – those trading in marginal areas with high rates of business
failure – involvement in the resale of stolen goods may well have
been the key to their commercial longevity.

The 'fencing' of long-firm goods has the advantage over other types of 'fencing' that it is less likely to result in conviction. On the other hand, it is correspondingly less profitable than other types of 'fencing', where the position of the thieves vis-a-vis the 'fences' is weaker. Estimates of the percentage profit that long-firm 'fences' make vary widely, but organizers appear to get between 60 and 95 per cent of the full market value of their goods. As one organiser said:

> When you're dealing in groceries, food, and stuff like that, the loss to the wholesaler is negligible. The l.f. would make maybe 90—95 per cent of the cost price, or even more sometimes, so the benefit to you would almost equal the cost to the creditors. In proprietory lines, the discount was greater, say, 12 per cent. It all depends on the supply and demand situation.

As I have shown, the 'fence' can make considerably more money by involving himself in the organization and financing of long firms, but this type of vertical integration increases manifold the risks to his liberty and to his reputation.

To summarize, the decision to 'fence' long-firm goods entails the consideration of two principal factors: the cost to one's self-image as a 'respectable person'; the fear of the stigma and commercial incapacitation that can result from arrest, conviction and possible imprisonment.

The first factor can be neutralized fairly easily, and the second can be guarded against without too much difficulty by the *modus operandi* which were discussed in Chapter III. However, the mere presence of motivation for 'fencing' long-firm goods is not a sufficient condition for action: crucial further constraints are contact between would-be 'fence' and fraudster, and a reasonable degree of congruence between the long-firm goods and those sold in the legitimate business role of the 'fence'.

Organizers The following are accounts of the reasons given by people I interviewed who have organized *at least five* long-firm frauds for their involvement in commercial crime. Because of my promise to those interviewed that their comments about others as well as themselves would not be readily identifiable, I have not intercorrelated statements made by any given individual at different stages of this chapter. It is hoped that this does not detract much from the value of the interview material.

(a) The problem was that we were discharged after the War having been trained to kill and used to excitement. Then, more so than now, you couldn't get a job in a big firm or a bank unless you had the right Old School Tie. They just didn't want to know you... And I wanted to get on in life, but in those days [puts on snobbish accent] you had to be the 'right sort of chap, don't you know'...

I turned to l.f.s through being in the wrong place at the wrong time, mixing with the wrong people. There were seven of us who formed a little circle. Some, who had extreme cunning, luck and background – and money – succeeded and became fantastically rich... Others did not make it, because they thought they were cleverer than they were... Myself and Blank were not so cunning, so we ended up as l.f. merchants... But in the beginning, at least, we were all the same. They are captains of industry, and I am a Prince of the l.f.! That's the way it goes...

Some people have a degree of honesty and then at the end have a twist. Take A, for example. I never understood why he went into l.f.s. He was wealthy in his own right, and he was married to a wealthy girl. Why should someone like that want to do l.f.s? It must be greed, or maybe something twisted inside...

Then you have the category of people with minds like a pirate whose only idea is to plunder as much as possible in as short a time as possible... They aren't l.f. merchants but pirates... Then, there are a third category of people, like myself, who are not born thieves or twisted businessmen, but who were unsettled by the War... the Richardsons and the Krays were all born abnormal, but circumstances made me a villain. I despise thieves because they have no self-control. This is why they can't run l.f.s.

I think really that l.f. merchants are people who have inferiority complexes or dreams of grandeur, and they do l.f.s so that they can impress birds with the High Life... I never had any capital, and although I started my businesses straight, I could never get them off the ground. So I turned to l.f.s.

(b) I suppose I went into l.f.s because I wanted too much too fast, and now, the people I used to muck around with are all better off than I am. I have run straight businesses, but the temptation is too great to stay in them. I reckon l.f.s are superior to ordinary crime because you have the scope to manipulate people and to cook the books afterwards. You can't do that in crimes like robbery. You can make a hell of a lot of money from l.f.s and the sentences are low because it's got no violence. The powers-that-be are really down on violence.

(c) I went into l.f.s purely for the money. I'm not a big spender or a High Liver like B. I'm a family man. B did it for fun, and must have gone through £1–2 million; others did it because it made them feel big; but I never was really interested in l.f.s for themselves. To me, they were just another type of business.

I had about 40 businesses in a number of fields, into which I channelled some of the l.f. gear... and I would have been a millionaire by legitimate means if I hadn't gone into l.f.s. Now, relatively speaking, I am fucked. I suppose I was trying to take too short a cut.

(d) When I started out, l.f.s were just a way of making a bit of money on the side. Just a little extra, you know. In the beginning, I just backed frauds and fenced some of the gear. Then, gradually, I got involved in the actual organization, and the whole thing snowballed.

The final motivational account of high-class organizers comes not from interviews with them but from one with a person close to them. Its reliability has, however, been checked and no inconsistencies have been found with 'the facts' as known to others. The people referred to here are not tied up with 'the underworld': they are what I have referred to earlier as 'pre-planned businessman-fraudsters'.

Green's father was a big businessman who died on the Continent and left him £150000. But unfortunately, Green had a taste for fast women and slow horses, and it didn't take him long to get through that. Fortunately, he had the sense to marry the daughter of a millionaire, who bailed out his gambling debts.

Then, he went into partnership with a man called Brown who was a sleeping partner [non-executive financier] while Green flogged his textiles stock for cash to pay for his gambling and female companionship. He ran this firm as an l.f. with his manager, who later did three years inside for the arson of three shops which were doing badly. Everybody was filching stock like mad, but the other partner knew nothing about it. Then, he had a *coup*. He had bought some rainwear from a large Hong Kong manufacturer, to the value of about a million pounds, and some, although very little, of it was faulty. So he got the letters of complaint and he showed them to the British manager of the firm, with whom he was very friendly. Somehow, he got him to sign a letter admitting that an unspecified amount of stock was faulty, and he then sued the Hong Kong manufacturers for breach of contract by delivering faulty goods. He got £120000 out of them.

Eventually, it all got too much for his partner, and he finished with him. The manager of the Hong Kong firm lost his job, and the firm will now never supply merchants in the City. And Green has lost his wife and her rich and helpful father. This is where a lot of them go wrong. They start to run around with these whores and they think it's big to lose a fortune in the casinos without blinking, which is all right if it's *your* money you're spending.

Then there's Pink, a similar sort of fellow. Rich background, brother comfortably off, but did lots of l.f.s that they could never prove. Every time he does a *coup*, he goes off to the Continent to celebrate, and spends half of it there living it up. Now he's settled down, though, and is straighter than straight. When these rich boys do l.f.s, it's generally because of the women and casinos and gee-gees [horses]. Otherwise, they have no reason for going 'bent'. They can earn a good living in the ordinary way of business.

Bearing in mind that these are retrospective accounts, it is all the more remarkable that they contain very few references blaming 'society' for their behaviour or alleging that they had little choice but crime. The nearest anyone comes to that is the 'blocked opportunity' hypothesis in the remarks of fraudster (a). The others justify their paths to wealth (and/or prison) as rational decisions which imprisonment may or may not lead them to regret.

Continuing with long-firm fraud

There is no *a priori* reason why the motives that led people into long-firm fraud in the first place should not remain intact. If the reason for involvement was a temporary shortage of money, then the offender should quit. The 'slippery-slope' fraudster should go on to do whatever people who go 'bust' normally do. The 'villain' seeking status in the underworld should carry on, or find some other type of high-status activity. Unfortunately, matters are rarely that simple. Along the way, people may find that they are 'turned on' or 'turned off' by what they have been doing. Active reflection concerning the potential *for them* of the experiences they have been through may lead them to reorient their lives in some measure.

The more or less respectable businessman who decides 'just this once' to 'fence' long-firm goods may be excited by the fun of it all as well as by the material profits. The people he meets may tell him that he has the *right* to have a little pleasure in life, that it is too 'square' to be just another boring little businessman, living out his humdrum little life, neither living nor dying. Mixing with 'the chaps' may open his eyes to a whole range of novel human experiences, in the areas of sex and gambling, which may encourage him to feel that his former 'respectable life' was unutterably dull. This is the sort of thing that has happened to many businessmen, and is particularly well described in one account of the way American crime syndicates get their hooks into businessmen on gambling junkets (Teresa, 1973). There are also some analogies with the hypothesis (Becker, 1963, p. 42) that 'instead of the deviant motives leading to the deviant behaviour, it is the other way around; the deviant behaviour in time produces the deviant motivation'.

Long-firm fraudsters do not need other people to teach them how to gain the maximum enjoyment out of their crimes, as Becker suggests marijuana users do. What happens to them is that they come to develop reasons for taking part in commercial crime rather than straight business, in the form of (i) the pleasure that the battle of wits with creditors and law enforcement agencies can bring; and (ii) the pleasure that the proceeds of crime can bring. What started out as a minor transgression, a banal way of supplementing one's income, may become a grand obsession or game in which the individual plays for high stakes against 'society' and his own nerves.

In the case of some former respectables, this process may be likened to a conversion. All of a sudden (or gradually) one is transformed from an ordinary fellow into a central participant in the High Life. One is surrounded by friends – one finds out only later that they are merely acquaintances or hangers on – and one is invited to clubs and to parties. One comes to identify with a *Grand Seigneur* self-image, which can be used to justify still further criminal activity. As Klapp (1969, pp. 197–8) points out, once the quest for personal identity is seen to lie in the direction of sensations, ever-greater 'kicks' must be found for temporary satisfaction.

Clearly, the analysis offered by Klapp is overdetermined: this slippery-slope theory of moral hedonism is belied by our experiences. However, for some long-firm fraudsters, the financial motivations which led them into fraud initially *do* become superseded by the fun and challenge involved in 'beating the system'. This challenge provides an excitement that is more difficult to attain in legitimate business – at least at their level – and this produces a psychological 'high'. The very risk this brings to their social identity as 'respectables' adds piquancy to their involvement, for this increases the stakes. They need not enter the 'underworld' to gain this satisfaction: the pleasure can be a purely private one. The attractiveness of being a 'secret deviant' is expressed very nicely by Steve McQueen in the film *The Thomas Crown Affair* and in the following illumination of the inner life of the political conspirator (West, 1952, p. 21):

> Complication is to the soul what condiments are to the palate and alcohol is to the nervous system . . . Sweet it is to be not what the next man thinks one, but far more powerful; to know what he wrote in the letter he was so careful to seal before he sent it for quite a different person's reading, to charm the confidences from the unsuspecting stranger; to put up one's finger through the whimsical darkness and touch the fabric of the State, and feel the unstable structure rock, and know it one's own doing and not a soul suspecting it.

Some long-firm fraudsters like to see themselves not as 'villains' but as 'adventurers', the latter-day equivalent of those piratic entrepreneurs who had won Britain her Empire. They feel that in an increasingly bureaucratic age, they are the sole carriers of the spirit of free enterprise. (Free, at any rate, to them.) They derive great pleasure from 'putting one over' on the creditors and salesmen who play out their dull and dreary lives. Despite having to remain constantly on the alert to avoid being cheated by their own partners, they enjoy a camaraderie reminiscent of *Butch Cassidy and the Sundance Kid*:

> We used to do this tough cop/soft cop routine with the salesmen. One of us would say that he wanted to order the stuff and the other – the tough cop – would say no. There would be a lot of argument, but the tough cop would be adamant. He would then leave the room for a bit, and you could almost bet your bottom dollar that the rep would offer the soft cop a bribe of some kind to persuade his partner to give the order. It was great fun.

> I used to love working with C because he was brilliant, a genius with his mouth. He had the ability after half an hour to make you feel that you were his very best friend. We used to sit in my office in Oxford St and he would say to me: 'Do you think that there is a *shmock* [fool] walking down Oxford St now?' I would reply 'of course' and he would go out and start to chat to some fellow and he would bring him in. We would spin him some nonsense, and he would go off and do something unbelievably stupid that we had suggested to him. With C you were never bored.

> There was this very funny occasion when we got a request to see a firm about selling them some furnishings. I was told some story by the buyer who wanted credit, while I was trying to get him to give me cash *pro forma* [before delivery]. We were to-ing and fro-ing for some time, each trying to persuade the other, when suddenly there was a burst of hysterical laughter from inside the office, and out comes D [another l.f. organizer]. It was one of his l.f.s. They didn't know it was my firm they were ordering from, and I was trying to get them to give me the money in advance and fuck them for the goods. We nearly died laughing about it.

Reactions to social control

So far, I have said little about the effects of social control upon long-firm fraudsters, except for the suggestion that although it may deter many from fraud, there are some who are actually *attracted* by the opportunity to 'beat the system'. Clearly, though, whether or not the individual is convicted for his offence(s), he knows that he cannot be indifferent to the activities of social control agencies or to the possible stigma he might suffer were his conduct to be treated as 'deviant' or criminal. He may not feel guilty about what he is doing, but he has the problem of coping with secrets. He must develop strategies for reducing the risks he takes upon himself. For example, a former 'respectable' businessman may have to enter existing fraudster and/or criminal networks if he wishes to find others to 'front' for him. The effects of these strategies may be to 'criminalize' him. He may spend the whole of his life as a background operator without being detected, prosecuted or convicted, but, in one sense, he will have taken on the social role of 'fraudster' because of the need to keep his deviance secret.

This process of 'secondary deviation' does not entail his separation from 'normal' society, however. As Maurer (1964, p. 11) observes: 'The big-time confidence men are flexible and equally at home in their own subculture or in the dominant culture – in fact they are able to simulate behaviour within the dominant culture to a high degree of perfection.'

There are very few long-firm fraudsters who conform to the image of the professional thief in the work of Sutherland (1937, pp. 165–6) as the man who lives 'largely in a world of his own and is rather completely isolated from general society. The majority of them do not care to contact society except professionally.'

Much criminological confusion has been generated by misunderstandings as to what counts as labelling and what it is that may tend to lead to further involvement in crime. (For a reasoned assessment, see Plummer, 1979.) The process of possible 'criminalization' referred to overleaf does not necessarily mean that the individual will commit either more or fewer crimes than he committed before or would have committed anyway: it relates solely to changes in his self-conception and way of looking at the world. I do not mean to imply that the activities of a long-firm fraudster lead him to question, in an explicit existentialist way, 'What kind of person am I *really?*' I met no-one who gave the slightest indication that he had ever woken up one morning and said to himself: 'My God, I am no longer a conventional businessman who, among other things, does the occasional l.f. but am now essentially a long-firm fraudster.' The process of psychological affiliation to deviance is more subtle than that: it insinuates into consciousness rather than smashes therein.

In this chapter, reactions to social control will be divided into four subcategories: reactions to arrest, reactions to trial, reactions to conviction, and reactions to imprisonment. When the reader assesses the material, he should bear in mind that (i) *some* of my interviews were short and were concerned more with organization and craft-work in fraud than with phenomenological subtleties: it seems somewhat over-optimistic to believe that one can enter someone's soul in less than three hours; (ii) no-one was interviewed who had been convicted but not sent to prison; and (iii) the interview data were *retrospective* and thus prone to biases of a kind different from those entailed in contemporaneous interviews.

Reaction to arrest

If a long-firm fraudster is arrested, the consequences of his criminal activities may be brought home rather sharply to him. Even then, however reflections tend to take the form: 'Why didn't I do x rather than y so that I wouldn't have been caught?' The following extracts may illustrate this point:

(a) It was all my fault in a way that I got arrested. What I should have done was to disappear until after the boy and the others had been tried, because they really had very little on me, but I suppose I was careless. That's the trouble with these diabolical conspiracy charges – the prosecution hammered my name till it was coming out of the jury's ears. I was the Mastermind, the Mr Big. When the judge sentenced me, I didn't know what hit me. I just couldn't believe it.

(b) The only reason I get nicked is because I am a perfectionist. You wouldn't believe the number of schemes that I have had that would have made me a millionaire if I had had reliable people working for me. But you can't get them: all these thieves want to know is grab, grab, grab. So I had to do things myself, and when you do that, you expose yourself.

(c) I suppose that I should have gone when I found out that no-one in C6 [the London Fraud Squad] was able to look at my file without the permission of the Commander. Maybe I wanted to get it all over with – I don't know. But I had so much going on here, and my wife was here . . . I just hoped it would never happen, but it did.

Two 'professional fraudsters' who were denied bail (for very good reason) subsequent to their arrest found that this presented considerable difficulties for their other legitimate business interests as well as for their families. However, in many cases long-firm frauds are *the* source of livelihood for the people concerned, so the issue of losing jobs does not arise. In this respect, they differ greatly from the 'white-collar criminals' interviewed in *open* prison by Breed (1979). Breed discusses the problems of his sample – who presumably were on bail until their imprisonment following conviction – in the following terms (p. 110):

For all of them, the mess deepens considerably months, or even years, before they appear in court. There is often a wide gap between their *indiscretions* [my italic] coming to light and the police being ready to proceed. Usually, they lose their job immediately, and, because they are under suspicion, find it impossible to obtain

work at a similar level... Their income is inevitably reduced...
the mess deepens... Sometimes there is also the threat of
bankruptcy, and this is the greatest worry of all.

This gap between suspicion and trial is often the worst period
for white-collar offenders: even though they are not yet officially
guilty, they usually are in the eyes of employers and most of the
people who know them. The slowness with which investigations
proceed... is extreme... The average wait for the men in the
sample was well over a year, and for a few the gap was between
two and three years.

The length of time taken by cases to reach trial did disturb
long-firm fraudsters also, but their primary reaction to arrest was to
blame themselves or others or both for their being arrested. Then,
they turned their minds to the serious business of 'getting off'. This
generally involved the normal task of preparing the best defence
possible (and getting the best barristers). Sometimes, however, it
extended to the attempted 'fixing' of witnesses, jurors and police
officers in a desperate attempt to keep out of prison:

B had been paying a fortune to the police before he got nicked. In
fact, it got to the stage where they were flocking to take an interest
in his affairs just so they could get in on the firm. After he was
nicked, he went to pieces. He offered this fellow he knew, a real
Mr Fixit, a load of money to get him out. This fellow was
supposed to have fixed the judge so that he would get a £12 000
fine, but when the sentence came, the judge must have misheard
what the deal was supposed to be! It turned out that all the time,
the fellow was really a police informant.

Being on trial
The kinds of 'accounts' put forward at long-firm fraud trials in an
attempt to achieve an acquittal take three principal forms: the claim
that what we done was not in fact proscribed by the criminal law;
the claim that although there was a crime, the particular defendant
in question was not a knowing party to it; and more rarely, the claim
that the defendant acted under duress: he took part only because he
or his family had been threatened in some way by 'heavies'.

Much attention has been paid to the alleged effects of trials as
'status degradation ceremonies' which mystify defendants and alter
their self-conceptions so as to reinforce their view of themselves as
'truly criminal'. As Becker (1969, p. 31) puts it:

One of the most crucial steps in the process of building up a stable
pattern of deviant behaviour is likely to be the experience of being
caught and publicly labelled as a deviant... being caught and
branded as a deviant has important consequences for one's
further social participation and self-image.

One might have thought that the act of preparing an account—whether justification or excuse – would be an important component in this process, for it would force the alleged deviant to make explicit to himself his rationale for acting as he did. However, although those to whom I spoke regarded their trials as highly artificial and mystifying in atmosphere – though less so than defendants described by Breed (1979) and Carlen (1976) – they did not suggest that their trials had made them feel *more* criminal than they had felt before. If anything, they said that their trial had almost made them believe their own defences! It seems likely that those who have a self-image of 'criminal' prior to their trials are able to cope with the acquittal-game more easily than those who rationalize away their crimes as, for example, 'borrowing', or who did not *really* believe that they would be caught.

Consequences of conviction for the long-firm fraudster

For the fraudster who is integrated socially into 'the underworld' prior to his conviction, the problem of stigma, of 'spoiled identity', is primarily a *practical* problem. He may ask himself how his conviction will affect his future criminal and law-abiding activities and how he will fare in prison. He may have to think about how his family will manage – if he has one – and about any other business interests he may have, which may require new management or even have to be put into liquidation. All these are major life-problems, but they seldom take the form of existential doubts. For the long-firm fraudster who has been a 'secret deviant', however, the consequences of conviction (or even arrest) may be very great. As Martin and Webster (1971) have pointed out, the English middle classes do not look kindly upon 'the criminal'. The long-firm merchant cannot expect the 'there but for the grace of God go I' tolerance which is extended so liberally to the motoring offender and to the tax 'fiddler'. His formerly friendly neighbours and golfing companions may ostracize his family and tell each other that 'I always thought that there was something *slightly* wrong about him': the retrospective re-evaluation of moral identity discussed so cogently by Kitsuse (1962).

There are strong grounds, then, for believing that someone is far better off *emotionally* if, prior to his conviction, he has accepted the label of 'fraudster' and has mixed socially with 'villains' or with those who find villainy *chic*. (However, this is only applicable to those who are *convicted*. For, as I have argued already, social mixing with 'the chaps' – known criminals – increases the risk that a fraudster will attract police interest and be defined as 'a villain'.)

One might also think that conviction would make more difference to the social identities of those who hold a view of themselves as 'respectable' than to those who have already accepted that they 'are' 'villains'. Unfortunately, however, I have no evidence on the post-conviction criminality of 'slippery-slope' fraudsters. As the sentencing study in Chapter X and Leigh's (1980) study of bankruptcy offenders indicate, many 'slippery-slopers' are not sent to prison. Breed's (1979) sample of 100 offenders in open prison appeared *to him* to be 'slippery-slope' offenders in the main, and they and their families suffered considerably from social and financial downfall. However, there has not yet been any substantial research on white-collar criminals who have *not* been sent to prison, so any remarks about them must remain speculative.

The other major category of long-firm fraudsters not sent to prison is that of the non-principals of conspiracies to defraud. In their case, it is difficult to assess the effects of conviction, because most people in this category were heavily involved in crime *before* their entry into long-firm fraud. One therefore has 'criminal data' which are more complex to interpret than are those relating to first-time offenders. Impressionistic remarks of some interviewees indicate that conviction has little effect on such individuals, but this too is somewhat speculative.

Long-firm fraudsters in prison

Long-firm fraudsters react to imprisonment in various ways, but the type of prison to which they are sent and the length of their sentence in relation to their expectations are crucial factors influencing their reactions. Some long-firm merchants, although doing what for fraud offenders are relatively long sentences such as five or six years, had expected longer and were relieved: others receiving similar sentences felt totally shattered. Some occupy their time in prison by campaigning endlessly against the injustice of their conviction and of their treatment as 'common criminals'. Others accept the situation philosophically and settle down to 'do their bird'. Indeed, some fraudsters doing less than three years at an open prison regard their 'time' as a not too unpleasant break from the hectic wheeling and dealing taking place outside: as a period of careful planning of future capers with their congenial and amusing fraudster friends 'inside'.

Most long-firm fraudsters manage quite successfully in prison, although its entertainments and amenities are hardly to their taste. As one first-time prisoner said: 'This place is really barbaric. I can make out all right: it's no worse than being in the army. But that doesn't mean that it isn't barbaric.' They are rarely troublesome prisoners, although they often continue their 'operator' habits while inside. It has been suggested that one organizer even ran long firms from prison! The normal prison 'fiddles' certainly present no problems for the expert fraudster and in this context, the report of one prisoner about 'long-term frauds' in tobacco is worthy of note (House of Commons, 1950–1). Some long-firm merchants, however, choose to adopt a disdainful indifference to 'prison rackets', thereby emphasizing their ability to rise above the common herd.

Long firmers are experienced manipulators, and they make entertaining company for both prisoners and staff. Consequently, unless there are 'gangsters' around, they usually manage to get the best jobs in the prison. The attitudes of others towards them, however, are tinged with ambivalence: on the one hand, they are admired for their *savoir-faire*; on the other, they are resented for that very quality by the class-conscious prisoners and prison officers. As far as prison officers are concerned, conmen have the advantage that they seldom present any physical risk, while the Governor grades clearly find them more congenial company than 'heavies' or 'thieves'. Indeed, some fraudsters are alleged to have spent most of their time in prison 'playing chess with the Governor'.

It might be argued that despite their relative success at 'making out' in prison, long-firm fraudsters suffer far greater 'relative deprivation' than do other prisoners. For on the outside, they live far more lavishly than do 'ordinary' criminals, and experience a correspondingly greater contrast between 'normal' and prison life. (This is one problem that must be faced by those who advocate a return to a retributivist model of punishment: how does one compare degrees of suffering between different people?) Although there is some truth in this relative deprivation argument, it is equally important to note that the pains of imprisonment are mitigated by pleasant recollections: to be doing 'a lot of bird' without having lived well seems far more futile and absurd than to be paying for the rich fruits that crime has already brought. At least there are benefits to be weighed against the costs!

In the illuminating analysis of strategies for coping with prison life put forward by Cohen and Taylor (1972), much space is devoted to the problems of killing time. Despite the fact that no long-firm fraudster has ever *served* more than six years 'inside', the problem of psychological survival is a very real one, particularly for those sentenced to terms longer than four years. Long-firm fraudsters are likely to be habituated to a higher level of arousal *outside* prison than are the majority of those given more than four years' imprisonment. For a man used to the intensity of organizing large-scale frauds and to thinking in terms of units of tens or even hundreds of thousands of pounds, the very slow pace of life inside prison, the absurdity of having to regard as consequential a few pence difference in wages, and the absence of any significant stimulation sometimes leads to a considerable degree of psychological disintegration. This need not take the form of overt 'mental illness'. The fraudster may continue to 'make out' successfully in the prison, while at the same time, his reactions may slow down and he may lose his sense of proportion and contact with the reality external to the prison.

During a long stretch of imprisonment, it is difficult for a long-firm merchant to avoid questioning seriously 'where he is at'. This need not take the form of an identity crisis – 'Am I essentially a villain?' – but rather the more practical forms: 'Is it really worth it?' 'Why did I really do it and do I want now what I wanted then?' In other words, he may call into question the attractions of a fraudster's life-style, with all its attendant consequences: 'Why did I spend all that money on those birds?'; 'Do I have any real friends?'; 'Who needs all those trips abroad and flash hotels?' The fraudster may 'grow out' of the desire to be a Big Spender, gambling heavily and impressing the ladies and neighbours with his generosity.

It is when a fraudster becomes disenchanted with his mode of life that change is most likely. It is not pleasant to live in a social world where no-one can be trusted and in which one constantly has to be on the alert to protect oneself against the police and one's partners. For one central feature of the life of the long-firm fraudster – and this applies equally to all professional criminals of high status – is that one lives all the time at a very high level of intensity and suppressed anxiety: one can never fully relax or unwind. This continual state of excitement is part of the attraction of professional crime, as the following quote from a leading bank robber, Bertie Smalls, in Ball *et al.*, (1978, p. 183) indicates:

> This nervous tension I used to feel before a job didn't stay with me all the time, only till I got started. Once I start I feel completely calm, one hundred percent, everything comes brilliant to me . . . I might be fogged up a minute or two before but the minute it's on it's like the sun coming out from behind a cloud.

However, it is also one of its most underrated costs.

Other kinds of reflections enter the minds of fraudsters in prison. There is concern about the impact prison may have on future criminal or legitimate commercial and social activities. For those with a wife and children, there is the worry about what a future prison sentence might do to their relationships. However, optimism about the reformative impact of these reflections should be guarded.

Experience shows that there is seldom any clear link between a genuine desire while 'inside' to reform and subsequent behaviour on the 'outside'. The latter is the world of action rather than existential contemplation.

Finally, it should not be thought that *all* prisoners who have committed long-firm fraud intend – while in prison – to go 'straight'. Some merely assert that 'next time, I won't make any mistakes'. For them, the main effect of prison is to sharpen their resolve to be more skilful on future occasions. In fact, however, they may find that although their *motivation* towards skill has increased, their performance has diminished. If it does little else, a long spell in prison takes the fine edge off a fraudster's judgement and operational cunning, and makes it more likely that he will be caught again.

Going straight (or not): exits from long-firm fraud

In one sense, long-firm fraudsters ought to make excellent candidates for 'going straight'. Apart from their deviousness – a quality not restricted to businessmen who are socially defined as fraudsters – they are clinically normal. As Eysenck (1977, p. 60) admits: 'conmen, incidentally, are high on E [extraversion] and low on N [neuroticism], as well as being low on P [psychoticism]; this is intelligible, as their trade demands normal social relationships'. These observations about *convicted* conmen are presumably still more true of those whose adeptness at managing social relationships keeps them out of the courts and out of prison.

Nor should it be thought that people become long-firm fraudsters because they are congenitally lazy, and this would make it difficult for them to reform. It is certainly true that many people turn to long-firm fraud because they wish to make money more quickly and easily than they could do legitimately. However, it would be quite erroneous to suppose that fraudsters do not work very hard while they are operating. Although long-firm merchants are in general hedonistic in their leisure pursuits, they are staunch 'protestant ethic' men in the workplace: a point that confirms the observations of Klockars (1975) about 'the professional fence'. Long-firm specialists work long hours under conditions of stress that would make most businessmen blanch. Indeed, there are few businessmen who could cope mentally with the strain of simultaneously 'conning' large numbers of creditors and the bank manager, making sure that one's employees and partners are not stealing for themselves the proceeds of the fraud, and keeping a watchful eye out for undercover investigators from the police, the Department of Trade, and HM Customs and Excise. No-one becomes a long-firm fraudster if he wishes to enjoy a peaceful, easy life. Given the stress of a fraudster's way of life, the possibility of being sent to prison once one has been reconvicted, and a relatively normal personality structure, one must ask oneself why anyone persists in carrying out long-firm frauds.

If those I interviewed or about whom I was told are in any sense typical, most long-firm fraudsters will say that their primary object in committing crime is to make enough money either to be able to afford to 'go legit' or to retire altogether. As one of them said: 'First, you must get on. Then, you want honours. And finally, you want to become honest.'

Some of them set themselves a goal, reach it and quit. They are the fraudsters one rarely meets or hears about (at least in a 'criminal' role). Somewhere along the line, many people find that 'enough' is an infinitely elastic concept. Mixing with the High Life in clubs and casinos, one tends to develop very expensive tastes in women, cars, holidays and gambling. One may even wish to acquire a Stately Home! This is the classic condition of anomie. It takes great self-discipline to stick to one's original targets – after all, long firms are so *easy* to do. As one organizer said (with some degree of self-deception):

> When I did an l.f., I used to always invest the money in my straight businesses. C, on the other hand, was a real high liver. We would split £10 000 on Friday afternoon, and by the Saturday his share would be gone, usually in the casino. Most of the l.f. people spend their money as they go along.

It is so tempting to save the proceeds from the *next* long firm! Another major fraudster reflected on his situation thus:

> When I started out, l.f.s were just a way of making a bit of money on the side... Then, gradually, I got involved in the actual organization, and the whole thing snowballed. It was like a drug – I couldn't stop. I had a wonderful wife and I was doing all right in straight business, but I was into the clubs and the casinos, I had a couple of mistresses, and birds all over the place. In the end, it was like you said, a kind of urge to destroy myself. I knew I would get caught and I carried on until I was. When I got nicked, I was shattered, but it was a relief in a way... I always had to have the best, and that costs a lot of money... Maybe that was insecurity, but that was the way it was.

Apart from the acquisition of expensive tastes, one may develop a taste for the excitement – the tension of knowing that one is risking one's liberty by one's actions. After a while, the twin elements of money-making and excitement – 'the game-like juggling with accounts, the constant split-second decision-making, the continual crises' – become inextricably fused, and the man is well on his way to becoming a professional fraudster. Although he may still regard money-making as his main aim, he finds that he becomes bored unless he is constantly immersed in wheeling and dealing. In this purely phenomenological sense, he becomes a 'fraud addict'. Even for those who are subsequently caught, there is great satisfaction in the fraudulent manipulation of creditors and salesmen.

Another aspect of 'the fraudster mentality' which makes it hard to 'go legit' is the deviousness and corner-cutting which becomes almost second-nature to him in the course of his career in fraud. The difficulty of 'thinking straight' is not confined to the professional criminal: it affects policemen, politicians, multinational corporation executives, and even some academics. However, it has a specific effect upon the professional criminal, for if he does not learn to 'think straight', he may go back to 'villainy' and end up in prison. Once someone has developed the techniques required of an effective burglar, it is hard for him to walk down the street without almost automatically 'casing' the houses and shops. Similarly, once someone has become skilful at getting goods on credit and disposing of them without paying creditors, it is difficult for him *not* to think of business in those terms.

In some respects, provided that he is not detected by social control agencies which misinterpret his motives, the long-firm merchant who is trying to go straight may be able to get away with some of the tricks of his former trade. After all, a certain amount of deceit concerning creditworthiness is almost universal. The problems arise when the fraudster feels that money is not coming quickly enough, or when he starts actually to begin making a loss. For many, the temptation to 'throw in the towel' and return to fraud becomes too great. The following is an illustration of a failed attempt by two professional long-firm organizers:

> We started this company as a legit business. My partner reckoned that he was a master confectioner, and we would be a second Cadburys. No way! The sweets he made were so bad he could't even get his kids to eat them, unless he paid them . . . We weren't selling them, and we had our overheads to pay, so we thought of going into voluntary liquidation. At that time, we would have lost our capital and about £2000 of trade debts. But when you're an l.f. expert, it seems crazy to lose money. So even though we half-expected to get nicked, we turned it into an l.f.

A further problem is that one's criminal colleagues are always searching for partners in joint ventures, and one gets frequent offers to participate in 'the perfect job'. So unless one moves away from temptation by living far from one's old haunts, the prospective 'big one' is never far away.

The combination of a 'bent' way of looking at the world and 'wide contacts' (both literally and metaphorically) among the fraudster fraternity make 'going straight' very difficult. While many fraudsters genuinely *believe* that they are going legitimate, they often have at least one eye on the fraudulent possibilities in situations where 'straight' people would not do so: *that* is their 'working perspective'. If they do not develop the ability to switch off from the temptations of taking short cuts, they may end their lives as 'professional fraudsters'. There have been men who have organized long-firm frauds until well into their seventies.

So far, I have tended to discount the labelling theorist's view that the social control of fraud leads to *increased* deviance by closing off options to the offender of rehabilitating himself. Rather, I have stressed the economic *rationality* of motivations for career fraud, the implications of which are that one would expect the attractiveness of long-firm fraud to *diminish* as social control increased. For if the police and the courts did not intervene against long-firm fraudsters, their only motivation for reform would be the desire for social respectability. There are, however, some aspects of social control which *may* provoke further deviance, along the lines suggested by Erikson (1964, pp. 15–17):

> Deviant activities often seem to derive support from the very agencies designed to suppress them. Prisons ... and similar agencies of control provide aid and shelter to large numbers of deviant persons ... But beyond this, such institutions gather marginal people into tightly segregated groups, give them an opportunity to teach one another the skills and attitudes of a deviant career, and often provoke them into employing these skills by reinforcing their sense of alienation from the rest of society. The deviant often returns home with no proper licence to resume a normal life in the community. Nothing has happened to cancel out the stigmas imposed upon him by former commitment ceremonies; from a formal point of view, the original verdict or diagnosis is still in effect. It should not be surprising, then, that the members of the community seem reluctant to accept the returning deviant on an equal footing. In a very real sense, they do not know who he is.

Prison does spread the notion and the techniques of long-firm fraud to other members of 'the criminal community'. It may also put fraudsters in touch with 'heavy villains', with whom they may team up subsequently, to commit either long-firm frauds or other types of crime. *One* consequence of the incarceration of long-firm fraudsters, then, is that the organization of long-firm fraud may shift towards integration with 'the underworld' and that other criminal activities may benefit from the organizational and commercial expertise of long-firm fraudsters. (This should not be misinterpreted as a call for solitary confinement! It may, however, imply that there are some social control benefits from the *de facto* segregation of 'underworld' and 'upperworld' criminals in closed and open prisons respectively.)

There is, however, another respect in which the activities of social control agencies may place obstacles in the way of the rehabilitation of long-firm fraudsters. For trade protection societies and credit agencies are extremely wary of granting credit to a convicted or suspected fraudster. The person who is perceived as a 'slippery-sloper' may be given another chance, but the 'deliberate villain' will be fortunate indeed to be granted credit next time. However, this stigma is not confined to those convicted or sent to prison. It extends to those who are suspected of organizing long-firm frauds, whether they have been convicted or not. Hence, one might regard this commercial incapacitation as a social consequence of suspicion rather than of conviction. Indeed, since the top suspected background operators seldom if ever come before the courts, the fact of being convicted makes less difference than one might have imagined. The implication of this observation is quite crucial, however, for it means that even if there were *less* formal social control (that is, policing and prosecution) of long-firm fraud, the process of commercial stigmatization would remain unchanged.

The paradox which results is this: if one appears 'upfront', one is unlikely to be granted credit; if one gets nominees to 'front' the enterprise but one is discovered to have some connection with it, this counts as a *prima facie* indicator of conspiracy to defraud. Once someone is a bankrupt or has a conviction for fraud, he must work extra-hard to rehabilitate himself in the eyes of his creditors. His problem is that he does not know if he will *ever* be rehabilitated. For what counts as evidence of rehabilitation? To have been 'straight' for years may be regarded as an indication of tremendous care and cunning in 'setting up a job'. Without credit, it is difficult to do well in any business, and the fraudster's problem is that he has literally been dis-credited: prior experience has shown that one cannot take his 'front' for what he 'is'. Although the better credit inquiry bureaux are sensitive to the problems facing the reforming fraudster, they feel, understandably, that their paramount duty is to protect their clients from fraud.

Two of the 'fraudsters' I interviewed said that this discrediting process had led to their legitimate business operations being misperceived as fraudulent. One actually claimed that he had never done a long firm:

> In 1947, I left the country owing a very large amount of tax. I spent nine years on the Continent, during which time an attempt to extradite me from France failed. My counsel saw the judge about the taxes, and it was agreed that the matter be dealt with by means of a fine. This antagonized the authorities.
>
> While I was in custody awaiting trial on these charges, large amounts of stock were stolen from my firms, and before I could remedy the situation, the police put my companies into liquidation. The only thing really wrong with these companies was that they had not kept proper books of account, because the amount for which they failed was very small. Although it was the manager's job, not mine, to keep the books, I was legally responsible and was convicted. Thereafter, the police conspiracy continued.
>
> For some reason, the police regard me as a dangerous man, and in accordance with their adversary system, they have pursued a vendetta against me. The next time they did this was over a firm in which I had been paid to act as negotiator by the people who intended to take it over. I didn't know and didn't care what they were going to do with it, but I certainly wasn't the organizer of the l.f., as the police claimed. During my case in the north of England, an officer from the Metropolitan Police was present, which was evidence of how much they wanted to 'get' me.
>
> When the last affair came up, I was again in a difficult situation. I had escaped from prison while on Home Leave, so with whom other than villains was I to associate? I was engaged as a financial consultant to take over businesses, et cetera, but I had no idea that they were to run an l.f. As I understood it, they were to build up a chain of 25 or more businesses, rationalize them, fix up the accounts to make them look good, and make a reverse take-over, injecting them into a shell limited company. We would then sell the shares. This was a kind of villainy, but no worse than anything else in the City.
>
> But the police treated it as an l.f. Why? Because they wanted revenge for the way I had put something over on them in the tax business. I gave money to one officer to stop myself being fitted up, but had done nothing wrong...
>
> The police have no moral right to step in to prevent what they believe is villainy from being committed. They should intervene if and only if they already have overwhelming evidence that a crime has been committed. In this case, they literally *created* the offence, because it did not exist except in their own minds. The judiciary are no better than they, and the DPP is the worst of the lot.

This man's fusion of the Inland Revenue, the police, the Director of Public Prosecutions, the judiciary and, presumably, the jurors who convicted him at his various trials, into one great Authority Conspiracy rivals Matza's (1969) use of Leviathan in its macrocosmic grandeur. It is almost miraculous that in the face of such overwhelming odds, he resisted the temptation to become the villain he was accused of being! (At the time of writing, there is a warrant out for his arrest on a number of other long-firm fraud charges alleged to have been committed subsequent to his release from prison.) Although I remain somewhat sceptical about the truth of this particular motivational account, however, it does contain the important gem of truth that distrust of the moral character of the person running a business can lead to mis-classification of an honest business as a 'fraud'. The lifelong 'master status' generated by the label of 'fraudster' does tend to lead to further deviance, or at least to continued deviousness. One of my informants expressed the problems facing the degraded businessman thus:

> After I was made bankrupt, I had to run my companies through nominees, because I couldn't get any credit for myself. If you've got no cash, the nominees you get are either villains or useless, and I couldn't appear on the premises to control the businesses in case the suppliers thought it was another l.f.! No wonder I kept on getting into trouble.

Despite all these obstacles, however, the degradation mechanisms of the state prove less effective and more leaky than labellists imply. Like most criminals, nearly all long-firm fraudsters go straight *eventually,* and when they do they often become straighter-than-straight. This may be a consequence of the fact that they remain, in a psychological sense, 'secondary deviants': their heightened awareness of 'bent' behaviour makes the slightest straying from the public norms of capitalism seems like the start of the 'slippery-slope' to fraud. Some of them make enough money to retire from work completely; some, including at least one *convicted* fraudster, have become directors of public limited companies; and same have faded into a decent obscurity as the owners of small businesses.

Those who have gone deeper into 'the underworld' have taken part in smuggling gold bullion, passing counterfeit currency, financing lorry hijackings, international 'car ringing', international bank frauds involving phoney bills of exchange, and organizing armed robberies. Others have remained in the twilight world of 'dodgy' commerce, seeking to find a niche in the interstices between 'fraud proper' and 'straight commerce'. Examples of this category are the running of 'funny banks' and pseudo-legitimate offshore companies; involvement in the supply of concrete to Nigeria; putting reputable labels on cheap whisky; setting up non-existent international loans for the Australian government; and engaging in fraudulent dollar-premium stripping, with the aid of corrupt stockbrokers and solicitors.

Finally, there are those who, like Mertonian ritualists, stick to what they know best: long-firm frauds.

Some go into only partial retirement, returning to long firms when times get hard or when they become bored with the drab routines of legitimate business. However, whatever the stage of their retirement or non-retirement, I know of no long-firm fraudsters who feel (or will admit) that what they have done is *wrong*. This ease of mind is not, in my opinion, merely superficial. To long-firm fraudsters, their crime is just one way among others of making a living, neither more nor less immoral than most lawful (or undetected) commercial activities. Like other ways of making money, long-firms frauds have both advantages and disadvantages, and among the latter, the stress of the fraudster's life and the experience or the risk of imprisonment stand out. The advantages of (and principal motivations for) a career in fraud are summed up nicely in the words of one of the most skilled and subtle of the long-firm merchant community thus:

> People can say what they like about the way I have earned my living, but I've had a good life. I've been around the world, stayed in the best hotels, drunk the best champagne and fucked a lot of beautiful women. There were some very bad times . . . but I've got no real regrets. The only reason I have stopped now is that I have changed: I'm just not interested in those things any more. But at least I've got something to look back on. There aren't many people who can say that for themselves.

VI. Informal Control of Long-Firm Fraud

It is an analytic truth that all victims bear some responsibility for their victimization. At its most trivial, one may make the *reductio ad absurdum* that a woman's status *qua* woman makes *her* responsible for her rape. In the case of long-firm fraud, the degree of 'victim-participation' is greater and more positive than it is in most types of property crime, because the victim parts with his property *voluntarily* to the offender.

Long-firm frauds arise within a broader political economy in which credit plays a central role. The importance of the credit mechanism occurs at all levels, for the acceptance by the people of a national currency as a medium of exchange is a form of credit. At a more prosaic level, there is a universal demand for credit to bridge the period between the obtaining of goods and their resale to 'final consumers'. Apart from the rare situation of near-monopoly, where there are high barriers to entry into a given product range, a firm which does not offer credit to its customers may be unable to sell large quantities of its goods. Even where there is relatively inelastic demand for goods, it is often profitable to extend credit in order to increase effective demand. Consequently, even those who are psychologically attuned to Victorian prudence are forced to accept credit as yet another commercial 'fact of life'.

The classic 'theory of the firm' states that at any given price, subject to the supply capacity of the firm, the object of the firm is to maximize sales. Implicit in this proposition is the assumption that sales are translated into revenue, that is, that goods sold are actually paid for. It is the easiest thing in the world to supply goods without charge: the object is to make a profit. Credit has an opportunity cost to any supplier, for in many cases, it creates problems of cash-flow and liquidity, and in all cases, it means that money is being deployed lending to customers when it could be profitably employed elsewhere. The actual cost to the lender depends upon the level of interest rates and upon the specific situation of any given firm, but in present inflationary times, it may amount to a considerable sum per annum.

On the other hand, the sale of goods is the source of profit, and if credit is necessary to sell the goods, the firm must, if it can, offer such credit. This, then, is the basic dilemma: there is a 'trade-off' between the desire of firms to maximize their profits/ sales and their desire to minimize the amount of credit they extend to purchasers. This 'trade-off' exists even in a risk-free world, for credit always possesses an opportunity cost.

In the real world, however, one has to introduce the concept of risk, and here, one has to place into proportion the 'problem of fraud'. The risk of being defrauded is only one among many types of commercial risk and, compared with the risk of losing money from the supply of goods to an honest trader, it is a risk which occurs with low frequency. It cannot be over-emphasized that credit is granted not only on the basis of a belief in the *integrity* of the debtor firm, but also on the basis of its predicted *ability* to pay for the goods supplied. Therefore, in a world characterized by economic uncertainty, caution would need to be exercised in the granting of credit even if there were *no* long-firm frauds and no social conception of the *possibility* of long-firm fraud. This is illustrated by the pattern of losses in manufacturing and wholesale business: even if one makes a high 'guesstimate' of 'hidden crime' figures for long-firm fraud, the category of 'losses to frauds' is very small in relation to that of 'losses to incompetent/unlucky firms'.

On a general level, the granting of credit is a positive function of the perceived 'need' of the donor to do so. Although this may appear to be a banal statement, it does draw attention to two crucial motivations for extending generous credit: first, the existence of a highly competitive market situation; and second, the existence of an aggressive marketing policy. These may arise simultaneously or independently, and they may apply to firms both great and small. It should not, however, be forgotten that the effect of credit on cash-flow is an important operational constraint which may override the enthusiasm of both sales and credit managers.

It is this light that I shall examine the role of the victim in long-firm fraud. The types of goods obtained by these frauds are not restricted to any particular area of commerce: they include anything from fresh fruit and vegetables to canned goods, from colour televisions to asphalt and road-making equipment. One of the most spectacular cases was that of the glass eyes mentioned in Chapter II, but the suppliers of £250 000 of mechanical grabs and road-making equipment must have been greatly surprised when they discovered that they had been the victims of a long-firm fraud. They might have been still more surprised if they had learned, as a normally reliable informant told me, that this equipment had been supplied to the

Richardsons' mining operations in South Africa. Similarly surprised were the victims of a massive £ 500 000 fraud upon suppliers in Covent Garden. How could they expect a fraudster to dispose of such a vast quantity of short-term perishable goods?

These cases are, however, the exception. Most long-firm frauds occur in more prosaic areas such as toiletries, fancy goods, canned foodstuffs and consumer durables. The first three are especially favoured because they can be sold through any number of outlets, have quick turnovers, and are not traceable by any registration numbers. In general, the victims are large companies, but small firms can also be victimized. In one case in 1977, fraudsters succeeded in obtaining virtually the entire output of one firm's Christmas trees, and the owner's delight at his sale was somewhat short-lived when he discovered that he had been defrauded.

The principal question to be answered relates to the measures taken by firms to protect themselves against loss. Here again, I must emphasize that the risk of being defrauded is a minor commercial risk, and the degree of sensitization of suppliers to it is extremely variable. Credit control as a commercial specialism is mainly concentrated in two areas: in the role of credit manager within a company or firm; and in the large organizations which exist to provide a reference service on the creditworthiness of firms or individuals.

The role of the credit manager

First, I shall discuss the problems of the credit manager. Two general problems present themselves: the question of 'political' power of the manager within the institution for which he works; and issues of technical judgement of the creditworthiness of applicants for credit. As often in organizational life, the issue of power often overrides that of the formal role.

Any business organization must possess some working definition, whether articulated or not, of the desired balance between sales and the granting of credit. This balance is not fixed – it varies with the conditions of the market, and with the situation of the firm within that market. In small firms, most management roles are played by the owner, and he personally must weigh up his desired balance: in larger, more bureaucratic firms, there is some division of labour, and the management of credit is given to a specific individual or group of individuals. There thus ensues a *personal* struggle between the 'tough cop' – the credit manager – and the 'soft cop' – the sales manager. Until recently, the credit manager was in a relatively weak position *vis-à-vis* the sales manager, for it is on the latter's ability that the firm's viability ultimately rests.

Discussions with businessmen indicate that three factors explain the growth in the importance of the credit manager: the growth in the number of large firms, which has led to a need for more sophisticated supply control and the keeping of efficient sales ledgers; inflation which, due to high interest rates and pressures on liquidity, has increased the opportunity cost of granting credit; and the high rate of business failures, which has increased the risk element in lending decisions.

In addition to these factors, there has been a trend to 'professionalization' within the 'credit industry', as evidenced by the growth of organizations such as the Institute of Credit Management. The 'search for respectability' has given an added impetus to the demand for recognition of the importance of their role in company management. To what extent an improvement in the general economic situation would reverse this trend is problematic, for although granting credit to 'bad risks' would no longer jeopardize the very existence of the firm, positions, once established, have a tendency to survive. That, however, is a hypothetical question for the future.

The second problem arises when, assuming that the credit manager has the power to make binding decisions, he attempts to evaluate his debtors. At this stage, it is worth nothing that a conscious management decision may be taken to sell goods on credit, whatever the risks of bad debts. For example, one crisp firm which was trying to break into the crisp market is reputed to have been so keen to get its goods onto shop shelves that it was extremely generous with its granting of credit. Fraudsters have stated to me that they obtained thousands of pounds worth of crisps at that time.

That, however, was an abnormal situation, as such huge promotional campaigns are very infrequent. Normally, credit practices vary between different-sized firms in different industries. Small firms keep a tighter reign on their credit than do large firms, from whom it is often easy to get up to £300 credit (at 1980 prices). The build-up of confidence depends upon the skill, resources and aims of the fraudsters, but the credit manager has three basic lines along which he may proceed:

(1) he may ask for references from trade creditors whose names he gets from the would-be debtor;

(2) he may trade on a *pro forma* (payment in advance) basis until

he feels that he knows the firm enough to begin granting credit; and

(3)   he may ask a credit inquiry firm for a reference on the firm requesting credit.

In the case of line (1), references from firms already known are preferable to those unknown: fraudsters may set up fraudulent references, or may keep respected firms 'sweet' for the purpose of obtaining good references. If the supplier attempts to get a reference from the debtor's bank, he may find it couched (for libel reasons) in very cagey terms, such as: 'X are a respectably constituted company, and we have no reason to suppose that they will not fulfil any obligations entered into. However, we cannot speak for any specific sum.'

Or the bank may be perfectly happy with the account, because any sophisticated fraudster takes good care to be on good terms with his bank; or the bank may itself be owed money, and, without actually 'conning' the supplier, may underestimate the potential 'naughtiness' of the would-be debtor.

The more careful supplier will insist upon cash for the first few orders. Here again, any skilled fraudster will be able to get round this obstacle, and he is likely to have sufficient backing to pay for goods. The danger for the credit manager is, however, that he will then relax his vigilance, for long-firm fraudsters usually work by 'doubling up' the amount of their orders, and 'flannelling' suppliers with grandiose expansion schemes. This applies equally to cases where credit is granted and is paid very promptly on or before time: few legitimate debtors choose to pay so promptly, even if they are able to do so, for most traders owe money to their banks, and can minimize their interest payments by paying trade bills at the last possible moment. Even where, as is usual, discounts are given for prompt or early payment, it is often uneconomic for firms to pay then, unless they have very good cash-flow or wish to remain on especially good terms with a supplier. Thus, if credit managers are sensitized to the behaviour of long-firm operators, they are very suspicious of early payers: they realize that they may be being 'set up' for the 'kill'. One of the major warning signs of fraud is a rapid build-up of orders, particularly if this does not appear to be warranted by the debtor's markets.

Finally, the manager may ask a credit inquiry agent to provide a reference. There are a large number of such organizations in existence, ranging from in-trade organizations such as the Tobacco Advisory Committee, through sleazy back-street operators, to profit-making firms such as Dun & Bradstreet Ltd, and non-profit seeking organizations such as the Manchester Guardian Society for the Protection of Trade. The reports given by them are of extremely variable quality. Groups such as the Tobacco Advisory Committee work in great secrecy. They provide security services and monitor hijackings, as well as seek to prevent fraud, and they collate information from their members about trading patterns, as well as maintain contacts with law-enforcement agencies. They tend to be staffed by retired police officers. The main obstacle in their path, apart from the difficulty of spotting 'villains', is the desire of firms to maintain commercial secrecy. Firms wish to keep details about their markets to themselves, and they must have great faith in the trade organization before they reveal such intimate trade secrets: in this sense, fraud control is counteracted by the entrepreneurial spirit and competition, a point also made by Rock (1973b).

Another grouping of inquiry agents are the 'independents'. This comprises a curious admixture of sub-Chandler 'private eyes'; powerfully connected, quasi-underworld figures who use rather dubious investigatory techniques, such as blackmail, to obtain information and recover debts; and rather more legitimate oper- ators, often retired Fraud Squad officers. Such firms are more often employed in the capacity of debt-recovery agents, a topic with which I shall deal later, than as credit inquiry agents for information on commercial firms. Finally, there are the well-established organiza- tions which deal with credit reporting on a large-scale national and international basis.

There are approximately 30 'professional' collators of commercial creditworthiness in the country, but the largest and best are undoubtedly the Manchester Guardian Society for the Protection of Trade, and Dun & Bradstreet Ltd. Both of these organizations work on similar lines: they provide reports on companies at home and abroad for subscribers, and will mount 'special investigations' if requested to do so. A fee is charged for each individual report, as well as an annual membership fee.

The Manchester Guardian Society, which has a good reputation among those tradesmen to whom I talked, possesses a stock of reports on existing companies. The procedure is as follows: when a member requests a report on a company not already registered on their books, they check the Companies Register, the register of liquidations, and other official documents kept at Companies House. They also send to the company a questionnaire asking for information about their trading position, the nature of their business, business antecedents of directors, and any references from other people with whom they have done business. The new accounts are then assessed by the senior credit reporter, and if he is satisfied by the information given, this is sent out on a report to the person requesting it.

If he is not completely satisfied, the reporter may authorize further inquiries, which may take the form of sending out a local agent, often a local businessman recruited in the days when there existed a general sense of social responsibility on the part of businessmen; or he may telephone the potential debtor and suggest a meeting. Since the Society can damage his prospects by issuing a bad report, this is normally agreed to.

Although local agents cannot effectively assess the nature of the firm's trading position, they may notice, for example, that goods appear to be going out of the back door shortly after they come in the front door. They may see that the firm has an apparent reluctance to be observed, obscuring the windows with whitewash, for instance, or large boxes. They may detect, then, that 'something is amiss'. Thus, local agents are useful in pointing out the existence of a shady, 'bucket shop' type of operation, rather than the more sophisticated type of long-firm fraud.

There are other major indicators of suspiciousness: there may be similarities in the letter-headings of the firm and its referees, which might indicate that they had been printed in the same place. Or there may be similarities in the type-face of the typewriters used by the firm and its referees. These suggest that the referees may be operating from an accommodation address, and may not actually be trading firms or companies – that the letters are all typed in the same place, but simply posted from different addresses, or even from the same area. The credit reporter may then decide to check out the referees, and if he is not satisfied, may issue a negative report. He may then, in less obvious cases, talk to the firm's directors, and ask them to clarify certain points about which he is unsure, and possibly, supply further information.

In most cases, there are no difficulties, and no reason to suspect any malpractice on the part of the directors. A report is made out and sent to the subscriber, and a file on the firm commenced. In other cases, however, although initially there are no grounds for suspicion, some degree of malpractice comes to be suspected. The major warning indicator takes the form of a sudden large increase in the number of reports requested on a given firm. For this implies that the firm is seeking to substantially widen its operations, and enlarge the amount of credit it is seeking from each individual supplier. This is the classic symptom of the long-firm fraud: nicely set up initially, with between £5000 and £50000 initial backing, with a speedy 'doubling up' for the 'kill'. In order to detect this, the flow of requests is supervised by senior staff, who are experienced in spotting this danger sign. It may be that the firm is a new one, or it may have been taken over by 'villains' bent on exploiting its good credit rating. In any event, the credit organization will institute further inquiries. Another important indicator is information concerning delayed payment of debts, which may come from contacts in the trade or from the debt-collection arm of the credit agency.

It may be seen from this account that good contacts and a good detective 'nose' are essential prerequisites for trade protection. These contacts comprise a huge grape-vine of people in commerce, in law, and in formal agencies such as the police and the Official Receiver's department. A telephone call from a sales representative to say that he has noticed that a warehouse is stocked with *empty*, rather than full, cardboard boxes, or from a police officer to state that he has seen X, a well-known fraudster, on the premises of company Y: all of these build up a pattern which enables the skilled eye to detect fraud before the company folds up and its principals disappear. The information flow tends to go *from* the credit inquiry agents *to* the police, but it is in the trade protection society's interest not only that fraud should be prevented but also that those who attempt it should be punished, both to take offenders out of circulation and *pour encourager les autres*. Their hope is that if a backer finds that his initial capital of £5–50000 is spent without reward, even if he is not himself charged, this will discourage 'investment' in long-firm fraud on future occasions.

Credit inquiries are an area in which there are considerable returns to scale. The charge for a basic credit report in 1979 is approximately £7·50 and the fees for the first few reports on a given firm do not cover the costs of the inquiries: profits are only made thereafter. Moreover, from the point of view of fraud detection, the fuller the pattern of trading which can be gathered from the requests of members for credit reports on company X, the more likely the detection of that steady or sudden upwards increase in 'borrowing' which is the hallmark of the long-firm fraud. If credit inquiry agents are only infrequently used, on the other hand, they will be in a poor position to evaluate the risk involved. Thus, a degree of oligopoly or even monopoly favours the detection and informal control of long-firm fraud by these agencies, since requests for credit information are concentrated among a small number of investigators.

The principal problem that credit investigators face relates to the reliability and current validity of the information they obtain. I have already alluded to the ways by which information is collated, and these normally offer a good system of checks and balances against inaccuracies, but it is very easy for information to become out of date, and some agencies can be accused of being insufficiently conscientious in updating their records. Once something is on file, it is cheaper simply to re-issue an existing report than to make additional inquiries. The Manchester Guardian Society date their information, so that they investigate again if the information has become old, but some other smaller agencies are less scrupulous.

The Consumer Credit Act (1974) provides that upon payment of a fee, private individuals and unincorporated traders may examine and criticize their own credit references (or that part of them which is down in writing for public access). Since credit agencies made successful representations to the government that the prevention of fraud would be hampered by 'drying up' sources of information, this provision does not apply to limited companies. Consequently, credit reports remain as confidential as their issuers and issuees care to make them, and the Manchester Guardian Society, for example, strenuously attempts to prevent any leakages to or infiltration by long-firm fraudsters, by carefully vetting their own staff and members. On occasions, members are tricked into showing firms the references upon them, and these may cause great embarrassment by revealing sources of information. The consequences of such revelations may be:

(1)   a damages suit for libel or for negligently or maliciously injuring trade;

(2)   if the agency is reluctant to 'burn' its informants, the loss of the case may not only lose it money but also harm its commercial reputation;

(3)   the loss of potential informants, fearful of being 'exposed'.

In order to provide some measure of protection against reports 'falling into the wrong hands', they are sometimes phrased in somewhat recondite language, although to a lesser extent than those given by banks, which has to be cautiously interpreted by members. Examples of this are given below. Although the absence of the ability of firms to critically examine reports upon their behaviour is justly a problem for civil libertarians, this does have to be balanced against the need for confidentiality and commercial protection against fraud, and it is clear to me that the extensive grape-vine of information would soon shrivel up if people felt that not only would they be exposed as a source, but also they would be legally liable if they were unable to *prove* the accuracy of their statements. The 'solution' may lie in the reform of the law of libel, but as matters stand at present, the government must have adjudged the protection against fraud as more important than the openness of *corporate* credit references to criticism.

A good example of a 'cagey' report upon a firm, which subsequently turned out *not* to be a long-firm fraud, is the following (all names here have been changed to avoid the possibility of identification):

> At present we are being inundated with inquiries on Spendalot Ltd and it is apparent that the company are seeking sources of credit throughout the country. The opinion has been expressed that Mr Fredericks would not be likely to commit the company to any commitment he could not see his way to fulfil but informants find it very difficult to assess the risk here or speak for specific figures at the moment. This can only be determined by those immediately involved and it is recommended that the account be kept to a one-order basis and under strict control.

Another, rather more forthright example, is the following extract:

> There are reports that one Davis has been seen on the premises – this may be Davis, ex ... and ... Both these companies failed and the manner in which affairs were conducted was investigated by the authorities. Messrs X and Y were recently sentenced to terms of imprisonment in the matter of ... Ltd, above. Davis was also a director of ... Ltd. He inspires no confidence in our informants.

There followed a long list of other dubious connections of people working for the company concerned. After a report such as that, no creditor with any faith in the credit reporters would extend any credit at all to the company concerned. From my own independent sources, I would confirm that the advice was well justified. Another good example of a perspicacious report is the following:

> ... The premises known as Stevenson Warehouse were previously occupied by ... Ltd, who failed and with whom ... was connected.
>
> Another supplier reports that they have done business to the extent of £2000 on monthly terms. This informant received numerous requests for trade references, a number much in excess of what would normally have been anticipated, and it was apparent that the company were seeking credit extensively.
>
> Stevensons were given as a reference by 'Goodvalue Supplies', who sought credit in many quarters and were freely inquired upon. It has been stated that Stevensons might have financed Goodvalue Supplies. We are aware that dealings took place between the two concerns, Stevenson supplying Goodvalue, and there was a mention of cheques from the last named in favour of

the former being returned unpaid. A. B. C., a partner in Goodvalue, was on or about X, charged and sentenced to 6 months' imprisonment for receiving.
Experience of payments is at variance.

Thus far, although nothing directly suggesting long-firm fraud has been mentioned, the reader might deduce that (1) a supplier with a good name in the trade has been 'set up' as a referee, so that other suppliers will be lulled into a false sense of security. This is the import of the statement that an abnormally large number of requests for credit information has been made to the supplier; and (2) that there appears to be a conspiratorial connection between Stevensons and a suspected long-firm fraud run by a very recent ex-convict.

The original owner of Stevensons then disposed of his shares to another trader, with obscure business antecedents. The report continues:

Stevensons Ltd is very much under-capitalized under the present director and dealings involving risk should be avoided.
Evidence is accumulating that since the change of control, Stevensons have been seeking credit on an increasing scale from existing suppliers and also opening new accounts with manufacturers. There have been a number of individuals seen on the premises of late, apparently in some way connected with running of affairs. They include X, [details of fraudulent career].
Messrs A and B [previous liquidation history] have also been seen on the premises. They are well known and not regarded with confidence.
We believe that Stevenson [the original owner] is still in the employ of the company.

There followed a list of the connections of a number of other Stevenson employees, including one who ran a business used by Stevensons as a reference. The report continues:

Since the above was compiled, we have heard of further dubious associations. The company continue to seek credit almost indiscriminately for all descriptions of goods and it cannot be appreciated by informants how a connection can have been established which would permit of the disposal of the quantities involved. Comment has also been passed by those who have received orders that the constitution of the order has given the impression that those placing the order had very limited, if any, knowledge of the market for such goods.
The credit opinion previously expressed remains the same.

This reference alone saved potential suppliers approximately £100 000 in orders for which credit had been requested, for the company subsequently went into liquidation for a substantial sum.

The sample of reports given here is a highly selected one from a large number to which I was granted access: it is typical only of the good quality reports of one of the best agencies. Other agencies vary considerably both in the competence of their reports and in the speed with which a fraudulent operation was detected by their compilers – this bears a direct relation to the quality and spread of an agency's carefully cultivated contacts. If one compares the caution recommended by the better agencies with the amount of credit requested by their subscribers' would-be creditors, they save their subscribers millions of pounds per annum. There is, however, a constant danger of over-prediction of risk in lending, with the consequence that some firms are denied credit who should have been granted it and a loss of potential profit to the subscribers of the reports. One London firm in particular has been strongly criticized by some of my business informants for their consistent underestimation of how much credit should be granted, and subscribers have the ultimate sanction, to the inadequate reporter, of withdrawal of their business.

The better credit reporters take their responsibility very seriously. They are well aware that their recommendation to grant no credit, or very little credit to a company could lead to its liquidation 'in a matter of days or weeks, rather than months'. In other words, a false suspicion of fraud or honest-but-poor trading could easily prove to be a self-fulfilling prophecy, for all companies depend on credit for their liquidity, and many limited companies – both public and private – exist on only a marginal cash-flow. A respected credit reporter therefore could effectively make redundant a large number of employees, as well as bankrupt the owners.

On the other hand, reporters dislike being 'conned', and place great store by their competence at spotting long-firm frauds and not being deceived by the fraudsters. A retired senior credit reporter told me about the way in which, in the late 1950s, a long-firm expert had persuaded him that the reason why he was not paying his bills was that the cloth he had been sold was substandard. He told him that he had sent off the cloth to the Chamber of Commerce for examination, and so he had, although in fact there was nothing wrong with it. By the time he discovered that he had made an error of judgement, the firm had folded and the fraudster absconded.

The detection of fraud is only one of the functions of most credit inquiry agencies. It is, however, a source of considerable prestige for an agency, in so far as it is able to prevent losses by its members or subscribers. The number of firms upon which recommendations of 'no credit' were issued and which were prosecuted subsequently for long-firm fraud is a good indicator of success, and the Manchester Guardian Society, in particular, enjoys an enviable reputation in this field. Although frauds are normally spotted by that agency, it is more difficult to evaluate the extent to which credit was wrongly denied to firms because their creditworthiness was misjudged. The observer tends to judge with the benefit of hindsight, and a decision may be 'correct' even if it turns out to be an inaccurate prediction: all such decisions are probabilistic in nature, predicting from experience on the basis of the best information that is available.

To summarize, the field of credit investigation is fraught with complex decisions which can have very far-reaching consequences for firms either positively or negatively 'labelled'. The standard of agencies is highly variable, and some of them provide what might be euphemistically termed a 'negatively beneficial' service. One important 'input' into the labelling process is the presumed character of the managers and owners of the firm being inquired upon. If a 'known fraudster', whether convicted or not, is seen about the premises, and appears to be involved in the management, alarm bells jingle in the ears of those preparing credit references. If credit is denied, and the firm fails, it may be that the prophecy has been causally self-fulfilling. On the other hand, it may equally be that the prophecy was merely an accurate one, which saved creditors from sustaining considerable losses. In view of this problem of balance of interests, it is perhaps fortunate that the more effective agencies display genuine concern about the danger of 'giving a dog a bad name', while the less effective ones are unlikely to detect the presence of 'known fraudsters' in any event.

However, notwithstanding all the fraud-spotting activities of credit inquiry agencies, ultimate decision-taking lies in the hands of suppliers. If they do not ask for a credit reference on a firm, or do not pay heed to the advice given, the only effect of detection is that the police may learn about the fraud. Many large firms will almost automatically grant credit of £300 to a purchaser, and will only request a status report when the debt passes that figure: as one shirt manufacturer discovered, the mis-classification of a record card into a 'good risk' category by a junior clerk can lead to thousands of pounds' worth of losses.

Once the decision to grant credit has been taken, there may come a stage when the creditor suspects that he may have a bad debt on his hands. In the case of the 'pre-planned' fraudster, he may not realize this until the long firm has closed down. Often, however, particularly in 'slippery-slope' cases, creditors have to decide what to do about debts and whether or not to extend credit further. Rock (1973b) provides considerable insight into this stage of the credit process, although his work is concerned almost exclusively with private rather than with commercial debtors and both credit management and debt collection have become considerably more 'professionalized' since he studied them. Basically, there is a conflict between the desire to recover bad debts and the fear of alienating a future customer, a conflict which is particularly intense when the sums involved are as large as they are in trade credit. I have been in business offices where the debtor has asked for a little time to pay and has had to reassure the creditor that he is not going 'bust', when the debtor knows that if the creditor pressed him, he *would* go 'bust'. Cues, gestures, the rendering of verbal 'accounts' and prior experience combine in the creditor's mind when he takes his decision. Particularly important is the issue of cultural homogeneity between debtor and creditor: Jews feel that they can trust other Jews; Asian subgroups feel that they can trust other members of their subgroup. Everyone feels that they are more likely to be seen as 'fair game' by out-group members, although, in reality, no-one is safe from the 'pre-planned' fraudster.

Some of the techniques by which payment is delayed are covered in Chapter III, and there is little point in repeating them here, but firms need to take great care that they do not become locked into an ever-increasing spiral of debt through the 'doubling up' of moneys owed to them. Otherwise, if they postpone the decision to regard a debtor as a 'bad debtor', they may find that they end up with huge losses rather than small ones. In the case of sophisticated long-firm frauds, there is little point in pursuing debts, because by the time that someone realizes that he has a bad debt, it is too late to do anything about it: there is no protracted period over which the debtor can be pressed for payment.

'Slippery-slope' frauds offer the most fruitful avenue for sociological analysis of the process of debt negotiation, but since my main concern has been with deliberate 'pre-planned' long firms, I have little detail to offer in this area. In some trades, creditors literally take debt collection into their own hands: the textiles printing trade, for example, is one in which creditors will readily use violence against people whom they feel have 'conned' them, for retributive reasons as well as in the hope of recovering debts. This observation applies also to sections of the car trade, and is more common than is generally realized among owner–managers of small- to medium-sized businesses. For not only are these businesses vulnerable to losses from bad debts but also the default is taken far more personally than it is in the case of large creditors. Some 'professional fraudsters' have stated that they avoid small businessmen for the very reason that they make the worst 'screamers' and will pursue them more vigorously than the large companies who 'put it down to experience'.

If the long-firm fraudsters are themselves well-connected with violent people, the self-recovery service can, however, be very counter-productive, and if it was known that the Kray or Richardson gangs were backing a fraud, strong-arm debt collection was out of the question. Physical security against aggrieved creditors is especially important when 'doing' small businessmen in 'heavy trades'.

At a more sophisticated level, other types of pressure tactics may be used, depending upon the 'street-knowledge' of the creditor in question. If he knows of something which might act to the legal or social or physical detriment of the people organizing the fraud, he may use this as a lever for the return of his goods or payment of the debt. This may involve 'threatening someone with the Fraud Squad', as one debt collector put it. The creditor may do this himself, or he may employ a private debt collector to do it for him. There is a very fine dividing line between 'putting the black on a villain' (that is, blackmailing a criminal) and suggesting to him that if he does not pay up the person 'will be obliged to inform the Fraud Squad', but agencies vary considerably in the extent to which they are prepared to go when obtaining payment. The more reputable organizations, such as the Manchester Guardian Society and Dun & Bradstreet Ltd, wear softer velvet gloves than do some others to whom I have spoken, but they can afford to do so, since debtors are wary of getting a bad name with such influential organizations. The due process of law is often ineffective in inducing the average long-firm fraudster to pay up, because by the time that his lawyers have given up resisting debt judgements and bankruptcy or insolvency petitions, he will often have disappeared, or the firm gone 'bust'.

The inadequacy of the civil law in coping with the skilled, deliberate fraudster may be further illustrated by reference to the increasing use in commerce of what are known as 'Romalpa' clauses, by which a vendor may transfer possession of goods without transferring ownership until payment is made. Thus, in theory, a 'Romalpa' creditor may reclaim his goods or their monetary value at any time after his debt becomes due, and he becomes a preferential creditor in liquidation or receivership. The criticisms that might be made about the general impact of this decision upon commerce, or about the general treatment of trade unsecured creditors in English law (see Hadden, 1977, pp. 181 ff.) are, however, of only marginal relevance in the case of long-firm frauds. For unless a 'Romalpa creditor' is quick to enforce his claim, he will find himself with a claim against an assetless company, and a preferential claim on zero is as valueless as an unsecured claim on it.

Finally, let us summarize the data in terms of Wilkins's (1965) notions of 'gates' and 'decision-stages'.

(1) Creditors see their primary task as the repayment of *their* debts, rather than the prosecution of every would-be evader of payment. This 'common-sense' morality is mirrored in the reluctance of the administrators of the law to treat commercial behaviour as fraud unless no other means of resolution seems possible.

(2) Many creditors would be willing to obtain repayment of *their* debts at the cost of some other creditor. If they then felt any qualms, they would 'cry all the way to the bank'. Thus, in exchange for the payment of a larger percentage of *their* debt, some creditors may agree to the appointment of a company liquidator whom they know to be in league with the fraudulent debtor.

(3) There is no easily discernible pattern in what happens subsequently. Some creditors will report suspected frauds to the police *after* they have been themselves repaid. Most will, however, simply do nothing further. Of those who are not repaid, some will be sufficiently indignant or optimistic about recovery to report matters to the police, pay £250 to put a trader into bankruptcy or into liquidation, or even hire private investigators to 'track down' the miscreants; others will simply 'put it down to experience'. As one small trader stated to me: 'What's the point of complaining to the Old Bill about villains like that? You're only going to give yourself a lot of aggravation for no result. In any case, up there, they're all bent, and they wouldn't do fuck all about it.'

(4) The system of reporting victimization by a long-firm fraud is not dependent upon the actual creditor. Apart from police, Department of Trade and Customs and Excise 'proactive' intervention as part of their normal role of seeking out crime, credit inquiry agents and debt collectors may inform the police as part of their normal grape-vine of information and favour-trading.

(5) The reaction of the police to reported fraud is highly variable, depending upon their case-loads, perception of seriousness, and the other factors discussed in Chapter VIII. It should, however, be emphasized that, in principle, only one complaint is needed to

trigger off an investigation. If the police decide that 'something should be done', they will then pursue other firms who may have been victimized by the long-firm fraud.

Conclusion

The informal control of long-firm fraud is fraught with contradictions and ambiguities. Although the major credit control agencies tend to co-operate with the police, individual creditors may not feel that the invocation of the formal social control process is worthwhile: it costs them time and money without any likely financial return. Many businessmen feel that they cannot afford the luxury of moral outrage at being defrauded. Morris (1976, p. 62) has observed that when the reporting of crime is contemplated, '*the cost to the victim* tends to be weighed against the *satisfaction to be derived from the law enforcement process*'. In many cases, as well shall see, these satisfactions may not appear to be very great. Creditors may perceive that they are unlikely to obtain either retribution or reparation. Hence, it is not surprising that – particularly in the case of international frauds – many of them do not seek to make use of the formal criminal justice system. No attempt has been made here to estimate the size of the 'dark figure' of unreported long-firm fraud. However, if my informal observations of the attitudes of businessmen are correct, this figure is likely to be considerable. The main thrust of the informal control system is towards the prevention of long-firm fraud. Once that has failed, the major impetus for crime control comes from the large credit control agencies, from proactive policing by police forces, and from the reactive processing of business failures by the Department of Trade Insolvency Service. If none of these agencies 'pick up' the long firm and define it as such, the actor and the act will remain outside the effective ambit of the criminal law.

VII. Long-Firm Fraud and the Criminal Law

At all times there will be people whose morality is so far below the average commercial morality of the age, that they do not scruple to take advantage of the credit which, in reliance upon the existence of that commercial morality, is given to them. If it is advantageous to commerce that the standard of commercial morality should be high, and that credit should be given, it is necessary to bring home to such people, in the only way in which they will feel it, the consequences of their conduct... [by] imprisonment. (Sir William Holdsworth, *A History of English Law*)

In most cases of property crime, the circumstances make it obvious that an offence has been committed. There may be evidence of breaking and entering, or goods may be missing from a home or a car without any explanation. This is not true of 'fraud'. In England, it is not an offence for someone to fail to pay his debts. This is an offence only when – by deception – someone obtains goods intending not to pay for them at all or neither knowing nor caring whether payment will be made. This is a very difficult matter to determine. This is not the place for a general discussion of *mens rea* – for an excellent discussion, see Glanville Williams (1978, ch. 3) – but the chapters hitherto indicate clearly the kinds of difficulties we might have in telling whether or not a businessman ordered goods with intent to defraud or by reckless deception. This is particularly true of 'slippery-slope' cases, where even if we had been present at the time, we might find it hard to attribute recklessness. But it is also true of the more sophisticated 'pre-planned' and 'intermediate' frauds. For such cases come to court at the end of a low-visibility *process*, during which time the 'criminal' has ample opportunity to cover his tracks and to throw up smoke-screens over the 'offence'. Consequently, although issues of identification are often important in long-firm fraud trials – was the alleged mastermind seen at the firm's premises? – a major burden on the Crown may be to prove that an offence was committed *at all*.

Fraud as a crime

Fraud...should be taken to mean... actual dishonesty involving, according to current notions of fair trading among commercial men, real moral blame. (MAUGHAM J, in *Re Patrick & Lyon Ltd* (1933), 1 ch. 786)

The real criminals in our society are not all those who inhabit the prisons of the State, but those who have stolen the wealth from the people. (Angela Davis, *If They Come in the Morning*)

The legal system is the means through which the State mediates conflicts between its citizens. The criminal law proscribes certain forms of conduct and – by not banning them – legitimates others. According to the conventional wisdom of the lawyer, it does so as a reflection of the customs and beliefs of the age. However, customs do not become embodied in law by magic but by human agency. Therefore, to understand the law, we must look at these agents (or what political scientists inelegantly term 'proximate decision-takers') to see what interests they reflect. Chambliss and Mankoff (1976) express this rationale nicely in the title of their book *Whose Law? What Order?* The conception of law as a reflection of 'the public interest' is empirically problematic, for there may or may not be a general consensus about the legitimacy of any given law, and conceptually problematic, for one may argue – as Marxists do – that even if people agree with the law, they may be suffering from 'false consciousness' concerning their 'true interests'. No attempt has been made here to provide the sort of sociological analysis of law-making offered by Paulus's (1974) study of pure-food legislation. However, the history of legislation concerning fraud reveals a marked reluctance on the part of any English Parliament to pass laws which might lead to the criminal conviction of businessmen pursuing 'legitimate' interests. Since it is difficult to draft legislation so finely as to penalize all 'undesirables' without also penalizing 'desirables', this has meant that some persons who are regarded by capitalists and by Parliament as 'undesirable' are able to remain outside the ambit of the criminal law. (See Gower, 1979; Hadden, 1967a, 1967b, 1977; Holdsworth, 1925; Levi, 1979, ch. 5; and Rock, 1973b, for detailed studies of the development of the criminal law governing credit fraud and debt.)

Early history of laws governing long-firm fraud

It was only gradually that English law began to distinguish between the 'honest' and the 'dishonest' debtor. By the reign of Edward III, the imprisonment of debtors had become the general method by which creditors could punish those who did not pay. However, by the mid-sixteenth century, the Court of the Star Chamber had begun to set the criminal law in motion against 'dishonest' debtors and, perhaps more importantly, the legislature enacted various laws so that creditors might get at the property of the bankrupt.

The first of these acts (33 Hen. VIII, c. 1) was passed in 1542. The class of individuals at whom it was aimed is nicely expressed thus: 'divers and sundry persons, craftily obtaining into their hands great substances of other persons' goods, do suddenly flee to parts unknown, or keep their houses, not minding to pay or restore to any of their creditors, their debts and duties'.

The Act empowered the Lord Chancellor, along with certain other officials and the two Chief Justices, to seize the property of the debtor and distribute it among the creditors. In addition, they could imprison the debtor and summons any persons suspected of owing money to, or holding the property of, the debtor, and require restitution of them. The provision for compulsory disclosure of any knowledge concerning the debtor's affairs is the precursor of the present bankruptcy examination. The Act also enabled debts paid to creditors who were unduly preferred by the absconding debtor to be set aside: the first attempt to regulate 'fraudulent preference'. Thereafter, large numbers of Acts were passed in relation to fraudulent bankruptcy, but non-fraudulent bankrupts were also treated savagely until the latter part of the nineteenth century.

The power of creditors to imprison debtors indefinitely by civil means and the fact that criminal prosecutions cost money meant that long-firm fraudsters were seldom prosecuted before the mid-nineteenth century. Indeed, despite the express criminal provisions of the Bankruptcy Act 1719, and the Consolidating Act, 1732, there were only two or three prosecutions under these Acts in the whole of the eighteenth century (Holdsworth, 1925, vol. VIII, pp. 229–45).

One interesting consequence of the overlapping of civil and criminal jurisdiction lay in the admissibility of bankruptcy examinations as evidence in criminal trials. For such proceedings have the power to compel answers of the bankrupt and, when used in criminal trials, thereby circumvent the normal protections of defendants' right not to answer questions. Mr Justice Coleridge – a latter-day Lord Denning – dissented from the majority of the Court for Crown Cases Reserved in the absorbing case of *R. v.Scott* (1856), 7 Cox CC 164, which ruled bankruptcy examinations admissible. However, the decision did not prove to be the 'thin end of the wedge' towards the destruction of English liberties that he had feared: in *ex parte* Schofield (1877), 6 Ch.D. 230, the Court for Crown Cases Reserved held that any witness *other* than the bankrupt who was examined under the Bankruptcy Act was entitled to refuse to answer questions if they tended to incriminate him. This remains the law at present.

It appears that it was quite common in the second half of the nineteenth century for the bankruptcy examination to be used as a prelude to prosecution, to gather evidence against the accused which could not otherwise be obtained. As one fair-minded solicitor, acting for the creditors in a long-firm fraud prosecution in my Old Bailey sample stated:

> I did not inform him [the accused] that I was getting up a prosecution against him, because I apprehended that he would abscond ... when we made up our minds to prosecute, we abstained even from examining the prisoner in the bankruptcy court – bankrupts are very frequently examined with a view to their prosecution – I thought that very unfair and did not examine the prisoner. (*R.* v. *Raudnitz* [1863], Central Criminal Court, unreported)

This principle is now followed more generally. Since the trial in 1974 of the bankrupt architect John Poulson for corruption, the public examination of debtors is now adjourned until *after* criminal proceedings have taken place, so that no disadvantage should accrue to bankrupts compared with other individuals on trial.

By 1914, when the Bankruptcy Act was passed which remains the basis of present law (see Thompson, 1977, for a full account), the Court of Bankruptcy had been given very extensive powers to compel evidence and to proceed against those it defined as 'criminal bankrupts'. Also, a clear distinction had come to be drawn between the unlucky/incompetent but honest businessman and the fraudulent debtor: those assigned to the former category received very few sanctions upon their conduct.

The limited liability company and long-firm fraud

By the latter part of the nineteenth century, the legal control of long-firm fraud was complicated further by the growth of the limited liability company. The general development of the law of limited liability is treated in the standard texts already mentioned (see also Shannon, 1931, 1933, for some illuminating analysis). However, the underlying philosophy of legislation is captured in Sir Robert Lowe's speech introducing the limited liability Act (19 & 20 Vic., c. 47) in 1856. He stated (Parliamentary Debates, 1856, vol. 140, col. 131) that

> the principle we should adopt is this, not to throw the slightest obstacle in the way of limited companies being formed ... and when difficulties arise, to arm the courts of justice with sufficient powers to check extravagance or roguery ... that is the only way

the legislature should interfere, with the single exception of giving the greatest publicity to the affairs of such companies that everyone may know on what grounds he is dealing.

Sir Robert denied the power or the desirability of the government to supply mankind with common sense, and contended that it was absurd to regulate ninety-nine companies simply to prevent the hundredth from committing fraud. The Act led to a massive increase in the use of limited liability and to large numbers of such companies going 'bust'. Shannon (1933) shows that of new companies floated between 1856 and 1863, 22·3 per cent were dissolved within three years of their formation. The corresponding figure for companies formed between 1866 and 1874 was 23·2 per cent and for those formed between 1875 and 1883 was a massive 36·2 per cent. These facts give a rough guide to the combined element of fraud, poor management and over-optimism which went into company formation. Unfortunately, it is impossible to partial out these factors, but there may be some truth in the assertion made by Chadwick before the Select Committee on the Companies Act, 1877 that thirty-nine out of every forty propositions for flotation came from firms on the downgrade, the general object being to defraud their creditors (Parliamentary Debates, 1877, S.C. viii, 365, Q. 2092).

The administration of corporate liquidations far outstripped that of bankruptcy in its inadequacy. Furthermore, the judiciary proved most reluctant to lift the corporate veil and allow for easy prosecution of directors (see Leigh, 1977a). It was not until the second quarter of the twentieth century that the criminal law even began to come to grips with the corporate form. In 1928, Section 75 of the Companies Act made it an offence for the directors of a company to carry on trading with intent to defraud creditors 'or for any other fraudulent purpose'. This provision was incorporated in the consolidating Companies Act, 1929, and received an authoritative interpretation by MAUGHAM J in *Re Leitch (Wm. C) Brothers Ltd (no. 1)* (1932), 2 Ch. 71 at page 77:

> If a company continues to carry on business and incur debts at a time when there is to the knowledge of the directors no reasonable prospect of the creditors ever receiving payment of those debts, it is, in general, a proper inference that the company is carrying on business with intent to defraud.

This case, like *Re Patrick & Lyon Ltd* (1933), 1 Ch. 786, concerned the attempt of the liquidator of the company to obtain a declaration that the directors of a company should be held personally responsible for its debts. However, the principles of what constituted 'fraudulent trading' remain valid. The difficulty remains of deciding what criteria should be employed when deciding (a) what each director knew, and (b) what is meant by a 'reasonable prospect' of repayment. For example, dismissing the charges under s. 332(3) of the Companies Act, 1948, in the case of *R.v. Poster Plywood Co. Ltd*, heard at the Old Bailey in 1956, the Common Sergeant stated that

> There is no doubt that there is a substantial deficiency. Well now, that by itself – I cannot say this too emphatically – cannot begin to be sufficient to establish an intention... to carry on business with intent to defraud creditors... What must be proved is that this man took a deliberate part in the calculated carrying on of the business at the expense of the creditors of that business knowing perfectly well that there was no prospect of the creditors being paid... All that you have got [in this case] is the fact... that [this company] continued to trade when... it would have been better if it had not. Well, this is nothing like enough to charge a director or a person concerned in the management of it with fraudulent trading.

(See also *Re Gerald Cooper Chemicals Ltd* (1978), 2 All ER 49, and *Re Sarflax Ltd* (1979), 2 WLR 202.)

The general law of criminal deception

I have summarized the principal features of bankruptcy and company law as they relate to long-firm fraud. However, long-firm frauds can also be prosecuted under the general criminal law covering what used to be known as 'false pretences'. During the twentieth century, it became increasingly clear to lawyers that the gaps and anomalies in the laws relating to larceny and fraud required a general overhaul. An example of the disquiet felt by them was the statement of Viscount Dilhorne in *Fisher* v. *Raven* (1964), 47 Cr. App. R. at page 195, to the effect that the result of the decision might be that 'some fraudulent persons may escape justice' and that a possible way of 'closing this gap in the criminal law' would be to 'change the law so that a false pretence need no longer be a pretence as to an existing fact'. (See Hadden (1967a) and Levi (1979) for detailed discussion of the history of 'false pretences' legislation.)

In 1959, the Home Secretary requested the Criminal Law Revision Committee to prepare a set of proposals for the reform of the law of larceny and fraud, a task which they completed in 1966. Section 15 of the Theft Act, 1968 was almost identical with the Committee's draft Bill, but Section 16 of the 1968 Act – which has now been replaced by Section 2 of the Theft Act, 1978 – was the creature of the House of Lords. Section 15 (1) of the Theft Act, 1968 states that

A person who by any deception dishonestly obtains property belonging to another, with the intention of permanently depriving the other of it, shall on conviction on indictment be liable to imprisonment for a term not exceeding ten years.

Sub-section (4) adds that

For the purposes of this section 'deception' means any deception (whether deliberate or reckless) by words or conduct as to fact or as to law, including a deception as to the present intentions of the person using the deception or any other person.

There is no room here for elaboration of the law relating to the Theft Act, 1968 (see Smith, 1979; and Williams, 1978). Suffice it to state that the new offence of obtaining property by deception removed many of the absurdities which arose from cases decided under false pretences and larceny legislation. Section 15 provides a useful way of making specific charges in relation to narrowly defined deceptions practised by long-firm fraudsters. It also provides a source of charges that may be relatively simply made for the purpose of extradition: a topic with which I will deal later this chapter.

Further measures against long-firm frauds of the 'intermediate' and 'slippery-slope' types were enacted by Section 16 of the Theft Act, 1968 (now replaced by Section 2 of the Theft Act, 1978). This covered the obtaining of a pecuniary advantage by deception, and could be used on those occasions when goods were ordered with intent to repay and with a belief in the ability to repay, but where subsequent to the obtaining, the debtor decided not to pay for the goods. It is quite clear from the case of *DPP* v. *Ray* (1973), 3 W.L.R. 361, that provided that the accused had made some further deception, express or implied, to defer or evade payment, he had committed an offence against Section 16. Furthermore, in the case of *R.* v. *Turner* (1973), 3 W.L.R. 352, the House of Lords held that a debt is 'evaded' even when the evasion falls short of being final or permanent, and is only for the time being. Therefore, even when no-one actually *ended up* by losing money, intending fraudsters who changed their minds under pressure from impending police or Department of Trade investigation and decided to repay creditors still fell within Section 16 (2) (a) of the Theft Act, 1968. Section 16 was applicable also if a debtor deferred payment by falsely stating that 'there is a cheque in the post' or that 'I am expecting a big cheque from one of my suppliers tomorrow and I will pay you then', or even if he deliberately left a necessary signature off a cheque or signed a cheque with non-matching words and figures.

The broad application of Section 16 led to considerable dissatisfaction within the legal profession. As the Criminal Law Revision Committee (1974) observed:

> It appears that Section 16 (2)(a) has been given an interpretation wide enough to make it an offence for a housewife to tell the talleyman that she cannot pay this week because her husband is off work sick, when this is not true. Lies of this kind must be commonplace, but the ordinary man or woman would, we think, be surprised to be told that such behaviour was criminal and not merely discreditable... We state here our view that the criminal law should not apply to cases where the only allegation is that a debtor has gained by deception the opportunity to delay paying a debt.

This view was accepted and was incorporated in the Theft Act, 1978, the relevant section of which, as regards long-firm fraudsters, is Section 2 (1)(b). This makes provision for the prosecution of any person who

> with intent to make permanent default in whole or in part on any existing liability to make a payment, or with intent to let another do so, dishonestly induces the creditor or any person claiming payment on behalf of the creditor to wait for payment (whether or not the due date for payment is deferred) or to forgo payment.

The need to prove intention to default *permanently* is likely to make it more difficult to sustain a charge against businessmen *before* their businesses have gone 'bust'. In this sense, it militates against the tendency of the police – discussed in the next chapter – to move towards what Reiss (1971) has termed 'proactive' policing strategies.

Finally, under the heading of criminal deception laws, it should be noted that whereas under the old false pretences legislation (and under the Bankruptcy Act, 1914 and the Companies Act, 1948), the maximum penalty was seldom more than two years' imprisonment, the maximum penalty on conviction on indictment was raised to ten years by Section 15 of the Theft Act, 1968. This alone made it more likely that the Crown would make use of charges of obtaining property by deception. For although the prime sources of dissatisfaction with the charge of false pretences were the technical difficulties of proof under case law, the low maxima also inclined prosecutors to prefer charges of conspiracy to defraud.

Conspiracies to defraud

The law of conspiracy is very ancient, and there has been a common law misdemeanour of conspiracy to cheat and defraud since at least the fourteenth century. According to Hadden (1967b), however, prior to the nineteenth century, the judiciary regarded with great disfavour attempts to use conspiracy counts where the evidence would not have supported substantive charges. From that time, they were used extensively to deal with what were euphemistically called 'industrial combinations', and this doubtless encouraged agile legal minds to search for ways of using conspiracy laws to circumvent the old and established principle that intentional failure to pay could never in itself be a crime: merely a breach of contract.

The ambit of indictments for conspiracy is well illustrated by the case of *R.* v. *Hudson* (1860), Bell 263, in which the defendants had combined to 'fix' the result of a bet in a public house. The only real falsehood that could be established was that the whole transaction had been implicitly represented as a genuine wager, when in fact, it was not. Yet the Court held that they were properly convicted of conspiracy to cheat and defraud. (This is now a statutory offence, covered by Section 2 of the Theft Act, 1978.)

A consequence of this was that the law could be used to prosecute as crimes acts which were merely tortious or in other ways unlawful, but which were not criminal by statute. For example, operators of 'fraudulent businesses' could be charged with conspiring to obtain goods by falsely pretending that the business was an honest and genuine business. What is an honest and genuine business? Why, one which intends to – and perhaps is able to – meet all its obligations.

The essence of the offence became the honesty of the *implied* representations as to intention, and the use of specific falsehoods, such as false references, was a buttress for but not a logical prerequisite of the charge. The popularity of the indictment of conspiracy to defraud as a substitute for the perceived inadequacy of the substantive criminal law of deception has continued, and remains the sole exception to the provisions of the Criminal Law Act, 1977 that conspiracy may be charged only in relation to substantive offences. This popularity is doubtless due to the fact that it enables the prosecution to put before the jury a relatively complete picture of the way in which the company has traded, thus bringing a broader compass to the allegation of fraud. It also illustrates the element of conspiracy which is almost invariably present in the operation of a long-firm fraud. This is something that is difficult to achieve by other means.

The conspiracy charge is also easier to *prove* than a substantive act of fraud. For example, in *Re Maidstone Building Provisions Ltd* (1971), 3 All E.R. 363, it was held that

> In order to be a party to the carrying on of the business of a company within Section 332 (1) of the Companies Act, a person must have taken some positive steps in the carrying on of a

company's business; accordingly, the mere failure of a secretary and financial adviser to advise the directors that the company was insolvent and should cease to trade did not constitute being a party to the carrying on of the company's business.

If 'mere failure' is taken in a narrow sense, this decision may be considered reasonable as well as a correct strict interpretation of the law. However, it should be noted that it is the practice in the more sophisticated types of long-firm fraud for the organizer of the fraud to use 'front men' as directors, while if he appears 'upfront' at all, he does so precisely in the role of 'financial adviser' whose criminal responsibility under the Companies Act is absolved in the above decision. It may be difficult to prove that such an adviser is party to the carrying on of the business under the Companies Act, but it is slightly easier to prove that he was party to a conspiracy to defraud.

One reason for this difference in the standards of proof lies in the rules of evidence in conspiracy cases, whereby the uncorroborated evidence of conspirator A is admissible against conspirator B: an exception to the general rule concerning the evidence of co-defendants.

The operational benefit to the police of the conspiracy charge is amply demonstrated by their practice of moving in and arresting suspected 'villains' while the alleged fraud is still in progress. This procedure, which enables them to gather forensic evidence before it is destroyed and to capture the participants before they disappear, would be impossible under the Companies Act (though not under the Theft Act). For the ruling of the House of Lords in *DPP* v. *Schildkamp* (1971), A.C. 1, made the liquidation of a company a *sine qua non* of prosecution under Section 332 (3) of the Companies Act, 1948. (The Companies (No. 2) Bill 1981 removes this restriction.)

Conspiracy charges have both the advantage and the disadvantage that they involve fewer technical disputes than commonly occur during the interpretation of statutes. This vagueness of ambit, however, has been the focus of recent criticisms of their use. Commenting on the use of conspiracy counts in the case of *DPP* v. *Withers* (1974), 3 All E.R. 984 – which related to the alleged use of corrupt surveillance techniques by private detectives – Lord Diplock stated (at p. 993): 'This branch of the criminal law is irrational in treating as a criminal offence an agreement to do that which if done is not a crime... If what the defendants did ought to be made a crime it is for Parliament to legislate accordingly.'

The logic of this argument is undeniable, but the problem in the control of what might tentatively be called 'fraudulent behaviour' is the clear definition of what constitutes 'fraud'. For those concerned with the finer issues of control, some hope may be gleaned from the judgement of Viscount Dilhorne, giving reasons in the case of Withers why he believed that the charge of conspiracy to cause a public mischief was *not* part of English law. At page 991 he declared that

> To say that there is now no power in the judges to declare new offences does not, of course, mean that well-established principles are not to be applied to new facts. Fraud, like contempt of court, may take many forms, and a conviction for conspiracy to defraud may well be sustained though the fraud has taken a novel form.

Although charges of conspiracy to defraud are broader than statutory offences, the usual control over judicial summings up and the rules of evidence still apply. For example, in the case of *R.* v. *Stock*, reported in *The Times*, 28 July 1961, the appellant sought to overturn his conviction on a charge of obtaining money and credit by false pretences. The false pretence alleged was that of falsely pretending to run an honest and genuine business. The Court of Criminal Appeal criticized the trial judge for saying to the jury: 'Do you think that this man was engaged upon a swindle?' and leaving his analysis of the law at that. In the appellate judgement, the Court differentiated between honesty and genuineness, observing that a business could be dishonestly run in many respects but yet be quite genuine. A business was neither honest nor genuine only if it was used merely as a sham, if the forms and apparatus of the business were used simply as the engine or vehicle of the fraudulent purpose. Although this offers only a general guideline to the conditions under which a business may be regarded as neither honest nor genuine, it does constrain the prosecution of indictments under that heading. Indeed, in one case that I witnessed, the judge dismissed a case that had lasted for several weeks at the end of the case put by the Crown because the defence counsel successfully argued that the business was dishonest but genuine. This illustrates the importance that technicalities of charge possess in fraud trials. (For an important ruling on the drawing-up of conspiracy to defraud indictments, see *R.* v. *Landy* (1981), 1 All E.R. 1172.)

Unfortunately, as frauds increase in complexity and the 'long' in 'long-firm fraud' begins to refer to the length of operation of the fraud, there is an increasing probability that genuine (or apparently genuine) trading will take place for a considerable time prior to the 'sting'. Under such circumstances, it would be inadvisable for this indictment to be charged, for it may be hard to prove that the business was not a genuine one. Indeed, given the capacity of many people for retrospective rationalization, they themselves might not be able to tell us 'validly' what their original motives were (see Appendix A).

The 1970s injected some clarity into the meaning of conspiracy to defraud. A leading case here is that of *Scott* v. *Metropolitan Police Commissioner* (1974), 3 All E.R. 1024, in which the appellants argued before the House of Lords that the offence of conspiracy to defraud had been abolished by the Theft Act, 1968. Rejecting the appeal, Lord Diplock stated that

> Where the intended victim of a 'conspiracy to defraud' is a private individual, the purpose of the conspirators must be to cause the victim economic loss by depriving him of some property or right, corporeal or incorporeal, to which he is or would or might become entitled. The intended means by which this is to be achieved must be dishonest. They need not involve fraudulent misrepresentation such as is needed to constitute the civil tort of deceit. Dishonesty of any kind is enough.

Elaborating further at page 1038, he added: 'If... "fraudulently" means "dishonestly", then "to defraud" ordinarily means... to deprive a person dishonestly of some thing which is his or something to which he is or would or might but for the perpetration of the fraud, be entitled.'

If the concept of dishonesty in the Theft Act, 1968 is followed, then the test of its existence is subjective: it is for the jury to decide whether or not the accused had an honest belief in the truth of his representation or in the legality of his course of conduct. It may be a difficult thing for any businessman contemplating a course of conduct to predict how a judge and jury will see his motives and his belief in the legality of his actions, but he may take comfort from the dictum of Lord Hailsham in *Kamara* v. *DPP* (1973), 2 All E.R. 1242, at page 1252: 'While a mistake of law is not a good defence, a sincere belief in a state of facts which if true would render the illegal conduct legal would be a good answer to any charge of conspiracy.'

The jurisdiction of the English courts

There is one final aspect of the criminal law that I consider to be of importance to the understanding of the control of long-firm fraud, and that is what is sometimes called the law of venue. As international fraud becomes increasingly popular with 'the criminal fraternity' – wherever that is to be found – legal disputes concerning 'venue-dodging' and extradition are likely to assume increasing significance.

There is nothing new about problems of jurisdiction *vis-à-vis* long-firm frauds. The False Pretences Act (30 Geo. III, c. 24) in

1757 enacted that 'any persons who knowingly by false pretences shall obtain from any person money, goods, etcetera, with intent to cheat or defraud any person, shall be deemed offenders against law'.

Prior to 1827, the entire offence of false pretences had to be completed within one *county* for it to be indictable at all. The question raised in venue cases was whether someone who allegedly had committed an offence under English law should be tried before a court whose jurors were drawn from one place rather than from another. This problem had in turn arisen from the origins of the jury system, in which jurors combined the functions of 'knowers of facts' and 'triers of facts'. Prisoners were entitled to have their guilt determined by jurors drawn from an area where the inhabitants would be most likely to know the facts alleged to constitute the crime with which they were charged.

In an eighteenth-century case, *R.* v. *Buttery*, which is unreported but mentioned in the libel case of *R.* v. *Burdett* (1820), 4 B & Ald. 95, Buttery was accused of obtaining goods by false pretences. He was indicted for this in Herefordshire, where the alleged false pretences had been made. However, the goods had actually been supplied in Monmouthshire and the judges who, according to the practice of the day, considered the matter at Serjeant's Inn, decided that he should have been indicted in Monmouthshire. The judges thought that the false pretence was a material circumstance which stamped the illegality of the obtaining of the goods, but that it was antecedent to, and not a part of, the obtaining. By this device, the judges sought to define the long-firm fraud as having been committed within one county.

This interpretation of the law survived the problems of venue from which it had arisen, and remained the basis for the resolution of jurisdictional disputes. For example, in the case of a firm, or two connected firms, operating both in England and in France, which obtains goods on credit from French firms and sends them to England, where it disposes of them and defrauds the creditors of the proceeds, are the goods obtained in England or in France? This was the type of problem which arose frequently in the nineteenth century, when there was a great deal of trade in textiles between England and France.

The venue difficulties were sometimes evaded by charging people with procuring goods otherwise than in the ordinary way of trade. Thus, in the case of *R.* v. *Raudnitz* (Central Criminal Court, 1863, unreported), referred to in Chapter II, the trial judge decided that it was up to the jury to decide whether the use of the Paris House to buy goods for the London House was a real and *bona fide* concern, or whether the premises in Paris were taken and used exclusively to enable the defendant and his partner to obtain goods to be sent to England. If the jury felt that the latter were the case, then the goods were obtained in England: if not, they were obtained in France, outside the jurisdiction of the courts.

The principle that it was the place of the obtaining of goods that is relevant for jurisdiction was confirmed in the case of *R.* v. *Ellis* (1898), Court for Crown Cases Reserved 210. This was a prosecution under Section 13 (1) of the Debtors Act, 1869. As HAWKINS J. stated in the judgement of the court:

> A false representation made to a London tradesman ... from, say, Paris ... must, according to every dictate of good sense, be intended by the maker of it to operate on and continue present in the mind of the tradesman until the goods are actually obtained from him; and by his conduct in obtaining the goods, he ought, in my opinion, be treated as having repeated his representations quite as effectively as if he had again put them into words.

This remains the law until the present, and is thus applicable to the increasingly popular attempts to defraud foreign suppliers of their goods. In recent years, however, a number of cases have come before the courts for decision which involve more complex issues of jurisdiction. The most significant case in this respect is *Treacy* v. *DPP* (1971), 1 All E.R. 115. Although directed towards the offence of blackmail contrary to Section 29 of the Theft Act, 1968 its impact goes far beyond that. In particular, the judgement of Lord Diplock is of interest. He stated (p. 123).

> The source of any presumption that Parliament intended that the right created by the Act to punish conduct should be subject to some territorial limitation on where the conduct takes place or where its consequences can take effect can, in my view, only be the rules of international comity. And the extent of the limitation, where none has been expressed in words, can only be determined by considering what compliance with those rules requires ... For reasons I have stated earlier, the rules of international comity, in my view, do not call for more than each Sovereign State should refrain from punishing persons for their conduct within the territory of another Sovereign State, where that conduct has no harmful consequences within the territory of the State which imposes the punishment. I see no reason for presuming that Parliament, in enacting the Theft Act 1968, intended to make the offences which it thereby created subject to any wider exclusion than this. In my view, where the definition of any such offence contains a requirement that the described conduct of the accused should be followed by described consequences, the implied

exclusion is limited to cases where *neither* the conduct *nor* its harmful consequences took place in England or Wales.

Despite certain ambiguities – for example, the definition of 'harmful consequences' – the adoption of this principle might have very considerable consequences regarding jurisdiction over international frauds. Indeed, this extension of the principle of territoriality has received major support subsequently in *Secretary of State* v. *Markus* (1975), 3 WLR 708 and, most interestingly, in *Reg.* v. *Stonehouse* (1977), 3 WLR 143 1.

Where the offender is not within the immediate jurisdiction of the English courts, extradition becomes necessary. Although fraud cases involving extradition do not come before the courts very often, the *potential* impact of such cases is enormous. In a work such as this, there is no place for a technical discussion of international extradition arrangements. However, I will crudely summarize the position *vis-à-vis* long-firm frauds.

An Engligh subject fleeing to England after committing a long-firm fraud abroad probably will be extradited back there provided that there is prima-facie evidence of his having committed an offence against that country's laws which is governed by the extradition treaty. In the case of Commonwealth countries, the rules are governed by the Fugitive Offenders Act, 1967, but in other cases, jurisdiction depends upon the country's individual extradition treaty. The requirement of *prima facie* evidence is by no means a mere formality, as the refusal of the courts to agree to the extradition of the English financier Jim Slater to Singapore in 1977 indicates. The same principles apply to foreigners who flee home after committing their offences entirely in this country. Englishmen defrauding creditors abroad commit an offence in this country as well as overseas, and may be tried here. Thus, the simple cases are reasonably well catered for, provided that there is a relevant extradition treaty.

However, when we arrive at cases for which there is no parity of offence between the countries concerned, the offender is no longer extraditable, although if not a citizen of Britain he may be deported as an undesirable alien. The lack of international parity gave rise to many problems with the False Pretences Act, 1757 and the Debtors Act, 1869, but is far less problematic since the incorporation of obtaining property by deception within the Theft Act, 1968. However, the requirement that only offences charged in the extradition warrant can be charged does hinder the prosecution of alleged long-firm fraudsters, since there is no extradition for conspiracies to defraud – the most common offence charged in England.

The technical problems of international fraud control could only be fully overcome if, first, there were a uniform, worldwide system of laws governing crimes of fraud which were incorporated in universally applicable extradition treaties; and secondly, there were no governments willing to be corrupted by rich fugitives from justice.

There are considerable differences in legal codes, in ideology, and in national interests that make it unlikely that the first condition will ever obtain; and one should not be over-sanguine about the diminution or the abolition of corrupt governments or judges. For these reasons, legal prescriptions for changes in the law of fraud would do well to avoid relying on perfect international co-operation.

As I have argued, simple bi-national frauds are adequately encompassed by present legal arrangements. In more complex cases, however, this is far from true. Let us take a case in which the subject of country A starts a company in country B. The company in country B establishes a subsidiary in country C. This subsidiary orders goods on credit from firms in country D, for which it does not pay. In such a case, the problems of enforcing judgements for civil debts are considerable. As far as the *criminal* law is concerned, it may be seen that once the businessman returns to country A, or goes on to country E, it is hardly conceivable that he could be extradited, *even in principle*. Now let us assume that Lord Diplock's views in *Treacy* v. *DPP* were accepted. The prosecution would have to prove that the fraud had harmful consequences upon trade in general, and therefore on trade in this country, *wheresoever it was committed*. Whilst this might be logical enough, it is doubtful if any English court would accept the argument.

But even if it were theoretically possible for an offender to be prosecuted, whose responsibility would this be? In every country, the resources of the police are continuously under strain, and international frauds, unless they are singularly sensational or seriously damage the interests of the nations concerned, understandably occupy a low priority in the allocation of these scarce resources. Moreover, from a human standpoint, it is normal for police officers to be concerned principally with offences that occur on *their* 'Manor'. Unless, as in the case of murder or sex crime, the behaviour grossly offends their moral sentiments, it is of only abstract concern. Multinational investigations of fraud are thus hampered both by gaps between legal jurisdictions of polities and by the absence of any great psychological investment in their prosecution.

Summary and conclusion

There has been a tendency for sociologists of deviance, particularly those in the interactionist school, to ignore the law and to focus upon the social creation of 'deviance'. However valid this may be in the case of offences such as vagrancy or juvenile delinquency, where the police and courts can define almost any behaviour as criminal and can impose penal sanctions accordingly, it is indefensible to adopt this position in respect of commercial 'crime'. With the possible exception of the broad common law offence of conspiracy to defraud, the English legislature has been very restrictive in setting the boundaries of the criminal law with respect to commercial conduct. The reason for this is that it is only with the greatest reluctance that any businessman is formally defined as an 'outsider'. As Lord Justice Brett stated in the case of *Wilson* v. *Clinch* (1879) (quoted in Shannon, 1933, p. 297): 'I must confess to such an abhorrence of fraud in business that I am always most unwilling to come to a conclusion that fraud has been committed.' The consequence is that the circumstances under which policing agencies may intervene in commercial affairs are tightly circumscribed. I have detailed the rather tortuous process by which an increasing amount of that conduct has become 'criminalized' but, even today, commercial criminal law is extremely complex and unwieldy.

It seems clear that the overriding principle on which the regulation of 'fraud' has been based has been that at all costs, 'free enterprise' must not be discouraged by fear of prosecution. The ideological underpinnings of this are discussed in Chapter XI, but capitalists pay a price for this principle in terms of their inability to find an adequate legal framework for the control of those of their fellows who are universally considered by them to be 'undesirable', for example, long-firm fraudsters.

The current legal position regarding the prosecution of long-firm frauds is nicely summarized by Glanville Williams (1978, pp. 739–40):

> The practice is to charge a single conspiracy to defraud, or, where a company is involved, the offence of fraudulent trading, giving particulars of A, B, C, etc. who have been defrauded. But there is no reason why the defendants should not be indicted for obtaining goods by deception from A, B, and C contrary to section 15(1) (in separate counts). You put each victim in the box and ask him: 'Why did you supply these goods to these men on credit?' Answer:

'because I thought they were an honest firm'. The mere ordering of goods is an implied representation of honesty.

These provisions work well enough when the police seek the conviction of the 'front men' after the long firm has gone 'bust', leaving few assets and a large deficiency. However, they are far less effective in the following circumstances:

(1)   where the true principals have remained in the background of the fraud and there is little direct evidence of their involvement. In such cases, only the minor actors may in practice be convicted;

(2)   where the police seek to close down the business and arrest the principals *before* the long firm's depredations become too great, it may be difficult to prove that the business was irredeemably insolvent or that there was an intent to defraud or criminal recklessness;

(3)   where the fraudsters dress up the books of account so that the fraudulent nature of the business and the true extent of its assets and liabilities are concealed, it may be hard to prove that a crime has taken place.

In brief, the more sophisticated the fraud, the more difficult it is to prove what an insider might regard as its criminality.

Philosophers of jurisprudence sometimes divide crimes into the categories of *mala in se* (crimes that 'we' take for granted to be wrong) and *mala prohibita* ('merely technical' crimes). One so-called explanation for the leniency with which 'white-collar crimes' are treated is that they are *mala prohibita* (compare Newman, 1977, pp. 53 ff.) In so far as this view rests upon the newness of the laws and the absence of the requirement to prove intent, long-firm frauds cannot be termed *mala prohibita*. This study has shown that many of the laws under which long-firm frauds are prosecuted are of considerable antiquity—even though most have been modified over the centuries—and that in nearly all cases, criminal intent or at least criminal recklessness must be proved. In other words, if there is any type of commercial crime which by reason of ancient lineage and injuriousness to 'capitalist interests' may lay claim to be considered as *malum in se* or as 'real' crime, it is long-firm fraud. In view of this, it is of considerable theoretical, as well as practical, interest to examine the way in which such frauds are *actually* treated by law-enforcement agencies and in the courts. This is the subject of the next three chapters.

VIII. Policing of Long-Firm Fraud

The investigation and proof of fraud have always presented considerable difficulties for policing agencies in Britain and America. For example, there is a contemporary ring about the following evidence of policeman John Bull in R *v* Gordon and Davidson, a £500 000 (at historic prices!) long-firm fraud tried at the Old Bailey in 1855:

> I was instructed to follow Davidson and Gordon – I left England on the 4th September 1854 and went to Neufchatel in Switzerland – I saw Gordon there in November 1854 – I was not able to take them into custody in consequence of the law of that country – after that, from information I received I went to Malta; the prisoners were apprehended previous to my going there – I arrived there on the 2nd April this year – I had come home in the meantime – I went with a warrant which the authorities there held to be illegal – they were discharged... they afterwards embarked upon the boat the 'Indus' on which I followed them and arrested them at Southampton.

However, until the 1960s, many of these difficulties were submerged because of the low profile adopted by most of the agencies concerned with the control of fraud. Until the late nineteenth century, the investigation and prosecution of fraud in England was left almost entirely to the wronged creditors, and since then, it has proceeded gradually along two basic fronts:

(1) the supervision of limited liability companies by the Board (now the Department) of Trade;

(2) the investigation of frauds by the police as part of their duty to enforce the general body of the criminal law.

An outline of the present control system vis-a-vis long-firm fraud is provided in Figure 8.1 overleaf, but the practical content of this system has undergone several changes. Before the Second World War, for instance, the investigation of fraud by the police was an *ad hoc* affair, in which individual officers with a personal interest in fraud were used as a 'resource' when frauds occurred in their 'Manor' (area). This is clear from the autobiographies of some police officers (Jackson, 1967; Millen, 1972; Thorp, 1954). The consequence of this was that if a fraud took place in an area where

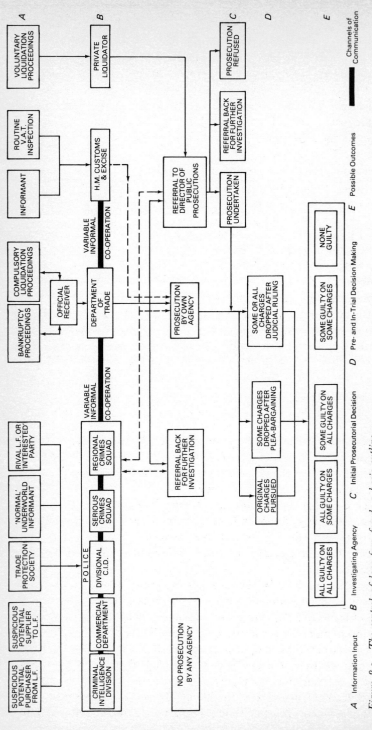

Figure 8.1 The control of long-firm fraud, a basic outline

A Information Input   B Investigating Agency   C Initial Prosecutorial Decision   D Pre- and In-Trial Decision Making   E Possible Outcomes

there was no experienced investigating officer, the chances of detection were low. Even the crude type of long firm, where the managers use false names and disappear at the end, was difficult to deal with unless it happened to be run by local 'villains'.

During the 1930s, however, Scotland Yard set up a small Sharepushing and Confidence Trickster Squad, and this trend towards specialisation was confirmed by the setting up in 1946 of a combined Metropolitan Police and City of London Police Fraud Squad to deal with the widespread frauds on demobilised Britons and Americans. This had two principal consequences:

(1) It improved co-ordination of efforts in the prevention and investigation of company frauds; and

(2) By creating a reservoir of expertise on the subject, it provided an organisational base for the mobilisation of the view that company fraud was a 'police problem'.

Although the impact of the latter is difficult to assess, it is noteworthy that the Fraud Squad has expanded gradually but consistently since the Second World War, while the number of 'frauds known to the Metropolitan Police' has increased fifteen-fold during this period. As with all official statistics, this apparent increase in crime has to be viewed with caution, since it may reflect reporting and police organisational changes as well as be the reason for these changes, but it is clear that there has been a major expansion in the visible face of fraud in Britain. (This observation also applies to the United States.)

There are no separate figures for long-firm frauds, but if one narrows one's consideration to this as a sub-category, it becomes possible to see that a number of variables may account for fluctuations in the amount 'known to the police':

(1) a change in the amount of long-firm fraud itself;

(2) increase in 'fraud' as a consequence of greater readiness on the part of the victims to regard their business losses as 'fraudulent losses', that is, a change in victim definition rather than 'actual' fraud;

(3) changes in beliefs about reporting crime. It may be the case that there has been a change in people's conception of their *duty* to report fraud *once they have perceived the loss as fraudulent*. For example, businessmen today are aware in a general sense of the possibility of being victimized by long-firm frauds, probably more aware than in the past, yet they may now be much less likely than in the past to feel that it is their duty to report such crimes;

(4) changes in expectations about *consequences* of reporting. For example, where reporting is done not out of a sense of duty but from

hope of recovery of goods or money, expectations of recovery may significantly influence reporting behaviour. Similarly, when desire for retribution is a motivation for reporting, changes in police efficiency in detection, in the probability of prosecution and conviction, and in the severity of sentences, may affect rates of reporting. It is important to emphasize the *subjective* nature of this category, as I have discovered widespread ignorance of the 'true picture' on the part of businessmen I have interviewed;

(5) changes in the organization and in the professionalism of the police with regard to fraud. The setting up of specialist commercial departments and specialist long-firm fraud sections within those departments leads not only to more efficient processing of information but also to more proactive policing strategies in the discovery and investigation of fraud;

(6) changes in the criminal organization of long-firm frauds. When frauds are operated and organized by apparently legitimate businessmen with no prior criminal record, the police are reliant upon their contacts in commerce for the identification of a business as 'suspect' and, up to a point, for information concerning the likely principals in the business.

When the businesses are operated by 'known villains', however, this picture changes. The police keep major 'villains' under observation, the intensity of which depends upon their perceived dangerousness. Consequently, their involvements with commerce are more likely to be discovered than the involvements of those not under police surveillance. Moreover, at any given stage in their operation, businesses run by 'known villains' are more likely to be labelled 'fraudulent' than those run by people outside the underworld.

The implication of this is that even though the 'real amount' of fraud remains constant, a change in the organization of long-firm fraud from individual businessmen with little or no underworld connection to 'professional villains' will lead to an increase in the amount of fraud 'known to the police'. This difference in the perception of fraud on the basis of working stereotypes of 'criminals' makes long-firm fraud a lower risk for the 'business criminal' than for the 'ordinary criminal'. As I hope to demonstrate later, this lower risk also applies to the probability of prosecution, conviction and to the severity of sentence.

The actual, as opposed to hypothetical, relevance of each of these factors is impossible to assess, since even if one carried out a longitudinal study, the act of researching would probably alter the actors' definitions of the situation, and I have not found the time to carry out a systematic victimization study either on a longitudinal or a cross-sectional basis. This does not mean, however, that 'guessti-mates' of the effects of such perceptions upon 'crime rates', independent of the 'objective' amount of crime, are not important to bear in mind when looking at 'the problem of fraud'.

Apart from the use of fraud statistics, another way of illustrating the development of fraud as a 'police problem' is to look at the comments about fraud made by the Commissioners of the Metropolitan Police in their annual reports.

Some of the Commissioner's reports make quite explicit the link between general economic conditions, commercial credit practices, and the amount of long-firm fraud:

> The number of long-firm frauds continued to increase, due no doubt to the anxiety of wholesalers to obtain markets. (1955)

> The prevalence of this type of offence is encouraged by the laxity of manufacturers and wholesalers in supplying goods without making proper enquiries of the financial standing and honesty of the buyers. (1964)

> Restrictions on credit generally are causing suppliers to reduce the credit they are prepared to give traders and this is accompanied by a closer scrutiny of new accounts, both of which are a serious handicap to the long-firm fraudsman. (1966)

What, then, determines the workload of the police with respect to long-firm fraud? There is no clear and consistent answer to this question. For example, although there is a general tendency for credit to be granted easily in prosperous times and sparingly in difficult times, this is not universal in its application. In hard times, firms in a competitive situation may be forced to grant credit to anyone with a good 'front' in order to preserve or increase their share of declining markets. In good times, firms in a monopolistic position may be able to give little credit and yet maximize their profits. Thus, the presence of 'hard times' does not necessarily discourage the professional long-firm fraudster. When one looks at 'slippery-slope' and 'intermediate' frauds, the position is somewhat simpler. In prosperous times, most businessmen survive adequately, and there is little temptation for a businessmen to turn to fraud. The number of 'slippery-slope' frauds increases in bad economic conditions, because businessmen attempt to salvage their businesses by continuing trading long past the period of insolvency, in the Micawber-like hope that 'something will turn up'. Thus, the ratio of 'pre-planned frauds' to *total* credit frauds rises in times of prosperity and falls in times of hardship.

Simplifying this picture, one may argue that two basic variables affect the amount of long-firm fraud at any given moment in time: the intensity of application and the sophistication of credit control techniques; and the skill, resources and mode of organization of intending fraudsters. These variables are themselves dependent, in ways explored in this book, but they are largely *in*dependent of direct police interventions.

The police can exhort suppliers to be sparing in the granting of credit to unknown firms, but apart from any possible resultant increase in awareness of the *risk* of fraud, this is likely to have little effect on what are essentially seen as profit-oriented decisions. Suppliers tend to act upon the principle 'nothing ventured, nothing gained', leaving the police to deal with any misadventures. This is not a unique situation for the police, in as much as they have no power to require anyone to protect his or her property carefully, yet they have the duty to investigate theft. However, the degree of consent, albeit unwitting consent, in the victimization of suppliers does make the prevention of fraud different from crime prevention generally.

The police have more influence over the organization of fraud. They influence its form, in so far as planned crimes are generally organized so as to minimize the risk of detection. They also exercise a different type of preventative influence, by detecting and building cases against the organizers of frauds. Many features of the criminal justice system, such as the criteria for 'sufficient evidence' to justify conviction and the disposition of convicted offenders, are outside their control. Yet when offenders are sent to prison, it is clear that their incapacitation means that detection at time (t) leads to prevention at time $(t + 1)$. In this sense, it may be seen that the traditional juxtaposition of prevention and detection is misplaced, for they are properly understood as time-lagged aspects of the same preventative ideal.

The problems raised for the police by long-firm fraudsters cannot therefore be treated ahistorically, since they relate to the prior successes and failures of control efforts. Similarly, the police base their control efforts in part on the lessons *they* have learned about the effectiveness of different ways of organizing *their* resources. The control of long-firm fraud resembles a permanent cat-and-mouse game, with continuous readjustment of tactics by the parties concerned.

Structure and operation of the Metropolitan and City Police Company Fraud Department

The Metropolitan Police Fraud Squad is characterized by a great deal of discussion, on matters of law, tactics, police and technical matters. It is this continual debate, as much as changes in the organization of long-firm fraud itself, which has led to the development of the policing of fraud. Initially, as I have already stated, the Fraud Squad served to integrate the rather *ad hoc* policing of company frauds. Gradually, the interests and abilities of some officers within the Squad led to an informal and incomplete specialization of 'domain', one such area being long-firm fraud.

In the early 1960s, professional fraudsters, often working under the aegis of the Kray or Richardson brothers, commenced large-scale operations in the field of long firms, and to deal with this, a number of officers were deputed in 1964 to specialize in long-firm frauds. This culminated in the formation, in 1971, of a long-firm fraud squad within the Fraud Squad in London.

As the Fraud Squad expanded its functions, the general criminal intelligence index became less useful, and in the mid-1960s, Sergeant Ray Dennis suggested that a Commercial Crime Index be compiled. In March 1968, a Commercial Intelligence Bureau was set up, to collate information on all commercial frauds within the Metropolitan and City Police districts. Since fraudulent operations tend to transcend police boundaries, this index was soon extended to cover the whole country, and became a resource for police forces throughout the country.

The Commercial Crime Intelligence Officers, of whom there were at the time of my research two, with one civilian assistant, are directly responsible to the Commander of the Fraud Squad. They maintain a basic card and computerized index, information on which commenced in 1965, of commercial enterprises convicted, suspected, or under investigation for crime and associated commercial offences; and persons concerned in the directorship, management or administration of such commercial enterprises.

By 1973, the index contained over 12 000 names of persons and over 12 000 names of companies. It acts mainly as a reference source, giving information about criminal record numbers, references to police file numbers, subsidiary companies and so forth. Partly for security reasons, the index, which is now computerized, contains little investigative information. It is available for reference by police officers, both within and outside the department, and there is no strict control of searches in the index.

The main function of the Commercial Intelligence Bureau is to act as a funnel and filter for incoming information, and as a centralized information resource for the company fraud investigators. Since informants are the life-blood of any police detective agency, its officers cultivate informants both in the underworld and in the upperworld. An important element in their job, therefore, is socializing or, less politely, 'hustling', with contacts outside. This is necessary not only to imporve detective work but also to generate confidence so that bankers, brokers, trade protection agents, credit controllers and others will report suspicious matters to them. In other words, the publicizing of Fraud Squad competence may increase the level of reporting of fraudulent activities.

Information may come from a number of sources. Trade protection agencies and credit inquiry agents frequently maintain close contacts with the Commercial Intelligence Bureau, and although the flow of information is generally from them to the bureau, there is a certain amount of information which passes from the bureau to the commercial firms. Underworld informants, or even rival teams of villains, may pass on information. Similarly, a supplier who receives a large order which arouses his suspicion may ring up the Fraud Squad, or an honest trader who is offered goods extremely cheaply may phone them up. Information also comes from other police squads or divisional CID. Nearly all of this passes routinely through the Commercial Intelligence Bureau, before being placed before operational officers, although people who habitually deal with the Fraud Squad may bypass the CIB.

The membership of the squad, or Company Fraud Department as it is more genteelly called, fluctuates in accordance with the demands placed on it and on the police force generally. In 1981, it comprised a Commander, five Chief Superintendents, eight Super-intendents, twenty Chief Inspectors, forty Inspectors, sixty Sergeants, and some eighty Constables.

All officers below the rank of Detective Chief Superintendent are fully operational, and most are engaged with a case-load of between three and five major inquiries at any one time. All correspondence has to be submitted through the Detective Chief Superintendents, and they and the Commander retain a general oversight over the work of the department, as well as supervising very important cases such as the Poulson local government corruption investigation. There is thus a fairly clear hierarchical structure of power and responsibility, although there is considerable operational autonomy at the lower end of the hierarchy.

Within this structure, there are two basic routes through which cases may be assigned to a particular unit. First, a senior officer may simply assign a case to the unit; and second, an officer may commence an investigation on the basis of information received from his 'own' informant, always subject to the consent of a senior officer. The very high case-loads which exist in the Fraud Squad mean that there is little interference with officers' conduct of cases, provided that this appears competent. Thus, each officer of the Fraud Squad, whether senior or junior, is expected to do his own inquiries into his own cases.

The long-firm section of the Company Fraud Department usually investigates cases with officers working in pairs, although in major investigations larger teams, sometimes incorporating divisional CID officers, may be used. If a complaint is received about a firm, or if an officer hears something from an informant, he may decide to go along to the suspect firm to interview the people who work there, or simply to take a look at the premises.

In the 1950s and early 1960s the usual police practice, both in London and the provinces, was to go along to the firm, look around and have a 'friendly chat' with the owners. If the officers were suspicious, but not certain, they might ask the manager if he knew what a long-firm fraud was, and suggest that he be careful lest anyone think he was running one. Alternatively, if their suspicions were stronger, they might specifically warn the manager that they knew what he was up to.

The object of this was primarily preventative. The warning was intended to induce the manager to repay his creditors or at least refrain from ordering more goods on credit. If he went on trading, and subsequently went bankrupt or into liquidation, the warning would buttress the case for the prosecution. In a sense, the police were operating a 'Wild West' system, to 'run the fraudsters out of town'. While the more confident fraudster might continue with his fraud, the policy undoubtedly succeeded in harassing some 'villains' out of carrying out a particular fraud. However, an unintended consequence was to drive the fraudsters to operate in areas where the police were less well organized to fight them.

Furthermore, this tactic can only be applied in cases where the police 'know' about the 'fraud' while the firm is still in operation. More usually, at least until the late 1960s, the police only knew about the fraud *after* it had closed down. In the 'hit-and-run' type of long firm, where the principals used false names and then simply disappeared, identification was frequently a problem, unless the individual was a 'known villain' who could be readily identified from photographs already in police files. The use of fingerprints on the premises for identification was not as common as it is today, and in any event, careful fraudsters would not leave any prints there, while prints on letters sent to creditors are often too blurred to provide adequate means of identification.

In the late 1960s and 1970s, the information flow on suspected companies improved greatly, and the police developed more effective methods of investigation, both prior to and subsequent to the closure of the business. Each case presents unique features, and therefore unique problems for investigation, but it is possible to make some generalizations about strategy.

One of the principal difficulties is the need to identify not only those who are actually operating the fraud, in the sense of working in the suspect premises, but also those who are organizing it and 'fencing' the goods. The narrower the scope of the police operation, the easier it becomes, in a non-linear fashion, because the problems of co-ordinating the timing of arrests and amassing evidence escalate dramatically when one tries to 'get' the entire network involved in the fraud. (This problem is neglected in Walsh, 1977, ch. 6.) When there is an international aspect to the fraud, these difficulties are compounded still further.

A number of tactics may be used. Attempts to get existing employees to act as informants are very rarely tried, since it is likely that all employees are parties to the fraud. If, however, instead of using their girl-friends as typists, the operators recruit from a typing agency, it is in theory possible to 'plant' an informant or even an undercover policeman. Officers may keep the premises under 24-hour surveillance, photograph everyone entering or leaving them, and follow goods vans and lorries from the firm to see where the goods are delivered. They may dress up as meter-readers, dustmen, plumbers or sewage engineers, to gain access to the premises. In this way they may obtain fingerprints or incriminating documents. A search of the contents of a dustbin, for example, may yield valuable evidence.

Some comparisons between the policing of fraud and 'normal' crimes

Thus far, I have emphasized the similarity between the investigation of long-firm fraud and other types of police work: problems of surveillance, of identification of suspects, of obtaining 'adequate standards of proof', of manipulating informants and so forth. The content of these categories naturally differs, for example, the longer exposure of people running a fraud to observation when compared with bank robbers, forgers, burglars and other groups of 'villains'. Yet the difficulty of compiling a case against the suspected organizer of a fraud, who has never been identified as having taken part in the running of the business, is not appreciably different from that of proving the complicity of the organizer of any other type of major crime. One can do a 'deal' with a potential witness who is a co-conspirator, or who is a potential defendant on some other charge. Where a very major fraud is suspected, or 'organised criminals' are involved, one may conceivably gain permission for telephones to be tapped, mail intercepted, 'target criminal' surveillance. This continual battle of wits is part of any investigation of a major criminal.

There are, however, some important differences between fraud work and other areas of police work, especially on division.

Four years in the Fraud Squad is OK, but then boredom sets in. You have a lot of time to think things over. Preparation tends to stretch to infinity. One does a lot of work with piles of documents, and then counsel says it is quite unnecessary. There is a tendency to put off jobs. You say to yourself: 'If the Director of Public Prosecutions can postpone it, so can I.'

All interviews are carefully thought out and you can compile a checklist or a formal questionnaire. When you are on division, you stand much more on your wits. In the Fraud Squad, you lose touch with ordinary reality, and when you leave, you have to reorient yourself to a completely different time scale for investigations. You also have to get used to the much smaller sums involved in petty crime: after thinking of bail in terms of between five and ten thousand pounds, you have to start thinking of fifty to a hundred pounds.

When you are on division, people are firing questions at you all the time for immediate decision, whereas on the Fraud Squad, if your superior is absent or busy, you simply wait till he has time to talk to you. You can mull over documents for hours or even days before making a decision.

The long gap between starting a case and its trial and the final verdict is very strenuous. One tends to become bored with it by the time it comes to trial. By then, one is already involved in an entirely different inquiry.

On division, the vast majority of inquiries are discrete, narrowly-bound entities. They may implicate someone who is smart by the standards of the street hustler, but rarely possess the complex ramifications of large-scale inquiries. Unless he is really determined to 'have a go', the junior or even middle-rank divisional CID officer does not have the time to pursue any latent undercurrents in an investigation.

Not that all long-firm frauds entail long-term complex investigations. There are the 'l.q.'s', or 'little quickies', as one wit called them. In other cases, officers may make a conscious decision that the pursuit of wider aspects of a case is not called for, and that they should let matters rest with the 'villains' they already 'have'. This may be a response to a high case-load, which in a sense determines the priorities of investigation, given the inelasticity in the number of personnel in the Fraud Squad. It may sometimes be due to a disillusionment with the legal process.

The police may take years preparing what they regard as an adequate case against a major operator, and then the person may be acquitted, or the judge may throw the case out. Some people who are well known by people in their élite circle in the underworld to be strongly involved in long-firm fraud have been acquitted on the rare occasions when they have been charged (see Chapter IX). One attained the admiration of his peers by successfully suing a senior officer for false imprisonment, although not, I might add, in connection with long-firm fraud. (The Court of Appeal rejected the decision of the lower court, and the case is not cited for reasons of possible libel.)

Although no great consensus is easily discernible among the police (indeed, there is no reason why this should be the case), certain beliefs about the nature of the 'justice' handed out by the courts do appear to be common. As one rather bitter officer expressed it to me:

> You spend months and months, poring over documents to make a case against someone you absolutely *know* is guilty. And then his counsel comes along, picks up his whacking great brief fee, and twists the case until you wonder whether he is talking about the same case that you have been investigating all these months. It seems to me that legal aid is a 'legitimate racket' laid on by society for the benefit of the legal profession. The lawyers seem to be the only people who really gain from the whole business, apart from some of the villains.
> When you consider the amount of time we spend preparing a major investigation, the failure rate is astonishingly high. If the DPP approves the charge, they monkey about with the plea-bargaining. If you get past the legal submissions to the judge, and the verdict of the jury, they start with the technicalities for appeal against conviction and against sentence. The whole legal process is totally demoralizing.

Having sat through trials lasting months, during which the counsel drag out flimsy defences over what seems like an eternity, one can sympathize with the feelings of the officer in question. On the other hand, many officers appear to successfully reconcile themselves with the role allotted to them in the judicial system:

> The lawyers get paid for doing one job: we get paid for doing another. Whatever society decides should happens to the villains we nick is nothing to do with us. If they let them out and they are

back 'at it', we will nick them again. As far as I am concerned, when we nick chummy [a criminal] that is the end of my problem. My books are cleared.

This represents the reaction of an experienced officer. He later added:

Some of the younger officers, they get really wound up over their cases. If chummy gets off, they get really upset. But in this job, you can't afford to let your emotions get the better of you. You just have to shrug your shoulders and put it down to experience.

Thus, the acceptance of a limited role for the police not only reflects the constitutional 'ideal type' – in the Weberian sense – for police work: it also represents an emotionally functional response to the reality of ultimate police impotence. It is, however, understandable that some policemen, faced with the arcane mysteries of an apparently irrational legal system wholly unsuited to the trial of complicated commercial crime allegations, resort to deviant practices to 'improve' a case that they believe is already substantial enough to justify conviction under a 'reasonable' system of adjudication. The extent of such 'improvements' is impossible to determine without the videotaping of all interviews, but when a sharp villain is reported to have said 'This was going to be one of the biggest l.f.s you ever saw', one is tempted to adopt a sceptical attitude towards the validity of the 'verbal'. Police officers suggest, sometimes rightly, that cunning criminals deliberately make these unconvincing statements in order to discredit their own admissions, but in the above case this was hard to believe.

Further complication sometimes arise in fraud investigations. The overlapping of areas of competence both within and between police forces may create major diplomatic problems as well as impose delays and a lack of coherence upon investigations. For example, as indicated in Figure 8.1, not only the Fraud Squad but also the Serious Crimes Squad, divisional CID, divisional Crime Squads, and non-Metropolitan Police Fraud and Regional Crime Squads may *all* theoretically find themselves investigating the *same* people. This overlapping occurs mainly when 'organized crime syndicates' are engaged systematically in long-firm fraud, but it may also occur when geographically disparate firms interlock in a fraudulent conspiracy. On such occasions, inter-force or intra-force rivalries and suspicions may act to the detriment of the inquiry. Informants may refuse to give evidence to Metropolitan Police officers, for example, because they fear that they may be 'bent'. If, in order to reassure them, the Regional Crime Squad handles the inquiry – as happened in the early stages of the Richardson gang investigation before a special combined Metropolitan and Regional Crime Squad team was set up – then the Metropolitan Police may take offence, however irrationally. Many Fraud Squad officers in the provinces feel that the London police treat them like country hicks and distrust the Londoners.

A national Fraud Investigation Unit might ease conflicts over jurisdiction in fraud inquiries, but jealousies and resentments between the 'Big City Wide Boys' and 'the Swedey' might well still remain. Moreover, such rivalries arise out of the fact that a certain amount of glory, not to mention promotion prospects, accrue from a successful investigation, and intra-force competition is thus endemic to the situation. Indeed, there is nothing ignoble about this, and it is the difficulty of providing adequate rewards for such major investigations that makes fraud work demoralizing and may make corruption more likely.

A more subtle problem arises from the different roles of respective teams. Any police squad must arrive at some *modus vivendi* with some underworld figures (compare Rock, 1973a, ch. 4). The informal deals and understandings represent an uneasy but pragmatic truce (except when corruption makes them cosy and friendly), but when 'outsiders' who have different goals and problems come along, this truce can be disturbed.

For example, the Regional Crime Squad may wittingly or unwittingly 'burn' the informants of a local divisional officer or squad, and this may have repercussions upon the latter's relationships with the underworld and upon other pending cases. Within the London region, the Serious Crimes Squad may disturb the investigations of the Commercial Branch, or vice versa. The Fraud Squad may take action which hampers an investigation by HM Customs and Excise into tax fraud, and so forth. The consequence can be something like a chess game, in which someone who was not visible as a player suddenly comes along and moves the pieces.

At present, there are about forty Fraud Squads in different parts of the country. These range from small units of two people to the dozen or so officers in large cities such as Birmingham, Manchester, Liverpool, Glasgow and Edinburgh, to the far larger Metropolitan and City Police Company Fraud Departments. Increasingly, co-operation between these various squads has become necessary, and significant efforts have been made to improve liaison. These efforts have taken a number of forms. First, information is exchanged via the Commercial Intelligence Bureau at New Scotland

Yard, and through the additional intelligence files kept by the long-firm squad at Holborn. Second, by the regionally-organized Fraud Squad conferences lasting two to three weeks where officers from Northern, Midlands and Southern squads get together in their respective areas and discuss common problems and pool expertise. And third, by the sort of gathering of officers on a national basis which occurred in the National Conference on the Investigation of Commercial Fraud, the first one being held in London in 1974. However, for reasons discussed more fully in Chapter XII, there is considerable scope for improvement in police training and co-ordination. One objection to the permanent placement of officers in fraud investigation units is the risk of continuing corruption, and it is consequently relevant to review the evidence regarding corruption under the present organisational system.

Police corruption and long-firm frauds

Neither in books nor in the news media has corruption within the Metropolitan Police Fraud Squad received much publicity to date. For instance, it is not mentioned in the accounts of corruption by Cox *et al.* (1977) or by Sir Robert Mark (1978). Whitaker (1979, p. 260) makes the bold assertion that corruption 'is localised – there has never been evidence of corruption in, for example, the Fraud Squad'. Clearly, the rebuttal of this assertion depends on what criteria of 'evidence' one adopts. But by 1976 (well before the publication of any of the books mentioned hitherto), one Fraud Squad Detective Inspector had been convicted in relation to long-firm corruption, two others had had their convictions quashed by the Court of Appeal (Criminal Division) as 'unsafe and unsatisfactory' (though co-defendants' appeals were dismissed), and a number of other officers had been transferred out of the Fraud Squad or the Force generally under a cloud of suspicion. Some of the police officers I interviewed (as well as informed outsiders) were willing to acknowledge that there were more than just one or two 'rotten apples' within the Metropolitan Police Fraud Squad during the late 1960s and early 1970s, though there is no hard evidence that corruption there was pervasive and 'organised' in the way it was in the Obscene Publications Squad and the Drugs Squad. To the best of my knowledge, no allegations of corruption regarding *long-firm* frauds were investigated by the 80 strong Operation Country-man team, but charges may result from allegations of corrupt involvement with other types of fraud in London.

A number of long-firm fraudsters made reference to both successful and unsuccessful attempts at corruption, but the truth of their rather vague (although purely spontaneous) allegations is difficult to evaluate. One fraudster informed me that a Divisional Chief Inspector had approached him with an offer to grant him a licence to operate long firms on his 'Manor' in exchange for suitable remuneration, but that he declined the offer, suspecting that he was being 'set up', i.e. that he would be prosecuted if he did operate the fraud. Another professional fraudster stated that a colleague had paid out vast sums via an intermediary in a vain attempt to obtain an acquittal. In a further case, I heard a tape recording which purported to be a discussion between a Detective Inspector on the 'long-firm squad' and a long-firm organiser on the run from prison who was engaged in some new frauds, arranging immunity from arrest in return for payment. (No charges were brought against this officer, though he was – coincidentally? – transferred to the uni-formed branch immediately afterwards. This example, if true, reveals the inadequacy of corrupt 'cover', since the fraudster concerned was subsequently arrested and convicted in relation to this fraud.)

Corruption relating to long firms was operated by virtue of the control that specialist officers in London were able to exercise over investigations and charges. In one case, for example, one branch of a long firm was set up in London so that a corrupt senior officer could make an initial visit to the premises there, thus ensuring that all subsequent police enquiries were referred through him. He could thus keep the fraudsters informed about the state of complaints and investigations against them. The idea was that the 'front men' could be arrested if necessary, but that the organisers would be left out of any charges. Thus, the crime would appear to be fully cleared up, satisfying superior officers and providing a credit on the officer's arrest record. Unfortunately for those involved in this case:

(1) one of the fraudsters was willing to implicate the others in the conspiracy;

(2) the organiser had left so many clues to his involvement in the fraud that any reasonable detective would have questioned him concerning it; and

(3) the senior officer persisted in not pursuing the organiser despite contrary instructions from his superior officer.

Consequently, they were all convicted. But had the organiser been more careful and stayed in the background, and had the officer not continued to protect him, it is doubtful whether either would have been convicted.

Although other officers and fraudsters allegedly working on similar *modus operandi* appear to have been more skilful and fortunate than those just mentioned, a number of factors reduce the likelihood of long-term pervasive organised corruption in respect of long-firm frauds. First, the relatively short periods spent by officers within the Fraud Squad, which means that fraudsters must be able to rely on the corruptability of a number of officers. Second, the geographical spread of many long firm operations, which makes it possible that other, non-corrupt officers from other Forces may become involved in the operational investigation, thus increasing the risk of conviction. Third, the overlapping police jurisdictions within the Metropolitan area: as I have indicated, the organisers may become the subjects of attention from the Fraud Squad, Regional Crimes Squad, Serious Crimes Squad, and divisional C.I.D. Fourth, long firms may be discovered, investigated, and prosecuted by officials of the Department of Trade or H.M. Customs & Excise. And fifth, unless superior officers and Police Complaints investigators are also negligent or corrupt, credit enquiry agencies or even creditors may become highly suspicious if their reports of the involvement of organiser X in long firms are not followed up, and this may lead to the exposure of the corruption.

The conviction of a number of major background operators during the 1970s supports the notion that there has been a marked reduction in corruption as well as a marked improvement in police efficiency. However, the fact that none of my underworld or police informants have told me about any continuing corruption is not logically adequate proof that it has been eliminated. *Prima facie*, it is unlikely that long-firm merchants will enjoy the sort of police protection offered in the pre-Mark era, but we can never be sure. What is clear is that suspicions of corruption within the Metropolitan Police led to reluctance on the part of credit inquiry agents and other police forces to give information to the London Fraud Squad during the early 1970s, and that the attempts to clean up the London police improved the flow of data into that force.

It appears, then, that fears of the impact that revelations of corruption might have upon police–public relations in the realm of long-firm fraud have proved unfounded. Those fears have been eased rather than exacerbated by the official recognition of the situation. My informants feel reasonably assured that in the present climate of policing, even though some miscreants within the force may have escaped retribution, they will be too cautious to succumb to temptation in the future, at least on the scale experienced hitherto.

Since the inception of the Metropolitan and City Police Company Fraud Department in 1946, the policing of long-firm fraud has undergone a number of changes. It has moved from a primarily *reactive* system, in which the police respond only to complaints received, to a more proactive system, in which the police keep a watching brief over suspected fraudsters and firms *before* any formal complaint is made (compare Reiss, 1971). This policy is not unique to the Fraud Squad: the Serious Crimes Squad, the Flying Squad and the Robbery Squad, for example, not only investigate robberies *after* they have occurred, but try to find out about planned robberies *before* they occur.

In the case of frauds, however, a great deal of interpretative work goes on at all stages of the inquiries. These inquiries normally entail three principal elements: whether or not the officers *believe* the behaviour under investigation is a crime; if they believe that it is a crime, how, if at all, can it be proved to be a crime? and, finally, the more usual type of CID problem, who are the principals and how can their involvement be proved to the satisfaction of the DPP and a court?

Although the judgements underlying these elements are seldom made explicit, it is possible to make some inferences about them. The first point relates to the constraints imposed by limited manpower, which arise in two principal ways: first, as stated earlier, by limiting the scope of any given investigation; and second, by affecting the definition by the police of a business failure as either 'crime' or 'no crime'. When officers dealing with fraud have very high case-loads, they sometimes classify possible frauds as 'no crime' unless either (a) a 'great deal' of money is involved (this may mean over £20 000 or over £50 000, depending upon the area and inflation), or (b) the victims are especially vocal or 'deserving'. This method of improving the 'clear-up rate' may be unorthodox, but since the officers would not in any event have the resources to undertake the investigation, its implications concern the validity of official crime statistics more than the administration of justice.

The 'low-visibility decision-making' in this field is, however, worthy of consideration. The police necessarily possess a crude 'working philosophy' about the boundaries between fraud and lawful business operations which does not completely coincide with the dictates of the law. This varies from individual to individual but, operationally, it centres around MAUGHAM J's dictum in *Re Patrick & Lyon Ltd* (1933), 1 Ch. 786, that fraud is 'actual dishonesty involving, according to current notions of fair trading among commercial men, real moral blame'. For not only do many officers share this definition of fraud, but their behaviour is determined by the acceptability of this definition to the Director of Public Prosecutions, to the judiciary and to jurors.

The ranking of business failures, then, proceeds along two dimensions. One is the 'badness' of the fraud in terms of its effects on the victims: some long-firm frauds literally ruin the small-time suppliers who sell them a large proportion of their output, while others are barely noticed by the large public companies. The other is based upon the perceived 'badness' of the people believed to be running the fraud, and may involve a number of decisions.

One of the most important of these decisions is, as I argued earlier, the criteria of 'suspiciousness' which makes a failure liable to investigation. A prior criminal record, association with criminals or a history of 'unfortunate business experiences', as they are ironically called, may lead to the initial characterization of someone as a 'fraudster type'. The absence of any of these attributes will not of itself enable anyone to 'get away with it', but will give him a relative advantage. For this reason, as well as to reduce the chance of identification, the ideal 'front man' does not possess a criminal record. The assessment of 'moral character' on this basis is not necessarily the result of any supposed 'prejudice' on the part of the police: it reflects not only their own probabilistic judgement about who is 'likely to be criminal' but also that of the judiciary and jurors. As one officer put it:

> These 'slippery-slope frauds' you talk about. They are more cases of fraudulent trading than proper l.f.s. The people who run them aren't really villains – they're mainly people who do stupid things when they get into a sticky financial situation . . . They won't face up to reality, and carry on when they ought to stop . . . But they're not proper villains . . .
>
> You won't find this in the rule book, but in practice, almost everybody is given one chance. If some 'bod' does a one-off fraud, he has got a bloody good chance of getting away with it. If we nicked everybody we thought might have done an l.f., we'd never finish our paperwork, the cases might never come to court, and if they did, they'd never have the room to try them.

Police investigatory decisions are also affected by their perceptions of the expectations of prosecutors and the courts (examined in the next chapter). On the one hand, pressure is put on the police to make their reports clear-cut and relatively simple; on the other hand, there is always the risk that those charged will put the blame on those not charged. Thus, at the risk of complicating the issues and prolonging the trial, it is tempting to charge most of the people who have taken part in the running of a long-firm fraud.

Here, too, the scenario is more complex than it *prima facie* appears. The warehouseman, or the driver, who may look as if he is only a minor character, is often the man put in by the organizer or by the 'backer' to safeguard his interests. The typist may be the girl-friend of one of the accused, and it may be expedient to charge her, to 'do a deal' with her boy-friend in exchange for dropping the charge, or to persuade her to give evidence for the Crown. This type of decision-making is learned on the job. It is part of the 'normal' police CID craft.

Other discretionary decisions sometimes arise in the evaluation of priorities concerning the relative 'dangerousness' of underworld figures. During the Richardson and Kray inquiries, as previously mentioned, it was decided that the fraudsters were less dangerous than the 'gangsters'. After the conviction of the 'gangsters', a number of the fraudsters who had given evidence committed further frauds: their usefulness gone, the police were able to prosecute them without sacrificing some more important objective. On occasions, the non-prosecution of a suspect, or the giving of evidence by a police officer in favour of an accused person may be wrongly attributed to corruption when in reality it is to serve some deeper 'game' the police are playing. In the world of long-firm fraud, things are rarely as they seem, and this is especially significant in the context of police strategies, which are generally inaccessible to the outsider.

In the preceding pages, I have tried to elucidate some of the significant features of the policing of long-firm fraud. The greatly increased professionalization of this policing in the last decade, not only in London but also in the regions, has led to the arrest of many, but by no means all, of the major figures involved in the backing and organization of long-firm frauds. At the time of writing, some of these figures have already been released from prison, some have been acquitted and others are awaiting trial.

As I have already stated, the specialization of police into units concerned with long-firm fraud is very variable, as is the extent to which the 'heavy squads' overlap onto their territory and the degree of 'proactivity' in operational style. Some features of policing are, however, omnipresent. The length of time taken to carry out inquiries, the methods of investigation, the long wait for processing through prosecuting authorities and the courts, the trouble taken to write clear, concise reports, and the problems created by the limited police powers of inspecting books and questioning suspects: these are common to all investigators. Sometimes, although these aspects of the job are *objectively* equally distributed, they are *perceived* differently in different areas. For example, Metropolitan police officers are inured to the long delays involved in obtaining authorizations from the DPP and in getting cases to trial: provincial officers, on the other hand, are used to relatively speedy decisions from their Chief Constable, and find waiting less tolerable. There are differences, too, in the perceptions of the seriousness of frauds; the same fraud may be large by Devonian standards, but small by those of London, and consequently, may be treated differently by the two forces.

It is important to understand the evaluation placed upon fraud work within the general police culture. As one officer stated:

> There are three things most policemen want nothing to do with: drugs, cars and fraud. The first because it's a social problem, the second because you have to spend all your time tracing kiddies, and the third because you get bogged down in boring paperwork and have to play silly-buggers with big City slickers.

Long-firm fraud is more akin to 'normal' police work than most other types of fraud: at least it is often practised by 'real villains'. Its investigation does, however, require a more introverted personality, and a more deferential and diplomatic style of manipulation from that which is needed for 'normal' crime. This does not mean that Fraud Squad officers are not lively people, but they must possess the ability to sit down and 'plod' for longer periods than might occur, for instance, even in a murder inquiry, which necessitates a similarly painstaking approach.

The investigation of fraud is an intellectually absorbing task. For example, how does one time one's arrests so as to simultaneously enable the business to be clearly categorized in court as a fraud; obtain adequate evidence against *all* the conspirators; and minimize the losses to the creditors? For the purposes of categorization as 'fraud', the *later* the police move in on the business, the better. On the other hand, from the point of view of arresting the principals, and saving creditors' money, the *sooner* the police move in the better. For the 'villains' may abscond, possibly out of the jurisdiction of the courts, documentary evidence may be destroyed, fingerprints wiped off, and the proceeds disappear. Thus, timing is crucial to the successful police operation, for if the arrests are made too early, insufficient evidence may exist of the intent to defraud to justify a criminal charge, and if they are made too late, there may be insufficient evidence to identify the fraudsters or to prove their connection with the fraudulent enterprise, despite the surveillance and photographic techniques currently employed. The investigation of long-firm fraud, then, does possess considerable appeal to the intellectual planning and hunting mentality, but it lacks the dimension of emotional identification with the victim which acts as a spur to police motivation.

Given the sort of stress which the prospect of 'bookwork' engenders in the proverbial 'man-in-the-street', and given the lack of in-depth training in company law and accountancy which the police receive, it is all the more impressive that long-firm fraud is investigated with the level of expertise that I observed in operation. When assessing the role of the police in such investigations, it is important to bear in mind not only the operational and cultural aspects of policing discussed earlier, but also that the police represent only one link, albeit a vital link, in the chain of the social control of long-firm fraud. It is to the other links that I must now turn.

Role of the Department of Trade

Under present arrangements, the police are the law-enforcement agency with primary responsibility for long-firm frauds. However, as part of their overall function of regulating corporate conduct, the Department of Trade (DoT) also plays an important role in their control. In assessing this role, it is useful to separate the powers of the Department into two categories: those relating to companies *before* liquidation; and those which arise *during* and *after* liquidation.

First, the pre-liquidation powers. Section 441 of the Companies Act, 1948 states:

> If an offence is suspected in connection with the management by an officer of the company's affairs, the Director of Public Prosecutions, the Board of Trade, or a Chief Officer of Police, may apply to a Judge in Chambers for an Order for the production of the Company's books, papers, etc.; or to inspect the said books, etc. . . .

A failure to keep and produce adequate books is now punishable under Section 12 of the 1976 Companies Act, which replaces Sections 147 & 331 of the 1948 Companies Act. It remains to be seen, however, whether the judiciary will be less reluctant to make an order than they were in cases where applications were made under the 1948 Act. If such orders become more common they may be useful in controlling fraud, since information obtained thereby is admissible in a criminal prosecution under other sections of the Companies Acts.

This reluctance may be attributable, as Hadden (1967, p. 587) believes, to the fact that: 'the preservation of commercial secrecy is felt to be more important than the active investigation of suspected offences', but there is no clear evidence on this point. Whatever the reason, the delays which arise from obtaining counsel's opinion and from preparing legal submissions make Section 441 of little value to either the police or the Department of Trade in the control of long-firm fraud, where rapid decision-making is essential. On the rare occasions when an order is sought and made, it is almost invariably a supplement to an already strong case rather than an aid in the early stages of an investigation. The position is well summarised by an officer as follows: 'As far as we are concerned, Section 441 might as well not exist on the Statute Book.' (For some further legal problems with the use of s. 441, see *In re Racal Communications Ltd., The Times,* 4th July 1980.)

The other major pre-liquidation power exercised by the Department of Trade with respect to long-firm frauds is Section 109 of the Companies Act, 1967, which gives the Department the power to carry out inspections of the books of limited companies when they suspect that fraud has taken place. When Hadden carried out his research in the mid-1960s, he was justifiable critical of what might be generously described as the 'low profile' of the Department's Investigative Branch. Since then, however, the Department has adopted a much more proactive stance, and Section 109 inspections have been utilized extensively throughout the 1970s. Although the vast majority of such inspections relate to public limited companies, the police are encouraged by the DoT to bring any suspected long-firm frauds to their attention, so that Section 109 can be used as an investigatory tool.

I have no figures for the actual use of Section 109 against long-firm frauds, but it is almost certainly of limited value. Deficiencies of some kind in a company's books are normal, since there is always some delay in the preparation of accounts for any small or medium-sized private limited company. The complete absence of *any* records is good grounds for suspicion that a company is being fraudulently operated, however, and the absence of such records is not only an offence itself under Section 109 (4), but also may lead to the search of any other suspect premises under Section 110 of the Companies Act, 1967.

The final sting in the tail of the Department of Trade is to be found is Section 114 of the Companies Act, 1967, in which

(1) A person who, in purported compliance with a requirement imposed under S. 109 to provide an explanation or make a statement, provides or makes an explanation or statement, which

he knows to be false in a material particular or recklessly provides
or makes an explanation or statement which is so false shall be
guilty of an offence...
On conviction on indictment, to 2 years imprisonment or a fine, or
both.
On summary conviction, to 3 months imprisonment or a £200
fine, or both.

The low penalties attached to Section 114 and (prior to the
increase in 1980) to the fraudulent trading provisions of Section 332
of the Companies Act, 1948 make them less appealing to the police
than the provisions of the 'ordinary' criminal law, but they are
useful as supplementary charges, to be brought when 'ordinary'
charges seem unlikely to succeed. Section 109 investigations are
more valuable in the case of a suspected fraud which has been
trading for a long time, or where there has been a change in
ownership, than when a quick 'in–out' long-firm fraud is in operation, for in the latter case, there is rarely the time needed for the
police to liaise successfully with the Department of Trade.

Finally, there are two major constraining factors upon the
proactive policing of companies by the Department of Trade. The
first is the effect that investigations have upon the trading positions
of the companies concerned. The confidence of creditors and
shareholders is indispensable to any company, and if news that a
Section 109 investigation is under way is leaked, as if often appears
to be, this can have a catastrophic effect on such confidence. Partly
because of the rarity of investigations, the attitude is common that
'they wouldn't investigate if they hadn't done something'. Consequently, the Department must take into account the risk that their
'labelling' may in some sense 'cause' the failure of the firm
concerned.

The other major constraint is the familiar one of manpower
limitations. The extremely heavy burden of work upon the
Companies Investigation Branch ensures that they tend to act on
long-firm frauds in response to specific requests by the police, rather
than on their own initiative. Moreover, since the Department's
officers do not ordinarily cultivate informants from the 'underworld', they are unlikely to receive 'tip-offs' in the ordinary course of
events. Consequently, given the increased capacity of police
agencies to cope satisfactorily with long-firm frauds, the *pre-
liquidation* role of the Department of Trade has become that of a
back-up rather than a primary investigative agency.

The main contact that the Department of Trade has with
long-firm frauds arises out of its responsibilities *vis-à-vis* company
liquidations, which I will briefly summarize.

A private limited company proceeds along one or more of the following basic paths. It may

(1) carry on trading at a profit;
(2) wind down without being formally wound up;
(3) go into voluntary liquidation;
(4) go into compulsory liquidation.

The Department of Trade is not concerned with the first category, unless it suspects that the profit is being obtained unlawfully or that a fraudulent operation is about to commence. Into the second category fall companies which have ceased to trade but which no-one has taken the trouble to wind up formally. As Hadden (1967a, p. 501) points out,

> There is no way of finding out how many of the companies that are permitted to lapse in this way have been utilised for fraudulent purposes. For if neither the shareholders nor the creditors complain, there is no reason why the fraud should come to light at all . . . It is only where the company has not been stripped of all its property that there is some point in arranging for the official distribution of what assets there remain.

Complaints can be made to the police or to the Department of Trade whether or not a company is in liquidation. However, where a company is assetless and its directors have flown, creditors may be reluctant to pay £250 plus time costs to put a company into liquidation for no financial return. Likewise, they may not see it as their business to inform the police of any fraudulent practices committed against them. The Registrars of Companies have the power to strike defunct companies from the Register under Section 353 of the Companies Act, 1948 so long-firm frauds may become formally extinct without being wound up on the initiative of creditors or 'police'.

A long-firm fraud which is incorporated will normally be processed via either a voluntary or a compulsory liquidation, the details of which are set out in Part V of the Companies Act, 1948 as amended slightly by the Companies Act, 1967. Whether or not the company can meet all its liabilities, it may be voluntarily wound up. Regarding long-firm frauds, the following is the usual procedure.

(1) A would-be fraudster becomes aware of police interest in his firm. If he has sufficient backing, he may be able to repay all his creditors in full. If he cannot do this, he may call a meeting of his creditors and ask them to agree to a settlement of 'x' pence in the pound. If more than three-quarters of the creditors, in number and value, agree, then the winding up may be done either by a professional liquidator or even by the director himself, subject to the

approval of the creditors. In such a case, there is unlikely to be any complaint, and the matter stops there, provided that nothing overtly 'naughty' happens during the sale and distribution of the assets.

(2) Although there is no known police interest, the fraudster may follow the lines mentioned in Chapter III and get the creditors to agree to a settlement which he has planned from the outset. From the fraudster's point of view, this represents the ideal crime, since he has 'cooled the marks out' with such success that they do not even realize that they have been defrauded. Since the police do not realize this either, he is free to retire or to commence all over again, *tabula rasa*.

In many cases, firms of professional liquidators are appointed, and in all cases, the liquidator has the duty to report to the Director of Public Prosecutions any cases in which he suspects that fraud has occurred. The Director may then refer the matter to the Department of Trade or may proceed himself. In practice, Hadden (1967a, pp. 502–3) argues, this is not done, because liquidators do not see it as their job to enforce the criminal law unless it is in the financial interest of the creditors or shareholders, which it rarely is. Trade representatives have stated to me that there is now greater awareness on the part of liquidators of their responsibilities for the prosecution of fraud than there was ten years ago, but they agree overall with Hadden's general conclusion.

An additional point is worth bearing in mind here. A number of sources have suggested to me that there is a remarkable coincidence involved in the use of certain firms of liquidators by certain groups of suspected fraudsters. Whilst I have been unable to confirm these 'coincidences', any such harmony of interests between fraudsters and liquidators would help to explain the low level of reporting to the DPP. The major reason, however, has nothing to do with malpractice: it is that for the average creditor, 'a bird in the hand is worth two in the bush', and he would far rather see in his bank account a 'reasonable' percentage of the money owed to him and 'put the rest down to experience' than become embroiled in a police or DoT investigation which would 'freeze' the assets of the company for some considerable period of time.

The general inferences from a study of voluntary liquidations are that any impetus for complaints about companies is likely to come either from trade protection societies or from the police themselves, despite the fact that those agencies are now easily able to obtain the support of creditors. Also, even when cases against companies are pursued, the intent to defraud will in marginal cases be difficult to prove (compare *R.* v. *Poster Plywood Co. Ltd*, 1956). One would therefore expect a high incidence of undetected fraud among those companies with 'substantial' deficits which are voluntarily wound up, although many such cases take the form of excessive 'milking' of assets by directors rather than long-firm fraud.

The less subtle operator, or the one who desires a greater ratio of liabilities to assets, is likely to find himself faced with compulsory liquidation. In practice, the major reason for such liquidation is the inability of the company to pay its debts, although Section 222 of the Companies Act, 1948 provides for other circumstances. If a creditor owed more than £200 is not paid within three weeks of demanding payment, or if a judgement, decree or order of any court remains unsatisfied by the debtor, the creditor may apply to the High Court or any court with jurisdiction under Section 218 of the Act for the company to be wound up. If the court grants the petition, permanent civil servants in the office of the Official Receiver carry out a preliminary investigation and submit a report to the Official Receiver.

If the Official Receiver does not suspect fraud, the company is wound up and the assets realized thereby are distributed among the creditors. If he does suspect fraud, he sends on the report to the Director of Public Prosecutions and to the Insolvency Service of the Department of Trade. The High Court may then authorize the Insolvency Examiners to examine publicly anyone concerned in the management of the company (a problematic issue in itself). The provision for the public examination of such persons is rarely utilized, but as in the case of bankruptcy examinations, the transcripts of the examinations may be used as evidence *against the debtor only* in any subsequent criminal proceedings apart from those under the Theft Act, 1968.

Here again, apparent rigour of the formal procedures is counteracted by the pressure of cases on limited resources. Insolvency Examiners are supposed to deal with fourteen cases per year, but the actual figure is approximately twice that number. Consequently, cases do not receive the detailed examination that the discovery of fraud might require, and only the more blatant instances are followed up. As a measure of this, out of 7466 liquidations in 1974, of which 1385 were compulsory, only 7 prosecutions for fraudulent trading, 18 prosecutions for failing to keep proper books of account, and 1 fraud by an officer of a company in liquidation, were authorized by the Department of Trade. It cannot be inferred that a very large number of these liquidations were of fraudulent companies, but one would expect that there were more than 26 such frauds.

The other major responsibility of the Official Receiver is the supervision of bankruptcies, which is governed by the Bankruptcy Acts of 1914 and 1926, as amended by the Insolvency Act, 1976. If a civil judgement for a debt is granted and the debt is not paid in full, the creditor may petition for the bankruptcy of the debtor. Alternatively, a person may file his own petition in bankruptcy. A registrar of the High Court or the county court grants a Receiving Order, at which stage the Official Receiver's Department is called in to supervise the preparation of a sworn statement of affairs. Unless the debts of the debtor can be paid in full, or unless he can prove that the order ought not to be made, a Bankruptcy Order will be made by the court.

At present, there is a preliminary examination of every debtor by a bankruptcy examiner. The examiner first interviews the debtor and questions him about his affairs. He attempts to discover what has happened to the debts, and ascertains the reason for the 'failure' of the person concerned. The Official Receiver then holds a public examination in court at which the creditors may question the bankrupt concerning his dealings. A notable example of this occurred at the examination of an architect named John Poulson in 1973, from which many revelations about corruption in local government ensued. At present, if the debtor's replies are accepted by the court, the public examination is concluded and the bankrupt is then in a position to apply for his discharge. If the court is not satisfied that the debtor is making a full and true disclosure of his debts and dealings, the public examination is adjourned, which until the implementation of the Insolvency Act, 1976 used to have the effect of permanently denying the bankrupt his discharge. Now, however, there is a review of all cases after five years, with a view to semi-automatic discharge, although the suspicion of fraud, failure to pay creditors at least 50 pence in the pound or keep proper books of account, and a number of other factors will still militate against discharge.

One important distinction between bankruptcy and liquidation is that if a bankrupt does not appear for his public examination, a warrant for his arrest is automatically issued. In the case of a company liquidation, however, not only are public examinations less frequent, but the consequences of non-attendance are far less serious. One director can always argue that the failure was the responsibility of one of the other directors, or, if he does not turn up, the examiner may write to another director, and matters may be thereby postponed for a considerable period of time. In this way, delaying tactics are more easily employed in the case of liquidations than in bankruptcies, and it is also correspondingly easier to diffuse responsibility in the former than in the latter cases.

A major problem for bankruptcy examiners is their workload. They have a statutory responsibility to investigate all bankruptcies, but they have limited resources. Consequently, in times of recession, it is easier for a fraud to 'slip through the net' than in prosperous times, when there are few bankruptcies. The operative criterion for recognizing the existence of a long-firm fraud is that a high ratio of liabilities to assets has been built up within a short time. This is the easy way of detecting a crude type of 'bust-out'. For the more sophisticated type, however, the examiner must 'use his nose' and, in this respect, examination is a *craft*, learned on the job, and for which some individuals appear to be naturally gifted. It is acknowledged, however, that a skilful fraud, incorporating perhaps a 'good' fire or robbery, in which a substantial proportion of the debts are paid, may escape detection.

In cases where long-firm frauds *are* suspected, the examiner has two options: he can prepare a report for the Department of Trade solicitors; or, where the police are involved, he can liaise with them, and get them or the Director of Public Prosecutions to prosecute. This latter is the preferred course of action, since the police wield bigger 'sticks' in terms of the charges they can prefer, and additionally, they are more experienced in preparing prosecutions against 'villains' than are the Department of Trade solicitors. A report for the latter takes an average of twelve months to prepare and then there are further delays while the solicitors and their counsel decide what to do with the report. The involvement of the police or the DPP may delay matters still further, but this is not felt to be important. Like the Canadian Mounties, they like to 'get their man' in the end!

The importance of bankruptcy examinations in the investigation of fraud has declined greatly since the nineteenth century. More recently, in the early 1960s, they were a major force in exposing the extent of the Kray and Richardson involvement in long-firm fraud – it was bankruptcy examiners who told the police that they had a hunch that a number of frauds around that time were connected. By the mid-1960s, however, it was normal for the cleverer fraudsters to use limited companies as the vehicle for fraud, because of the lesser amount of investigation, and because of the absence of personal liability thereby entailed. This remains the case to the present.

The overall problem of policing for the Department of Trade, as for the police, is one of resources. One important resource is the law which proscribes the behaviour. Conversations with numerous officials have convinced me that if the law were worded differently, many more firms and companies could be proceeded against. The obstacles to such revision have been discussed in the previous chapter, but, as long as this situation remains, it seems likely that there will be a substantial amount of unprosecuted 'fraud'. From the point of view of personnel resources, a situation in which there are seven senior and a few hundred ordinary bankruptcy examiners for the whole country must be held inadequate to investigate the number of frauds, whether long-firm or other, which one suspects must occur. Consequently, one must hypothesize a very large 'dark figure' of undetected fraud.

When Hadden carried out his research, he was extremely critical of the wasteful overlap between the police and the Department of Trade (though he did not acknowledge its latent function of reducing the probability of corruption). The basic situation has remained unchanged since then, but the co-ordination between the agencies has much improved, so it is no longer such a problem. It does generate delays, but the duplicate investigations are not identical: frauds about which 'normal' police informants are ignorant (or are unwilling to reveal); frauds about which there have been no formal complaints to the police – these *may* be noticed by the Official Receiver. One would expect the role of the Department of Trade to be particularly important in the detection of the 'intermediate' and the 'slippery-slope' fraud, or the 'middle-class' fraudster who does not need to mix with the 'underworld'. Even if the long firm is a crude fraud, the Official Receiver may still uncover extra evidence, especially in the case of a bankruptcy rather than a liquidation. The delays involved are, however, important to the understanding of the control process, and in this context, insolvency and bankruptcy examiners experience similar frustrations to those of the police already mentioned. The experience of cases being 'sat upon', of the reluctance of everyone concerned to authorize prosecutions, of acquittals or of 'pathetic sentences being handed out by the judges': all these are universal to fraud investigators. They learn not to get involved in cases, for the consequences of getting involved are emotionally destructive. Many investigators feel that the social and legal system does not do fraudsters justice, for they escape too lightly at every stage of the process. This is a theme to which I shall return later.

The third and final major investigatory agency to deal with long-firm frauds is the Customs and Excise department. In the days of purchase tax, the more sophisticated type of long-firm fraudster would attempt to widen the gap between his buying and selling price by buying goods tax-free. To do this, three strategies were possible:

(1) the company or firm could register with HM Customs and Excise, so that it could agree to pay purchase tax at a later date. This, however, meant that the Customs and Excise would investigate the company's credentials, a risky enterprise for a long-firm merchant;

(2) the aid of a dishonest trader might be enlisted, so that his purchase-tax number might be borrowed;

(3) most crudely, a company might be formed with a name similar to that of a well-established company, and both their name and their purchase-tax number would be used. Naturally, the company or firm could not then be registered with the Registrar of Business Names or the Registrar of Companies, because it would be disallowed if too close to a pre-existing trader.

In these cases, the Customs and Excise inspectors became involved with long-firm frauds, and they were greatly feared by the underworld, because of their considerable powers of interrogation, seizure of documents, and expertise. (This fear, incidentally, extended to the ordinary business world. Many businessmen who habitually defrauded the Inland Revenue without concern at being caught or punished 'would never touch purchase-tax fraud with a barge-pole'.) In cases where long-firm fraudsters bought goods tax-free, the Customs and Excise overlapped with the police and DoT jurisdictions.

When value-added tax replaced purchase tax, considerable unease was expressed, both in the underworld and in the 'legitimate' business world, about the consequences of the change. First, on a general level, it meant that any fraud on the Inland Revenue was likely to be a fraud on the Customs and Excise also. By extension, this would apply to the long-firm fraudster, and it would also mean that the fraudster would have to decide whether or not he would register for VAT. If he did not, he might have investigators asking why he did not do so, and suppliers would assume that he was only a small venture, since all companies doing more than £15 000 turnover per annum have to register. If he did, then the Customs and Excise might require detailed records from him, and would be able to trace his transactions. In the event, it appears that the change to VAT has had a neutral impact, partly because HM Customs and Excise has become overloaded and has been unable to investigate with the degree of thoroughness that was present in the past.

My principal aims in this section of the book have been to provide a historical and contemporary account of attempts by law-enforcement agencies to control long-firm fraud; and to convey something of the organizational and cultural *ambience* in which this enforcement is sociologically located.

As I stated at the beginning, the control process can only be properly understood as part of a total feedback mechanism incorporating the organization of fraud itself: as a sort of 'cat-and-mouse' game in which each side continuously adjusts to the other's moves, as imperfectly perceived by it. On the control side, two strong impressions are of significance: first, the self-perception of control agencies as an under-staffed, under-publicized, beleaguered army of fraud-fighters, waiting despairingly for a relief army that they do not expect to come; and second, the almost universal frustration of these officials at their lack of power to 'nail' their quarry. They feel that they can usually 'knock off' the front men and the middle-rank men, but are powerless to 'put away' the 'really top men'.

Since the Second World War, and even since Hadden carried out his research in the mid-1960s, there had been a considerable strengthening of the control process, which may be attributed in part to the sensitization of agency policy-makers to 'the problem of fraud'. Some points of criticism remain, such as the length of time it takes for a complex long-firm fraud to be 'processed' through the control system, and the occasional reluctance of the Department of Trade to inform the police when they investigate a company under Section 109 of the Companies Act, 1967. These criticisms are, however, more a reflection on the paucity of investigatory resources than 'faults' of the agencies concerned.

Sometimes, too, new legislation can affect the pattern of control in an unanticipated way. For example, one side-effect of the Employment Protection Act, 1975, which makes the state liable in the last resort for redundancy payments, is that the state has become a preferential creditor in any liquidation in which any of the staff have not been fully paid off. If, as has been suggested to me, the state tends to pursue defaulters on a 'money-no-object' basis, this is likely to lead to a higher rate of reporting and prosecution of fraud than occurred prior to the passing of this Act. In many long-firm frauds, all the employees are either brought in by the fraudsters or hired as casual labour from Job Centres, so the provisions of the Act will not affect them. In other cases, however, when fraudsters take over an existing firm, the state is likely to become a creditor because of its obligation under the Employment Protection Act. Consequently, long-firm fraudsters may find themselves at risk from yet another state agency.

The present picture of enforcement is that of a number of agencies bearing down upon would-be fraudsters, co-ordinating, rather than merely duplicating, their inquiries. Although, for reasons discussed earlier, there are personal and institutional factors which limit this harmonization, it is now common, for example, for the police to ask the Department of Trade or HM Customs and Excise to 'help out' if they feel that *their* powers are appropriate to the situation, and vice versa. This informal co-operation is crucial to the whole process, and the insider may readily observe its impact by the 'incapacitation' of many of the leading figures in the world of long-firm fraud.

Notwithstanding the great improvement in control which has led to the present lull in crude long-firm frauds, the supremacy of the police is always tentative, and they often wonder who is the cat and who is the mouse. Their effectiveness is ultimately dependent upon the ability of the legal system to process their investigations and to transform them into convictions, and it is this set of 'filters' that I must now examine.

IX. Prosecution and Trial of Long-Firm Fraudsters

It was argued in the last chapter that the detection and investigation of long-firm frauds was a complex process which often necessitated the simultaneous or sequential involvement of a number of state policing agencies. The same observation may be made with respect to decisions about and the actual conduct of the prosecution of long-firm fraudsters. This process is represented in Figure 8.1. Prosecutions may be undertaken by the police, the Director of Public Prosecutions, the Department of Trade, and HM Customs and Excise.

Although I did not have the opportunity of making a detailed study of these agencies, some general remarks can be made about their policies. First, there appears to be a general consensus among all agencies that only 'rogues' should be prosecuted for business offences, and that criminal prosecution should be seen as a measure of the last rather than the first resort against 'failed' businessmen. This is a finding which is common throughout the field of the control of 'white-collar crime' (for English studies, see Carson, 1970, 1974; Gunningham, 1974; Paulus, 1974; and Leigh, 1980).

It is not uncommon, especially in times of proactive policing, for warrants to be obtained or charges laid against people for involvement in long-firm frauds *before* they have been formally interviewed. In many cases, however, the decision to prosecute is taken only *after* one or more interviews with the 'suspect' or 'suspects': this is particularly frequent in the case of bankruptcy offences. In this sense, prosecution can be regarded as a stage in the negotiation of the businessman's moral character, entailing decisions about his culpability and integrity. The co-operativeness of the individual in providing information is an important 'sign' in this process: lack of co-operation is generally perceived as an indicator of negative moral character but co-operation is not in itself sufficient to make the police regard the individual in a positive light. If investigators believe that he is 'trying to pull the wool over their eyes' and his co-operation is more apparent than real, it may be seen as an indication of the devious and 'bad' character of the businessman. This definitional process is common to crime generally (Cicourel, 1968; Werthman and Piliavin, 1967; Piliavin and Briar, 1964), but takes a different form in the case of frauds, where *mens rea* is such a problematic issue.

The decision to prosecute entails two analytically distinct processes. First, the policing agency concerned must make its own categorization of the act and actors on a dimension of seriousness, for example, 'villainous', 'bad', 'naughty', 'unfortunate'. This is done for the internal satisfaction of the officers. Second, these internally-held views must be re-translated in terms of the legal rules governing the admissibility of evidence, the criteria for evidence and the burden of proof. This second process may be called categorization-by-due-process. Together, they comprise the issue of the social production of crime rates discussed by Kitsuse and Cicourel (1963).

The tension between the process of internal categorization and categorization-by-due-process is sometimes reflected in conflicts between investigative officers and prosecuting officers. If the former feel that they 'know' that X is a 'villain', they often urge prosecution; the latter are seldom involved sufficiently to let their *private* beliefs intrude upon their perceptions of the 'convictability' of the suspects, and have to bear in mind more general considerations of public policy. Some police officers have complained that prosecutors 'take too legalistic a view' and 'get too involved in legal technicalities instead of taking note of the way the jury are going to see the case'. This reflects both the conflict between 'public' and 'private' 'knowledge' *and* the separation of the investigative role from the prosecutorial role. For the individuals who take the decision to prosecute rarely meet beforehand the people about whom they take the decisions, and this encourages investigators to regard them as 'too remote from the ground', whereas the *real* reason for the frustrations of the latter may lie in the legal rules themselves which constrain the decision to prosecute. Police officers may correctly judge that a jury might convict on the evidence presented, but judges may well adopt a formalistic view of the evidence and reject the case before it is put to a jury.

The meaning of this process is revealed when 'known fraudsters' or 'known villains' appear to be involved in the running of companies, whether as background or foreground figures. Such involvements by people regarded as 'fraudsters' are always looked upon askance by police and trade credit agencies. Yet in spite of the fact that the dealings of the individual may be following the classic pattern of long-firm fraud, the police or the Department of Trade may find that they have very limited powers to intervene under civil or criminal law.

For example, the wife of a man with numerous previous convictions for fraud purchased a substantial private limited company on credit terms. When his connection with the company was discovered, the Department of Trade suspected that a long-firm fraud was in the offing, and used their powers under Section 109 of the Companies Act, 1967 to inspect the books of account. Although they could find no evidence of irregularities, they decided to use Section 35 of the Act to ask the court to wind up the company. The ultimate twist to this case occurred when, having sacked his counsel, the 'fraudster' was told that he had no standing to appear in person to represent the company in the civil action, since his wife had written a letter earlier to disclaim his connection with the company. The company was duly wound up, but for some time, it was doubtful whether or not the action would succeed.

Although in this instance, civil remedies were sought, it provides an excellent illustration of the social production of 'crime'. Had the same manoeuvres been carried out by someone of respectable antecedents, no suspicion would have been aroused, and no action would have been taken or even contemplated. In this case, action was justified on two grounds: the 'known' moral character of the man concerned; and the great similarity between the *modus operandi* of the instant case and that of a business in connection with which he had been convicted previously. Irrespective of whether or not the firm was 'in fact' intended as a fraud, the case illustrates the way in which the superficially harmless 'intrinsic' qualities of a set of actions become translated into '*dangerous*' acts as a consequence of imputations of moral identity made upon the actor by agencies of social control. The 'dangerous offender' does not have to be incarcerated to become the object of penal action: he may be incapacitated on the outside!

In the above instance, the Department of Trade could initially only use its *civil* powers to intervene (although a prosecution is pending at the time of writing). In other cases, however, criminal prosecutions may ensue immediately. These may take two principal forms: 'normal' criminal charges, in which *mens rea* has to be proven; and 'strict liability' charges, where the process of classification is much simpler, for one does not have to assess the state of mind of the accused. For example, it is an offence for a bankrupt or someone subject to disqualification under Section 188 of the Companies Act, 1948, to take part in the management of a business without leave of the court. Further, it is an offence for a bankrupt to obtain credit of more than £50 without disclosing to the creditor his bankrupt status. However, whether the charges entail 'strict' or 'normal' liability, categorization-by-due-process cannot take place *solely* on the basis of the presumed *moral* character of the suspect. The suspect's acts must be capable of being defined convincingly as *criminal* before a judge anxious to preserve the rule of law *and* before a jury who normally will know nothing of the antecedent history of the accused.

As stated in Chapter VII, the definition of the *actus reus qua* 'crime' and the linking of the criminal intent of individuals to this *actus reus* provide formidable conceptual difficulties. These difficulties present practical problems: some cases go through a lengthy procedure at the magistrates' court and a further lengthy and expensive trial at the Crown Court, only to end at the close of the prosecution case, when the judge rules that either the act itself did not fulfil the criteria for the crime charged in the indictment or there was no case for a particular accused person to answer. In theory, this should not happen, for the resolution of these issues is the reason for the delays in bringing cases to trial that arouse the ire of some police officers and Hadden (1967a). In practice, however, it sometimes does happen. In 1981, one case was dismissed by the judge after a trial lasting 103 days.

Use of discretion in long-firm fraud prosecutions

The normal reason for the rejection of a case for prosecution by any prosecuting authority is the inadequacy of the evidence to establish a sufficient *prima facie* case to provide a reasonable prospect of conviction. Very occasionally, when police inquiries are particularly protracted, prosecutions are not undertaken because of the extreme staleness of the offence by comparison with its perceived gravity; some prosecuting authorities state that they have been castigated by judges for bringing such 'stale' cases to trial.

Informal discussions (which I have agreed not to attribute) with a number of officials from prosecuting agencies indicate that once a failed business is categorized as a 'prosecutable' long-firm fraud, prosecution is the routine practice. The only exceptions are:

(1)   where an individual has played a comparatively minor part in the fraud and his evidence as a witness is essential to establish the case against one or more of the principal culprits;

(2)   when the person who is the main culprit cannot for some reason be identified or prosecuted and it is considered that without him the prosecution of the minor offender would be evidentially difficult, oppressive or 'not in the public interest';

(3)   when there is reliable medical evidence that someone is so

seriously ill that he could not stand trial and would never be likely to be fit to be tried without the risk of gravely affecting his prospects of recovery and possibly endangering his life;

(4) when the person is outside the jurisdiction of the English courts, and either (a) he is in a country which does not have a relevant extradition treaty with England; or (b) the authorities do not consider that his offence warrants the complications and expense of obtaining an extradition order.

In some cases, potential witnesses who have committed an offence are *both* prosecuted *and* used as witnesses. In such cases, in order to forestall allegations by the defence that the witness is perjuring himself as part of a dubious 'deal' concocted behind the scenes, the usual procedure is for them to be tried and sentenced *before* giving evidence. On the other hand, it is well recognized that persons turning Queen's evidence may expect to receive lighter sentences as a consequence, and this has been approved by the Court of Appeal in 1977 (*Lowe* v. *R.*, 66 Cr. App. R. 122). In some further cases, where criminals have been sentenced to very long periods of imprisonment, cases against 'fraudsters' who were to be tried with them subsequently for long-firm frauds are not proceeded with. This occurred in both the Kray and Richardson cases, and has been justified on the grounds of avoiding unnecessary public expense (*R.* v. *Richardson* et al., 1967).

These categories are problematic, and I have been unable to expand upon the manner in which they are employed. I can add, however, that my contacts with the business and criminal 'fraternities' have revealed only one case of a non-prosecution which falls outside categories (1), (3), and (4a), that of Leslie Payne, the principal witness against the Kray gang. It appears, therefore, that the overt and conscious use of the discretion not to prosecute is probably rare in cases of long-firm fraud, though it may be much less rare with regard to other kinds of fraud.

Behind this, however, lie the consequences of the kind of corruption discussed in the previous chapter and the 'non-decision process' whereby some commercial activities fail to be considered as criminal (compare Bachrach and Baratz, 1963). If police officers do not present to prosecutors the evidence which would enable them to take the decision to prosecute, it follows that those fortunate individuals concerned will escape prosecution, at least for the moment. Similarly, if social control is so organized that some deliberate non-payers of commercial debts are able to remain outside the legal and investigative nets, those individuals too will not be prosecuted. In this sense, human and organizational processes may pre-determine the content of the decisions which prosecutors *can* make.

Many prosecutions of long-firm fraudsters are undertaken by officials of the various police authorities and the Department of Trade. Some, however, are undertaken by the Director of Public Prosecutions. The cases dealt with by the Director fall into two basic categories:

(1)   those for which he has statutory responsibility, such as prosecutions on indictment for failing to keep proper books of account and for reckless gambling by bankrupts contrary to the Bankruptcy Act, 1914 (a duty conferred by Section 165 of that Act), and proceedings involving extradition;

(2)   those referred to him by police authorities or by the Department of Trade which do not fall within category (1).

Except for those few cases which overlap with category (1), most long-firm frauds are not among those which the police are obliged to refer to the DPP under the Prosecution of Offences Regulations, 1946.

In practice, however, the Department of Trade, provincial police forces, and the Metropolitan Police refer most of the difficult and complex cases to the Director's Office. Such references may follow a number of paths, the most common ones being:

(1)   those which arise *after* a report on a fraud has been made by the investigating officers. Such reports are often very complicated, with large numbers of statements and written exhibits running into hundreds of pages. The DPP may find that the evidence is adequate for a prosecution to be instituted, or that further inquiries are necessary, or that there is no prospect of worthwhile prosecution resulting;

(2)   those cases, especially those involving the Metropolitan Police, where the practice has developed of close consultation from an early stage in the police inquiries between the DPP and the police. The latter make interim reports on their investigations, and are given advice, sometimes by counsel, on what further inquiries may have to be made.

In most cases, the final report of the police is sent by the DPP to counsel for an opinion on the case and to settle what charges should be brought. Counsel will eventually bring the prosecution on behalf of the Crown, since the restrictive practices of the Bar prevent *any* full-time professional legal advisers from conducting a case (other than their own) in court.

The period which can elapse between initial police inquiries and court hearings may vary from months to years, and Hadden (1967a, pp. 569–74) was scathing about the duplication of resources which are involved in this process. Some of these delays, however, are quite unavoidable. Hadden states that (p. 569)

> Long periods may be spent . . . in attempting to trace a suspect, or in waiting for the outcome of prior proceedings . . . and in those cases where the fraudulent operation has been completed long before a complaint is made, even the tracing of witnesses may be a matter of some difficulty.

However, he did underestimate the complexity of police investigative and arrest strategies. In cases of international fraud especially, the police often have difficulty in obtaining evidence from witnesses, who may be reluctant to become involved in a trial in far-off England, or a conspirator may be out of the country at a critical moment. In one case at the end of the 1960s, the police waited for months for the return of two principals who were abroad. Eventually, when only one had returned, they felt that they could wait no longer. The other stayed away for six years, and when he returned, he was arrested, pleaded guilty and was given a suspended prison sentence, presumably because of the 'staleness' of the offence. The point here is that there may be considerable gap between the decision to prosecute and the execution of that decision, a gap which arises from strategic considerations rather than inefficiency. It may be the case that the preparation of reports for external bodies and the duplication of decision-making organizations make for further delays, but informants suggest that these are not the *principal* causes of delay, at least in respect of long-firm frauds.

Since Hadden carried out his study, disfunctional delays have been reduced in two principal respects: first, proactive policing strategies have in most cases overcome the problem of identifying the people running the fraud; and secondly, closer co-ordination between policing and prosecuting authorities has lessened the procrastination entailed by what one might call 'decision-making by committee'.

Nevertheless, there appears to be much scope for speeding up the decison-taking process. In particular, the inability of qualified officials of the DPP, the police, and the Department of Trade to undertake prosecutions without employing unattached counsel, and the often lengthy waits for written decisions and opinions by those counsel are the source of much resentment and apparently unnecessary delay.

Pre-trial process: plea negotiation and long-firm fraud

Once a suspect is arrested and charged, he enters a new and more critical phase of the criminal justice process. Although I did not carry out any systematic study of the use of bail, it appears that in most major conspiracies, especially those involving 'gangland figures', the principal defendants were refused bail. It should be noted that my study occurred before the introduction of the Bail Act, 1976, but in many cases, the refusal of bail could still be justified on the grounds of potential interference with witnesses or the likelihood of absconding. The latter is a common strategy, both for principals and 'front men', in the hope that by the time they return, the staleness of the case will diminish the likelihood of successful prosecution or even identification by witnesses, and may effect a lesser sentence: counsel may claim that there is no longer any point in fixing a long sentence as an active deterrent.

Defendants are usually able to claim full legal aid, and because of the seriousness and complexity of the charges, they are almost invariably given Queen's Counsel to represent them. At this stage, they must make a crucial decision: whether to plead guilty or not guilty to the charges against them. To the best of my knowledge, there is only one thing that will induce a long-firm fraudster to plead guilty: the hope or expectation of a reduction in sentence. This may seem to be a truism, yet it is not so, for some offenders do experience genuine contrition for their offence, in addition to the fact that they have been caught. I have yet to meet or hear of a long-firm fraudster who genuinely feels ashamed of what he has done.

Following up this theme, there is an essential contradiction which underlies the judicial expositions of the conditions under which a plea of guilty should lead to the imposition of a lesser sentence than would have been imposed otherwise. This contradiction is nicely, though unwittingly, expressed in the Court of Appeal's ruling in the leading case of *R. v. Turner* (1970):

> Counsel must be completely free to do what is his duty, namely to give the accused the best advice he can and if need be advice in strong terms. This will often include advice that a plea of guilty, showing an element of remorse, is a mitigating factor which may well enable the Court to give a lesser sentence than would otherwise be the case...
> The judge should, subject to the one exception referred to hereafter, never indicate the sentence which he is minded to

impose. A statement that on a plea of not guilty he would impose a severer sentence is one which should never be made. This could be taken to be undue pressure on the accused, thus depriving him of that complete freedom of choice which is essential. (*R.* v. *Turner* (1970), 2 W.L.R. 1093)

It is difficult to see how it is possible to have a system in which someone can expect to be rewarded for pleading guilty *and* have a 'complete freedom of choice'. All the long-firm fraudsters I have ever met *believe* that an unsuccessful plea of not guilty will result in a heavier sentence, and some support for this view may be found in the dicta of the Court of Appeal (Criminal Division) in the case of R. v. *Staples* et al. Discussing the sentence of one defendant in a conspiracy case, the court stated:

> It was, however, in his favour that at the Central Criminal Court, he pleaded guilty. But for that, his sentence would probably have been more... The other brother... was one of those who did not plead guilty, and therefore did not, like his brother, get a reduced sentence on that account. (*R.* v. *Staples* et al. (1971). (Criminal Appeal Nos. 6510/B/70, 6618/B/70, 6706/B/70, 69/B/71, 71/B/71).

It is clear that there is an *institutionalized* expectation that a plea of guilty will lead to a reduction in sentence. In view of this, it is perhaps surprising that so few people plead guilty to long-firm fraud charges at the Central Criminal Court: 53 out of 171 people (31 per cent) in the 1948–61 period, and 54 out of 258 people (23·2 per cent) in the 1962–72 period. (15 out of 53 people charged with long-firm frauds at Manchester Crown Court between 1961 and 1971 pleaded guilty – 28·3 per cent). (These were obtained from an exhaustive survey of the court files.) These are very much lower figures than average (compare Baldwin and McConville, 1977, 1979; Home Office, 1979).

What is far less clear, however, is the extent of *direct* negotiations between prosecution, defence and judge regarding pleas of guilty in long-firm fraud cases. In some cases of which I have knowledge, defendants have been promised light sentences if they plead guilty and turn Queen's evidence against their co-conspirators. There is no evidence, however, that judges were party to these offers. In any case, it is important to distinguish between cases in which the *defendant* makes the initial approach and those in which the *prosecutor* or the *judge* does so. In long-firm fraud cases, it is usually the defendant who takes the initiative in the plea negotiations, often promising to 'grass' on the background figures. I know of no long-firm fraud prosecutions in which barristers have placed pressure on clients who assert their innocence, to induce them to plead guilty on occasions when they have reasonable chances of acquittal. Indeed, there is good probative evidence for the belief that many defendants plead *not* guilty when there seems very little likelihood of an acquittal. There is little support here, then, for the existence of plea-bargaining of the kind strikingly illustrated by Baldwin and McConville (1977).

Interviews with long-firm fraudsters indicate that two principal factors explain their reluctance to plead guilty: first, they believe that they have a good fighting chance of acquittal: approximately 17 per cent of those *charged* at the Old Bailey between 1948 and 1972 were acquitted; and secondly, long-firm fraudsters believe that in any event, they are unlikely to receive a very long sentence. This view is amply borne out by the data on sentencing presented in Chapter X. The consequence is that since the range of likely sentences is so limited, there is relatively little leverage to induce a plea of guilty. The main exception to this is a choice between a prison and a non-custodial sentence, which might prove particularly tempting for a businessman with a respectable image and/or with existing business interests which might be prejudiced by his incarceration. It is also possible that the social consequences of conviction may be greater for long-firm fraudsters than for the people in Baldwin and McConville's sample, and that therefore, the former have greater inducements to plead *not* guilty.

Despite the possibility that a plea of guilty may not make a great deal of difference to sentence, the choice of plea is often very difficult. The following illustrations provide some guide to the range of possible decisions: they are taken from actual cases.

(1) A defendant in a large conspiracy case may plead guilty if his part has been a minor one and he does not want to attract the opprobrium of the judge by participating in a lengthy and expensive trial which 'wastes the time of the court'.

(2) A 'front man' in a conspiracy trial may be offered a 'deal' by the prosecution to receive a light sentence in exchange for turning Queen's evidence, yet reject the offer because of fears that his co-defendants will 'shoot his legs off'.

(3) A criminal with a long record may expect to receive a severe sentence whether or not he pleads guilty, but none the less regards his case as so hopeless that he pleads guilty on the outside chance that the judge will give him 'one last opportunity to make good'.

(4) A criminal with a long record and a poor case may plead not guilty in the hope that he will be acquitted, even though he does not expect this result and is aware of the risk of getting a heavier sentence for pleading not guilty.

The choice of plea 'somehow emerges' from a constellation of factors: the defendant's perception of the strength of his case and the consequences of his plea – both of these mediated through his lawyers; his confidence in his barrister; and finally, the personality of the defendant himself – whether or not he is a 'fighter', whatever the odds. There is, of course, one further factor of some importance: the innocence or guilt of the accused. However, although I do not believe that every person charged in connection with a long-firm fraud is guilty, the reader should remember that the decision to prosecute a businessman for fraud is not taken lightly. Consequently, one should view the legal processing of business offenders in a different way from that of the generality of offenders, where the burden of proving *mens rea* is less great. Discussions with lawyers have led me to conclude that the choice of plea in long-firm fraud cases revolves around a more or less rational assessment of the consequences rather than around severe protestations of innocence. In other words, defendants see their plea as a highly consequential move in an unpredictable game.

Apart from the probability of an acquittal, the major element of uncertainty arises from the estimation of how much mitigation a plea of guilty will attract. The methodology adopted in Chapter X is inappropriate for this task, but it should be noted that there was only a very moderate and *inverse* relationship between plea and sentence ($r = -0.01455$). This does little more than refute the hypothesis that 'minor' fraudsters consistently plead guilty and receive light sentences while 'major' fraudsters consistently plead *not* guilty and receive heavy sentences. Furthermore, although the data were discarded from this study because the subsamples were too small to be statistically significant, the ability of plea to predict the sentence of any one judge was very erratic, and in the absence of a specific plea-bargain, it would be most unwise for any barrister to use the judge's decisions in previous long-firm fraud cases as a basis for advising his clients on their choice of plea. The most relevant conclusion here would be that it seems unlikely that a plea of guilty would reduce sentence by more than two years' imprisonment at the outside, though it might lead to the substitution of a non-custodial for a custodial sentence. Whether this risk is worthwhile depends on the defendant and on the strength of the case against him.

Trials of long-firm fraudsters

If a defendant makes an initial decision to plead not guilty, he may opt either for full committal hearings or for what is known as a voluntary bill of indictment. In the former case, the prosecution must substantiate before a magistrate that they have a *prima facie* case against each of the accused. The defence counsel may cross-examine witnesses, but need not call any witnesses for the defence. A voluntary bill of indictment means that the defendants waive their right to hear the case against them presented at the magistrates' court, and the case proceeds direct to the Crown Court. Since there are usually delays of three to twelve months between the end of committal proceedings and trial at the Old Bailey, proceedings by voluntary bill speed up the hearing of the case considerably. However, if a defendant is guilty (but wishes to plead not guilty), and if he is to be refused bail anyway, he may prefer to go through full committal hearings. This is because prisoners on remand are permitted greater privileges than convicted prisoners, and time spent in custody on remand counts as part of the sentence for the purpose of determining both remission and parole. In addition, committal proceedings delay the full trial still further and create an atmosphere of staleness around the case which defendants hope may get them a lighter sentence.

Fraud prosecutions often involve large numbers of witnesses. When evidence is agreed by prosecution and all defence counsel, it may be read out at the trial without the donor having to be present. If, however, there is any dispute, the witness must appear in person. In 1974, an attempt was made at the Old Bailey to cut down on unnecessary time and expense by holding pre-trial meetings between all counsel and the trial judge to agree on as much of the evidence as possible. These meetings have not been a notable success, partly because complex cases may be handed to the trial judge only a few days before the hearings.

The major problem appears to be the often contradictory interests of co-defendants. It was also asserted, however, that another reason for the relative lack of success was the fact that counsel are paid daily, and that this encourages them to prolong cases unduly. I am not in a position to test this interpretation, but although there does not appear to be any great shortage of 'criminal work' for Queen's Counsel, it is also true that to remain in court while relatively unimportant witnesses are giving evidence is not excessively stressful.

When the parties assemble for trial, the first task is the swearing in of a jury. This consists of a random sample of the general population who are present on the electoral register of each jurisdiction. Basically, this includes almost all persons over the age of 18 years at the time the registers are compiled other than those who are highly mobile. It should be noted that the sample of jurors which forms the jury for a fraud case is not different from that for any other type of case. The only *formal* positive qualification is that one should be able to read the oath, although there is even then no guarantee that the juror can read – he or she may simply have remembered the wording.

Before any trial, all counsel are able to receive a list of the names and addresses of *all* the empanelled jurors. At the time of my research, the jurors' occupations were also furnished, but this is no longer the case. Counsel are entitled to make inquiries regarding individuals on this list, although not to seek to approach any of them. The formal disqualifications from jury service are set out in Section 14 of the Criminal Justice Act, 1967. Those sentenced to three months' imprisonment or more (including detention or Borstal) are disqualified from jury service for ten years; those sentenced to five years' imprisonment or more are disqualified for life. There is no disqualification, however, for those currently subject to probation orders or even suspended sentences, nor for those who are on bail awaiting their own trials. In the context of long-firm frauds, the 63 persons in my sample (see Chapter X) who received non-custodial sentences would be eligible to sit as jurors immediately on another long-firm fraud trial.

On some rare occasions, extensive efforts to vet jurors in advance of trials have been made. This vetting consists of checking the jurors against the Criminal Records Register and against Criminal Intelligence files. The names of those jurors who appear in the files are then given to counsel for the Crown. It should be emphasized that this process is expensive and time-consuming, and is only employed in cases where the police feel that there is a strong likelihood of jurors being 'got at' *and* where the persons on trial are given a very high 'Public Enemy' rating. In two very major long-firm fraud trials, involving 'gangland figures', the juries were vetted in advance, and it was found that in both cases, over 20 per cent of the jurors empanelled (that is, the pool from which the actual jurors would be drawn) were named in police files. The tacit assumption made is that jurors with some *direct* association with crime are likely to adjudicate unfairly, both in absolute terms and relative to other jurors with no such *known* contacts.

Long-firm fraud trials: some observations in court
This section is based upon the author's observation of four fraud trials and his interviews with a number of lawyers. In the Central Criminal Court (the Old Bailey), the practice is for the empanelled jurors to gather at the trial court, where they are in full view of counsel and the defendants. It is here that a certain amount of 'gamesmanship' can enter the proceedings. My own direct observations, confirmed by discussions with a number of lawyers, indicate

that the address (and, formerly, occupation) of potential jurors is an important criterion in the assessment of their likely opinions. Crudely put, an address in Hampstead will be presumed to indicate trendy liberalism, one in Westminster deep conservatism, and one in a 'working-class area' such as Tottenham, Harringay or a dockland borough, cheerful disdain for the law generally. Whether or not these working hypotheses about the moral characteristics of the inhabitants of various London boroughs are correct is not sociologically relevant, but they take the form of real probabilistic expectations employed by at least some lawyers. (See Baldwin and McConville, 1979 for some hard data on factors influencing jury verdicts.)

As the jurors enter the court-room, they are searchingly scrutinized by counsel and by the defendants for 'clues' regarding their general disposition. The wearing of horn-rimmed spectacles (or indeed any kind of spectacles) immediately symbolizes The Reader. Suits and tweed jackets form the basis of categorization, depending on their quality and condition. The nature of the newspaper one carries is a major symbol of moral identity, and those who take with them a copy of the conservative middle-brow newspaper *The Daily Telegraph* are anxiously regarded by defence counsel and their clients.

After this period of great initial suspense, the Clerk of the Court reads out the names of the jurors, who must verbally indicate their presence. The manner in which the juror responds is an additional clue in the assessment of his disposition. A clear, loud 'Present' in a barking or cultured voice indicates 'Army' or 'Public School' or some kind of authoritarian/disciplined character; a challenging assertive or drawled 'Yeh' indicates 'I don't care what he's done: the best of British luck to him'.

These categorizations are by no means unique to the English jury system. They tend to occur wherever people's life-chances can be crucially affected by the decisions of others. If, for example, the system of trial in fraud cases were to change from jury trial to trial by judge alone, defendants and counsel would still attempt to assess the character and temperament of 'their' judge. Within the present English system, however, this type of prediction has relevance for a particular form of action: the decision whether or not to object to a particular juror. In other words, a defendant can presently change a juror if he objects to him, but it is barely conceivable that he could successfully object to a particular judge. (One defendant in the case of *R.* v. *Richardson* (1967), Central Criminal Court, attempted to obtain a retrial by falsely claiming that he had had acrimonious prior personal dealings with the trial judge. His claim was rejected by the judge.)

Objections to jurors can be raised under two headings. First, defendants and the prosecution can object 'for cause' to an indefinite number of jurors. The criteria for this have been the cause of much debate, but as most of this is irrelevant to long-firm fraud trials, I shall not discuss it here. Suffice it to say that no real precedent exists for American-style cross-examination of jurors except in rare cases of severe potential prejudice. (At the trial of the 'Angry Brigade terrorists' in 1972, Judge James permitted the defence to exclude all members of the Conservative Party on the grounds that their political beliefs might preclude a fair trial. At the trial of the Kray brothers for the murder of Frank Mitchell, all jurors were cross-examined because of the great publicity arising from the conviction of the Krays for other murders at an earlier trial.) The only long-firm fraud trials in which objections 'for cause' have been raised and sustained to my knowledge involved prior dealings between the juror and persons connected with the case.

The second heading under which objections to jurors can be raised is that of the well-established right of peremptory challenge, where no reason for the objection need be given. When I carried out my research, each accused was permitted seven such challenges, normally exercised through his counsel. Since then, however, the Criminal Law Act, 1977 has reduced the number to three.

The general elements of the peremptory challenge are nicely, if somewhat evasively, expressed by Mr John Platt-Mills, QC, in the following extract from the case of *R.* v. *Kray and Others* (1969), Central Criminal Court:

> the whole history of the challenge, the use of the peremptory challenge was based on the off-hand, first-hand view of the intended juror by the accused. 'I don't like the cut of his Jib' – his clothes – the way he walks – whatever it may be. I am not saying [*sic*] any case here would be because of those grounds – people's homes, their dress, the kind of company they keep – but all these can influence the accused and his counsel in making a peremptory challenge. (Trial transcript, day 1, page 43C).

The 'common-sense typifications' referred to earlier form the basis for the use of peremptory challenges in those long-firm fraud trials of which I have knowledge. The general aim of counsel is to maximize the probability of the acquittal of their clients, subject to the law and their professional codes of conduct. Part of this acquittal-maximization process is the attempt to eliminate from the jury persons who are believed to be potentially ill-disposed towards their clients. Consequently, in spite of the principle that jurors should form a representative cross-section of the community (Morris Committee on the Jury, 1965, para. 54), counsel employ the over-riding principle of acting in what they believe to be their clients' best interests.

My own observations and discussions with lawyers have led me to conclude that defence counsel generally prefer either a very 'upper crust' jury or a very 'rough' jury, avoiding wherever possible people in the middle- to upper-working class bracket. A short-haired bespectacled man in a tweed jacket, carrying a copy of *The Daily Telegraph* in his hand, is a prime candidate for peremptory challenge by the defence. *Ex hypothesi*, a man *known* to have committed four previous long-firm frauds without receiving a custodial sentence is a prime candidate for peremptory challenge by the Crown. Since *each* defendant is permitted three peremptory challenges, the number of jurors who can be objected to in this way in a conspiracy trial is large. Defendants sometimes collaborate in this process, and others will make challenges once the quota of one of them is used up.

If there are no objections to a juror by either the prosecution or the defence, the trial judge gives some estimate of the time that the trial is expected to take, and gives the juror the opportunity to justify his or her excusal on the grounds mainly of already booked holidays or extreme hardship to self or others. These grounds are very restrictively interpreted by judges, but the owner of a one-man business or a crucial and indispensable employee or manager would normally be excused duty on a long case. Since long-firm fraud cases are almost invariably expected to last at least twenty working days (the record to date is 102 working days), it is very unlikely that any jury would contain a businessman or anyone closely acquainted with commercial *mores*. In one case, however, the dangers of mis-labelling were well illustrated when the defence mistakenly permitted onto the jury a rather scruffy-looking individual who turned out to be a qualified accountant in a distinguished London firm, while objecting to a man wearing a pin-striped suit, with bowler hat and rolled umbrella, who was in fact a market porter in his 'Sunday best'.

The juror then takes the oath or affirms. In one case I witnessed, a juror stated that he could not read the oath because he had forgotten his glasses. The trial was commenced, but on the second day he admitted that he could not read at all. The entire jury was discharged, and another one sworn in.

All trials commence with an opening speech by prosecuting

counsel. At the Old Bailey, the prosecutors are full-time counsel with the title of Treasury Counsel who only prosecute and never defend cases. In the provinces, prosecutions are led by any chosen counsel attached to the circuit in question: those counsel are not exclusively prosecutors. The opening speech is the only occasion on which the jury are likely to hear an uninterrupted, rounded analysis of the conduct of the firm's business and the role of each of the defendants (albeit as seen by the Crown.) As such, it is a vital opportunity for the prosecution to generate an image of the accused within which the jurors will 'frame' subsequent data and argument.

Counsel vary widely in their styles of presentation. Prosecutors generally try to avoid aggressive presentation, lest the jury think that the defendants are being hounded: they tend to range from the leisurely-avuncular-patronizing to the sincere-talking-to-equals. Subjectively, I was always conscious of the immense social distance separating counsel from the jury and some if not all of the defendants: the Crown Court equivalent of Carlen's (1976) observations on magistrates' courts. This distance was symbolized by the very different dress and accents of the various parties, and was heightened by the general consciousness of the fact that they were at 'The Old Bailey', whose awesome historical importance was diminished only slightly by the artificially-lit bright modernity of the new courts in which long-firm fraud trials are normally held.

At the conclusion of the opening speech for the Crown, the prosecution witnesses are called in a carefully predetermined order. Each witness is first examined by Crown counsel, who studiously avoids any obvious leading of the witness. Then, each defence counsel who wishes to do so may cross-examine the witness. The general strategy appeared to be to discredit the witness's memory or integrity, subject to the underlying constraint that too obvious an attack on the integrity of the witness may lead to a successful claim by the prosecutor to introduce the criminal record of the counsel's client before the jury.

In many instances, each defence counsel makes substantially the same point in cross-examination: the only apparent distinction is that that point is made in respect of a different defendant. There is nothing improper in this, for the aim of each is to secure the acquittal of his own client, but it had the consequence that although I was actively interested in the trials I attended, I found difficulty in maintaining concentration, and it was very easy to lose the thread of the cases. This loss of grip on reality is a phenomenon confirmed by some of the defendants to whom I spoke: they sometimes wondered whether the case was truly about them.

Notwithstanding this air of unreality, however, there appears to be far less alienation of the defendants from 'the action' in long-firm fraud trials than Carlen (1976) observed in magistrates' trials. At times, there was much frenetic passing of notes from accused to solicitor to counsel and, occasionally, vice versa. (This derives from the convention that defendants employ solicitors who have the sole right to instruct counsel.) Behind the scenes, defendants often seek to advise their counsel on what line they should adopt with various witnesses, and often recommend a more hostile line of questioning than counsel actually adopt. The image in the minds of defendants seems to be that of 'point-scoring', whereas counsel act within a more measured, case-long frame. This desire of defendants to interfere constantly with the conduct of their case is a source of friction between them and their lawyers, who generally prefer to be free to 'get on with it'. This is a reflection of the belief of most lawyers that they have a 'reserved area' of professional competence, the invasion of which is only permitted in rare cases by exceptionally bright and sophisticated clients. In view of the fact that most defendants in fraud cases are represented by Queen's Counsel, this professional hubris is only to be expected, just as one would expect relatively articulate 'fraudsters' to play a more active part in their trials than those on trial in magistrates' courts.

The 'rules' of the trial 'game' are very tightly circumscribed. Witnesses, for example, are not permitted to 'go on the attack' in their 'fencing' with counsel: one witness who not unreasonably suspected that counsel was pre-structuring his questions in such a way that a 'false' picture would be created in the minds of the jury was strongly rebuked by the judge when he expounded his answers at length in an attempt to generate a different and more 'accurate' frame.

Compared with other trials for different crimes that I have witnessed, long-firm fraud trials normally lack drama: there is little scope for the kind of theatricality enjoyed by both counsel and the general public. This opinion may derive some support from the fact that the public galleries are very sparsely populated, even in the height of the tourist season when other courts are full. The few who wander into the public gallery are carefully scrutinized by defendants, defence counsel and the police. Many of them leave after a short while, to continue sight-seeing or to observe some more glamorous trial of a more comprehensible nature. Judge, jury, counsel, solicitors and defendants settle down for what they know will be a long session, and the police officer or officers who also attend sit at their desks, conscious of all the fraud investigations that they could undertake if they were back at their offices in Holborn.

Although the working day is the apparently brief period from 10.30 to 13.00 hours, and 14.05 to (normally) 16.15, it would be difficult for all concerned to concentrate for any longer period. The only dramatic breaks occur when the jury are asked to retire to the jury room while some complex point of law is being debated by counsel before the judge. These debates often occur right at the beginning of the case, when the indictment itself may be discussed and applications made for separate trials, and at the end of the case for the Crown, when counsel may argue that their clients have no case to answer and that the case should proceed no further. They also occur, however, when disputes arise over the admissibility of evidence in the trial. In one extremely dramatic trial, after lengthy argument, the judge decided to admit in evidence a tape-recording of an alleged conversation between the principal defendant (later convicted) and the Inspector at the Fraud Squad who was in charge of the investigation. The defendant himself introduced the recording in evidence, and as we listened to the tape of a telephone conversation on excellent equipment, we could barely make out the words of the officer allegedly accepting a bribe from the defendant to keep him out of the case.

The drama was heightened still further when, without in any way admitting that the conversation recorded was authentic, Treasury Counsel stated that he would proceed on the basis that the officer had acted corruptly and told the jury to disregard evidence given by him. (A police investigation later concluded that the poor quality of the recording and the possibility of its having been 'fixed' meant that there was insufficient evidence to justify the prosecution of the officer concerned.)

As the judge summed up the case, it seemed to all concerned that the conviction of all the principals was likely. However, by coincidence, the sister of one of the defendants was allegedly seen talking to a juror in the case, so the jury had to be discharged and a fresh trial ordered. Some of the defendants then alleged that the judge was biased and applied to have their case tried by a different judge: their request was refused. (I heard nothing to suggest that the judge was biased – his summing-up accurately reflected the strength of the evidence as seen by me.)

This amount of excitement is, however, a rarity in long-firm fraud trials. Normally, they appear to drag on interminably until the end of the prosecution case. Then, greater expectations are aroused by the prospective entry of the accused into the witness box. This entry, however, is far from certain. An effective cross-examination can totally shatter the fabric of the defence by revealing that the 'front man' is a mediocre puppet rather than the grand businessman he has claimed to be. Consequently, his counsel must carefully balance his assessment of the likely performance of his client 'in the box' against the suspicions that are presumed to arise in the minds of the jury when an accused does not give evidence on his own behalf. In the case discussed above, for example, the principal defendant (and two co-accused) did not go into the witness box. Instead, as he was perfectly entitled to do, he made an unsworn statement from the dock, on which he could not be cross-examined. In this way, he found a loophole in the rules of procedure, for the prosecution cannot introduce the previous convictions of a man who does not go into the witness box, even though his counsel has previously cross-examined Crown witnesses 'as to credit' (that is, impugned their integrity).

At the close of the defence cases, the prosecuting counsel sums up for the Crown, and each defence counsel in turn then makes a final speech on behalf of 'his' defendant. These defence speeches are often very repetitive and, together, they may take up two working weeks. However, each counsel has an obligation to 're-frame' the evidence so that the best possible light is cast upon the person he represents. At this stage, counsel are sometimes confronted starkly with a problem that may have been implict throughout the trial proceedings. It arises from the fact that they do not have an unfettered choice concerning the line of defence which has the best (estimated) chance of securing acquittal for their individual clients: they must negotiate the 'account' with each client himself. In some cases, the defendant chooses not to maximize his chances of acquittal, because to do so, he would have to blame either a co-accused or someone not on trial as the '*real* villain', and he has been threatened with violence if he does so. Consequently, unless counsel can persuade his client to ignore the threat, he will be unable to put forward the 'best' case for him.

In so far as my perceptions were typical, it appeared that there was an air of ritual about the closing speeches. Most jurors seemed somewhat listless during them, and I myself found it difficult to maintain interest. Some lawyers expressed the view that the final speeches were probably a 'waste of time'. I observed a marked difference in the atmosphere between the end of the closing speeches and the final stage; the judge's summing-up. The judge first reviews the law relating to the fraud, and then analyses the evidence in terms of the legal requirements of proof, corroboration, and so forth. Throughout this process, great attention is paid by everyone in court to 'clues' concerning 'what the judge is thinking'. The judge's summing-up often repeats points just made in the closing speeches by counsel, but he must be both thorough and lucid in order to forestall the success of an appeal against conviction on the grounds of an inadequate or biased summing-up (compare *R.* v. *Stock* (1961), *The Times*, 28 July 1961 with *R.* v. *Landy* (1981), 1 All E.R. 1172).

When the judge finishes, the jurors are sent out to see if they can arrive at a unanimous verdict. In only one of the three trials that I attended which went as far as a jury verdict did the jury return to ask a question of the judge, and on that occasion, it was to ask the meaning of 'estoppel', a technical term buried in the fine print of one of a hundred exhibits. Finally, the jury come back and the foreman or forewoman announces the verdict. (A critical discussion of the jury system may be found in Chapter XII.)

Acquittals in jury trials of long-firm frauds

Table 9.1 sets out some details of acquittals at the Old Bailey in *all* long-firm frauds tried between 1948 and 1972, and those tried at Manchester Crown Court between 1961 and 1971.

TABLE 9.1 Results of long-firm fraud trials

Data	Acquitted (percentage)	Convicted after not guilty plea (percentage)	Convicted after guilty plea (percentage)	Total
Old Bailey (1962–72)	16·7	62·4	20·9	100 (N = 258)
Old Bailey (1948–61)	18·7	50·3	31·0	100 (N = 171)
Manchester (1961–71)	18·9	52·8	28·3	100 (N = 53)
All frauds (Old Bailey, 1977)	23·6	29·4	47·0	100 (N = 242)

Long-firm fraudsters do not appear to do as well as those charged with fraud generally do in terms of acquittal. However, their overall acquittal rate is on a par with that of Crown Courts generally, and is greater than that found by Zander (1974) in his study of fraud and forgery cases at the Old Bailey. Comparisons with other types of crime may be slightly misleading, since (a few bankruptcy offences apart) no long-firm frauds are 'siphoned off' at the Magistrates'

Court level, as happens with most property crime. The only other relevant comparison is with Baldwin and McConville (1979, pp. 64–5) who found that two out of eight persons charged with fraud at Birmingham Crown Court were acquitted, although this hardly constitutes a large sample! However, because long-firm fraudsters are so over-optimistic in pleading not guilty, far greater proportions of them are convicted on such pleas than is usual.

Breaking down the data further, it becomes apparent that one group of alleged fraudsters does particularly well in jury trials: those 'businessman-fraudsters' *without* previous convictions. During the period 1948–61, 37·2 per cent of those without previous convictions were acquitted, compared with a mere 3·3 per cent of those who *had* been previously convicted. During the period 1962–72, 31 per cent of the 84 people *without* previous convictions were acquitted, compared with only 9·8 per cent of those *with* previous convictions.

My reading of the court depositions (and discussions with lawyers about more recent cases) gave me no reason to suspect that those who pleaded guilty did so for plea-bargaining purposes even where the prosecution had a weak case. Consequently, although Baldwin and McConville (1977) have demonstrated that many defendants who plead guilty stand a good chance of being acquitted, it seems reasonable to assume here that all those who pleaded guilty would have been convicted had they pleaded *not* guilty. On this assumption, we may note that taking the period 1948–72 overall, long-firm

TABLE 9.2 Acquittals in long-firm fraud trials at the Central Criminal Court, London

| Type of trial | Period | Number charged | | Number of defendants acquitted | | | |
| | | | | with previous convictions | | without previous convictions | |
		number	percent-age	number	percent-age	number	percent-age
Trials in which only one person was charged	1948–61	86	(100)	0	(0·0)	4	(4·7)
	1962–72	27	(100)	0	(0·0)	2	(7·4)
Trials in which more than one person was charged	1948–61	85	(100)	3	(3·5)	25[1]	(29·5)
	1962–72	231	(100)	17	(7·4)	24	(10·4)

NOTE:
1. Four of whom were involved in trials in which no co-defendant was convicted.

fraudsters have a one in six chance of acquittal. If they have *no* previous convictions, the probability of acquittal rises to one in three; if they *do* have previous convictions, the probability of acquittal falls to about one in fourteen.

When I examined the sorts of cases in which defendants were acquitted, it became apparent that these were overwhelmingly conspiracy cases. Table 9.2 indicates that very few long-firm fraud *cases* were prosecuted where the judge and jury did not regard the act as a *crime*, but that jurors sometimes dispute the prosecutor's judgement that a given individual is guilty of criminal involvement in a business which they agree is a long-firm fraud.

Are those who are acquitted 'professional criminals'?

There is no space here for an extended critique of the flaws in existing studies of the acquittal rates of so-called 'professional criminals' (see Levi, 1979, ch. 8; and Baldwin and McConville, 1977, 1979). However, it may be useful to present a brief profile of those acquitted.

Out of the forty-three people acquitted in long-firm fraud trials at the Old Bailey between 1962 and 1972, fourteen had played a minor role in frauds for which others were convicted: only two of these had previous convictions, both for very trivial offences. If we examine the criminal records of those acquitted who had been accused of playing moderately serious roles in a long-firm fraud, we note that all nine had previously been sent to prison for more than one year. Eight of them were employed in the transportation of goods either out of or within the warehouse: a role earlier stated to be associated with that of the 'minder'. The jury presumably took the view – in the absence of knowledge of their prior convictions – that none of them had guilty knowledge of the purpose of the business, and this may have been so. The other 'moderately serious' alleged role was played by a 71-year-old man with seven previous fraud convictions who had worked as a clerk for a long firm. He was one of four judge-directed acquittals, and although he had been to prison several times before, there is no evidence from my informants that he was an *éminence grise* in that or in any other fraud.

Finally, let us examine the criminal records of those acquitted of playing major roles in long-firm frauds. Two people were acquitted of turning their legitimate businesses into long-firm frauds, and eighteen were acquitted of charges of conspiracy to defraud. Of these latter, seven were alleged to have been 'fences', eight to have been 'background organizers', and three to have been 'fence-cum-organizers'.

Fourteen of the alleged major role-players had *no* previous convictions, and of those who *had* previous convictions, only two had been sent to prison for a year or more previously. If we examine the histories of my top twenty 'professional fraudsters' (see pp. 276–8), we discover that six of them have been acquitted of long-firm fraud charges at the Old Bailey or Manchester Crown Court at one time or another. Of these six, two have *never* been convicted for *any* offence. Indeed, one of them has been acquitted three times.

However, a focus on acquittals is far too narrow to enable the reader to begin to consider the 'adequacy' of the criminal justice system. Discussions with police, prosecuting officials and fraudsters indicate that 'due process' rules governing the collection of evidence and its use in court have their major effect at the stage of the *decision to prosecute* rather than at the *trial* stage. It may be that Chief Constables and the Director of Public Prosecutions are more hesitant in approving *fraud* prosecutions than lower-ranked prosecutors are with 'ordinary' crimes: the acquittal of someone with a substantial legitimate 'front' can lead to a great deal of aggravation, and senior officials are wary of putting someone's livelihood at risk unless there are very strong grounds for doing so. But clearly, if 'professional fraudsters' are able to conceal their connection with long firms by staying in the background and if police and prosecutors are far from 'prosecution happy' with regard to them, it follows that the examination of those people who are acquitted will tell us very little about whether or not 'professional long-firm fraudsters' are avoiding conviction. For prosecutorial 'second-guessing' of the reactions of judge and jury is an integral component of the processing of 'suspected criminals' through the courts, a matter largely neglected in the debate on 'professional criminals' to date.

In the past chapters, I have attempted to tease out some of the social and technical processes which underlie the labelling of some business failures as 'fraudulent' and of some individuals who take part in these operations as 'fraudsters'. *Pace* those who believe that the only criminals are those who are labelled as such, it seems that levels of policing, legal rules, and social stereotyping combine to produce an officially defined 'criminal population' which by no means comprises the entire 'real' criminal population. Many offences go unreported or unrecorded, while many offenders go unprosecuted or unconvicted. However, formal penal sanctions may only be applied to those offenders who *are* convicted by due process of law, and it is to the fate of these convicted long-firm fraudsters that I now turn.

X. Sentencing of Long-Firm Fraudsters

This credit card situation... does not speak of the sort of activity where the public screams for protection, Your Honor... I think that in the vernacular the defendant stands before you convicted of having committed a white-collar crime and... I suggest to the Court that he should be sentenced in conformity with people who have been convicted of white-collar crimes, and not... on the basis of his being Salvatore Bonnano. (Gay Talese, *Honor Thy Father*)

If the jury return a verdict of guilty, the sentencing phase begins. A police officer enters the witness box and reads out the 'antecedent history' of the defendant. Since the end of the 1960s, these antecedents have tended to be rather mundane statements about previous convictions, employment history, and family income and circumstances. However, earlier court records reveal items such as a list of 'criminal associates' and of prior 'unfortunate business experiences'. Defence counsel may then cross-examine on these facts and, if he thinks it wise, may ask about the co-operativeness of his client during questioning. (Beliefs by suspects about the impact that the police can have upon their sentences as well as on whether or not they are prosecuted influence their co-operation during investigations.) If he thinks it wise, counsel may also ask whether or not his client is regarded as the 'true' principal of the fraud.

The counsel for each defendant then makes use of his knowledge of the judge's general approach to sentencing and his instinct about the judge's attitude towards his client to marshal his speech of mitigation. In long-firm fraud trials, there are very few pleas on the grounds of 'broken homes' or 'poverty', not so much because of the social class of defendants – which in fact is rather mixed – but rather for the following reasons. First, the age of most defendants – half of those convicted at the Old Bailey between 1962 and 1972 were over 38 years old and only 5 per cent were under 25 – makes the connection between crime and family pathology rather remote. Secondly, there is no 'conventional wisdom' which enables *business* crime to be explained in terms of *social* pathology. This gives an ironic confirmation to Sutherland's critique of 'pathological' explanations of criminality on the grounds that they could not account for white-collar crime: the stereotype of the man of business as a normal, non-pathological individual affects the accounts that can be put forward on behalf of commercial criminals to mitigate blame.

However, the absence of childhood deprivation-type explanations for involvement in crime does not eliminate *all* 'social problem' factors from mitigation speeches. These remain in the form of more directly situational elements which either 'explain' the behaviour or serve as reasons for leniency in sentence. In the case of a 'slippery-slope' fraudster with no previous convictions, the 'momentary departure of my client from his normal standards of commercial propriety' may be accounted for as the consequence of family stress or 'bad influences'. Great emphasis will be laid upon the 'fact' that the case was not a 'grave' one in which a man began with the intention to defraud but rather one in which a man of unblemished reputation came to hold an over-sanguine view of his business affairs. There may be a plea for leniency on the basis that the individual has 'suffered enough' by the loss of his livelihood, and by the social disgrace of himself and his family. (These arguments are also put forward by Breed, 1979, in his plea for lighter sentencing of white-collar criminals.) Finally, further mitigating factors, such as the age of the defendant, his health, or the presence of family dependants, may be brought into play.

In trials involving conspiracies between 'professional criminals', this type of mitigation is not possible. Those principals of frauds who possess a number of previous convictions have to rely on humanitarian appeals and on 'the gravity of the offence', that is, how much money was involved. Co-defendants may plead that their role in the fraud was a minor one, or that in some degree they had been coerced by 'gangsters' into co-operation. They too may point to family circumstances or to their prior record. This type of mitigation is common to all trials, but, as we shall see, the 'criminal backgrounds' of commercial criminals may lend special force to pleas for leniency on behalf of long-firm fraudsters.

Prior criminal records of convicted long-firm fraudsters

One clue for sentencers regarding 'the kind of person' the offender before them 'is' lies in his criminal record. If he has a long record for 'serious' offences, he is likely to be regarded as a rogue: if he does not have a bad record, he may stand a better chance of being regarded as someone who is 'essentially' respectable. In reality, of course, the length of a man's criminal record may be a very poor guide to his prior involvement in crime, but sentencers are not supposed to speculate about such matters.

TABLE 10.1 Ages and number of previous convictions of long-firm fraud
principals[1] convicted at the Central Criminal Court, London,
1962–72

Number of previous convictions	Number in sample	Percentage of total sample	Average age
0	26	31·3	41·5
1	13	15·7	46·0
2	11	13·3	36·5
3	13	15·7	38·8
4	8	9·6	39·0
5	6	7·2	33·5
6	2	2·4	39·0
8	3	3·6	37·3
15	1	1·2	55·0
Total	83	100·0	40·3

NOTE:
1. The judgement of whether or not someone was a principal was based upon my
reading of the court depositions. In many cases, there are several principals, and
the major ones may not come before the court at all.

In 18 of the cases for which I had details of previous convictions, I was unable to
decide whether or not the person was a principal. These are excluded from the
breakdown of figures.

An examination of the criminal records of those persons convicted
at the Old Bailey in relation to long-firm frauds would indicate that
they are a fairly 'non-criminal' bunch of people. Half of the principals
convicted there between 1962 and 1972 had fewer than three
previous convictions (see Table 10.1) and half of the non-principals
had fewer than two previous convictions (see Table 10.2). Furthermore, the light records of the offenders below the half-way mark
cannot be explained away simply as the result of the amount of time
they have spent 'at risk' of conviction. Indeed, if we discount the
case of the 55-year-old man with 15 previous convictions, Table 10.1
indicates an almost *inverse* relationship between age and number of
previous convictions. The data do *not* follow the popular image of
'the criminal' as someone who progresses from juvenile to adult
crime, picking up an increasing number of convictions along the
way. This too may lead sentencers to regard them as different from
the general body of criminals who come before them.

One useful perspective in which criminal records can be viewed is
to examine them in relation to the time that the offender has spent

TABLE 10.2 Ages and number of previous convictions of non-principals of long-firm frauds convicted at the Central Criminal Court, London, 1962–72

Number of previous convictions	Number in sample	Percentage of total sample	Average age
0	20	25·3	37·6
1	21	26·6	34·2
2	9	11·4	42·2
3	12	15·2	33·6
4	9	11·4	41·8
5	4	5·1	46·7
6	3	3·8	33·0
10	1	1·3	42·0
Total	79	100·0	37·4

'at risk' of conviction since the age of 17. Some of the relevant data from the Old Bailey sample are as follows: 35 per cent of long-firm fraudsters convicted during the period 1948–61 had *no* previous convictions, despite having spent an average of 21·9 years at risk of conviction. A further 19 per cent had only *one* conviction, despite having spent an average of 20·7 years at risk. During the period 1962–72, 31·2 per cent of convicted *principals* had no previous convictions, despite having spent an average of 24·5 years 'at risk'. 47 per cent had less than two convictions, despite an average of 27·5 years at risk since the age of 17. During the same period, 25·3 per cent of convicted *non-principals* at the Old Bailey had no previous convictions, having spent an average of 20·6 years at risk. Over half of the non-principals had less than two convictions despite having spent an average of 18·9 years at risk since the age of 17.

Given the low probability of prosecution for any given commercial crime, it would be naive to assume that the samples had never been involved in any earlier criminal activities and were in fact a 'non-criminal' bunch of people. As Kitsuse and Cicourel (1963) point out, criminal statistics are as much indices of law enforcement as they are of criminal behaviour. In so far as this is this is true, it is true *a fortiori* in the case of long-firm frauds. As Kitsuse (1962, p. 256) has argued, 'In modern society, the socially significant differentiation of deviants from non-deviants is increasingly contingent upon circumstances of situation, place, social and personal biography, and bureaucratically organised agencies of social control.'

TABLE 10.3 Total previous prison sentences imposed upon principals and non-principals convicted for long-firm fraud at the Central Criminal Court, London, 1962–72

Total prior sentences imposed[1] (years)	Number in sample		Cumulative percentage of total sample	
	Principals	Non-principals	Principals	Non-principals
0	47	54	50·5	58·1
0–0·99	10	15	61·3	74·2
1–1·99	6	5	67·7	79·6
2–2·99	6	7	74·1	85·1
3–3·99	6	1	80·5	86·2
4–4·99	5	2	85·9	88·4
5–5·99	1	4	87·0	92·7
6–6·99	4	2	91·3	94·9
7–7·99	2	0	93·5	94·9
8–8·99	0	1	93·5	96·0
9–9·99	4	0	97·8	96·0
10–17	2	2	100·0	100·0
Total[2]	93	93	100·0	100·0

NOTES:
1. One would expected time actually served to be two-thirds of these figures.
2. There were 29 cases in which I was unable to decide whether or not the individual was a principal.

The thrust of this argument applies equally to the prior imprisonment records of those convicted of long-firm fraud. As Table 10.3 reveals, over half of principals *and* non-principals had never been to prison, and less than 10 per cent in each category had actually *served* more than five years in prison prior to their present conviction. Although there is some difference between the principals and non-principals in terms of length of prison records, it is not very great. The lightness of the prison records of principals may owe something to the predominance among them of convictions for commercial crime only: as we shall see, such convictions attract relatively light sentences as well as being hard to obtain.

Long-firm fraud sentencing in the appellate courts
The only major English work that has devoted explicit empirical attention to sentencing in fraud cases is Thomas's (1970, 1978) research on the sentencing practices of the English Court of Appeal (Criminal Division). After examining those cases dealt with on

appeal (that is, those in which barristers felt there was some chance of obtaining a reduction in sentence), Thomas (1970, p. 151) observes that

> The Court's basic policy in cases of fraud is similar to that found in the theft cases. Deterrent sentences are considered appropriate for highly organised offences, offences involving a breach of trust, and offences of a kind which is considered to be particularly prevalent... Rehabilitative measures are usually considered in the types of situations where an individualised approach is generally favoured, particularly in the cases of inadequate recidivists.

As far as the Court of Appeal is concerned, the 'individualized approach' would not then be considered appropriate in a case where a fraud was 'highly organized' unless there were exceptional mitigating circumstances. My distinction between the 'slippery-slope' fraud and the others is recognized as a basis for discrimination in sentencing, for as Thomas (1970, p. 151) states,

> It seems clear that in the context of company frauds, the Court draws a broad distinction between cases where companies are set up or acquired in the execution of a preconceived fraudulent scheme and those where the management of a company resorts to fraud in an attempt to rescue a sinking business from disaster.

This is supported by reference to a number of well-chosen cases. In one (presumably) 'slippery-slope' case, the court reduced a sentence for a fraud involving losses to creditors of £17 000 (at historic prices) from seven to four years' imprisonment, on the grounds that (*Criminal Law Review*, 1964, p. 238) 'it is...much more the case of a fool rather than a knave, a man in a moment of enthusiasm starting a business which he was quite incapable of managing'. Thomas (1970, p. 153) comments that 'sentences below this level in cases involving thousands are rarely considered appropriate except where exceptional mitigation is present'.

This is a fair summary of the approach of members of the Court of Appeal (Criminal Division) to cases of long-firm fraud. It appears from the cases cited that the 'tariff' for such planned frauds is about five years.

If we examine those judgements subsequent to Thomas's book, we see broadly similar decisions. (All cases were supplied through the generous assistance of officials of the Court of Appeal.) In the case of *R.* v. *Staples* et al., heard in 1971, the court upheld sentences of two years, twelve months and nine months, upon various defendants in a long-firm fraud involving £4300. It did not state that these sentences were too low, however, and it was clear that most of the problems in deciding on the appropriate sentence lay in balancing the previous records of the defendants against the roles they played in the fraud.

In another case, *R. v. Green, Lukover and Schallamach*, heard in 1972, the court felt it important that the appellants had been sentenced on the basis that their fraud had involved losses of some £60 000, when in fact the losses had been more like £30 000:

> though this was a long-firm fraud, it was not an exceptionally bad long-firm fraud, it was an ordinary long-firm fraud, it was a long-firm fraud which involved not £60 000 but a very much smaller sum as the deficiency suffered by the creditors and that a sentence of nine years could only be justified in the case of an exceptionally serious long-firm fraud which this was not. [Counsel] points to the fact of a report from the Prison Medical Officer showing that this man was a nervous type, and contains the doctor's impression that he is a man with little self-confidence; he is a man who has [two] previous convictions for receiving ... But although he has not got a good character, he has got no record that would justify a sentence of nine years in the circumstances of this case, but furthermore, he has shown remorse particularly with regard to the effect that his conviction has had upon his family. (Criminal Appeals Nos. 3463/A/71 3633/C/71 3703/C/71)

Of another appellant, it was said that he was much younger than the others, and that despite having a father with convictions for receiving, he himself had no previous convictions:

> he had tried hard after the bombshell about purchase tax had fallen, to repair the matter and went to Schallamach to try and get money. He had had a breakdown and indeed had been in a mental hospital, and eventually he had confessed to the Board of Trade pretty well the whole of the facts of the conspiracy except his own guilty part in it. For a young man of good character, tempted to put money into a business and advised by his father to put it in, he has lost all that investment ... (ibid.)

The court went on to reduce his sentence from five to three years, and that of the principal from nine to five years. On the facts of the matter as presented in the court's judgement, these sentences were in line with the norms elaborated by Thomas (1970). This case does, however, illustrate two general difficulties faced by sentencers, especially by Court of Appeal judges who have not had the benefit of observing at first hand the general demeanour of and the evidence against each of the persons sentenced:

(1) what was the 'true' role played by each of the accused in the fraud;

(2)   what are the criteria for establishing the 'wickedness' of the persons sentenced?

The first question is difficult enough even for the police to answer, and involves assessing the characters and competence of the appellants and those people concerned who were not convicted or who did not appeal against sentence.

On the second point, 'hidden crime' is important. For the courts are only entitled to use previous *convictions* as the criterion for prior criminality. An offender may be suspected of having been a professional backer or organizer or fence for some time previously, but this unproven fact cannot be taken into account when he is sentenced, officially at least. In this context, we may observe what Mack (1976, pp. 241–67) has depicted as the conflict between 'legal' and 'sociological' evidence.

The irony of this judgement was that the following year, the same appellant made a further appeal in respect of another case, for which he had been given a sentence of five years *consecutive* to the one he was already serving. His counsel argued that this meant that he had been given a sentence of ten years in all, which was excessive: it was out of proportion and was more than would be passed in a case involving a large number of offences committed over a period of intervening years.

His counsel further argued that there was no previous deterrent sentence operating on the mind of his client at the time of his offences, and the Court of Appeal (Criminal Division) held that in such a case,

> it was appropriate to asses first of all what is the proper sentence for each group of offences and where there is already in being a previous sentence then to have another look ... at the totality and see to what the effect of the total amount of years' imprisonment comes. (*R.* v. *Schallamach* (1973), Criminal Appeal No. 5872/B/72)

It was finally decided to make the second sentence concurrent with the first, except that the second sentence should operate from the date of its passing. The import of this is that in most circumstances, once a 'villain' has 'got away with' a crime, he is in a far better position *vis-à-vis* sentence than someone who is caught, released after a term of imprisonment, and commits a further offence. It is therefore 'better' for a fraudster to commit a number of frauds at approximately the same time than it is for him to leave any major gaps between his fraudulent activities.

The most general problem for sentencers in long-firm fraud cases arises out of the element of conspiracy involved. It often seems inequitable that any participant should be given a sentence more severe than that given to the principal organizer. If, therefore, there is any reason why the principal should be given a relatively light sentence, fairness demands that all the other sentences should be scaled down correspondingly. The principle of balance applies to the benefit of co-defendants.

A good illustration of this is *R*. v. *Caldori*, heard in 1974. Outlining the background to the case, the Court of Appeal (Criminal Division) stated that

> the learned Judge [at the Central Criminal Court] indicated that the kind of sentence customarily imposed for offences of this sort might be in the order of five years and he indicated in imposing, as he did, in this case a sentence of three years that he had knocked a lot off the sentence because of the personal problems in the case.

The Court continued, discussing the sentences in general, and stated that

> Although these persons who were before the Court and were sentenced mostly to three years imprisonment can be described as being only the supporting team, and although their parts varied between the comparatively substantial and the comparatively minor, it needs to be recognised that in a complicated scheme of this kind, all those who take part, even those who take a comparatively subordinate role, are playing a very necessary and essential part in the general scheme, and if they are caught and convicted they can expect to receive substantial terms of imprisonment.
> That being said ... the Court does feel that the minor nature of the parts they played should have been acknowledged by the learned Judge in passing sentence, and should have been reflected by a somewhat, but not very much, lower sentence than that passed upon the other members of the supporting team. (*R*. v. *Falco and Caldori* (1974), Criminal Appeal Nos. 3696/A/73, 3769/A/73)

The court cut the three-year sentences to two years. The main difficulty here appears to be the mingling of 'individualized justice' with the 'tariff' for the severity of the crime. Where single defendants are involved, the problem of parity does not arise. In the case quoted above, however, light sentences for *major* conspirators on grounds of 'individualized justice' made it unfair for the court to deal with the appellants in any other way. It should, however, be noted that there is nothing here to suggest that light sentences given to the most *minor* defendants on the basis of 'individualized justice' should have any mitigating impact on the sentences handed out to the principals. This seems to be quite consistent.

Sentencing of long-firm fraudsters: the Central Criminal Court

The work of Thomas (1970, 1978) in deducing general principles from the *rationes decidendi* of the Court of Appeal (Criminal Division) is a valuable guide to the thinking of the members of that court during the periods he studied. Tradition assumes an important role in English law, and it may be reasonable to assume that his findings are true of the court today, not least because of his systematization of the previously tacit criteria which underlay their decisions.

The important question remains, however, of the extent to which the views on sentencing held by the Court of Appeal are also held by the lower judiciary. It is beyond the scope of this study to examine the effect of elevation to the Court of Appeal on the judiciary: it may be that this change of role results in profound alterations in their sentencing decisions, making them pay explicit attention to more general criteria. For present purposes, however, suffice it to say that although all Court of Appeal judges are derived from the 'stock' of other judges, the traffic is strictly one-way: judges do not leave the Court of Appeal to return to the 'ordinary' bench. Consequently, both the communication 'downwards' of principles of sentencing and the use made of them by judges in the lower courts remain problematic.

Discretion in sentencing is greatly valued by judges, and has survived without much difficulty the concern of many criminologists with disparities in sentencing. Although my study has not sought to achieve the methodological rigour of the work of Hood (1962, 1972) and Hogarth (1971), it does provide data on the degree of correspondence between the decisions of the Court of Appeal and those of the judges at the Central Criminal Court (the Old Bailey) between 1962 and 1972, and examines some hypotheses about factors influencing sentencing *at that time*. Since then, the use of Thomas's book by many judges as a guide to sentencing may have affected their dispositions: a tribute to their search for consistency and fairness.

The Clerk at the Central Criminal Court generously gave the author full access to court records for the period studied. Having first excluded all cases which did not, from the charges made, appear to involve fraud, I examined each fraud file and further excluded each case which did not fall within the definition of long-firm fraud. The cases analysed here comprise *all* long-firm frauds tried between 1962 and 1972, and are not a sample in the normal sense of that word.

A comprehensive study of the factors influencing sentence would entail the assessment of the impact on the judge of the conduct of witnesses and defendants during the trial and also the mitigation speeches by defence counsel. The retrospective nature of this study made that impossible, and my inferences should not be accepted without reservation. However, the data are the best that could be obtained from the court files and they do permit the falsification of some sentencing hypotheses in regard to long-firm fraud.

Sentencing data 1962–72

The sentences imposed on long-firm fraudsters during this period ranged over almost the complete spectrum of possible sentences. Either alone or in combination, they included imprisonment, suspended sentences of imprisonment, probation, fines, conditional discharges and binding-over orders.

Counting all sentences except immediate imprisonment as 0, the most common sentence did not involve imprisonment at all; the average sentence was seventeen months' imprisonment; and half the fraudsters sentenced were given less than fifteen months' imprisonment. Half the fraudsters in the study were involved in frauds which netted over £19 000, one-quarter in those which took £40 000 or more, and 7·15 per cent (16 people) were involved in frauds which obtained over £130 000 in goods. It should be noted that the sums given here represent nominal values which have not been adjusted to account for inflation: the *real* sums at contemporary prices would be treble this. Yet in a mere 18 out of 215 cases was the sentence four years' or more imprisonment. There is thus a clear gap between the sentences imposed at the Old Bailey and Thomas's deduction from appellate cases that 'sentences below [four years] in cases involving thousands are rarely considered appropriate except where exceptional mitigation is present'.

My data suggest the converse. Indeed, in no less than 63 cases (29·2 per cent), mitigation presumably was considered so exceptional that no sentence of immediate imprisonment was imposed. Two people were bound over for three years; three were conditionally discharged for three years and another for twelve months; one person was put on probation for three years and another for two years; 24 people were fined (only one by more than £300); and 31 people were given suspended sentences of imprisonment. The maximum prison sentence imposed was nine years, but it is clear from the distribution of sentences in Table 10.4 that the majority of long-firm fraudsters do not appear to be regarded as 'serious villains' by the judges at the Central Criminal Court.

TABLE 10·4 Sentences imposed upon all long-firm fraudsters convicted at the Central Criminal Court, London, between 1962 and 1972 in relation to long-firm fraud[1]

Sentence (months)	Percentage on whom sentence was imposed (percentage)	Cumulative percentage	Number of persons	Percentage with previous convictions (percentage)	Percentage who had been sent to prison before (percentage)
0	29·3	29·3	63	58·0	19·0
6	2·3	31·6	5	25·0	0·0
9	7·4	39·1	16	66·7	43·8
12	9·3	48·4	20	81·3	35·0
15	5·1	53·5	11	100·0	54·5
18	12·6	66·0	27	66·7	44·4
21	2·8	68·8	6	100·0	50·0
24	13·0	81·9	28	80·0	60·7
27	0·9	82·8	2	100·0	100·0
30	3·7	86·5	8	100·0	87·5
36	5·1	91·6	11	90·0	63·6
48	3·7	95·3	8	83·3	87·5
60	2·8	98·1	6	83·3	83·3
72	0·5	98·6	1	0·0	0·0
84	0·5	99·1	1	100·0	100·0
96	0·5	99·5	1	100·0	0·0
108	0·5	100·0	1	100·0	100·0

NOTE:

1. There were 215 long-firm fraudsters convicted at the Old Bailey during this period.

Suspended sentence and long-firm frauds

The statutory basis for suspending sentences has changed since the period studied here. Section 20 of the Powers of Criminal Courts Act, 1973 specifies that custodial terms of imprisonment should be avoided where possible in the case of an adult first offender, and in principle, at least, there has been some degree of official encouragement to the judiciary to relieve pressure on prisons by making use of non-custodial alternatives to imprisonment. Nevertheless, the basic principles underlying the use of the suspended sentence have changed little since the measure was introduced in 1967. They are outlined by Thomas (1970, pp. 227–8) as follows:

> The trial court...must consider whether an individualised measure such as probation is appropriate and if it decides in favour of the tariff it must determine the length of the sentence in accordance with normal tariff principles; the sentence should reflect the gravity of the offence subject to allowance for mitigation. If, at the conclusion of this process, the sentence is not more than two years imprisonment, the question of suspension arises.
> ...It appears that the process is essentially one of eliminating cases where the sentence must be ordered to take effect immediately, rather than looking for positive factors justifying suspension...long before the question of suspension has been reached the court considered and rejected the claims of the offender in positive terms to individualised treatment.

Thomas states that for a sentence to be suspended, the offender should not normally have undergone a previous sentence of imprisonment in the relatively recent past, although the absence of previous convictions is not so important. He adds (pp. 229–30) that

> The Court [of Appeal] has refused to order suspension of a sentence passed for what amounted to a series of offences rather than an individual one; in cases where the offence exhibits a degree of careful premeditation, or where the offence amounts to a serious breach of trust. *The Court is also reluctant to order suspension where the length of the term of imprisonment imposed already makes substantial allowance for the mitigating factors which are urged as a basis for suspension....* The kind of offender left at the end of this process of elimination is typically a man of good character, possibly with one or two minor convictions, who is not considered a suitable person for probation, and who has committed a more or less isolated offence of a moderately serious nature. [my italic]

The policies of the Court of Appeal have changed somewhat since this was written (compare Thomas, 1978), but since the criteria laid down in the court decisions from which Thomas made his deductions were the relevant guidelines for trial courts to follow in *my* period of study, I have left Thomas's early work as it stands.

It seems clear *prima facie* that long-firm fraudsters would be extremely unlikely to receive suspended sentences on the basis of the criteria set out by the Court of Appeal. However, if we examine the decisions of judges at the Central Criminal Court, we note that almost 30 per cent of all those sentenced for long-firm frauds between 1967 and 1972 received suspended sentences. Analysing the cases in detail, it seems that suspended sentences were used for two main 'types' of offender: first, those who were relatively minor co-accused in 'organized conspiracy cases'; and second, those who were the principals of frauds other than 'organized conspiracies' and had no more than one previous conviction.

Although one might have expected that suspended sentences would be most commonly used for first offenders, the data show only a slight trend in that direction. First offenders comprise 38·7 per cent of those given suspended terms of imprisonment, compared with 26·7 per cent of the sample as a whole. If we combine this figure with those who had only one previous conviction, we arrive at a proportion of 58 per cent of those given suspended sentences, whereas 48·3 per cent of the sample a whole had fewer than two convictions. 29 per cent of those given suspended sentences had more than three previous convictions, and 10 per cent had more than twenty of them. In brief, the use of suspended sentences against long-firm fraudsters fits rather badly against Thomas's model.

If we take the prior imprisonment of those given suspended sentences as our baseline, there still remains a gap between appellate decisions and those of the Old Bailey judges. No fewer than eight out of the thirty-one people given suspended sentences had been to prison before, for periods of up to eleven years – 25·8 per cent in all. In only two of these eight cases were the people clearly identifiable as 'front men', and the most likely 'explanation' for the suspension of their sentences is that the judge's desire for retribution and deterrence had already been satisfied by sending a co-defendant to prison.

On closer analysis, it appears that those cases in which people who had already been to prison were given suspended sentences could be justified as 'special cases'. One man had only just finished a 9-month sentence for long-firm fraud when he was charged and convicted in connection with another fraud, which he had committed *before* his previous sentence. In a similar case, in 1969, two men had edged out the previous owner from an old-established business and, in three months, they ran the company into liquidation with a deficit of £56 000. One of the men was then given a three-year sentence for another long-firm fraud, and on his release, they were both charged with conspiracy to defraud. The other person had a number of previous convictions, but his last prison sentence and conviction was in 1943. Although this was a clear case of a planned and profitable fraud, the sentences were suspended, presumably because the fraud had occurred before the 1969 prison sentence had been imposed. However, both defendants may be deemed fortunate in 'getting away' with a fraud of this nature, especially since presumably, the man sentenced to three years had received that sentence on the basis of only *one* fraud.

Other 'special cases' involved a man with a prison record totalling eleven years who ran a long-firm fraud which netted £19 000 – he was given a suspended sentence, fined £400, and disqualified from taking part in the management of a company for five years, probably because he had settled down in a steady job since the fraud; and a 'fence' with previous prison sentences for theft and receiving, who had carried out a £7000 long-firm fraud – here, the apparent grounds were his age, for he was 60 years old. It should be noted, however, that all of these 'special cases' were well planned and organized frauds, and one might query whether the same generosity would have been extended to those committing 'normal thefts' for the same amount of money.

If we look at those cases in which the persons had *not* been given a prison sentence previously, some appear to fall well outside the guidelines given by the Court of Appeal. The following examples may illustrate the point.

In 1959, one of the two defendants began a textiles company, which was run semi-respectably until 1967, when it was turned into a sophisticated long-firm operation and finally was wound up with a deficiency of £63 000. Although neither of the co-directors had been to prison before, and they each had only one conviction, the person mentioned above had had a previous liquidation involving some £23 000. In any event, there was little apparent reason why he should have been given a twelve-month sentence suspended for two years and disqualified from taking part in the management of a company for a mere two years. (The co-director was conditionally discharged on the lesser offence of failing to keep proper books of account – they both changed their pleas to guilty after their trial had gone on for seven days.)

In another case, two men ran a company which defrauded both customers who paid deposits on freezers and the suppliers of freezers and frozen goods. They went into liquidation with a deficiency of £100 000. Neither of the men had many previous convictions, and neither of them had been to prison before, but it seems surprising, nevertheless, that they should have been sentenced to twenty-one months' imprisonment suspended for two years, fined £500, and ordered to pay £500 costs towards their defence.

Some of those given suspended sentences of imprisonment were minor associates of the Kray and Richardson gangs. Indeed, two of them had attempted earlier to obtain acquittals by pleading that they had taken part in the frauds only under duress, while a further one said this in mitigation. Despite this, however, no-one given a suspended sentence we a 'major villain' in the conventional sense of that term, although three of them had had a number of 'unfortunate' prior business experiences, to take a charitable view. This leads me to a problem connected with the implementation of the criteria for suspending sentences laid down by the Court of Appeal.

I stated earlier that many people who commit long-firm frauds are not prosecuted or detected. I have just demonstrated that many long-firm fraudsters are not given prison sentences even when convicted. It follows that if one adopts the 'previous imprisonment' criterion laid down by the Court of Appeal, many fraudsters who have escaped legal or social definition as 'villains' in the past may be eligible for a suspended sentence when eventually they are convicted. Although no court is *obliged* to give a first offender a non-custodial sentence, there is increasing social pressure in that direction, and one might expect that, other things being equal, business criminals are in a good position to benefit from the 'trend away from punishment' that Sutherland (1961, p. 136) identified as one reason why white-collar criminals were not treated as 'real' criminals. This view is given some support by Leigh's analysis of sentencing in what he terms 'minor' bankruptcy frauds, in which he concludes that such fraudsters generally receive suspended sentences in the Crown Court and fines in Magistrates' Courts (Leigh, 1980). Indeed, recent Old Bailey cases show that overcrowded prisons have become the justification for fining offenders who otherwise might have been imprisoned (R. v. Bhasker and Ramji, The Daily Telegraph, 20 March 1981).

In conclusion, one 'low-level' inference that could be made about the use of the suspended sentence in long-firm fraud cases is that it occurred when judges felt either that retribution was not required or that individual rather than general deterrence was appropriate and could be adequately assured by the passing of a non-custodial sentence. In a number of cases, an attempt at incapacitation without incarceration was made by the use of Section 188 of the Companies Act, 1948 to disqualify fraudsters from participation in the management of companies. The use of Section 188 did not vary with the length of sentence imposed, however, as Table 10.5 indicates.

Sentencing in conspiracy cases

The data presented hitherto provide ample evidence for the view that many long-firm fraudsters are treated on a light 'tariff' or on 'individualized justice' criteria. One might seek to account for this

TABLE 10.5 Use of the suspended sentence in long-firm fraud trials at the Central Criminal Court, London, 1967–72

Length of sentence (months)	Number of persons sentenced[1]
6	1
9	5 (2 of whom had S. 188 orders in addition)
12	7 (5 of whom had S. 188 orders, of whom 2 also had costs awarded against them)
15	2
15	3 (1 of whom was given a S. 188 order)
18	3 (2 of whom were fined £250 plus costs, and 2 of whom were fined £500)
24	9 (1 with S. 188 order alone; 1 with S. 188 order plus fine; 1 with S. 188 order plus fine plus costs)

NOTE:

1. A total of 31 persons were given suspended sentences in long-firm fraud trials at the Old Bailey during this period.

by stating that those persons either fit the stereotype of the 'white-collar criminal' or, as Leigh (1977b, 1980) concluded, are perceived by sentencers as 'minor' offenders. One hypothesis that might be put forward is that although *some* offenders may be treated 'leniently', the principal organizers of 'professional frauds' would be sentenced on a 'deterrence tariff' as 'professional thieves'.

In an effort to test this, sentencing in *conspiracy* cases was analysed. Although a reading of the depositions convinced me that many single-defendant cases were in fact conspiracy cases, the definition adopted excluded these. In order for a case to count as an organized conspiracy, two conditions had to be met: first, three or more people had to be *convicted* for the offence; *and*, second, a reading of the court depositions had to produce clear indications of a well-organized conspiracy. The use of this somewhat restrictive definition avoids the pitfalls of overstating the number of 'serious conspiracies': a problem lucidly analysed in one critique of 'organized crime studies' (Morris and Hawkins, 1970, ch. 8).

In *no* conspiracy case was every defendant given the same sentence. The range of sentences varied from twelve months' imprisonment to a non-custodial sentence in the 'lightest' case, to the 'heaviest' case, where they varied from nine *years'* imprisonment to a non-custodial sentence. The indications are that there would be still more variation in the sentencing of co-conspirators if the 'top' sentences were higher.

Thomas (1970, p. 153) suggests that there is a tariff' of five years' imprisonment for highly organized frauds. This hypothesis is tested against the sentences imposed on the *principals* in conspiracy cases, which are listed in descending order in Table 10.6. If we include the persons of both principals in those cases where there are two, but do not double-count the money involved in their frauds, we arrive at a

TABLE 10.6 Sentencing of principals in highly organized long-firm frauds at the Central Criminal Court, London, 1962–72

Sentence (years)	Amount taken (pounds)	Previous prison served (months)	
9	200 000	94	(Joint principals)
8	200 000	0	
7	42 800	192	
5	190 000	81	
5	8000	84	
4	8300	75	
4	6500	117	
4	2650	0	
2½	85 000	36	
2½	6000	0	
2¼	14 000	64	
2	27 000	9	(Joint principals)
2	27 000	8	
2	16 000	0	
2	8800	48	(Joint principals)
2	8800	28	
2	3500	36	
1½	40 000	36	
1½	30 000	117	(Joint principals)
1½	30 000	33	
1½	25 000	0	
1½	24 000	48	
1½	10 000	57	(Joint principals)
1½	10 000	0	
1½	2500	0	
1	16 000	0	
1	8000	0	(Joint principals)
1	8000	0	

mean figure for the amount at stake of £26 691, and a median figure of £16 000. (Sums are calculated at historic prices, so they must be inflated.) If we take all the sentences together, we find that the average sentence is 2·82 years, 50 per cent of principals are sentenced to no more than two years, and the most commonly occurring sentence is eighteen months. All these figures are well below the 'tariff norm' found in Court of Appeal cases, and it should be remembered that that court ordered a sentence of five years for the organizer of a £30 000 long-firm fraud who had only two minor convictions for receiving and had never been to prison before (*R. v. Schallamach* (1973), op. cit. – sentence reduced from nine years). Indeed, the sentence was five years or more for only five out of the twenty-nine principals in the foregoing sample, and frauds involving £85 000, £40 000 and £30 000 attracted sentences of thirty months, eighteen months and eighteen months respectively. None of the principals involved in these three frauds had served less than thirty-three months' imprisonment before their present sentence. One is therefore driven to conclude, either (i) that the judges at the Central Criminal Court are either ignorant of, or disregard, or interpret differently the view of the Court of Appeal that deterrent sentences are called for in cases of highly organized deliberate frauds, or (ii) that when the Court of Appeal is asked to make a *declaratory* judgement in cases where a man appeals against an inflated sentence, *it* is ignorant of the general level of sentencing in the courts. In this context, it is important to realize that Thomas's work derives only from those relatively few cases whose appeals reach the final stage of decision by the Court of Appeal.

It is clear from these data that although the principals of organized conspiracies are sentenced more harshly than their co-defendants and 'non-conspirators', they are not sentenced on the basis that they are 'professional thieves'.

Relationship between 'the tariff' and the sentencing of long-firm fraudsters

Hogarth (1971), Hood (1962, 1972), and Thomas (1970) discuss at length the importance of sentencing tariffs, and it was considered worthwhile to examine the data in this chapter in order to see if there were any strong relationships between tariff elements and sentences.

One may break down 'the tariff' into three major components:

(1) the 'seriousness' of the offence and the degree of responsibility/ culpability of the offender;

(2) mitigating factors relating to the previous record of the offender;

(3) mitigating factors of a different nature.

Given the constraints of a documentary study, some fairly crude measures of these components were devised. The first element was measured by two variables: the amount of money involved in the fraud and whether or not the person was a principal in it. The second was measured by three variables: number of previous convictions, number of previous *fraud* convictions and total previous prison sentences imposed. The third component of the tariff was measured by two variables: age of the offender and plea of guilty/not guilty.

Although these measures are neither comprehensive nor ideal, they do at least provide some basis against which sentencing can be evaluated, for although a strong relationship between any one variable and sentence is not proof of any causal influence, the absence of any such relationship indicates that the variable has a relatively minor causal influence. Bearing this in mind, Table 10.7 below presents the results of a three-step multiple regression analysis which was carried out on the data as a whole, in an attempt to 'explain' the variations in sentence noted earlier this chapter.

TABLE 10.7 Predictors of sentencing variations in long-firm fraud cases

Variable	Percentage of sentencing variations accounted for by variable[1]
Principal in fraud	7·595
Total prison sentences imposed previously	9·153
Plea	0·848
Age	0·766
Number of previous fraud convictions	3·348
Number of previous convictions	0·247
Amount of money defrauded	15·310
Total	37·418

NOTE:
1. derived from r^2 change figures (see statistical Appendix B).

It is not possible to make any causal inferences from these figures alone, but it appears that component (1) in the 'tariff' is the best predictor of sentence: the amount of money defrauded and the fact of being a principal together predict 22·9 per cent of variations in sentence. Component (2) of the 'tariff' was far less significant, accounting for only 12·7 per cent of variations in sentence; and component (3) was the least important, being able to 'explain' a mere 1·6 per cent of sentence variations. All the variables taken together could account for only 37·4 per cent of the variations in sentence, and this suggests that long-firm fraudsters are not sentenced consistently on the basis of any form of 'tariff'.

The statistical analysis was supplemented with interviews with two judges who were kind enough to discuss sentencing with me. These discussions confirmed the inferences drawn from the data analysis that 'human' factors other than the 'objective' variables used in that analysis played the most important role in sentencing. It was stated that three factors 'explained' the relative leniency of sentences: the absence of violence, the comparative affluence of the victims and the carelessness of some of them in failing to make proper credit inquiries before supplying the goods. Much account was also taken of special personal mitigating circumstances, something that could not be allowed for in my analysis: in this sense, it may be said that considerations of 'individualized justice' are prominent in the sentencing of long-firm fraudsters.

This is illustrated by the following case. The principal defendant in a major organized long-firm fraud had been in prison more or less continuously in the decade before the offence for which he was to be sentenced. Although the man was eligible for an extended sentence, and although his record gave no evidence of any great desire for reformation, the judge sentenced him to five years' imprisonment – a lighter sentence than he had received on his previous conviction.

The reasons given for this *relative* leniency were first, humanitarian – no human being should have to serve a number of long sentences more or less unbroken unless there is a 'serious' and tangible danger to the public; and secondly, humanitarian/reformative – the man was in his late fifties, and the judge felt that unless he was given one last chance to reform, he might well spend the rest of his life in crime or in prison.

Even though the judge believed that the principal and some of his co-defendants 'deserved' harsher sentences, five years was his psychological limit in *this* case. Having given the principal architect of the fraud that sentence, equity demanded that the sentences of the others be scaled down in accordance with the roles they played in the fraud. In so far as this decision-making process is typical, it is perhaps not surprising, though still interesting, that 'tariff' elements could not explain a large proportion of variations in sentences.

This does, however, raise an interesting conceptual problem in the notion of 'equitable sentencing'. For if someone who is not a principal is given a lighter sentence than he would have received had he been sentenced alone, the grounds being those of equity between co-defendants, is this not itself inequitable? For a person similar in all other respects save that he was sentenced alone might have good reason to feel that he had been unfairly treated. As a final point in this section, it should be noted that this type of distinction would not show up on the variables used here, and consequently, such a case would be thrown up by my statistical analysis as an example of inconsistent sentencing.

Some additional aspects of sentencing in fraud cases

In addition to the normal powers of the courts, two further penalties may be imposed upon long-firm fraudsters. One of these is the Criminal Bankruptcy Order, discussed in Chapter XII, which is excluded here because it did not come into existence until 1973. The other is the power granted under Section 188 of the Companies Act, 1948 that in the case of persons convicted of fraud in relation to the management of companies,

> the court may make an order that the person shall not, without leave of the court, be a director of or in any way, whether directly or indirectly, be concerned or take part in the management of a company for such period not exceeding five years as may be specified in the order. (Note: The Companies (No. 2) Bill 1981 recommends that this maximum be raised to fifteen years.)

It should be noted that this ban applies from the date of sentence, and not from the date of release into the community. The first order under Section 188 against a long-firm fraudster at the Old Bailey was made in 1951. During the period 1951–61, such orders were made in 27 out of 122 cases: 22·1 per cent. There were 20 five-year orders, 1 four-year, 4 three-year and 2 two-year orders made. Only one person given a non-custodial sentence was made subject to a Section 188 order, and he was fined £1000 in addition to the five-year ban.

During the period 1962–72, Section 188 orders were made in 39 out of 215 cases: 18·1 per cent. Orders for five years were given in 14 cases in which imprisonment was imposed, 8 cases involving only suspended sentences, 4 further cases involving *both* suspended sentences *and* either fines or costs, and 2 cases in which offenders were fined. Four-year orders were made in 2 cases, one involving a suspended sentence and the other a fine. Three-year orders were made in eight cases, including for prison sentences, two suspended sentences, one fine and one conditional discharge. Finally, one two-year order was made upon a person given a suspended sentence. In all cases where S. 188 orders were made, they were made upon the principals of long-firm frauds, and appear to have been intended as additional weapons in the armoury of individual deterrence, although the maximum sentence for violation is two years imprisonment and a £500 fine for conviction on indictment. In many cases, however, the principals of frauds were not made subject to a S. 188 order, and one is left without any clear indication regarding what criteria inform its use or relative lack of use. For example, does one take the absence of a S. 188 order as an indication of the judge's belief that the individual concerned should *not* be discouraged from taking part in the management of a company? This must remain a matter merely for speculation at present.

The sentencing of long-firm fraudsters at the London Central Criminal Court, 1948–1961

The sentences imposed upon all long-firm fraudsters convicted during this period are set out in Table 10. 8. The average sentence was 18·8 months imprisonment. One quarter of the sample were sentenced to 12 months imprisonment or less, half were sentenced to 18 months or less, and three quarters to 30 months imprisonment or less. In contrast with the 1962–1972 period, in which the most common sentence was a non-custodial one, the most common sentence between 1948 and 1961 was that of 12 months imprisonment.

None of the 10 people given non-custodial sentences had been to prison before, and only 2 had previous convictions. Three of them were conditionally discharged; one placed on probation for three years; one person was fined £75, two were fined £250, one fined £500, one £600 plus costs, and one person was fined £1000. Just over 7 per cent of the sample were given non-custodial sentences, in contrast with the 29·3 per cent of people convicted between 1962 and 1972 who were given non-custodial sentences. The percentage of people sentenced to six months' or less imprisonment is almost identical in the two periods, however, and this indicates the replacement of short prison sentences by non-custodial ones – a change that is probably connected with the introduction in 1967 of the suspended sentence.

Table 10.8 reveals no clear and consistent association between sentence and the number of previous convictions, but there is a general tendency for those given severe sentences to have been convicted and sent to prison previously. The general pattern of sentencing in the 1948–61 period follows a more normal distribution than is found in the later period, a fact that may reflect the increasing tendency of trials to include a number of co-defendants and a correspondingly greater differentiation is sentences.

Finally, it should be noted that five women were convicted of long-firm fraud during this period, compared with only two women in the 1962–72 period. Three of them had no previous convictions, two of whom were conditionally discharged and one given a £75 fine; one had 15 convictions for soliciting, and was sentenced to twelve months' imprisonment; and one had two convictions for fraud and was sentenced to two years' imprisonment. The two women convicted in the 1962–72 period were given probation and a suspended sentence respectively.

TABLE 10.8 Sentences imposed upon all long-firm fraudsters convicted at the Central Criminal Court, London, 1948–61

Sentences (months)	Percentage on whom sentence was imposed	Cumulative percentage	Number of persons	Percentage with previous convictions	Percentage who had been to prison before
0	7·2	7·2	10	20·0	0·0
3	2·2	9·4	3	0·0	0·0
6	4·3	13·7	6	33·3	33·3
9	10·1	23·8	14	50·0	28·5
12	15·8	39·6	22	45·5	27·3
15	8·6	48·2	12	91·7	75·0
18	11·5	59·7	16	68·7	43·7
21	3·6	63·3	5	80·0	60·0
24	11·5	74·8	16	75·0	62·5
30	3·6	78·4	5	60·0	60·0
36	10·1	88·5	14	64·3	57·1
48	6·5	95·0	9	100·0	88·9
60	2·2	97·2	3	100·0	100·0
72	1·4	98·6	2	0·0	0·0
84	1·4	100·0	2	100·0	100·0
Totals	100·0	100·0	139[1]	100·0	100·0

NOTE:

1. In addition, one person with a previous conviction for long-firm fraud was held on arraignment to be insane, and was sentenced to be detained at Her Majesty's pleasure.

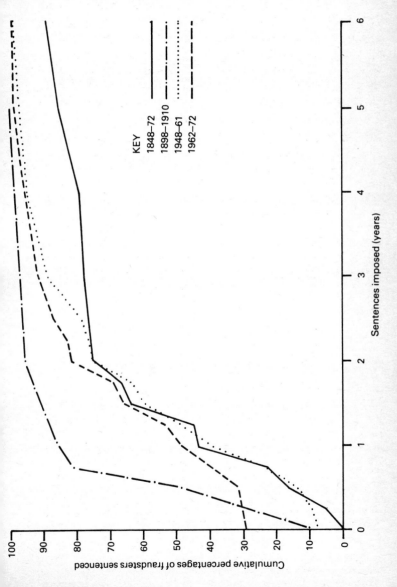

Figure 10.1 A historical comparison of sentences imposed upon all long-firm fraudsters convicted at the Central Criminal Court, London, during the periods: 1848–72, 1898–1910, 1948–61 and 1962–72.

The sentencing of long-firm fraudsters at the London Central Criminal Court: a comparative historical analysis

The main thrust of this chapter has been to demonstrate that most long-firm fraudsters are sentenced as if they were errant business-men rather than arrant knaves. It is interesting to examine whether or not this has always been the case, and Figure 10.1 and Table 10.9 bring together some core data relating to this question. The 1898–1910 period stands out as a very lenient time for long-firm fraudsters, but even if one excludes this period from the analysis on the grounds that there were relatively few cases then, Table 10.9 provides evidence of only a slight trend towards lighter sentences over the last century, principally in the form of a 'take-off' of non-custodial sentences in the 1962–1972 period.

TABLE 10.9 A historical comparison of sentences imposed upon long-firm fraudsters at the Central Criminal Court, London

Period	1848–1872	1898–1910	1948–1961	1962–1972
Number sentenced	80	21	139	215
Proportion given non-custodial sentences	0	9·5	7·2	29·3
Average sentence (months)	31·8	8·2	18·8	17
Most commonly occurring sentence	17	9	12	0
25% quartile	12	3	12	0
median sentence	18	9	18	15
75% quartile	24	9	30	24

However, if we examine the data more closely (see Figure 10.1), we may observe that Table 10.9 obscures some significant differ-ences in the patterns of sentencing in the periods studied. For example, in the 1848–1872 period, 21·4 per cent of long-firm fraudsters were sentenced to four years or more imprisonment, compared with 11·5 per cent in the 1948–1961 and 8·4 per cent in the 1962–72 periods. At the other end of the scale, we may observe that in the 1848–1872 period, 22·5 per cent of convicted long-firm fraudsters were sentenced to less than twelve months' imprison-ment, compared with 23·8 per cent in the 1948–61 and 39·1 per cent in the 1962–72 periods. The contrast is greater still when we observe the growth in the use of non-custodial sentences (counting sus-pended prison sentences as non-custodial measures).

Taking the period 1948–72 as a whole, we note that the proportion of people sentenced to four years' or more imprisonment fell by 123 per cent compared with the period 1848–72, to 9·6 per cent of the total sentenced; and that the proportion of people sentenced to *less than* twelve months' imprisonment increased by 47 per cent between 1848–72 and 1948–72, to form 33·1 per cent of the total sentenced. In brief, the pattern of sentencing has shifted in the direction of far fewer long sentences and the far more frequent use of very short sentences, although there remains a strong bunching between the twelve- and twenty-four-month sentence intervals.

The sentencing of long-firm fraudsters at Manchester Crown Court: a geographical comparison

The average sentence imposed on long-firm fraudsters at Manchester Crown Court between 1961 and 1971 was 26·2 months' imprisonment. One-quarter of those convicted were sentenced to twelve months' imprisonment or less; one-half to two years' imprisonment or less; and three-quarters to three years' imprisonment or less. These figures are higher than the equivalents at the Central Criminal Court since 1948, the sole exception being that a greater proportion of the Manchester group were given non-custodial sentences than were those sentenced at the Old Bailey in the period 1948–61.

The proportion of those sentenced to six months' imprisonment or less, however, was almost identical in the Manchester and the early Old Bailey groups, giving further support to the notion that the 1960s saw the demise of the three-month sentence and its replacement by the non-custodial one. Neither in Manchester nor at the Old Bailey was anyone convicted of long-firm fraud given an immediate custodial sentence of between nothing and six months in the 1960s and early 1970s. Of the five people given non-custodial sentences, three (co-defendants) were fined £200, one was fined £250 and one was given a prison sentence of twelve months suspended for two years. The person fined £250 was also disqualified under Section 188 of the Companies Act, 1948 from taking part in the management of a limited company without the permission of the court: he was 68 years old and had no previous convictions. In all, six Section 188 orders were made, all of them for five years.

The rest of the data in the sample are inadequate for proper comparison with the Old Bailey samples. Even if there were less missing data, the total number of cases would not enable any statistically significant results to be obtained. The main object has been to provide an independent sample against which the uniqueness of the Old Bailey data can be measured and evaluated. Although the sentences at Manchester tend to be higher than those

Table 10.10 Sentences imposed upon all long-firm fraudsters convicted at
Manchester Crown Court, 1961–71

Sentence (months)	Percentage on whom sentence was imposed	Cumulative percentage	Number of persons	Percentage with previous convictions	Percentage who had been sent to prison before
0	11·6	11·6	5	20·0	20·0
6	2·3	13·9	1	0·0	0·0
9	2·3	16·2	1	NI	NI
12	16·3	32·5	7	0·0[1]	0·0[1]
18	11·6	44·1	5	0·0	0·0
24	14·0	58·1	6	0·0[2]	0·0[2]
30	4·7	62·8	2	0·0	0·0
36	23·3	86·1	10	30·0[3]	30·0[3]
48	4·7	90·8	2	100·0	100·0
60	4·7	95·5	2	50·0[4]	50·0[4]
72	2·3	97·8	1	100·0	100·0
84	2·3	100·1	1	NI	NI
Totals	100·1	100·1	43		

NOTES:
1 No information available on four persons (57 per cent).
2 No information available on four persons (67 per cent).
3 No information available on four persons (40 per cent).
4 No information available on one person (50 per cent).

in London, it should be noted that only 2 out of the 43 cases
exceeded Thomas's five-year tariff' for 'professional frauds', and
that only 14 per cent of the Manchester group were sentenced to
longer than three years' imprisonment. There is no evidence, then,
for the proposition that long-firm fraudsters are sentenced on a high
tariff.

Conclusions
The sentencing of long-firm fraudsters, at least at the Central
Criminal Court, appears to make use of the same 'common-sense'
typifications employed by creditors, police officers, Department of
Trade officials and the Director of Public Prosecutions, discussed
earlier in Chapters VIII and IX. Offenders tend to be classified into
at least three basic categories: the 'slippery-slope' first offender, who
is generally regarded as 'naughty' rather than 'bad'; the principal in

the 'highly organized' fraud, who is commonly regarded as 'bad' though almost always redeemable; and miscellaneous others, such as the co-accused in 'organized frauds'.

These categorizations are reflected in a general manner in sentences. Table 10.6 shows that no principal in a fraud for which three or more people were convicted was given less than twelve months' imprisonment. On the other hand, of the 11 people whom after reading the court depositions I classified as 'slippery-slope' or intermediate fraudsters, only one was given a sentence longer than twelve months' immediate imprisonment. The sentences of other 'types' of offender were distributed in no apparently consistent manner. Even though judges might disagree with policing agencies over which fraudsters should be allocated to which category, the distinction they both make between the 'slippery slope' fraudster and the 'real' fraudster corresponds to the difference between someone who is regarded as having done a criminal act and someone who is regarded as 'a criminal'. In the former case, the fraud is only one 'auxiliary' aspect of the man to be sentenced: in the latter case, it is taken as representative of the man – what has been called a 'master status' (Hughes, 1945). One of the interesting findings of my study is that although these distinctions were reflected in sentence, the prior criminality of the person did not appear to be strongly or consistently relevant to his being categorized as 'naughty', 'bad' or 'very bad'. This is demonstrated by the results in Table 10.4. In the Manchester group (Table 10.10), there was a strong association between length of sentence and the presence of previous convictions and a previous sentence of imprisonment, but it is possible that this association might disappear if missing data were known.

Even in those cases where the presence of a large number of previous convictions might be expected to 'cue in' the treatment of fraudulent conduct as a master status of the individual concerned, the sentence imposed is very seldom outside the working maximum of five years' imprisonment. It seems reasonable to suggest, then, that almost *all* long-firm fraudsters are sentenced on the basis that they are 'white-collar law violators' rather than 'villains'. It could be argued that this observation applies equally to burglars and thieves, and is less than remarkable: indeed, a Home Office study has revealed that 90 per cent of burglars and thieves were sentenced to three years' imprisonment or less between 1974 and 1976 (Advisory Council, 1978, p. 148) – the same proportion as the long-firm fraudsters in my study (compare Table 10.4). However, the analogy is quite inappropriate, since the sums of money involved in the long-firm frauds are so much vaster than the proceeds of all but a tiny minority of thefts and burglaries. Were it not for the violence threatened against the victims thereof, armed robbery would be a closer crime for comparison with long-firm fraud, since in both cases, the victims are usually large rich organizations.

It is difficult to ascertain precisely the reasons for this leniency in sentencing. Some clues may be found in the judicial comments reported on page 239, but they do not explain why judges hold the views they do hold. The absence of violence and the carelessness of some victims certainly appear to be important. However, I should like to add the following possibilities.

(1) Despite the fact that the long-firm fraudster is one of the types of business criminal most prone to be regarded as an anti-capitalist 'outsider', judges find it easier to empathize with such men than they do with other types of criminal. This is an extension of the point made by Sutherland (1961, p. 248) when he stressed the cultural homogeneity between government officials and white-collar criminals.

(2) Compared with many of the 'major criminals' (a category that is itself highly problematic) who appear at the Old Bailey, long-firm fraudsters may appear to be relatively benign criminals. This is consistent with the harsher sentences imposed in Manchester, where other crimes are less 'organized' and where, consequently, long-firm fraudsters may appear relatively more 'villainous' than they do to judges in London.

(3) An offence of fraud generates less of a master status *qua* 'criminal' than does one of violence, sexual molestation or conventional theft. This enables a note of redeemability to be introduced into mitigation speeches in a more *confident* way than is normally possible. At the very least, the offence itself seems to generate a less emotive *gestalt* which may make it less likely that appeals for leniency and 'individualized justice' will be dismissed out of hand.

Be that as it may, the serious threat that long-firm fraudsters pose to the trust which must underpin commercial relations seems inconsistent with the apparent reluctance of judges to sentence them to more than three years' imprisonment. One might have thought that they would regard long-firm fraud as a deterrable offence *par excellence*, except in the case of some (though by no means all) 'slippery-slope' fraudsters. It is surely no less deterrable than burglary or bank robbery, where the rhetoric of retribution, of incapacitation, and of both individual and general deterrence is so commonplace. It appears, then, that *individual* deterrence – the attempt to deter the offender from future crime – plays little part in the penal philosophy which underlies the sentencing of long-firm fraudsters, perhaps because they are seen as less 'criminally-minded people' than other criminals and are not expected to offend again anyway.

Let us now turn our attention to *general* deterrence. We have no precise way of knowing whether these individuals would have committed fraud in the first instance had they believed that they would receive a harsher sentence. Some tentative inferences may, however, be made from my interviews with the fraudsters themselves:

> You can make a hell of a lot of money from l.f.s and the sentences are really low because it's got no violence. The powers-that-be are really down on violence.

> When we were thinking of running an l.f., we reckoned that even if we got done, fuck all would happen to us. You get less for a l.f. in toiletries than you would for knocking off a bog roll from Woollies [stealing a toilet roll from Woolworths].

These statements suggest that low sentence expectations may have influenced the decision to take part in a long-firm fraud. On the other hand, one fraudster told me that he expected to be given *more* than the six years he actually received, so the expectation of a long sentence *if caught* is not necessarily a deterrent.

Long-firm fraudsters form a heterogeneous category: among them, we find the 'gangster', the 'professional underworld fraudster', the 'petty thief', the scheming 'businessman-fraudster' who remains aloof from the conventionally defined underworld, and, finally, the 'slippery-slope' fraudster who begins with honest intentions but ends in fraud. These labels are socially and legally negotiated – what labels are not? – but there is clearly ample scope for distinguishing between offenders in terms of common-sense perceptions of their 'wickedness'. This is basically what judges appear to have done. However, the reader may be surprised at the relatively short sentences imposed upon the *principals* of conspiracies to defraud, for they undermine the trust between those who transact business on credit, on which the capitalist system depends, and one might have expected that the threat they pose to the interests of commerce would attract the wrath of the judiciary.

Sutherland (1961, p. 136) sought to explain society's failure to regard 'white-collar crime' as 'real' crime in terms of 'the status of the businessman, the trend away from punishment, and the relatively unorganised resentment of the public against white-collar criminals'. Faced with a study showing that businessmen received light sentences for frauds involving large sums of money, a believer in a crude ruling-class conspiracy theory of criminal justice might respond: 'So what else do you expect? Of course they look after their own kind.' The data in this chapter, however, reveal that Sutherland's observations apply even when the business criminals are not 'white-collar criminals' proper, but rather are predators upon the *corpus capitalisti* itself.

XI. Towards a Theory of Long-Firm Fraud

(The Lilliputians) look upon fraud as a greater crime than theft, and therefore seldom fail to punish it with death; for, they allege, that care and vigilance, with a very common understanding, may preserve a man's goods from thieves; but honesty hath no fence against superior cunning; and since it is necessary that there should be a perpetual intercourse of buying and selling, and dealing upon credit; where fraud is permitted or connived at, or hath no law to punish it, the honest dealer is always undone, and the knave gets the advantage. (Jonathan Swift, *Gulliver's Travels*)

The phrase 'white-collar crime' is a singularly potent and interesting one. It serves to differentiate business crimes symbolically from the 'real' crimes that form the subject matter of 'law and order' campaigns throughout the West. The low levels of enforcement of laws which govern offences by businessmen and by employees in the workplace have the unintended consequence of maintaining the myth that there is a vast, law-abiding majority in society. In reality, however, the presence of this 'law-abiding majority' may be an artefact of the reporting and recording of different crimes and of the selection for criminal prosecution of only some groups of 'offenders'. Tacit recognition of this fact is given by a recent report which calls for the decriminalisation (*de jure* as well as *de facto*) of a vast number of allegedly non-serious offences which, if enforced, 'might make criminals of us all' (Justice, 1980).

Fraud and corruption in high places now receive far more attention from the media and from law enforcement agencies than they did before the 1970s. Nevertheless, however seriously such 'white-collar crimes' may be regarded by the media, the general public, and by radical criminologists, those who contemplate practising such activities remain able to differentiate them *morally* from 'true' crime, as Section A illustrates. Section B of this chapter supports the hypothesis that high social status, as measured by the absence of a criminal record and/or contact with major underworld figures, is an important insulator against the risk that a businessman will be defined (socially and legally) as a 'fraudulent trader'. For example, the police are most likely to learn of the existence of those frauds committed by 'known villains' and consequently, these frauds constitute the great proportion of 'frauds known to the police'.

Where frauds involve less than a million pounds, intensive investigation by the police or by the Department of Trade is more likely to occur if the individual(s) involved has a criminal record or is suspected of having committed a fraud or some other type of crime previously. Furthermore, judgements made by creditors or by the police about 'what sort of person' a failed businessman 'is' affect the decision to prosecute; and an accused person stands a far better chance of being acquitted if he has no previous convictions than if he already has a criminal record. Judges, too, appear to take the view that it is less villainous to deceive a man into parting voluntarily with his property than to take goods by stealth or by force; they also tend to treat those who have run their businesses legitimately (or apparently so) for a number of years prior to the offence for which they have been convicted more leniently than they treat other, 'pre-planned' offenders.

The concentration of police forces upon street crimes and upon 'front-line' rather than background criminal operators means that even those 'professional villains' who turn to commercial crime enjoy a high level of immunity from conviction compared with their colleagues in 'ordinary' crime. The consequence of this, in the graphic words of one former leading American mobster (Teresa, 1973, p. 142) is that 'the cops could show a good record fighting crime in the streets. Meanwhile, the mob was stealing the streets.' This general observation is confirmed in Section C, which presents an analysis of the ways in which 'criminal organisations' and the criminal justice system interact to produce specific forms of organising long-firm frauds.

Aubert (1977, p. 168) has argued that

> One main obstacle to the development of a fruitful theoretical orientation is to be found in the tendency to treat criminal behaviour, on the one hand, and the system of criminal sanctions, on the other, as two separate problems. In our opinion, crime and punishment are most fruitfully handled as two aspects of a group process or two links in a specific type of social interaction.

It is in this context that I should like this study to be judged, for I hope that it provides ample confirmation of the value of the perspective that Aubert has advocated.

Section A Towards the explanation of the 'causes' of long-firm fraud

(i) *Genesis of 'slippery-slope' frauds*
The delineation of the category of 'slippery-slope' *fraud* presents considerable difficulties. It appears that in practice, a 'bust'

businessman is likely to be defined as a criminal only if he has continued to trade after any reasonable person ought to have realized that he would be unable to pay for the goods. The 'reasonableness' test clearly contains an element of subjectivity although specific acts, such as selling goods below cost price in order to repay existing creditors, serve as indicators of criminal reckless-ness or fraud.

There are two principal sub-types of 'slippery-sloper':

(1)   those who, although they are clearly insolvent in 'objective' terms, do not realize this until they actually go 'bust';

(2)   those who recognize that they are insolvent at the moment, but who carry on trading in the Micawber-like hope that 'some-thing will turn up'.

The latter category are relatively easy to differentiate both from the 'knowing' long-firm fraudsters and from other failed business-men. They have been successful in satisfying themselves that they are not going to go 'bust' and that their creditors will be better off in the long run by their continuing to trade. It follows, then, that lying to creditors and selling goods under cost price are not 'really' criminal, since creditors would agree to the behaviour if only they were as perspicacious as the debtor about his business prospects. Just as Cressey's trust violators 'discovered' the cultural store of motivational accounts sanctioning trust violation and applied them to their own conduct, so too do 'slippery-slopers' draw upon culturally approved patterns of thought and action to justify their transgressions to themselves. Equally apposite to them is Cressey's (1953) quotation from Alexander Dumas's *The Money Question*: 'What is business? That's easy. It's other people's money, of course.'

The behaviour of the type (2) 'slippery-sloper' can be made intelligible by the same type of analysis used by Cressey (1953). As in that study, however, we remain ignorant of why a particular definition of the situation should be adopted by some persons and not by others. There may be some physiological or personality differences which explain why some conform rapidly to 'the reality principle' while others cast their business prospects in such a roseate hue that they are able to reconcile continuing to trade with their view of themselves as 'honest' and 'normal' businessmen. The methodology adopted here has not thrown any light upon this issue, however, as I have been interested mainly in wilful long-firm fraud.

Type (2) 'slippery-slopers' do at least recognize that they are insolvent, even though they may justify continued trading by denying injury and by asserting that they are doing nothing abnormal. One may contend that their behaviour is recklessly, if not wilfully, criminal. The type (1) category, however, present more conceptual problems, for the behaviour appears to lack any significant degree of *mens rea*. Type (1) 'slippery-slopers' carry to extremes the failure to associate their actions with abnormal risks to creditors. They do not see what they are doing as rule-breaking in any sense at all, and consequently do not need to 'normalize' it by reference to some technique of neutralization or special motivational account. The slide down the slippery slope is as unselfconscious as anything the individual does, which is not to say that it is 'motiveless' behaviour but that it is not differentiated perceptually from normal conduct. In other words, it does not call for the performance of any conscious 'remedial work' at the time.

At present, we can only attribute this inadvertent, non-wilful depredation to some random and unspecifiable phenomenological process. We know only that in respect of these 'slippery-slopers', the condition of irredeemable insolvency remains outside the realm of consciousness. One may hypothesize, for example, that 'slippery-slopers' of type (1) have developed such a stake in their continued business activities and attendant status and life-style that their 'unconscious repression mechanism' seeks to 'solve' the situation by blotting out their awareness. However, the present writer shares the scepticism evinced, for example, by Vold (1958, ch. 7) with regard to the scientific validity of Freudian theories. Until we can specify the mechanism through which this happy state of ignorance is maintained, the 'explanation' of thought-processes presented here is no more than a heuristic low-level analytical framework. The search for prediction may be illusory within the context of a non-deterministic model of human behaviour, but even the postulate of a 'repression mechanism' fails to illuminate *differential* responses to apparently similar life-situations.

An account of business conduct along the lines of my type (1) framework would tend to raise the defence of 'accidental' behaviour, thus enabling the person to excuse himself and to avoid a charge of reckless or fraudulent trading. If the claim strains the credulity of defining audiences such as Department of Trade officials, however, the type (1) individual could find himself classed as a type (2) fraudster, though given the rarity of prosecutions for this sort of offence, this mis-diagnosis probably affects few businessmen. The analyses presented here, however, should make abundantly clear to the reader the problematic nature of the use of the label 'fraudulent', even within the context of *existing* legal definitions. (See Ditton, 1979, for an elaboration of this theme with regard to employees who are 'part-time criminals'.)

(ii) *Genesis of 'intermediate' long-firm frauds*

One fruitful perspective for the analysis of criminal behaviour is that of 'control theory'. Hirschi (1970, p. 26) argues that 'delinquency is not caused by beliefs that require delinquency, but rather is made possible by the absence of (effective) beliefs that forbid delinquency'.

The ability of individuals to withstand temptations to commit deviant or criminal acts depends upon the subjective meaning they give to the attachments they form, the commitments they develop, and the beliefs they accept (Hirschi, 1970, pp. 13–34). As Becker (1963, pp. 27–8) expresses it:

> The 'normal' person becomes progressively involved in conventional institutions and behaviour...several kinds of interests become bound up with carrying out certain lines of behaviour to which they seem formally extraneous... The individual, as a consequence of actions...taken in the past...finds he must adhere to certain lines of behaviour, because many other activities than the one he is immediately engaged in will be adversely affected if he does not. The 'normal' person, when he discovers a deviant impulse in himself, is able to check that impulse by thinking of the manifold consequences acting on it would produce for him. He has staked too much on continuing to be normal to allow himself to be swayed by unconventional impulses.

Although this aspect of the model is not discussed in detail, one might add that the 'manifold consequences' to which Becker refers depend not only on the individual's perception of what is likely to happen to him if he gets caught but also on his perception of the risk of being caught. Furthermore, the situation applies only to people who have 'deviant impulses'. Becker would have to require (a) that the impulse arises; and (b) that the impulse should be recognized as a 'deviant' one which would attract the sanctions of which he is afraid. If either of these conditions were not fulfilled, the 'normal' individual would remain normal in his own eyes.

We can apply this Becker–Hirschi model to the analysis of business criminality. Most people who go into business subscribe to the central dream of capitalist society that by owning and running one's own business, one can acquire wealth, status, independence and power. They are socialized into a 'normal' orientation towards making profits by buying cheap and selling dear. Sometimes, during the course of business, someone may be given the opportunity to buy goods particularly cheaply. Provided that no risk is believed to be attached to the transaction – either materially, in terms of criminal prosecution for handling stolen goods, or else psychologically, in terms of one's self-image as a 'respectable person' – the transaction may be entered into. After all, as Cressey (1965) has pointed out,

'Business is business'. Some businessmen are sharper than others; some have more initial capital, luck and contacts than others. In any event, some make more money than others.

Sometimes, a businessman may look around him and come to the conclusion that he is 'relatively deprived' and begin to feel strongly dissatisfied. He may then begin to 'fiddle' his income tax and/or value-added tax returns beyond the 'normal' level or perhaps 'fence' stolen goods. On the other hand, it may occur to him, either by introspection or by 'differential association' with those who know the techniques, that he could make a considerable amount of money through bankruptcy fraud. His commitment to the 'legitimate order' has already been weakened by his perception that he is not getting what he considers to be his 'needs' or 'just deserts'. He may develop verbalizations which justify fraud (or other types of deviance) on the lines suggested in Chapter V. However, if he is afraid of the consequences of apprehension (for example, what would his wife, family and friends think of him if he was prosecuted as a 'criminal'?), then he may be deterred, as Becker suggests, from putting his deviant impulses into action. If he is confident of his ability to manipulate the authorities, or if he does not fear the consequences of his being 'done', then involvement in crime is more probable. The expectation that in any event, he is likely to go 'bust' is likely to diminish the consequences of being 'done' in the mind of a businessman *to whom the idea of 'doing an l.f.' occurs*. It cannot be over-emphasized, however, that the idea of 'doing an l.f.' probably occurs to few businessmen who find themselves in that situation. Although businessmen have suggested to me that the concealment of assets from the liquidator or bankruptcy examiner is common – 'to save a few pennies for my wife and children' – the socialization patterns of most businessmen do not normally include sensitization to the possibility of long-firm fraud as a method of obtaining extra income, *though they might succumb to temptation if the idea arose in their mind*.

The essence of my argument is that instead of assuming that temptations are all around us and what we must do is to explain why people respond differently to those temptations, we should also try to explain differences in perceptions of situations as possessing *potential* for crime. The phenomenologically problematic nature of 'the criminal idea' deserves more attention than it has received hitherto from criminologists. Although I have followed Clinard (1952) in rejecting Sutherland's differential association theory as a complete explanation of business crime, on the grounds that people can arrive at long-firm fraud by 'creative introspection', the absence of contact with those who have discussed long-firm frauds does diminish the probability that such frauds will be committed. Creditors should be grateful, then, for the fact that most smallish businessmen are trapped into a ritualistic way of looking at the world (in the Mertonian sense) and are not socialized into what one might term 'deviant imaginings'.

The notion that a major difference between people who commit crimes and those who do not lies in their different susceptibility to 'deviant perceptions' (as well as in social learning experiences) has an interesting analogy with Austin's discussion of the nature of 'opposite' adverbs. Austin (1979, p. 193) states that

> There is no use for 'advertently' at the *same* level as 'inadvertently': in passing the butter I do not knock over the cream-jug, though I do (inadvertently) knock over the teacup – yet I do not by pass the cream-jug *advertently*: for at this level, below supervision in detail, *anything* we do is, if you like, inadvert, though we only call it so, and indeed only call it something we have done, if there is something untoward about it.

In other words, the principal line of social defence against long-firm fraud lies in its 'inadvertent' nature: the fact that few people think of doing it. It is only when long-firm fraud becomes an *advertent* issue that 'stakes in conformity' and 'active deterrents' become relevant.

Having teased out some of the factors that influence advertence to long-firm fraud, let us now assume that someone in business has become thus advertent. Following a non-deterministic 'control theory' perspective, Box (1971, pp. 150 ff.) suggests the following:

> Whether or not an individual with the option to deviate decides to, depends to some extent on what he makes of the issues of *secrecy, skills, supply, social* and *symbolic support*... One pivotal issue in the transformation of willingness into behaviour is that of *secrecy*. That is, the degree to which an individual perceives that a deviant act can be concealed and hence detection avoided... The most important risks are giving off information and being apprehended... the perceived certainty of not being caught may well unhinge even those whose commitments are normally binding and those whose attachments are usually sufficient to keep them on the 'straight and narrow'. Thus even having something to lose may not be an adequate constraint against criminal behaviour, for under certain circumstances particular forms of law-violation carry such low risks that an individual's physical and social possessions are relatively secure.

Problems surrounding the operational impact of deterrence are manifold – for excellent discussions, see Beyleveld (1978) and Gibbs (1975) – and not being caught is by no means certain for the 'intermediate fraudster'. However, the discussion does point towards one feature of significance for those seriously considering such fraud: the low *de facto* level of surveillance by the Department of Trade (still less by the police) of company liquidations other than those which are blatantly fraudulent. For someone already in charge of a business, the supply of 'the tools of crime' is no problem. Skill may present a greater problem: long-firm fraud is not quite as easy as embezzlement (Cressey, 1953) or cheque fraud (Lemert, 1972). The businessman may not know anyone to whom he can sell large quantities of goods rapidly for cash, or he may not know how to manipulate the books of account in order to conceal the true nature of his defalcations. In such a case, however, it is unlikely that the idea of long-firm fraud would have occurred to him anyway, since I would hypothesize that the skills to perform a long-firm fraud normally precede the idea of committing one. To the extent that this is not so, the lack of skill could stop the businessman from committing a *long-firm* fraud, though not, perhaps, the fraudulent concealment of assets from the liquidator and creditors.

Unless the prospective 'intermediate fraudster' is part of a coterie of 'businessman-fraudsters' or mixes with 'the chaps' – criminals – he is unlikely to obtain direct social support for his actions. He may, however, find *symbolic* support, along the lines suggested by Cressey (1953), Hartung (1965) and Sykes and Matza (1957). Using the Sykes and Matza typology, I have noted that he may justify his conduct to himself by appealing to higher loyalties, for example, the need for continued financial support for his wife and children, and by a mixture of denial of injury – the creditors can afford it – and denial of the victim – 'they made enough money out of me all these years'.

This model of the influences which bear upon the decision to turn a licit business into a long-firm fraud has implications for social control which are discussed in the next chapter. For the moment, however, I wish to return to one of the primary factors which influences commitment to law-abiding norms: the businessman's perception of what will happen to him if he does *not* go 'bent'. *Prima facie*, it would seem unlikely that someone would turn to fraud if he could make a living which appeared adequate to him by lawful means. Hence, although lack of opportunities is not a *sufficient* condition for criminality, the distribution of life-chances in society at large may be thought to *influence* the businessman's predisposition towards fraud. On this subject, Bonger (1961, pp. 600–2) has some interesting comments:

Picture to yourself the state of mind of one who has led a more or less comfortable life, who has been independent, and enjoyed the esteem granted to one who is well-to-do, and who sees that the time is approaching when all this will come to an end, and that there remains nothing for him to do but to accept some minor poorly paid employment, and lead henceforth an existence that cannot satisfy him in any way. Imagine also that chance throws in his way an opportunity to commit a crime with good hope of success. It must be granted that here we find very powerful determinants to crime... it is the present organisation of society that makes it possible for a man to be in charge of an enterprise which he is not fitted to conduct, while another who is fitted for it cannot find employment for his talents...

It may be observed, perhaps, that if it is true that a special disposition on the part of the individual is unnecessary for the explanation of these crimes, they ought to be more numerous than they are... but... first... these crimes are more numerous than the criminal statistics show; second... there are those who, as a consequence of the struggle for existence, have lost all courage and give up the fight, even the fight with dishonest weapons; others, prudent by nature, take into consideration the fact that, bad as their situation may be, it would be worse if the crime were discovered, etc.

Extrapolating Bonger's views, one may argue that the ultimate cause of 'intermediate' long-firm frauds is the private ownership of the means of production, which allocates managerial responsibility to people on the basis of inherited wealth rather than ability, and which provides only the crude alternatives of capitalist wealth and poorly paid employment: the gap which tempts the failing bourgeois to crime. It is naïve to blame all business failures on 'bad management', and the income gap between workers and capitalists is not as great as it was in Bonger's day, but the basic frame of analysis is useful, even if Bonger's attempt to avoid overpredicting bourgeois criminality is inadequate for explanatory purposes. One would predict that under conditions which favoured large businesses and made small businesses struggle for survival, commercial frauds of all kinds would tend to flourish. Walsh (1977, p. 42) makes this point in relation to 'fencing', and Paulus (1974, pp. 92–3) states that

Periodic business depressions in the last quarter of the nineteenth century were particularly hard on small shopkeepers. Watering of spirits, beverages, milk, and the admixture of expensive goods with inferior although harmless ones... allowed some shopkeepers to remain solvent.

This general model would apply to long-firm frauds also, although whether or not the failures would be defined as fraudulent would depend upon the formal social control processes. *Pace* labellists such as Ditton (1979), increased criminal behaviour may not lead to increased rates of officially recorded crime.

Bonger (1916, p. 600) also provides a quality-of-conditioning argument which illuminates the dissonance between self-perceptions as 'law-abiding' and commercial criminal behaviour, and helps to explain why people who would not commit 'ordinary crime' would be prepared to commit long-firm (or other types of) fraud:

> What is the environment in which many . . . who are guilty of such crimes are brought up? Certainly, they have learned that one must be honest, that it is wrong to pick pockets, etc., and they will not fail in this regard. But they have learned also that the principal end in life is to grow rich, to succeed . . . Those whose probity has this for a basis have only a weak check to prevent them from becoming a criminal, when the thought of a wrong act arises within them. They remain honest so long as it is to their advantage, but woe to society when this is no longer the case . . . the environment in which these persons have lived after their youth has not contributed to reinforce the social sentiments . . . He who is compelled always to have his own interests at heart can give very little thought to the interests of others.

The primacy of the goal of material success, combined with a lack of negative reinforcement of business crime, means that businessmen are released from the moral bind of law and thus are free to calculate the costs and benefits of long-firm fraud (and other possible courses of action) in relation to their fears and aspirations and what they perceive as the 'objective' consequences of lawbreaking. Thus it is that 'intermediate' frauds may come about.

(iii) *Becoming a 'pre-planned' long-firm fraudster*

Unlike 'intermediate' and 'slippery-slope' fraudsters, the criminal motivations of 'pre-planned' long-firm merchants *precede* the formation of their businesses. However, those I interviewed did not appear to view their behaviour as morally problematic. The reason for this was the rather jaundiced view they took of 'legitimate business'. Essentially, they regarded themselves as no different from any successful self-made men, all of whom committed crimes in the running of their present businesses or had done so on their way to the top. In their view, only those who have made or inherited considerable wealth, so that they can make huge sums of money within the law, can afford to be honest. Whereas the 'intermediates' and the 'slippery-slopers' accord legitimacy to the 'public norms' of capitalism, the 'pre-planned' fraudsters regard the notion that success is achieved by law-abiding industry as 'strictly for the birds'.

The vocabularies of motive they employ indicate the cynicism with which they view the difference between 'legitimate' and 'illegitimate' capitalism. In terms of the typology developed by Sykes and Matza (1957), they make use of the denial of injury – 'I only "do" big companies who can afford it', 'I have never taken any money from poor people'; of denial of the victim – 'These big firms are so lax in their credit control that they deserve to get conned'; of condemnation of the condemners – 'what we do is no different to what the boys in the City do all the time'; of denial of responsibility – 'After the War, you couldn't get into commerce unless you had the Old School Tie'; and a mixture of denial of responsibility and condemnation of the condemners – 'Some of the reps virtually force gear onto you, especially the stuff they can't get rid of anywhere else, if they think that you're a sucker'. It would be a gross mistake, however, to regard their cynicism as *positively* radical, except in the sense that any lack of belief in the moral validity of legal norms may be termed 'radical'. Provided that they can obtain a larger share of the cake for themselves, they display no great dissatisfaction with capitalist organization, apart from when it lands them in prison.

The presence of such scepticism is not, however, a sufficient condition for someone to become a 'pre-planned' long-firm fraudster. It supplies the necessary *symbolic* support for crime, but, as stated earlier, the problems of secrecy, supply, skills and social support remain.

The skills required to run a long-firm fraud have been described extensively in Chapter III, and there is no need to repeat them here. In principle, there may be no reason why anyone who knows what to do should not be able to run a long-firm fraud of some kind, but, in practice, many who are not brought up in a commercial environment do not have the self-confidence to set up a business, order goods, pay some creditors, stall others, dispose of the goods and so forth. This is particularly true now that the improved social control of credit has made it more difficult to carry out a 'little quickie'. Except under the tutelage of experts, the role of 'businessman-fraudster' appears to them to be beyond their range of abilities. Part of this role is the ability to counterfeit oneself as legitimate, perhaps for the duration of the fraud only but preferably at a more general level. As Maurer (1964, p. 11) notes: 'The big-time confidence men are flexible and are equally at home in their own subculture or in the dominant culture – in fact they are able to simulate behaviour within the dominant culture to a high degree of perfection.'

Concern about whether or not one will pass muster in society is related to the issue of secrecy, for it depends on how closely one will be examined by others. An excellent discussion of this is provided by Rock (1973a, pp. 70 ff.):

> While the counterfeit may pass if he is an object which lies in the other's zone of ignorance or 'knowledge about', he will not manage to do so if he is the centre of explicit expertise... If, on cursory inspection, he appears other than deviant and is not then subject to knowing scrutiny, the more or less esoteric clues which might betray him will remain unnoticed or misunderstood... In some cases the problems are those experienced by the spy, the traitor, or impostor. They revolve around maintaining the semblance of an adequate level of commitment to the normal world; explaining other commitments which prevent full involvement in conventional activity... The deviant must prepare two presentations of himself... Of course, the strain and complexities of such an accomplishment may simply be excessive. The deviant may decisively opt for full commitment to one life-style. He may also reduce the burden by resigning himself to the penalties attendant on deviant status, mitigating them only by presenting the status in its most acceptable form.

The prospect of this strain may deter some would-be fraudsters, but some may feel confident about their ability to play counterfeit and pass. Indeed, this represents an attraction for some of those to whom I spoke, though they recognized the costs it entails. The strain of running a business is too much for some, but the low level of surveillance by crime control agencies helps to reduce the strain of 'passing' for those who 'know' how easy it is.

The degree of social support received by the person contemplating long-firm fraud can be important here. Mixing with others who have carried out long-firm frauds can provide information about techniques, confidence in the *practicability* of fraud, information about the functioning of the formal social control system, and moral support which may facilitate the 'normalization' of the prospective action. The relative absence of negative societal reaction is equally important, however. Although I have not carried out any systematic survey of social attitudes towards long-firm fraudsters, conversations with some city businessmen indicate that some respectable merchants *are* prepared to mix socially with people whom they know to be long-firm merchants, though some will not do so, particularly if the fraudsters are connected with 'the underworld'. Furthermore, it appears that some respectables will not inform the police even when they know that a long firm is taking place, though they take care themselves not to grant credit to the fraudsters. There are fairly strong conventions in commercial circles that one does not question other people's 'deals' too closely. If some high status persons are prepared to *tolerate* long-firm fraudsters, even though they do not support their actions and have no direct interest in their frauds, then *positive* subcultural support may not be as necessary to long-firm fraudsters as it is to people whose crimes attract more condemnation from society as a whole or from the more powerful groups therein. However, this should not be misinterpreted to mean that there are no social costs attached to being known as a 'fraudster': few businessmen want to be too close to someone who may become involved with the police.

Finally, we come to the question of supply. The perception that one is insufficiently skilled and has an inadequate supply of money and business contacts are the principal 'supply problems' facing an intending long-firm fraudster. Many legitimate businessmen have the necessary skills, but as I have observed already, have enough of a stake in lawful enterprise to insulate them from temptation, while many 'villains' are too unversed in the ways of sophisticated business to try their hand at long firms. However, the social mixing of the 'criminal' and 'commercial' classes in night clubs, casinos and prisons has diminished the separation of ability from motive, thus spreading commercial crime beyond the confines of 'secretly deviant' businessmen. Nevertheless, the obtaining of sufficient finance to get long firms off the ground and finding outlets to dispose of the goods still present problems for long-firm fraudsters. Finance is a particular problem, for the success of police proactive strategies against pre-planned frauds appears to have made businessmen wary of risking their investments in this area.

The financial rewards and excitement derived from their first venture into long-firm fraud may induce some first-timers to continue in this line, while others may count their blessings and quit. Of those who commit more than one long firm, some make sufficient money to enable them to feel that they can now afford to be honest: they find some profitable line of lawful commerce. As the criminal-turned-capitalist MacHeath states (Brecht, 1976, pp. 225–6):

> Grooch...you are an old burglar. Your profession is burglary. I wouldn't think of suggesting that your profession, in itself, is out of date...Only in its form, Grooch, does it lag behind the times. You are an artisan...That class is on the wane...What is a pick-lock compared to a debenture share? What is the burglary of a bank compared to the founding of a bank? What...is the murder of a man compared to the employment of a man?...Take our business, for example: we break into shops at night in order to get the goods we want to sell. Why? When the shops go bankrupt through being uneconomically run, we can buy their goods with perfect legality at prices far below the costs of burgling...In this

present age one uses more peaceful methods ... Why send out murderers when one can employ bailiffs? We must build up, not pull down.

The more long firms they commit, however, the more difficult it is for merchants to avoid being labelled as 'fraudsters' by trade organizations or the police or the Department of Trade. Once they have been so defined, it becomes difficult for them to obtain credit 'upfront', and since nearly all businesses require credit, this forces them to use 'front men' and to act deviously, even when they want to run a *legitimate* business. It is hard to run a straight business under such conditions, thus providing further reinforcement for deviant motivations. In spite of this, however, most long-firm fraudsters eventually either become very 'straight' or find some grey area of semi-licit commerce where their deviousness can be employed to good advantage. In the final analysis, most long-firm fraudsters desire respectability, and with advancing age, the social, psychological and penal costs of continued law-breaking begin to outweigh the excitement and the financial rewards therefrom. The strain of being a career criminal becomes too great to bear, and the fraudster lowers his sights and returns to the fold.

Long-firm fraudsters are not impelled into crime by personality defects or by the stigmatizing activities of social control agencies (except in the tautological sense that there can be no crime without rule-makers to define it as such). Being defined as a 'villain' by such agencies does make it more difficult to go 'straight' but is neither a necessary nor a sufficient condition for career long-firm fraud: even if they are not caught, persistent long-firm merchants know that they are violating the criminal law. Given the potential to commit long-firm frauds, continued involvement in them at any given time is determined by the reasoned calculation of costs and benefits, as defined subjectively by each individual in terms of the things *he* values and fears.

Section B   Towards an explanation of societal reaction to long-firm fraud

(i) *Making of criminal law in relation to long-firm fraud*
Although long-firm fraud is not defined in law as a specific type of crime, criminal laws relating to it have existed since at least the sixteenth century. The effectiveness of those laws, that is, the extent to which wilful and 'slippery-slope' 'fraudsters' can be found guilty under due process rules, has been highly variable, however. This sort of observation is not uncommon in the area of business crime, as

Hadden (1967a), Hall (1952), and Paulus (1974) have found; but as the work of Hall (1952) demonstrates, the constraining influence of precedent is not exclusive to crimes committed by the powerful.

Legislators have found great difficulty in expressing in legal terminology the distinction they have in mind between 'lawful' and 'criminal' obtaining of goods. Furthermore, judges have at times expressed considerable conservatism in the way they have applied Statute and Common Law to the conduct of businessmen: until the nineteenth century, judges were prone to dismiss prosecutions for credit 'fraud' unless the suppliers had exercised a very great degree of prudence before granting credit. However, as the nature of commercial relationships changed from primarily *local* trading to trade between physically distant *strangers*, judicial conceptions of what degree of prudence it was reasonable to expect altered gradually, and it became easier to sustain criminal prosecutions for fraud. For example, as Hadden (1967a) points out, deceptions that were merely implied by conduct and deceptions regarding future events came to be 'criminalized' by judges.

The most notable feature of legislation affecting long-firm frauds has been the caution with which law-makers have approached the subject: their desire not to criminalize 'legitimate' commercial conduct and not to discourage trade has been paramount. The unwillingness to provide for effective law which is consequent upon these considerations is illustrated by the rejection of the proposals for a general offence of deception made by the Criminal Law Revision Committee (1974, clause 12(3)), and by the *de*criminalization of the offence of delaying payment by deception when one intends to pay eventually, in Section 2 of the Theft Act, 1978. This may make it harder to convict some 'slippery-slope' traders, who may successfully claim that they believed that their losses were retrievable.

From the perspective of Marxism or conflict theory, it is not unexpected that a capitalist society should have difficulty in differentiating the 'legitimate' from the 'criminal' in areas such as commerce where class interests make morality difficult to define precisely. In order to ensure that the 'vast majority of respectable businessmen' are not criminalized and are not at risk of the major status degradation entailed in the transition from 'businessman' to 'fraudster', law-makers are willing to grant effective immunity from the criminal law to a few people whom they regard as 'villains'. If the stalling of creditors and similar deceptions were restricted to the *petit bourgeoisie*, one might have expected the larger capitalists to support more wide-ranging laws 'in the public interest', just as they did in the development of factory legislation (Carson, 1974, 1979) and pure food laws (Paulus, 1974). However, large capitalists are as prone as small ones to stall their creditors by deception, and in so far as strict criminal laws might discourage business and reduce turnover, they have no strong interest in extending the ambit of the law in this context.

In addition to these practical considerations, however, there are more general ideas about the 'essential nature of capitalism' which may shape laws governing commerce. One of the central premises of Anglo-American culture is that it is founded upon 'free enterprise', that capitalism is open to all. The history of the criminal law shows that law-makers have been loath to enact legislation that might put initiative at risk, for to do so might undermine economic growth. Furthermore, even if capitalism has in fact moved towards an oligopolistic model, it would be contrary to the interests of any hypothetical power élite to demystify the 'real' social order by discouraging the belief that capitalism *is* open to everyone. In so far as this belief is an important source of social consensus (or false consciousness) in western societies, it is vital for capitalists to preserve it, even at the cost of considerable losses from long-firm frauds. In brief, it might prove more threatening to enact laws which might control fraudulent trading effectively than to allow 'fraudsters' to evade the criminal justice system.

Although I reject the ruling-class conspiracy theory of the emergence of criminal law, not least because it is too vague to give any practical guide to the actual content of law, the absence of any strong capitalist interest in strong laws governing commerce may help us to understand why there has been no great pressure for wide-ranging criminal laws in this area. For example, although capitalists might *like* to give the police more powers to investigate unwelcome predators such as long-firm fraudsters, they cannot do so without putting their *own* activities at risk of detection, or without subjecting their businesses to 'intolerable' disruption by investigators. It is not surprising, then, that the extra powers granted to the Inland Revenue under the Finance Act, 1976 should have attracted the wrath of traditionalist judges such as Lord Denning (*R.* v. *Inland Revenue and others, ex parte Rossminster* (1979), 3 All E.R. 385), nor that letter-writers to *The Times* should observe (15 December 1979) that 'it is but a short time until 1984'. For businessmen are not part of 'the criminal classes'!

This analysis also yields some predictions regarding future trends in law. One may expect stiff opposition from the 'privacy lobby' to proposals to reform the Bankers' Books (Evidence) Act, 1879, to enable the police to examine bank accounts in circumstances where they do not yet have enough evidence to justify charging someone with a criminal offence. The powers of the Inland Revenue and HM Customs and Excise may be restricted further following criticisms by the Law Society and by businessmen in submissions to the Keith Committee on Enforcement Powers of Revenue Departments in 1981.

Substantive and procedural law has been devised so as to maximize the safeguards against the conviction of all but the most blatant types of 'fraudster'. The fundamental reason for this is that most legislators (and media men) take the view that the vast majority of capitalist conduct is not morally reprehensible and should not be made liable to the slightest risk of conviction as 'criminal'. Self-interest undoubtedly plays a part in this, but the social construction of the meaning of 'fraud' is not reducible to mere self-interest. As Rock (1973a, pp. 144–9) states:

> Neither the conspiracy nor the consensus theorists have attained mastery over the problem of what law, as a set of enforceable definitions of deviant phenomena, can be shown to consist of... The transformation of behaviour into *crime* must be understood largely as a result of a moral world's active interpretation of that behaviour. It cannot be usefully discussed as if it were no more than a rational and straightforward response of a society to threatening acts. The emergence of law is founded upon processes which mediate between behaviour, its construction as threatening by the powerful, and its translation into crime.

(ii) *Enforcement of the criminal laws relating to long-firm fraud*
There has been much heated debate within criminology between Marxists and 'non-partisan' conflict theorists such as Turk (1969) and Chambliss and Seidman (1971) over the importance of specifically *class* interests in the law-making and law enforcement processes. One Marxist (Pearce, 1976, p. 104) has argued that

> When examining specific kinds of criminal acts and the actual societal response to them, I have shown that the major determinant of police action is the relationship between the criminal activity and the 'real social order' (i.e. class interests). Actions that pose a threat to this must be controlled e.g. embezzlement or lower-class attacks on private property.

Long-firm frauds represent at least as real a threat to the 'real social order' as do embezzlement and theft. After all, as well as injuring the rich, the offence strikes at the very heart of the commercial trust on which inter-capitalist social relations depend. Consequently, Pearce's hypothesis would require that law enforcement against long-firm fraud would be severe and be undertaken by 'ordinary' crime control agencies. The evidence on the latter point does nothing to refute his argument. Long-firm frauds not only are banned under the *general* criminal law but also are dealt with by the police as well as by the Department of Trade. This contrasts with the enforcement of most business regulatory law, which is undertaken almost entirely by administrative agencies such as the Health and Safety Executive, the Office of Fair Trading, the Inland Revenue, the Department of Trade, and by municipal authority Trading Standards Officers. (This sort of demarcation is also present in the United States.)

However, as we have seen in earlier chapters, the enforcement of laws against long-firm fraudsters has been far from severe. In order for such a situation to be compatible with Marxian analysis, we need to apply to it the notion of the 'relative autonomy of the legal sphere' from 'class interests'. As Hall *et al.* (1978, p. 208) argue in their study of 'mugging', the State is not, except in *mediated* form, "the executive committee of the ruling class". Such a theoretical development, though apparently immune from empirical falsifiability, represents an advance on the views of Pearce (1976).

A more subtle analysis would indicate that law-enforcement agencies themselves are subject to the more general positive stereotype that is attached to the role of the businessman. One of the tacit assumptions that is built into the structure of policing is that businessmen are not a class of individuals among whom many *real* criminals are to be found. For the police or the Department of Trade to direct policing on any other assumption would require a conceptual leap which senior policy-makers are unlikely to take, even if politicians were to permit it.

Many police officers are in fact extremely cynical about what they regard as the myth that businessmen are law-abiding. They do not share the view expressed by Vold (1958, p. 253) that 'There is an obvious and basic incongruity involved in the proposition that a community's leaders and more responsible elements are also its criminals.' However, their scepticism is not translated into increased levels of policing. Police manpower is allocated largely on the basis of cultural typifications of 'the crime problem'. The police are neither psychologically nor organizationally geared up to deal with commercial crime, and in the absence of strong pressure from 'society' for increased resources to deal with it, few police will be allocated thereto. Many victims of fraudulent traders do not perceive that they are victims of *crime* or, when they do, do not report it to the police, and, under these circumstances, the amount of 'fraudulent trading known to the police' is a direct function of their powers, efficiency and numbers. The creation of Fraud Squads in most large police forces has increased police sensitization to this type of crime (as well as being a reflection of increased social concern about it). However, until Chief Constables provide more personnel, many examples of long-firm fraud, particularly those *not* committed by members of 'the underworld', will go undetected.

The pressures on the police to provide a high 'clear-up rate' may also contribute to the low level of policing of commercial fraud. A man may work for a year or more on a single fraud, yet at the end of the day, only one crime will have been cleared up, though the sums involved may run into millions of pounds. Fraud inquiries, then, are highly labour-intensive for little numerical reward, so unless they are given some kind of extra weighting *vis-à-vis* the 'clear-up' figures, the under-policing may be expected to continue.

These observations apply also to the policing undertaken by the Department of Trade, albeit in a somewhat different way. British studies of the field of 'white-collar crime', such as those by Carson (1970), Gunningham (1974) and Paulus (1974), have noted that administrative agencies do not regard their primary purpose as that of 'crime control' but rather as a back-stop to ensure some degree of compliance with the law and ethical practice. Officials in the Department of Trade do not work on the basis that 'crime is all around' in a large proportion of liquidations or in businesses still extant. Like the police, they differentiate liquidations into the 'diabolical' and the 'normal', and concentrate on the 'diabolical' business*es* (or, when a 'known defaulter' is at work, business*men*) among those who go 'bust'. There is, however, one operational 'fact of life' which makes a crucial contribution to this lack of prosecution-mindedness: the manpower stresses entailed by the preparation and conduct of prosecution cases. The task of proving fraud is so great that a great deal of effort must be expended in the careful build-up of a prosecution case. Furthermore, while the case is in progress, an operational officer has to be present in court, possibly for months. The consequence of this is that in order to prosecute one offender, a large number of other cases can be given only cursory attention and the back-log of work in the department increases considerably. This principle applies not only to the area of long-firm fraud and fraudulent trading: it applies throughout the field of business malpractice, to the police, the Inland Revenue and to value-added tax frauds investigated by HM Customs and Excise.

The 'trade-off' between prosecutions and 'normal' workload is inevitable, but its impact is exacerbated by the understaffing of the relevant departments.

Another factor which affects the level of prosecutions in long-firm fraud cases is their cost. The relevance of cost has been denied by senior personnel in the police and in the Office of the Director of Public Prosecutions, except where extradition is involved, but some junior personnel have stated that it plays a part in their decision-making. In terms of police and specialist adviser man-hours, administrative costs, travel and such like, even a minor fraud investigation can cost thousands of pounds: major investigations can exceed the hundred thousand pound mark. The costs of trial also can be enormous. After one exceptionally long long-firm fraud trial in 1972, Judge King-Hamilton said:

> This trial and the earlier one occupied 151 working days and the only reason it was divided up was because it was considered it would be unfair to make any jury sit on any one case for seven and a half months. I am told that the total costs to the public will exceed a quarter of a million pounds and in the present trial they are £65 000.

A long trial that I attended cost over £50 000 in legal fees. A fairly routine long-firm fraud trial, involving four defendants, would last about four weeks. At least three of the defendants would be represented by Queen's Counsel and a junior counsel each, and there might well be four QCs for the defence. At 1978 prices, each QC would receive approximately £800 as a 'brief fee', plus daily 'refreshers' of £110. His junior would receive half these sums, making £165 per day for counsel for each client. Each defendant might have a separate solicitor, each of whom would receive about £2000 plus daily attendance allowances. Assuming that all defendants are on full legal aid – the normal state of affairs – the cost to public funds for such a trial would be about £27 000. This sum *excludes* the cost of the prosecution, judge, jurors, court staff and accommodation. Since fraud cases take so long and so few defendants plead guilty – 23·2 per cent at the Old Bailey between 1962 and 1972 – a major increase in such cases would clog up the courts still further, take out of active duties a number of operational officers from whatever agencies are involved, cause added strains (and delays) in the processing of cases in the Office of the Director of Public Prosecutions, and cost the taxpayer still more money in court costs. When investigating officers consider the possibility of acquittal and the kinds of sentences that commonly are imposed, it is hardly surprising that they are reluctant to proceed except in the most 'grave' frauds and against those persons who play the clearest roles in the allegedly fraudulent operations.

If the acts of long-firm fraudsters were beneficial to major business interests, the conflict theorist might find nothing puzzling in the under-enforcement of the criminal law in this area. However, their under-enforcement despite their being injurious to dominant class interests is rather more difficult to explain away. The most fruitful avenue for speculation is that serious attempts at law enforcement might actually prove to be *dys*functional for capitalists, even though they might prevent long firms. Many businesses might not be able to withstand close scrutiny by the police, and functionalists, who ignore meanings held by those involved, might hypothesize that capitalists do not press for very vigorous enforcement because they may feel that 'there but for the grace of God go I' and because they may be afraid that if they mobilize the police against long-firm merchants, the authorities may not stop there. Long-firm fraud does not constitute a sufficiently great threat to commercial interests to justify risking these consequences of intensive enforcement programmes.

In brief, one may argue that capitalists have a vested interest in maintaining what Schattschneider (1960, p. 71) has called a 'mobilization of bias', whereby the police and society at large do not regard commercial crime as 'real' crime. For if the public began to think seriously about the matter, they might not concur with the distinction the criminal law presently makes between 'legitimate' and 'criminal' capitalist conduct: they might want to draw the line at a different point. The price that capitalists pay for this mobilization of bias is that many potential fraudsters consider it worthwhile to commit fraud and that many 'fraudsters' go unpunished.

These arguments are highly reified: I doubt if there has ever been a capitalist who has thought through a policy on fraud with the logic that I have outlined, and they cannot explain the changes that may be observed in the control of fraud during the postwar period. Furthermore, Chief Constables probably respond more to general public and media pressure than to 'capitalist interests' in their resource allocation, and although the media now pay far more attention to fraud than they used to, there is greater pressure on police agencies to give more resources to the control of 'mugging' and 'vandalism' than to fraud, and resources are finite. Nevertheless, the reified arguments may help to explain why there has been so little vigorous moral entrepreneurship in the field of credit control and the surveillance of 'failed businesses'.

Finally, one should note that the anxiety displayed by social control agencies lest they mis-define someone of high status as a 'deviant' or as a 'criminal' contrasts fairly sharply with their readiness to label other 'social types' such as 'muggers' (Hall *et al.*, 1978), vagrants (Chambliss and Mankoff, 1976), or 'young toughs' (Piliavin and Briar, 1964; Werthman and Piliavin, 1967). This confirms other studies of 'white-collar criminality' (Carson, 1970, 1974, 1979; Gunningham, 1974; Paulus, 1974). The severe extent of the status reduction as a consequence of the classification of a businessman as 'a criminal' is a central background element in the way that social control is activated. Rightly or wrongly, formal control agencies perceive that status degradation is more consequential to businessmen than to others, and they act in accordance with that perception, though they may not recognise that that is the criterion they are adopting.

(iii) *Sentencing of long-firm fraudsters*
The data on the sentencing of long-firm fraudsters indicate that judges at the Old Bailey and at Manchester Crown Court do not perceive long-firm fraudsters as *major* property criminals, in spite of the fact that the money they 'steal' is equivalent to that obtained in serious armed robberies and in spite of the symbolic threat that they pose to commercial interests. Half the long-firm fraudsters convicted at the Old Bailey received sentences of eighteen months or less in the 1948–61 period, and fifteen months or less in the 1962–72 period. In this latter period, almost one-third of offenders were not sentenced to a term of immediate imprisonment. Moreover, even the principals of highly organized conspiracies were sentenced to an average of only 2·82 years' imprisonment, though by the mid-1970s, 'Mr Bigs' in the world of long-firm fraud tended to be given five-year sentences. These data are represented pictorially in Figure 11.1.

The relative leniency of the sentences imposed upon principals appears to be due to the absence of violence and the lack of public concern in this area. Since judges also make use of a 'relative blame' concept when sentencing co-conspirators, the punishment imposed upon others is correspondingly lower, accounting for the low average sentence. One may hypothesize that where an offence is perceived as 'very serious' by sentencers, there will be little scope for 'individualization' of sentences, but where it is perceived as 'non-serious', the scope for individualization is far greater. This also corresponds to a difference in the rhetoric of punishment: in the former 'serious' cases, judges refer to the 'need' for retribution, *general* deterrence or the protection of the public, and these needs

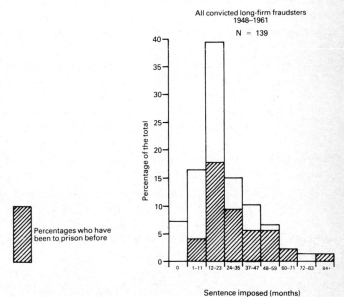

Principals of highly organized conspiracies
1962–1972

N = 28

All convicted long-firm fraudsters
1962–1972

N = 215

Percentage of the total

Sentence imposed (months)

All convicted long-firm fraudsters
1948–1961

N = 139

Percentage of the total

Sentence imposed (months)

Percentages who have
been to prison before

Figure 11.1   Sentences imposed upon long-firm fraudsters at the Central Criminal
Court, London, with proportions who have received previous prison sentences

override all other considerations of motivation or circumstance; in the latter 'less serious' cases, *individual* deterrence or rehabilitation become politically possible philosophies of punishment.

Long-firm fraudsters, even those who are connected with 'organized crime', do not have any political influence with the English judiciary, as they might do in the United States. Furthermore, their actions do not benefit *any* politically significant section of the 'industrial' or 'finance' capitalist classes. Consequently, one cannot attribute the light sentences imposed upon them to class interest. To explain this dissonance between material depredation and sentences, we must examine the culturally derived stock of 'seriousness ratings' which affect judicial perceptions of the 'dangerousness' of different types of offender.

In his brilliant essay on 'The Stranger', Schutz (1967b, p. 93) distinguishes between two types of knowledge: direct 'knowledge of acquaintance' and indirect 'knowledge about' people. Developing this distinction, we may hold that, provided that the offence is not perceived as heinous, people with direct 'knowledge of' offenders may 'normalize' the rule-breaking of the latter rather than regard it as representative of their essential badness. The logic at work here appears to be that if *real* criminals are 'not-like-us', then someone who *is* (or appears to be) 'like-us' cannot really be 'a criminal'. Support for this may be found in the work of Paulus (1974, p. 127), who argues that when businessmen are convicted of food adulteration, they retain their master status as businessmen when sentence is imposed.

Rubington and Weinberg (1968, p. 10) contend that

> A set of cultural rules for typing deviants exists. These rules are not necessarily fully explicated; rather they are tacit, and therefore known usually after the fact. One rule on typing, inferred from many observations, may be summarised as the greater the social distance between the typer and the person singled out for typing, the broader the type and the quicker it may be applied.

Where 'normal' predatory criminals are concerned, social distance between judge and offender is natural (at least in our judicial system), arising out of their different backgrounds. However, where long-firm fraudsters are concerned, the apparent nature of the offence, that is, its business-like character, inhibits the assumption of social distance. The level of public concern about long-firm fraud, which probably relates to its lack of dramatic quality compared with armed robbery or even burglary, is not high enough to overturn the tacit assumption of the judiciary that business criminals are not *real* criminals. In so far as Crown Court judges respond in their sentencing practices to what they perceive as the 'demands of the public', it is not surprising that long-firm fraudsters, like many of the less sensational 'white-collar criminals', receive relatively light sentences: there is no outcry in the media when they are given suspended prison or non-custodial sentences.

Appellate judges, however, possess a broader and more abstract view than Crown Court judges of what sentencing practices are required to serve 'the public interest'. Consequently, as Thomas (1970, 1978) observes, they recommend that people who take part in highly organized long-firm frauds should be given five-year prison sentences. It appears that the more thought that is given to the socio-economic consequences of long-firm frauds, the more punitive is the response that is elicited. This hypothesis is given some support by the observation of one former member of the Parole Board that its lay members tend to take a lenient view of long-firm fraudsters and recommend them for parole, while the 'professional' members take the view that they are 'villains' in 'slippery-slope' clothing and tend to oppose parole. (See also Leigh (1977a, p. 126), who – on the authority of the Chairman and a judicial member of the Parole Board – states that 'white-collar criminals' are seldom considered to be suitable candidates for parole.)

Contrary to what a crude 'judges are puppets of the ruling class' theory of sentencing might suggest, long-firm fraudsters are treated with relative leniency in the courts, even when the premeditated quality of their crimes and their prior criminal records might lead one to expect severe retribution and/or a deterrent sentence. The general positive stereotype attached to business activities helps to inhibit the development of a view of fraudsters as *truly* evil. The data on the sentencing of long-firm fraudsters reveal that judges are as prone as anyone else to make sentencing decisions on the basis of socially defined conceptions of the 'seriousness' of offen*ces* and of the 'wickedness' of offen*ders*. Although underworld-connected 'professional criminals' tend to be sentenced more severely than businessmen without any prior criminal record, this study has shown that the 'objective class interests' of capitalists cannot account fully for the sentencing practices of the criminal courts.

Section C Impact of social control measures upon the freedom of 'professional long-firm fraudsters' and upon the organization of long-firm frauds

(i) *'Professional long-firm fraudsters' in the criminal justice system*
The social control of long-firm fraud has become considerably more

effective during the 1970s. One index of this is the increase in the number of background organizers who have been convicted during this period; another is the improved prevention of long-firm frauds. It is contended that one conviction is not a sufficient condition for the assertion that someone's criminal behaviour is being dealt with 'adequately' in the criminal courts: one must also examine the ratio of crimes to convictions, profits per crime and the penal sanctions imposed upon those convicted.

Mack (1976) suggests that 'full-time' major professional criminals enjoy a considerable degree of immunity from imprisonment compared with their less skilful brethren, and that their immunity would be greater still were it not for the fact that they receive heavy sentences when convicted. He supports this hypothesis by the use of data on the numbers of charges made which did not result in conviction and on the proportion of their lives since the age of 17 that alleged professionals spend *outside* prison. This 'prison-free ratio' is 70 per cent for organizers, 92 per cent for receivers, 82 per cent for thieves, and 80 per cent for the 'providers', that is, servicing middlemen. The ratio for 'professionals' overall was 74 per cent, mainly because the violent offenders received long prison sentences (Mack, 1976, pp. 252–6).

There are comparatively few long-firm fraudsters who are persistent but not skilled, so I am unable to validate Mack's data fully against this study of long-firm fraudsters. However, although the 'professional' background operators behind long-firm frauds receive longer sentences than their 'front men' and than 'intermediate' or 'slippery-slope' fraudsters do *when convicted*, the former have higher ratios of offences to convictions and seldom receive very long prison sentences anyway. This is illustrated both by the data on the sentencing of principals of highly organized frauds in Figure 11.1 and by the prison-free time of professional long-firm fraudsters which is detailed in Table 11.1.

The criterion I have adopted for 'professionalism' is that more than one of my informants – whether 'criminal' or 'respectable' – have stated their firm conviction that a given individual has been involved at a major organizational level in *at least four* long-firm frauds within the past twenty years.

In some cases, these views are backed by some criminal convictions (though none of the sample has been convicted four times for long-firm fraud). In others, however, I have tried to validate them by reference to composite pictures built up from interviews with different informants, however imperfect this procedure may be. This list of professionals may not be exhaustive, but *a*

TABLE 11.1 Proportion of the lives of suspected major long-firm fraudsters not spent in prison since age 17[1] compared with data on major professional criminals in Mack[2, 3]

Percentage of time not in prison	Number		Percentage	
	long-firm fraudsters	*professional criminals (Mack)*	*long-firm fraudsters*	*professional criminals (Mack)*
100	4	8	20	8
90–99·9	9	21	45	21
80–89·9	5	20	25	20
60–79·9	2	26	10	26
>60	20	75	100	75
<60	0	25	0	25
Total	20	100	100	100

NOTES:
1 The data on suspected major long-firm fraudster in this table relate to the period from each suspect's seventeenth birthday to 30 April 1979.
2 See Mack (1976, p. 252).
3 No long-firm fraudster is younger than the average age of 'professionals' given by Mack (1976, p. 256). Only his receivers have an average age as high as that of long-firm merchants.

priori it seems likely that persons *not* known to my informants will have lighter criminal records than those who *are* known to them. (To use the terminology of Mack, 1975, the unknown professionals will be 'substantial incomers' or 'substantial upcomers'.) If this assumption is correct, then inferences from Table 11.1 regarding the small proportion of their lives that major long-firm fraudsters spend in prison will be true *a fortiori* of the *unknown* 'professional long-firm fraudsters'.

Of the twenty people who are regarded by my police, 'underworld' and business informants as 'high class' long-firm fraudsters, four have convictions for both business and theft offences, twelve have convictions for business offences only, and four have no convictions at all to date. None of the twenty has any criminal record for violence, although a number of them have used violence to control their 'front men' and to ward off competitors who have sought to muscle in on their activities. Although half of them are over 50 years old and none of them is under 40, only six of them have served more than four years in prison during their entire lives, and only three have received sentences of longer than five years' imprisonment on any one occasion. Three of them have had their sentences reduced by the Court of Appeal (Criminal Division) and, in one case, the trial judge was criticized for having imposed a prison sentence on a 'first offender' (*sic!*).

Six of the twenty have been acquitted of involvement in long-firm frauds. Of these six, only two are believed to have given up crime: one of the two was convicted subsequent to his acquittal, while the other was not. Of the six acquitted, only four had previous convictions at the time of their acquittal: the remaining two have never been convicted at any time. These data may understate the true acquittal rate of 'professional long-firm fraudsters', however, for they relate only to long-firm fraud cases tried at the London Central Criminal Court and at Manchester Crown Court. None of the 'professionals' has been convicted for *all* the long-firm frauds he has committed: this is true according to both police and underworld sources. However, the main reason for the non-convictions is that prosecuting officials consider that there is insufficient evidence for a judge and jury to convict and therefore advise against prosecution rather than that suspected 'professionals' are acquitted when tried. This analysis reveals the poverty of using acquittal rates as a measure of the adequacy of the conviction rates of 'professional criminals'.

The concept of the 'full-time criminal' is difficult to apply to these principal fraudsters, just as it is to the 'fences' studied by Walsh (1977). The amount of time that each of them spends organizing, backing and 'fencing' long-firm frauds is variable and impossible for me to calculate. Most of the background operators combine long-firm frauds with ostensibly legitimate business interests: long firms are either an occasional activity when they feel they have nothing better to do or an adjunct to their legitimate businesses. To the best of my knowledge, only eight out of the twenty have *never* earned 'much money' through lawful activity. Nevertheless, it would seem curious if a discussion of 'professional long-firm fraudsters' were to exclude the twelve who have been involved, albeit intermittently, in the background organization of at least four long-firm frauds: to do so would be to confirm the somewhat artificial criminological concentration on 'the underworld' and to neglect the links which exist between 'professional criminals' and 'legitimate society'. This is a fault of which Mack (1975) is guilty, in spite of his criticism of Fordham (1972) for giving a somewhat old-fashioned picture of 'the underworld'.

The principal conclusion of my study of the social control of long-firm fraud is that the amount of time that 'professionals' spend in prison is remarkably small in relation to the amount of money they obtain from long-firm frauds. Each long firm brings in over £ 12 500 on average to each principal background operator, so at 1980 prices, all of the twenty people discussed here have obtained at least £ 50 000 from crime. Yet in spite of this, no less than 65 per cent of the group have spent less than 10 per cent of their time 'at risk' (that is, since the age of 17) in prison. Although recent years have seen the conviction of most of the principal long-firm fraudsters suspected by the police, there seems little doubt that the 1960s, in particular, offered long-firm merchants very substantial rewards without a great deal of inconvenience from the agencies formally entrusted with the control of long-firm fraud. Even today, provided that a large fraud can get off the ground, the probability of conviction and the sentences that are imposed when one *is* convicted may make long-firm frauds a fairly good gamble in comparison with traditional forms of property crime.

(ii) *A model of the determinants of the modes of criminal organization of*
     pre-planned long-firm frauds
McIntosh (1975) has suggested that the most fruitful way of examining the organization of crime is to relate it to the technology and the pervasiveness of social control in any given area. When losses to individual victims are slight, efforts at crime prevention and policing tend to be weak, and small groups of criminals can practise crime routinely as a *craft*. When the size of depredations increases, societal reaction follows suit in intensity, and 'one-off' *project* crimes become the norm, their participants dispersing after each operation. Finally, where police corruption can be arranged, as most notably in the United States, *business* type organization of crime becomes possible, even though the crime is visible to law-enforcement agencies.

McIntosh implies that these modes of organization exist at *different* historical periods. However, in the case of long-firm frauds, we have seen that they can co-exist simultaneously, suggesting perhaps that the level of societal reaction has never been very high in this area of crime. The analysis of long-firm fraud in the nineteenth century reveals that 'criminal families' carried out series of long-firm frauds in different places under different names – *craft* organization; that businessmen both with and without 'underworld contacts' carried out 'one-off' project crimes; and that Germans living in England operated large-scale criminal syndicates to run long firms on business lines. The last example presumably counts as 'business organization', although it entailed no apparent police corruption and was different in degree rather than in kind from 'craft organization', that is, it had wider tentacles and greater background organization: the craft/business distinction is difficult to apply here.

Eventually, however, business-type organization of long-firm frauds declined due to a combination of pressure from 'moral entrepreneurs' such as Reuschel (1895); the development of trade magazines such as the Trade Protection Circular and of trade protection societies such as the Manchester Guardian which warned their subscribers of 'gangs of swindlers'; the general sensitization of traders to the existence and *modus operandi* of long-firm fraudsters; changes in the law; and improvements in the organization and integrity of the police. There is no evidence of any *large*-scale syndicated organization of long-firm fraud between the beginning of the twentieth century and the 1960s, though we cannot infer that such organization did not exist. The main feature of organization in Britain in this period was project crime, although Moore (1933) points to the existence of bands of swindlers, who may have been craft or small-scale 'business' criminals under McIntosh's typology.

At the beginning of the 1960s, long firms began to be organized along syndicated lines once again, although this time they were incorporated within the *general* criminal activities of the Kray and Richardson gangs. Syndicated fraud was mainly London-based, but it extended from the Midlands to the south coast of England as far west as Plymouth. The 'gangsters' offered long-firm merchants the apparent benefits of vertical integration: finance to set up long firms, 'faces' to front the business, outlets for the disposal of goods, and 'protection' from parasitic 'heavies'. They also offered the prospect of security from the police, since the 'front men' were too frightened of the 'heavies' to inform against the organizers to the police. (There is no reliable evidence of police corruption in this respect during that period.) However, the fraudsters quickly learned that if they did not agree to syndicate control, the gangsters would 'grass' on *them* to the police and/or commit acts of violence against them. The hegemony of the syndicates over long-firm fraud was incomplete, however, because they could not learn about the activities of long-firm merchants who had access to legitimate trade outlets and who could finance their frauds from their own or from 'non-underworld' capital. None the less, there was a marked trend towards the centralized organization of long-firm fraud during the 1960s, though craft and project organizational forms managed to coexist therewith. These organizational changes are reflected in the criminal records of those convicted for long-firm fraud at the London Central Criminal Court, depicted in Figure 11.2 overleaf.

The moral panic generated by the presence of what were dubbed by the media as Mafia-style gangs in Britain led to the formation of special gangbuster squads by the police. Eventually, the gangsters were incarcerated, and this broke up the syndicated organization of long-firm fraud. However, the long-firm merchants were needed as prosecution witnesses against the gangsters, and got off very lightly themselves. After the Richardson and Kray trials in 1967 and 1968 respectively, they continued at long-firm fraud, this time on the basis of project organization.

In the late 1960s, some long-firm fraudsters who had not been involved to any significant extent with the gangsters reinstated a limited form of business organization by corrupting key officers in the Metropolitan Police Fraud Squad However, to the best of my knowledge, this corruption in respect of long-firm fraud lasted only for four to five years, until Sir Robert Mark's fairly successful anti-corruption drive began to generate greater circumspection within the police. Some of the criminals and police officers concerned were sent to prison. By 1977, inflation had made it difficult for non-established businesses to get credit, proactive intervention strategies by the police had made it more difficult for the fraudsters to get away with their goods and money, and many of the top fraudsters were either in prison or still chastened by recent imprisonment. All these factors combined to eliminate continuous business-type organization of long-firm fraud during the late 1970s, at least as regards those persons known to my informants: there may be some very high-level 'background operators' who are still continuously active.

It may be appropriate to examine at a very general level the costs and benefits of business-type organization of long-firm fraud. In an analysis of the relationships between thieves and fences, McIntosh (1976, p. 262) observes that 'the beauty of the system of the autonomous fence and thief is that it reduces risks for everyone involved'.

Although this is true also of long-firm fraudsters and their 'fences', it should be remembered that long-firm 'fences' and organizers already possess greater protection from the criminal law than do 'ordinary' criminals. The ability of long-firm 'fences' to produce quasi-legitimate accounts for their purchases and to organize frauds *sub rosa* will protect them from conviction at normal levels of police activity, unless their 'front men' become disloyal or courageous enough to 'grass them up'. They need to expose themselves 'upfront'

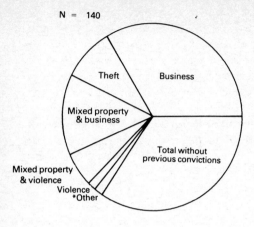

1948–61

N = 140

Business

Theft

Mixed property
& business

Total without
previous convictions

Mixed property
& violence

Violence
*Other

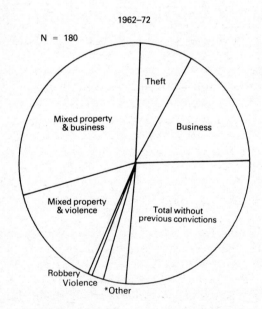

1962–72

N = 180

Theft

Mixed property
& business

Business

Mixed property
& violence

Total without
previous convictions

Robbery
Violence
*Other

*Includes taking and driving away, motoring offences, bigamy
and soliciting.

*Figure 11.2   Criminal backgrounds of persons convicted for long-firm frauds at the
Central Criminal Court, London, 1948–72*

only if they do not have enough control over their 'front men' to remain in the background. It is only if they do so expose themselves that police corruption becomes a necessary condition for business-type organization of long-firm fraud. Even if they expose themselves, however, the crime may not be reported to the police or the police may be inefficient and, in the short term, the 'Mr Bigs' may be fortunate enough to escape prosecution.

The typology devised by McIntosh (1975), then, appears to be incomplete, in so far as it neglects the protection offered to organizers by virtue of their ability to remain in the shadows: the 'front men' may be highly visible, but the background personnel may remain unknown to the police or unconvictable by the due process criteria adopted in the courts. Consequently, it is doubtful whether long-firm background organizers need 'the fix' (corruption) to avoid conviction, in the way that professional thieves (Sutherland, 1937) and confidence men (Maurer, 1940) are said to do.

Police corruption, then, is neither a necessary nor a sufficient condition for the business-type organization of long-firm fraud. It is not sufficient, because improved supplier liaison may inhibit long firms at source and because 'organized crime' requires the presence of people with entrepreneurial and organizational flair. It is not necessary because long firms do not have to be highly visible as 'crimes' and because not *all* their perpetrators are clearly identifiable. It is true that police corruption makes business organization of long firms *easier*, but ironically, the confidence generated thereby may lead background operators to expose themselves in the foreground of their frauds, rendering them liable to conviction if their 'protection' fails: this happened to some prominent figures in the early 1970s. The last observation, however, does not invalidate my critique of McIntosh's typology, since it represents a human failing rather than an analytic necessity.

Inter-fraudster relationships and the organization of fraud Another important influence upon the organization of long-firm fraud is the set of expectations which develop out of the interpersonal experiences of fraudsters. The central characteristic of these expectations is distrust. For whereas the professional thieves described by Sutherland (1937) form a solidary network, co-operatively adhering to clear rules regarding the distribution of profits, the sharing of information, and suchlike, the working philosophy of long-firm fraudsters is the example *par excellence* of what Schutz (1967a, p. 229) has called the '*epoché* of the natural attitude'. Unless they have good grounds to suspect the contrary, they expect all around them to cheat and betray them if they have the opportunity or the need to do so. Under these conditions, a genuinely cohesive subculture cannot develop, for no-one can afford to relax their surveillance over their colleagues to the point where smooth business organization of crime can be assured. Even those who would prefer to be loyal and who understand the benefits of continuous organization feel that they cannot afford to act in support of long-term interests. As one person who was involved in a car racket with a top long-firm organizer said in a statement to the police: 'Blank got [the stolen Mercedes] over here... but I didn't want to know. With Blank, he either stitches you up with the law or he fucks you... I have decided to tell the truth because with Blank you always end up losing and I want to get in first.'

It is difficult to explain fully the general lack of trust between long-firm merchants. At a more abstract level, one may relate the code of loyalty to the necessity to mitigate violence among people who must work together over long periods in a circumscribed geographical area. Loyalty also facilitates the performance of criminal activities, since it enables one to take certain things for granted. However, not all things that are functional actually exist. In the case of long-firm fraud, organizers are relatively mobile and devious, are often multilingual, and their confidence in their social skills may enable them to transcend the geographical rationale for loyalty. There may also be personality differences: long-firm fraudsters may be more individualistic (or anomic) than most 'villains' who are still working-class community-based, despite demographic changes (compare Mack, 1964, 1975; Ball *et al.*, 1978). Be that as it may, the constant 'grassing' and financial cheating inhibit the development of business-type organization of long-firm fraud, and make project organization its most *socially* viable form. If the police are corrupt or inefficient, business organization may be sustained because of the carrots and sticks offered by syndicated criminals, but most long-firm organizers would not hesitate to 'grass' if it became expedient to do so and if they trusted the police to protect them. We may verify this hypothesis by reference to the Kray and Richardson trials in the 1960s and to the attempt of the long-firm organizer for the Dixon gang in the early 1970s to turn Queen's evidence in exchange for non-prosecution.

The model of distrust presented here is a little extreme: there have been many occasions when organizers have not betrayed each other to the police when to have done so would have been to their advantage. However, the general absence of a code of silence stands in marked contrast to the behaviour of *most* bank robbers as revealed in Ball *et al.* (1978), though it is almost certain that the solidary subcultures of armed robbers and burglars will disintegrate in time through the disloyalty and suspicion generated by the 'super-grasses'.

Although organizers may inform upon their colleagues or against 'heavier villains', their 'front men' seldom inform upon them or – where the roles of organizers and fence are distinct – upon the 'fences'. This superior morality may be due to their expectation that if they become known as 'grasses' they may find it difficult to obtain future criminal employment; or to their healthy fear of the violence that can be summoned by powerful background operators. However, fair treatment by organizers does seem to have some influence on the decision to remain silent. It may be, too, that the present levels of sentencing for 'front men' do not provide them with any great incentive to 'grass'. The principal occasions when 'front men' have given evidence against organizers have been when police corruption has also been charged, though there is no obvious reason why this should have been so.

Despite the fact that long-firm organizers are not as dependent upon knowing 'fences' as are other types of 'villain', I know of no cases where they have 'grassed' upon them. Organizers may think that they may need the 'fence' at some future date, that the word of their treachery may deter other 'fences' from dealing with them, that the 'fence' could easily 'grass' on *them* in the future, and that the police are unlikely to let *them* off lightly in order to 'do' a 'fence' in the way that they would if they wanted to 'do' a 'gangster'. Equally, however, in contrast to the general trend, it is rare for 'fences' to 'grass up' organizers. When they do so, their motivation is to punish organizers for cheating them or for taking their business elsewhere. One may account for the difference between 'ordinary' and long-firm 'fencing' by the fact that long-firm 'fences' already possess legal security against a charge of handling stolen goods by virtue of the legal title of the vendors, and do not need to trade with the police to ensure their own survival. Finally, on the topic of 'grassing', it should be noted that the absence of insurance rewards for the recovery of long-firm goods removes one major underworld incentive for non-conspirators to leak information to the police.

However, although there is limited trust between organizers and 'fences' on the subject of betrayal, there is now little trust with respect to finance. By contrast with the situation which existed before the mid-1960s, 'backers' and 'fences' are unwilling to loan money to finance long firms in advance of the delivery of goods. This lack of trust discourages some long firms, since organizers who are not already rich may find it very difficult to raise enough money to finance a 'big one'. On the other hand, it encourages vertical integration as 'fences' and 'backers' become more closely involved in organization to prevent themselves from being 'ripped off' by the 'front men' and organizers. When this happens, however, the relative immunity from conviction that is afforded by background status is sacrificed.

McIntosh (1976, p. 265) comments that

> Looking at professional crime as a rational economic activity, geared to making money and minimising risks, enables us to see that the arrangement of autonomous thieves and fences engaging in market relations is not likely to give way to an arrangement of fences exercising central control over thieves. There may be individuals in the underworld who will wish to attempt such control, but they are unlikely to succeed unless they can offer thieves some real economic advantages without increasing the risks of crime too much.

The 'fences' and 'backers' of long-firm frauds can maintain physical and financial control over the organisation of long firms (1) by allying themselves with gangsters who can keep the others in line, and (2) by cutting out the middleman and organising the frauds themselves. The latter – vertical integration – is particularly profitable. However, such centralised control does bring attendant risks, in the form of altering society's perception of the dangerousness of the activity. The phrase 'organised crime' is a potent negative image which tends to spark off more intensive efforts at social control.

Conclusions

Those criminologists who have devoted any significant attention to white-collar crime have tended to assume that the general public is fairly apathetic about it, though the public may regard it more seriously than do businessmen (Aubert, 1977; Clinard, 1977) or sentencers (Newman, 1977). This supposed fact is explained by Marxists (Pearce, 1976) as the result of ideological mystification, and by others (Smigel & Ross, 1970, p. 7) as the consequence of our having an ethical system developed from life in small communities which cannot yet cope with obligations between individuals and large impersonal organisations.

However, recent research in America has called into question assumptions about low public reactions to organisational crime. Schrager & Short (1980) have revealed that those white-collar crimes – such as the manufacture and sale of drugs known to be harmful or of dangerous automobiles – which may cause serious *physical* damage are regarded by the public with roughly as much seriousness as 'ordinary' violent crime; while 'purely financial' business crimes are perceived as being roughly as serious as 'ordinary' property crimes. (For earlier research, see Conklin, 1977.) In London, Sparks *et al.* (1977) found that the public regarded long-firm fraud more seriously than they did non-violent property crime. Consequently, we should treat as problematic the notion that white-collar crime is not 'real' crime in the eyes of the public. Moreover, we should not theorise about 'white-collar crime' as if this were a homogeneous concept.

Nevertheless, whatever the general public may or may not feel, under normal circumstances, formal social reaction to long-firm fraud is fairly modest. The long-firm fraudster is tolerated if not wanted or liked, for he benefits from the general deference with which businesspeople are treated in the Criminal Justice System, as well as from the distribution of policing resources which takes it for granted that criminals are seldom to be found in the business world. As Morris (1965, pp. 32–34) argues:

> Tolerance spreads over into the business world where the sharp man may spend much of his time on the margin between legal and illegal behaviour.... Such offences are seen for the most part as 'administrative' offences, yet they relate to a standard of integrity in business that in the long run may be just as important as ordinary honesty with money.... Most of the individuals who are convicted of 'orthodox' crime are lower class. Our society is predominantly middle class and the law makers and the judges are for the most part upper class. There is no problem in condemning the criminal because he is conveniently different from the majority of those who have to evaluate his behaviour and decide upon his fate.... Attitudes towards crime and criminals, then, vary, not so much in terms of the intrinsic nature of the criminal act, but in terms of the likelihood of the act being an established part of the observer's own social world. Crime in the last analysis is what the other person does. What I do, if it is against the law, is susceptible to redefinition through rationalisation. Even if the observer is unlikely to commit the particular crime in question, his attitude to it will be conditioned by a degree of identification which may result in either a lenient tolerance or a punitive rejection, depending upon how far the crime threatens the observer, or the group to which they all belong.

Although it seems unlikely that many businessmen will feel ready to identify with the 'pre-planned' or even 'intermediate' long-firm fraudster, the latter are often able to stay out of the criminal limelight. It is possible that one reason for this is that long-firm fraud generally remains a crime without a readily visualisable 'villain', and as Walsh (1977, p. 28) argues in her excellent study of 'fencing' in America, 'criminal characterisations and even carica-tures are a *useful* [my italic] device for the conceptualisation and description of criminal behaviour. Without them, the proscriptions regarding behaviour can remain very remote indeed.' This analysis applies both to the moral control exerted by the law on potentially deviant individuals and to the nature of societal reaction. However, by becoming 'organized' and teaming up with 'gangsters', long-firm fraudsters removed the protective veil afforded by their status as 'businessmen' and laid themselves open to what Tannenbaum (1938) has termed 'the dramatization of evil': to some extent, they were transformed from mere 'law-violators' into *criminal* social types, attracting more severe social condemnation and more active social control. Whether these levels of social control (modest though they are still) will persist, only time will tell. It is quite feasible that if 'traditional criminals' cease to involve themselves in 'white-collar crime', the levels of policing of the latter will decline. However, as one of the most subtle long-firm merchants of the 1960s stated to me:

> The l.f. used to be a real doddle for us: a great way to earn a few readies when times were hard. But then along came the gangsters and flogged the l.f. scene to death. Creditors started screaming and trade organizations started screaming, and the police got all excited about gangsters moving into commerce, and now it's all over. It's no longer worth the aggravation to run an l.f. Maybe things will quieten down eventually, but one thing's for certain: they'll never be the same again.

In conclusion, we may note that the organization of capitalism generates a framework of social control which is conducive to the perpetration of long-firm frauds. First, it promotes a value system which concentrates attention upon the goals of material success rather than on the means by which these goals are to be attained. Second, it provides inadequate means for the realization of these goals by all who wish to attain them. Third, in order to provide incentives for risk-taking and to encourage people to believe that success is open to all, it allows for the formation of limited liability companies. Fourth, it makes the acquisition of such companies easy by allowing specialist firms to sell 'ready-made' companies 'off the shelf'. Fifth, to enable vendors to make larger profits by increasing their turnover, it provides a ready source of credit to retail and wholesale customers. Sixth, it does not institute severe inquisitions and/or penalties for those businessmen who go 'bust'. And seventh, it provides a set of criteria for the attribution of criminality to businessmen which makes it relatively easy for many long-firm merchants and their 'fences' to remain outside the *practical* ambit of the criminal law. For example, the rules which make it lawful for businessmen to buy stolen goods provided that they have done so 'in good faith' protect the long-firm 'fences' who merely appear to do so; and the rules which make it lawful for creditors to delay payment by deceiving their debtors (provided that they intend to pay eventually) make it difficult to convict 'slippery-slopers'.

Society creates the venue for its own victimization, for the organization and quantity of 'crime' is moulded by the moral and practical organization of society in respect of the behaviour in question. In the case of fraudulent trading, the 'crime rate' is subject *a fortiori* than is normally the case to the crime-defining activities of social control agencies, because many victims do not perceive that they have been the victims of *crime*. Furthermore, under present social arrangements, the label of 'fraudster' is not only difficult to assign to businessmen but is also relatively inconsequential in terms of formal punishment for those so labelled.

The perceived seriousness of any given crime determines the nature of societal reaction to it, and this in turn determines both the internal and external constraints which influence the decision to act in a criminal manner. By sustaining a conception of long-firm fraud as relatively non-serious crime, society both ensures that its police discover only a small proportion of the total amount of fraudulent trading and makes it easier for businessmen to commit such frauds in the belief that what they are doing is not *really* criminal.

XII. Control of Long-Firm Fraud: Some Issues for the Future

The past fifty years have witnessed a massive expansion in the importance – both relative and absolute – of fraud within the criminal justice process. Frauds now comprise some 4·7 per cent of all recorded indictable crime in England and Wales, compared with a mere 0·5 per cent in 1928. During the last decade, this trend has accelerated. Between 1968 and 1978, convictions for fraud in the higher courts rose by 230 per cent, while the amount of money involved in frauds handled by the London Metropolitan and City Police Fraud Squad increased tenfold to approximately £300 million per annum. During 1980, the latter figure rose to £400 million.

This growth has placed a strain upon all levels of the system for controlling fraud. In respect of policing, there are still only 25 full-time investigators employed by the Department of Trade to monitor the increased incidence of reported corporate malpractice, and there is only one Fraud Squad officer for every hundred officers in the Metropolitan Police. Fraud cases now impose a heavy burden upon the time and manpower of the Director of Public Prosecutions. And the number and length of fraud trials are creating blockages in some of our criminal courts, as well as leading to heavy expenses for the Legal Aid Fund. These problems are not unique to Britain: they are occurring also in the United States (see, for example, Edelhertz and Rogovin, 1980).

The London Central Criminal Court (the 'Old Bailey') is not typical of English higher courts, but the situation there may be a portent of future problems elsewhere. The average length of long-firm fraud trials there has *quadrupled* since the 1940s. Taking all fraud cases committed to the Old Bailey in 1977 (and tried mainly in 1978 and 1979), we may observe that the *average* length of contested conspiracy to defraud cases was five and a half working weeks, and that even the relatively simple prosecutions for fraud taken out under the Theft Act 1968 lasted an average of more than three weeks. Indeed, one in five contested fraud trials lasted over six working weeks. (To put this in perspective, it should be noted that less than half the defendants charged with fraud pleaded guilty.)

Judicial concern has been aroused also by the fact that some fraud trials last for more than six months, only to be abandoned or expensively retried. In 1979, a trial that had cost over £1 million in legal fees was stopped because of a prejudicial newspaper report which revealed that some of the defendants had experienced previous problems with the law; in March 1981, an Old Bailey judge directed the acquittal of a man whose fraud trial had lasted 103 days, finding that the prosecution had failed to prove their case; and on 1 May 1981, a trial for a fraud involving £25 million finally ended in the conviction of the principal suspects, after *two* trials lasting 137 days each. (The first of the trials, which cost £1 250 000, was abandoned by the judge after suspicions that an attempt had been made to bribe two jurors.) Lord Elwyn Jones, who was Lord Chancellor during the Labour government of 1974–1979, has observed that despite exhortations to speed up and simplify fraud trials, they increased in duration by ten per cent per annum while he was in office.

The cumulative impact of these stresses – even if we set aside the issue of the 'dark figure' of unrecorded fraud – requires us to rethink radically the future direction that the control of fraud should take. A small beginning has been made, with the reforms of company investigation procedures proposed by the Secretary of State for Trade in May 1980, but there is little evidence of fundamental thought elsewhere. For example, the Conservative Attorney-General, Sir Michael Havers, has responded to concern about the length and cost of fraud trials by suggesting three changes: shorter judicial summings-up; longer, unbroken sittings in court; and less complicated, all-embracing indictments, with only 'the real villains' being subject to criminal charges. However, these proposals are either undesirable or not feasible. First, although judges should provide more acute and illuminating summings-up (see in particular *R.* v. *Landy* (1981), 1 All E.R. 1172), they may find that convictions are quashed in the Court of Appeal if they fail to give sufficient weight to all the defence evidence. Second, if sittings are longer and unbroken, the primarily working-class, inexpert jurors may find even more difficulty in maintaining their concentration than they do at present. And third, those suspects who *are* charged with fraud will undoubtedly seek to cast the blame for the fraud upon those – allegedly on the margins – who are *not* charged. Moreover, why should someone obtain *de facto* immunity from prosecution simply because he is a 'minor' co-defendant rather than a minor criminal acting alone?

Against this background, there are four principal directions in which the control of long-firm fraud (and fraud generally) could move. First, we could continue to muddle through as we do at the moment, prosecuting only the more blatant cases within a criminal justice system that is singularly ill-adapted to the investigation and trial of accusations of sophisticated fraud. Second, we could reverse the last century's trend towards the increased involvement of the State in the policing of commerce. We might even *de*criminalise fraud, on the grounds that the careful businessman and the general public should not have to subsidise those businessmen who are too greedy or mean to carry out proper commercial credit enquiries. (However, this is an argument that could be applied to most law-enforcement functions, and except in a tautological sense, most victims of intermediate, slippery-slope, and sophisticated frauds cannot reasonably be blamed for their 'negligence'.) Most long-firm fraudsters make charming and amusing company, support the free enterprise system, and are no more likely than law-abiding businessmen to beat their wives or go on 'mugging' expeditions. Most of them only want to be able to make enough money to be able to afford to be honest. So why worry about them?

Third, we might move towards a system of informal community control, such as Henry (1978) has advocated in relation to the trial of pilferers by courts composed of workers. We might, for instance, bring debtors who are alleged to have infringed commercial norms in front of 'community courts' composed of businessmen, where they would be tried without formal rules of evidence and procedure. The fourth and final possibility is that we might universalise our concern with 'Law and Order' to incorporate 'crime in the suites' as well as 'crime on the streets'.

All law enforcement entails social costs as well as social benefits, but our preference for each option depends on how seriously we want to treat the acts of long-firm fraudsters and other commercial criminals. If we are indifferent to (or even approve of) the fraudulent behaviour under consideration, then the first two options may seem attractive. We may be happy with the *de facto* non-enforcement of much company and bankruptcy law due to the slender resources that are devoted to them. And we may support the Conservative Government's proposals to reduce the *existing* levels of surveillance over commercial activities (including fraud), as indicated in the 1980 consultative 'Green Paper' on bankruptcy and in the Companies (no. 2) Bill, 1981. It is an interesting reflection of the government's conception of 'the crime problem' that, in a period of alleged maintenance of expenditure on law and order, it proposed the abolition of the Registry of Business Names in order to save £3 million. (The 570 jobs lost here may be contrasted with the employment of an extra 1,000 staff to deal with suspected social security fraud.)

The suggested denationalisation of bankruptcy control will probably result in fewer bankruptcies, since creditors will not wish to bear the costs of placing people into bankruptcy as well as accountants' fees unless there are substantial assets to be recovered. It may also lead to less thorough investigation of those persons who *are* made bankrupt and who may have committed fraud, since private accountants tend to take the duty of pursuing fraud less seriously than do bankruptcy examiners, and there will be poorer liaison with the police if bankruptcies are handled by private liquidators rather than by the Official Receiver. In short, government measures can obscure the public face of fraud, thus reducing the apparent scale of 'the fraud problem'.

If, on the other hand, we wish to take commercial credit (or other) frauds *more* seriously than we do at present – and it is important to note that the public in London rated the obtaining of £1000 worth of goods on credit from large manufacturers by a bogus firm as being *substantially more* serious than any other non-violent property offence (Sparks *et al.*, 1977, p. 184) – then what might we do about this, short of abolishing the capitalist system altogether? It appears to me that informal 'community courts' might be effective as well as fair ways of dealing with 'slippery-slope' frauds, but they are unlikely to be effective in dealing with 'pre-planned' fraudsters. For non-punitive community control depends for its effectiveness upon the presence of close social, geographical, and affective ties between judges and defendants, and this does not meet the case of the mobile and individualistic world of the professional long-firm fraudster. It is difficult, then, to see how such a 'community control' system would work in practice, even if one regarded it as desirable in theory.

In this chapter, I shall pursue the logic of the reformist line advocated by the late Judge Morris Finer (1966, p. 588), who was highly critical of the procedures for processing company frauds:

> The complaint is not that these problems have not been solved but that they are not being seriously considered. The history of the Companies Acts could be written in terms of a century of sporadic and ill-planned endeavour to mitigate the more intolerable consequences of a basic premise that business, even when conducted under the special conditions of limited liability, is an affair between consenting male adults. We need to build carefully, but anew, from a different premise – that limited liablity is an artifice sanctioned by the community, derived as a privilege from them, and subject, accordingly, to the paramount rule of their welfare.

Informal control of long-firm frauds

The primary line of defence against long-firm fraudsters is the decision not to grant them credit. Historically, trade protection societies have been the major source of social defence in this field, and they will continue to possess a better overall view of any given trader than is possible for any one firm's credit controller. The grocery, tobacco, and the wine and spirits trades have their own industry-wide trade protection organizations, but given the lack of corresponding specialism in the goods ordered by many long firms, multi-trade credit bureaux should in principle be more effective than single-trade ones. The more that suppliers use such agencies, the lower the price that the latter can charge per enquiry and the better the flow of information regarding the trading pattern of the would-be debtor. Hence the control of fraud – and the provision of good advice – might be improved by a monopolistic or oligopolistic system of commercial credit inquiry.

The best means of preventing any long firm which seeks major increases in credit is through the use of efficient trade protection organizations. This is true of 'little quickies', of formerly licit businesses which are taken over by long-firm fraudsters, and of long firms which employ references from banks or merchants of dubious integrity. However, the more sophisticated long firms, in which credit ratings are built up very gradually and no abrupt increase in credit requests is made, are very difficult for both individual credit managers and trade protection organizations to detect. For part of the art of the skilled long-firm merchant is to lull the supplier into taking his worth for granted.

In the latter *modus operandi*, there is no direct clue which triggers off suspicion. The only real protections for businessmen are a *permanently* suspicious attitude towards supplicants for credit, however well they think that they know them, and a good 'nose' for the honesty of intentions (in the 'pre-planned' and 'intermediate' cases) and for the solvency of their debtors (in 'slippery-slope' cases). Sometimes, an individual creditor can be paid in full because the fraudster robs Peter to pay Paul, but general losses to 'slippery-slopers' can be prevented only when trade is so good that everyone is making profits. Similarly, general losses of large sums to 'pre-planned' and to 'intermediate' fraudsters who set up their 'marks' slowly and carefully can be prevented only if *general* business conditions are so bad that *no-one* is allowed substantial sums of credit. (Although, as we have seen in Chapter V, motivation for running an 'intermediate' long firm is less in prosperous times than it is in hard times). In all situations, however, the professionalism of the credit manager and the weight given to his opinion are crucial to the minimization of the risk of losing money to a fraud (and to a legitimate business).

Organization of the police in relation to long-firm fraud

In his opening address to the first National Conference on the Investigation of Commercial Fraud, held in New Scotland Yard in 1973, the Metropolitan Police Commissioner, Sir Robert Mark, stated (personal communication, unpublished) that

> There is no doubt that from a really professional police viewpoint, [fraud] is becoming one of the most important problems of today. What is even more important is that if we fail to appreciate this properly and if we fail to take the necessary measures, it will grow at an inordinate rate and it may well have international complications which will make our task exceedingly difficult.

Although it is probably the case that long-firm fraud is the type of commercial crime that the police are best equipped to handle, its investigation is hampered by the general lack of priority given to fraud as a form of crime – it is conspicuous by its absence from Mark's (1978) account of the problems he tackled in office – and by the general organization of the police. One of the principal difficulties here is caused by the combination of small Fraud Squads and relatively inflexible rank structures. Although Fraud Squad officers within the Metropolitan Police can rise to Commander level, the most senior rank within any provincial Fraud Squad is that of Detective Superintendent, and that applies only in a few larger forces. The average senior rank of fraud investigators is that of Chief Inspector, and many complicated frauds involving less than a million pounds are dealt with by constables or at most a sergeant, something that would be unimaginable with other types of crime. As Whitaker (1979) observes, very few officers spend their entire working lives in the investigation of fraud, because promotion tends to be based upon the concept of the 'good all-rounder', even in the Metropolitan Police where specialization is at its greatest. Since most bright people in the police are ambitious for status, power and money, it follows that the present organization of the police is disadvantageous for those who wish to acquire *and maintain* expertise in the investigation of fraud.

Furthermore, the greater part of police training is 'on the job': in most forces, there is little or no training except for the short courses organized in London, Birmingham and Manchester, which do little more than provide some basic information about the varieties of fraud and (importantly) enable officers in different forces to meet, exchange views and build up informal networks which may aid subsequent investigations. If long-firm frauds and commercial crimes generally are to be investigated properly, there is a need for far greater manpower and professionalism. Moreover, in so far as one of the obstacles to the investigation of fraud lies in the fear of tackling the unknown and making a mess of it, there would seem to be a case for spreading knowledge about fraud to as many officers of Sergeant and Inspector rank as possible. At present, however, fraud barely reaches backwater status in police training courses.

Most fraud investigations are extremely labour-intensive, and any given number of officers can deal with far fewer frauds than any other type of crime. Yet because the public and Chief Officers of police do not press strongly for greater resources in this area (possibly because of their fear that a redistribution of resources from 'normal' crime to fraud would have negative effects on their 'clear-up' rates for other crimes), there are very few officers in Fraud Squads in comparison with the amount of money that is involved in fraud offences. It appears that in order to increase the number of fraud investigators, a change in police attitudes is required.

This need for change applies also to the present system of interchange between fraud and other police tasks. The present system is advantageous in two principal respects: first, it reduces (probably) the risk of systematic corruption; and second, after a few years of fraud work, the motivation of *some* officers diminishes greatly, and they begin to work slowly and inefficiently. Nevertheless, there does appear to be a case for specialist Fraud Squad recruitment from inside and outside the police service. This can only be achieved by special merit awards for specialization independent of promotion or by the creation and maintenance of a disproportionate number of middle and senior ranks within Fraud Squads. Otherwise, despite major improvements in police pay, remuneration will be inadequate to attract people of sufficient calibre. This might well create considerable tension within the police service, but it is the only long-term solution to the problems of ensuring professionalism and continuity in the investigation of fraud. The need for these factors is particularly acute in the investigation of international frauds, the special difficulties of which have been recognized by the setting up in 1980 of a squad to pursue frauds which occur between Commonwealth members.

Prosecution of long-firm frauds

The prosecution of long-firm fraudsters has become considerably more efficient since Hadden (1967a) studied the control of company fraud. However, provincial officers in particular are highly critical of the delays which occur when they submit a case for decision to the Director of Public Prosecutions. Some of these complaints are attributable simply to frustration and to a lack of understanding of legal niceties. However, the large and growing burden of cases which reach the Director's Office means that 'non-priority' cases go to the bottom of the queue for attention. It may be that what is required here is a major improvement in the local or regional provision of expert advice in fraud cases. This could be achieved by expanding the Director's staff and devolving them more than at present, or by creating more or less autonomous Task Force Regional Prosecution Units (on the European and American model), paid for either out of central funds or by pooling the resources of local police authorities. Speedy advice and decision-taking is essential for fraud investigators, because unless they receive it, the trail of the long-firm merchants may go cold and the background operators, in particular, may escape prosecution. Although liaison between the Director's staff and police officers (and between the police and the Department of Trade) has improved considerably in the last decade, particularly in the holding of joint case conferences in London, there is still room for considerable improvement with regard to fraud and corruption investigations which occur outside London.

Changes in criminal law and criminal procedure

It is clear that the large increase in the numbers and complexity of fraud cases which reach the stage of prosecution have generated something of a crisis in the criminal justice system. Although Baldwin and McConville (1979, p. 64) state that 'there was not a single fraud trial in the London sample which lasted as long as seven days and most of those which lasted as long as three days resulted in conviction', this belies the state of affairs at the Old Bailey, where half or more of the courts are often occupied with fraud cases which may last several months. It is very rare for long-firm fraud trials to last less than twenty working days, and they are relatively simple. The time and costs of such prosecutions and investigations has led some forces to write off frauds which obtain less than £50 000.

Discussions with people involved in the control of fraud indicate that they experience less difficulty with long firms than with other types of fraud. Nevertheless, effective control is inhibited in the following ways:

(1) the police find it very difficult to obtain access to the bank accounts of suspects prior to their arrest;

(2)   neither the police nor the Department of Trade have the power to inspect the books of unincorporated businesses;

(3)   it is extremely difficult for anyone to investigate, arrest or prosecute successfully those who engage in international frauds;

(4)   *all* agencies involved in the control of commercial crime suffer from a lack of resources in terms both of quality and quantity: this is a claim that is made by all subsections of the police, but the ratio of resources to the costs of crime seems to be particularly low in the case of frauds;

(5)   considerable doubts are expressed regarding the ability of the criminal justice system to process commercial crime in a way that is fair both to the accused and to the Crown.

Let us first examine the issue of access to commercial records and to bank accounts. The Royal Commission on Criminal Procedure (1981, pp. 34–35) has recommended increased investigating powers, so that accounts may be examined before arrest or the issuance of a summons. The granting of this change in police powers – restricted though it is – may have far less effect on long-firm frauds than on the financial and accounting frauds which are at present extremely difficult to investigate. However, one may predict the following consequences for the control of long-firm fraud:

Provided that they learn of the suspect firm while it is still in operation, the police will have better information than they can lawfully obtain at present about its state of solvency, so they should be able to judge the optimal timing of arrests. (The Department of Trade can obtain permission to inspect the books of limited companies under Section 109 of the Companies Act, 1967, but the company finds out that it is being monitored.) Fearing police access to their accounts, fraudsters may be tempted to withdraw funds from the business at the last moment, instead of doing so gradually, thereby increasing the risk to their capital if the police close down the business early. They may also be induced to enter into circumlocutory laundering operations with the proceeds of their crimes, to provide better protection against police inspections of their personal bank accounts. However, the larger the number of complicated transactions they enter into, the better the chance that they will slip up somewhere along the line or that someone will 'grass' on them. The operational effectiveness of 'backers' and organizers may be diminished by the time they waste covering their tracks: some may even be deterred from participation by the effort involved, or by their lack of access to the more sophisticated world of 'dirty money' operators.

However, the consequences of the proposed new powers for an increased *conviction* rate in long-firm fraud cases should not be overestimated. For example, 'fences' will still be able to obtain secret 'kick-backs' from organizers, while presenting them with cheques for the full market price of their goods. Also, there will still be no way of tracing transactions which take place *sub rosa* for cash, and bank accounts held in countries which enforce strict banking secrecy rules will remain beyond the purview of the English police and courts.

I have already mentioned the policing problems entailed by international frauds, and these are matched by legal difficulties to which few practical solutions are in sight. In my view, the harmonization of EEC substantive law which is taking place – slowly – is unlikely to make any major impact on the control of international crime. Improvements in the law of venue – discussed in Chapter VII – might be useful, but as long as there is no universal international agreement regarding extradition of commercial offenders and there are corrupt governments willing to shelter them, multinational fraudsters will be able to avoid *ex post facto* prosecution.

Finally, let us examine the possible consequences for long-firm fraudsters of some changes in the criminal justice system that have been under discussion during the 1970s.

(1) *Introduction of the previous convictions of accused persons into the case put forward by the prosecution*

One-quarter of those convicted at the Old Bailey between 1962 and 1972 in connection with long-firm fraud had no previous convictions, and almost half had less than two previous convictions. In other words, as measured by their previous convictions, those convicted at present are not a heavily criminal group. Of those *acquitted* during this period, no fewer than 60 per cent had no previous convictions and only a quarter had received total prison sentences of longer than twelve months prior to their present conviction. (For further details, see Levi, 1979, ch. 8.)

If we look at the alleged 'professional long-firm fraudsters', of whom nine were acquitted at the Old Bailey between 1950 and 1976, we may note that at the time of their acquittal, only three had received sentences totalling more than twelve months' imprisonment, one had a previous twelve-months sentence, one had two previous convictions but had never been sent to prison, and four had no previous convictions at all. However, all five who had criminal records had at least one conviction for commercial crime and, in their cases, the introduction of previous convictions *might* have had some effect upon the jury's decisions, although precisely what effect is a matter for speculation. On the assumption that all five would have been convicted had their prior convictions been known, then 55 per cent of the acquitted 'professional long-firm fraudsters' would have been convicted.

However, there is a further possible consequence of the proposal that the Crown be entitled to introduce into evidence the prior convictions of accused persons: it might encourage the police to prosecute in cases where at present they would not prosecute. In other words, the police might think that the prejudicial effect of jurors' knowledge of the previous convictions of an alleged 'professional criminal' might lead to a conviction where, under the present rules, there would be an expectation of an acquittal which would deter prosecution. So the ratio of suspected involvements in crimes to prosecutions might *decrease* as a result of the change in procedural rules. This would apply principally to those professionals who already have a record, and the great majority of those 'professionals' below the top level do have *some* kind of record, even if their convictions are in no way equal to their crimes. If, however, the view that the knowledge of previous convictions will increase the chances of conviction turns out to be ill-founded, we might then see an *increase* in the rates of acquittal of 'professional long-firm fraudsters': a most paradoxical ending to Mark's (1973) allegations regarding the high levels of acquittal of professional criminals.

(2) *Power either to compel a defendant to give evidence on oath or to permit the prosecution and judge to draw an adverse inference from his refusal to do so*

In the only case I witnessed in which a defendant in a long-firm fraud case refused to give evidence on oath but instead read a statement from the dock, the defendant was convicted. It is not beyond the bounds of reason to conjecture that jurors presently ask themselves what a defendant has to hide if he fails to give evidence on oath. They may not always convict after such speculation – the acquittal of the English politician Jeremy Thorpe being a case in point – but, in the view of those counsel to whom I have spoken, not giving evidence is regarded as the last resort of a desperate case or of a case where the client is assessed as a dismal performer in the witness box. In my view, the suggested reform would have little impact upon long-firm fraud cases unless it went further and compelled defendants to answer questions on oath: something that might smack of the Spanish Inquisition.

On the subject of the rules of evidence, there is an anomaly regarding the conditions under which previous convictions of defendants can be introduced. Normally, subject to the judge's discretion, such convictions may be revealed if defendants attack the integrity of prosecution witnesses. Yet if a defendant does impugn the honesty of the police (or any other Crown witnesses) but chooses not to give evidence on oath – for example, if he makes an unsworn statement from the dock – the prosecution is not entitled to introduce evidence of his previous convictions. If, as I have suggested, jurors usually are prejudiced against people who do not go into the witness box, the effects of this subtle defence ploy may be negated, but it remains an anomaly nevertheless. (The Royal Commission on Criminal Procedure in 1981 recommended the abolition of the right to make an unsworn statement from the dock.)

To summarize my arguments concerning the likely effects of proposals to increase police powers and change some rules of procedure in court, I list them in descending order of predicted effect:

(1) easier police access to private and commercial books of account;
(2) the introduction of previous convictions into the Crown case as of right;
(3) the power to make adverse comment should a defendant choose not to give evidence on oath.

However, with the possible exception of the first proposal, none of these reforms would make as much impact as an increase in police and Department of Trade manpower devoted to the surveillance of fraud or as increased specialization within a Fraud Squad career-structure.

The fundamental reasons why background operators are seldom convicted for *all* their crimes are that their *modus operandi* make it very difficult to discover what they are up to all the time, and, also, to prove to the satisfaction of the courts the organizational links between them and their 'front-line' operators. Police successes against these background operators have been due principally to the facts that the anti-corruption drive caught out those who had become over-confident and had exposed their connections with long-firm frauds, and that their inability to trust their 'front-liners' sometimes induced them to move 'upfront', thereby giving the police reasonably clear evidence of conspiracy to defraud.

Long-firm frauds and trial by jury
Finer (1966, p. 588), who before his elevation to the judiciary had been a distinguished commercial lawyer, once wrote that

It is rare in a working life to undergo a dream sequence of exquisite fantasy, but such has been the experience of one former barrister seeking – as a preliminary to more complicated matters – to explain the inwardness of a cumulative non-participating preference share to a manifestly hostile inspector of sewers, a lady with a bag of knitting, and several others whose gaze of rapt attention would have been more encouraging had they found it easier to read the oath.

I am not sure that in the present condition of things, where it is generally only the more gross and palpable frauds that are prosecuted, that the jury causes much injustice in the end. To smell bad fish does not require the nose of a connoisseur, and by the end of the trial, and by dint of repetition, and repetition of repetition, the bulk of the jury no doubt obtain some broad understanding of the facts they are supposed to be trying.

What is involved is a most profligate expenditure of time and money on the paper, speeches, and explanations adduced in striving to convey a glimmer to the darkest intelligence present... the jury in this class of cases should be special, not common – that is to say, should be selected from persons who by occupation and experience are likely to bring into court with them some modicum of ability to follow the evidence.

These sentiments of concern about fraud trials by jury were echoed in two 'leaders' in *The Times* (28 March 1972, and 16 January 1973), which advocated trial by judge and expert assessors, and which pointed out that the abolition of the property qualification for jurors would make it still more likely that a jury would be selected who would fail to understand the case. (In Chapter IX, I observed that defence counsel seek to object to jurors who look capable of understanding financial matters.) *The Times* added that in order to avoid the risk of perverse jury acquittals, the prosecution sometimes felt obliged to accept pleas of guilty on lesser charges. (No mention was made of the cost of trials as a factor which might lead to the same result.)

In contrast to these critiques of the jury system in fraud cases, Baldwin and McConville (1979, pp. 62–5) report no general dissatisfaction with juries among fraud investigators *from the police*, and observe that the fraud acquittal rates are no greater than the norm. There remains, however, no hard evidence about the ability of jurors to understand fraud cases.

Perhaps one useful starting point would be to assume that we were asked to devise from scratch an ideal system of trial for fraud allegations. What would be the advantages and disadvantages of different systems of trial? In a letter to *The Times* (16 January 1973), Michael Sherrard, QC, observed that the common jury system was unsuited to fraud trials:

The ends of justice are not always served by over-simplification ...
the complexity of cases involving elements of foreign commercial
practice and documentation will prove even more daunting to
jurors ... Possibly the Commercial Court should develop an extra
arm with which to embrace criminal as well as civil cases. One
result is certain: there would be speedier disposal of other
comparatively simple cases otherwise queuing behind a long
fraud.

Although I agree with his criticism of existing juries, his
suggestion regarding the expansion of the Commercial Court should
be viewed with care, not because it represents an irrational way of
trying cases but because it may lead to a further devaluation of the
treatment of fraud as *crime*. There would probably be even less press
publicity for fraud cases if they were taken out of the Crown Courts,
and this in turn might lessen whatever deterrent impact public trial
has.

The use of special juries or expert assessors within the existing
Crown Courts is not without its problems either. It may be argued
that some criminal offences in the area of 'white-collar crime' *do*
reflect common commercial practices, and that 'offenders' might be
acquitted by a jury of their peers in the way that is alleged to happen
to motoring offenders. To a limited extent, this objection might
extend to the use of expert assessors. Unless the age-limit for jury
service were raised so that retired people could be used, it would
undoubtedly prove difficult to recruit special juries for the large
number of cases now before the courts.

The use of special juries would be a more traditionalist change, for
it was only a century ago that the use of special juries to try
misdemeanours such as conspiracies to defraud and the falsification
of documents was abolished. Moreover, this would represent a
return to the principle that the jury should consist of persons
acquainted with the customs of the area, something that is certainly
not true of fraud juries as they are presently composed.

The introduction of special juries or expert assessors in place of
the present jury system might lead to an increase in the numbers
prosecuted as well as – perhaps – in the proportion of those prosecuted who are convicted. This would apply particularly to those
suspected 'slippery-slope' and 'intermediate' fraudsters who are
presently given the benefit of jurors' perceived incompetence and are
not prosecuted at all. Furthermore, it is unlikely that the proposed
changes will lead to injustice, for there is no reason *prima facie* why
special jurors should be more likely than common ones to convict
innocent *businessmen*: the high social status of the latter should

protect them against possible 'prosecution-mindedness' on the part of professional jurors.

However, even if one were to accept the arguments set out above, there are several reasons why one might wish to reject the proposal to introduce trial of fraud cases by special jury or by judge with expert assessors, which in 1981 was accepted in principle by the Law Society.

First, it may be feared that this is the 'thin end of the wedge' which prepares the ground for the abolition of trial by jury altogether. While it is probably the case that many of those who support the abolitionist argument in respect of fraud cases would also oppose juries for other criminal trials, there are ample technical and intellectual grounds for arguing that fraud cases present particularly extreme difficulties. Besides, the principle that juries should be acquainted with the inhabitants and customs of the area would support the maintenance of 'common juries' in other spheres.

Second, it may be argued that jury trial is as necessary as *mens rea* to public acceptance of fraud as 'real crime'. Although I argued against the transfer of fraud cases to the Commercial Court on this kind of ground, it applies less cogently to trials in the Crown Courts. Moreover, there may be little point in the public regarding fraud as 'bad' if their inability to comprehend the details thereof makes them feel unjustified in convicting those who are tried for fraud.

Finally, enthusiasts for a 'People's Court' system of justice may wish to retain the common jury system in the hope that 'immoral' businessmen will be convicted of crimes when, in fact, the behaviour in question has not been proscribed by law. However, irrespective of the *general* merits of this approach, it should be noted that such conduct is unlikely to be prosecuted or, if prosecuted, the defendant is likely to be acquitted on the direction of the trial or appellate judge.

However, unless people are willing to accept lower standards of proof, *no* reforms of police powers and criminal procedure will make it easy to convict background operators: this, after all, is the principal reason why people *become* background operators. Readers may feel that despite the effects on the fabric of trust which is so necessary to the capitalist economy, and despite the built-in advantage to business criminals offered by present levels of control, long-firm (and other) frauds do not represent as great a threat as they would require to induce them to agree to any further invasion of civil liberties. However, they must accept that if they do not agree to these measures, commercial criminals – whether they be 'villains' or apparent 'respectables' – will continue to enjoy their fairly high levels of immunity from conviction.

The data and arguments presented here and by Baldwin and McConville (1977, 1979) cannot of themselves justify increased measures of control. It is hoped, however, that they will lead to a more considered judgement about 'the problem of professional fraud' (and of crime in general) than is provided by the largely irrelevant debate about acquittals in those cases that *are* brought to court. Only if *all* criminals were prosecuted for *all* their *actual* crimes, and not only for those crimes that are both 'known to the police' and brought to court, would the acquittal rate provide an adequate baseline for measuring the extent to which alleged 'major criminals' are avoiding conviction.

If the reader accepts the thrust of my arguments, he or she will conclude that there is almost certainly a vast 'dark figure' of undetected and/or unprosecuted 'fraudulent trading'. The precise nature of this 'dark figure' will always be problematic, for it is not theoretically possible to generate unambiguous procedures for the imputation of 'fraudulent intent' or 'recklessness'. It seems likely, however, that the dark figure of undetected 'slippery-slope' fraud is greater than that of 'intermediate' fraud, which, in turn, is greater than that of 'pre-planned' fraud. Furthermore, in those cases of business failure that *are* prosecuted as fraudulent and which involve some degree of conspiratorial background organization, it is *rare* for *all* of those concerned to be charged, though the 'background operators' seldom are acquitted when they are brought to trial. It is for the reader to consider whether or not this constitutes an important 'social problem'.

Sentencing of long-firm fraudsters

Disillusionment with 'the rehabilitative ideal' and concern about 'law and order' have led to considerable debate about alternative penal strategies during the 1970s. One of the primary new directions being considered is that of incapacitating the so-called 'dangerous offenders', that is, keeping them out of circulation for the protection of society. Van den Haag (1975) and James Q. Wilson (1975) have argued that *all* people who commit certain defined 'serious crimes' should be incarcerated for long periods. Alternatively, it has been argued that certain selected *individuals* should be incapacitated on the basis of predictive tables of 'background variables'.

These incapacitation strategies have been criticized on a number of grounds, of which two are most noteworthy. First, the predictions of who will become a 'dangerous offender' are highly inaccurate and will lead to the long-term incarceration of many people who would not have committed another 'serious offence'. Second, they will not reduce the crime rate by a large amount, since the vast majority of offences are committed by people who have not been convicted of such offences previously. (For these critiques, see Bottoms, 1977; Monahan, 1975; Pease and Wolfson, 1979; Radzinowicz and Hood, 1978; Van Dine *et al.*, 1977; Von Hirsch, 1972, 1976.)

Furthermore, as Petersilia (1977) has noted, since the peak of criminal behaviour occurs in early adulthood, traditional incapacitation measures are applied only when most offenders have already passed their major 'active' periods. The debate about such sentencing strategies has taken place almost entirely in the context of conventionally defined 'violent crime'. However, there is no reason why this should necessarily be the case. Let us examine the effects of such a strategy upon 'professional long-firm fraudsters'.

One of the principal difficulties here is our inability to predict future involvement in fraud with any degree of accuracy. People may turn to long-firm fraud from commercial or from 'ordinary' crime at any age between their twenties and their seventies, and they may 'mature out' early on or may continue until their seventies. There seem to be no discernible criteria from which one might predict who will give up fraud and who will return to it.

Petersilia's (1977) analysis would appear to imply that if we impose light criteria for eligibility as candidates for incapacitation, we are likely to overpredict career criminality, while if we impose stringent criteria for eligibility, we may catch 'the habituals' only when they have already passed their peak of activity, that is, when it is less necessary to protect the public from them. This is a particular problem when the probability of conviction for each crime is as low as it is for commercial crime. For under these conditions, the predictive power of previous convictions as a discriminator between occasional and frequent offenders is considerably reduced.

If the reader is not disturbed by the potential for injustice of the incapacitatory 'crime control' model, then he may feel that long sentences should be imposed upon the second or third convictions. However, if we look at the criminal conviction records of my top twenty professional long-firm fraudsters, we note that four have no convictions *at all*, eight have no convictions for long-firm fraud, twelve have no more than *one* conviction, and seventeen have no more than *two* convictions for long-firm fraud. (These figures include all convictions registered by the end of April, 1979.) None of the twenty has been convicted of long-firm fraud on more than three separate occasions. In brief, an incapacitation strategy based on previous convictions for long-firm fraud would not enable us to incapacitate more than half of the 'top professionals' unless it were to apply at the first conviction stage. If it were applied then, we would also incapacitate many first-timers who would have ceased crime subsequently in any event.

The logic of this approach applies equally when *individually* deterrent sentences are contemplated: either overprediction or underprediction will occur. However, there may be a case for more severe sentencing of long-firm fraudsters on the grounds of *general* deterrence and retribution.

If we examine the practice of sentencing in long-firm fraud cases, we may note that judges rarely impose severe sentences for 'social defence' reasons. For example, few fraudsters are incapacitated for very long periods, and judges do not hand out severe sentences to 'front men' in order to make it more difficult for organizers to find willing recruits or to encourage them to 'grass' upon the organizers. Judges appear to follow a policy that Walker (1972, p. 30) has termed 'limited retributivism': 'the unpleasantness of a penal measure must not exceed the limit that is appropriate to the culpability of the offence'.

If it is the case that judges do use retributivist criteria when they sentence long-firm fraudsters, we have to determine: (a) whether or not we agree with their perception of the gravity of the offence; and (b) whether or not we agree with their philosophy of sentencing.

Agreement on the 'just deserts' for different offences does present difficulties which may deter those who are tempted by Von Hirsch's (1976) call for a return to retributive justice. However, since those kinds of decisions are being made at present, it seems to be a 'cop out' to evade the issue. (See also Cohen, 1979, for a thoughtful discussion of these matters.)

At present, the culpability of even the most persistent long-firm fraudsters is not perceived as being very great, and co-defendants benefit still further from this fact, since their punishments are scaled down in accordance with the roles they have played in the frauds. *Prima facie*, in terms both of the perception of gravity and the philosophy of sentencing that are applied to their behaviour, long-firm fraudsters are treated more leniently than other 'substantial property criminals'. This sentencing gap (which applies even more strongly to fraudsters in general) may be expected to increase, for because of the apparent lack of public concern about them, fraudsters are in a good position to benefit from the economic and political pressures on sentencers to reduce prison overcrowding and cut the costs of imprisonment. (This will be despite the facts that the open prisons to which many fraudsters are sent are not over-crowded, and that it is the incarceration of petty persistent offenders which is generating the crisis in the British prison system at present.)

One model for the alleviation of the penal crisis is contained in the controversial report of the Advisory Council of the Penal System (1978) on *Sentences of Imprisonment*. This report sought to differentiate so-called 'dangerous' offenders from 'ordinary' criminals, recommending lighter sentence maxima for the latter (for a fuller analysis, see Levi, 1979a). It is interesting to note that long-firm and most other fraudsters appear to be excluded from the category of 'dangerous offenders', so the maximum possible sentence recommended for them is 4 years imprisonment. Although the report is politically moribund at present, due to the public outcry at the apparent leniency of general sentencing it advocated, it may herald future directions of sentencing in Britain and the United States.

Criminal Bankruptcy Order

The Advisory Council report provides an interesting discussion of the use of the Criminal Bankruptcy Order, which was introduced to provide a measure of restitution for the victims of 'serious' crime. Out of the 71 fraudsters on whom Criminal Bankruptcy Orders have been imposed to date, 22 had received a prison sentence of two years or less: of these, 7 had been given non-custodial sentences (figures deduced from Advisory Council, 1978, pp. 231–4). Unfortunately, as the Report acknowledges, the Criminal Bankruptcy Orders (CBOs) have not proved very effective to date. A number of suggestions for improvement are then made, the aim being to enable judges to impose wholly or partially suspended sentences instead of fully custodial sentences by giving them confidence that the criminal will not retain the profits from his crime and that the victim will benefit. It is not argued that the CBO is an undesirable penalty to be imposed upon long-firm fraudsters (or any other type of large-scale property criminal). However, if the CBO is to be promoted as an alternative to imprisonment for fraudsters, a serious attempt must be made to evaluate its potential recovery power.

At present, there is very little incentive for someone sent to prison to co-operate with the Official Receiver in recovering his assets. For effectively, there are few sanctions that can be employed: committing him to prison for contempt of court is irrelevant, since he is already there! Moreover, the high lower-limit of £15 000 for the imposition of the Criminal Bankruptcy Order means that relatively few criminals are liable to it.

The Council makes a number of proposals to improve the scope and effectiveness of the CBO, of which three are particularly important:

(1)   the statutory limit on the amount of loss or damage from the offence which qualifies the offender for the imposition of a CBO should be reduced from £15 000 to £10 000;

(2)   the Official Receiver should be asked to indicate to the Parole Board at the moment of eligibility for parole (and at intervals thereafter) the extent of the prisoner's co-operation with him;

(3)   if a criminal bankrupt is committed to prison by the Bankruptcy Court for failure to disclose all his assets to, or otherwise co-operate with, the Official Receiver, this should provide sufficient grounds for the activation of any suspended sentence to which he may be subject.

In theory, the strengthening of the CBO should release large amounts for restitution to victims and should prove a veritable Sword of Damocles in the struggle against organized crime: one can imagine major robbers, 'thieves' and underworld-connected fraudsters queuing up to 'grass' upon their 'fences' and financial backers in the hope of getting parole and avoiding a further sentence for non-compliance with the Official Receiver's investigations (Advisory Council, 1978, para. 302, p. 132). However, before the reader becomes overwhelmed with joy at these Draconian consequences, he should take note of the following problems of which the Council seems only dimly aware.

(1) Despite the proposed reduction to £10 000 in the lower limit of crimes for which CBOs can be imposed, there may be far fewer cases than the Council expects. The reason for this is the unanimous decision of the House of Lords in the case of *DPP* v. *Keith Anthony Anderson* (1978), 2 All E.R. 512, which was heard subsequent to the writing of the Council Report. At present, if a long-firm fraudster defrauds large numbers of creditors of smallish sums each, the police often charge him with a few specimen counts under the Theft Act, 1968 and hand the judge and the defence a schedule alleging other cases of a similar nature. This saves the time of the court and consequently legal aid costs. However, the decision in *DPP* v. *Anderson* has ruled this procedure useless for the fulfilment of the criteria for a CBO: their lordships have held that only offences that have been proved formally may be taken into account in reaching the present £15 000 figure. Consequently, a change in the law beyond that recommended by the Advisory Council will be needed to extend the scope of the CBO, unless inflation performs the function for it. The potential impact of the CBO limits upon

plea-bargaining must also be considered: long-firm fraudsters may be induced to plead guilty in exchange for a promise not to charge specimen counts 'over the limit', though this is unlikely in conspiracy to defraud cases.

(2) As the Advisory Council (1978, p. 128) acknowledges, only to ignore the implications of its observations: 'There remains the fundamental obstacle that in many cases, the profit from the crime is dissipated before offenders are brought to trial, and they do not have the wherewithal to make reparation.' Evidence concerning the life-style of many long-firm fraudsters (and 'professional criminals' generally) suggests that the money they obtain is spent very quickly indeed. Even that money which is not spent immediately tends to disappear into the coffers of wives, girl-friends, secretly owned businesses, and secret bank accounts in this country or abroad. It is only the amateurs who fail either to spend or to secrete away their profits.

(3) The Advisory Council (1978, para. 299, pp. 131–2) makes great play with the fact that

> under criminal bankruptcy (unlike civil bankruptcy), any gifts or under-valued sales made on or after the earliest date on which the criminal offence has been committed can, on application to the Bankruptcy Court by the Official Receiver, be ordered to be transferred by any person acquiring the whole or part of the property given or sold at under-value.

Fur coats and expensive jewellery purchased for wives and/or girl-friends with the proceeds of crime are zealously pursued at present by Official Receivers, and they provide some measure of compensation for victims, even though their resale value is lower than their purchase price. However, since much of criminals' money is spent in casinos, betting shops, night clubs, hotels, airlines and on 'hostesses', which, according to current conceptions of the social order, provide value-for-money, the financial returns to victims from criminal bankruptcy will continue to be small. Furthermore, the determination of 'the earliest date on which the criminal offence has been committed' is highly problematic in cases of fraudulent trading: this would be a rich source of legal wrangles.

(4) The Council recommends that criminal bankrupts be prosecuted if they fail to answer the Official Receiver's questions or furnish him with false information. Unfortunately, there is a large gap between believing that someone has given false information and being able to prove this. Let us apply this problem to the area of the 'fencing' of long-firm goods. Long-firm 'fences' are normally quasi-legitimate businessmen, who merge the cheaply-acquired

produce with their ordinarily purchased stock. To provide security against a charge of dishonest handling, the 'fence' issues the fraudster with a cheque for the full market price of the goods, but receives a secret kick-back in cash. In such a case, even if the fraudster were to 'grass' upon the businessman, the Official Receiver would rarely be able to prove that he bought the goods under-value. (If he *were* able to prove this, the 'fence' could be charged with conspiracy to defraud or with dishonest handling in any case.) Conversely, however, the Official Receiver would find it difficult to prove (or to be certain) that the fraudster had given him false information, for the fraudster could claim that the nature of the transaction prevented him from proving it to the satisfaction of the court.

(5) For the foreseeable future, the Insolvency Service of the Department of Trade will continue to be hard-pressed and under-staffed. At present, CBOs are dealt with by senior bankruptcy examiners, who may have about 50 cases, including 10 highly active ones, to deal with at any one time. They make heavy demands upon the extremely scarce resources of the examiners, and in many cases, these efforts are wasted because, through no fault of their own, the officials in the Office of the Director of Public Prosecutions who decide whether or not to activate the CBOs are not expert judges of the possibilities of recovering money from fraudsters. The proposals of the Advisory Council may reduce the strain on the Insolvency Service by increasing the stick it can wield over criminal bankrupts, thereby speeding up the proceedings as well as recovering more money. However, unless more staff are brought in to deal with the increased workload, the zero-sum game situation will lead to *other* cases being investigated *less* thoroughly than they are at present. In other words, there is a trade-off between uncovering the assets of criminal bankrupts – a respectable aim of penal policy – and the investigation, detection, and prosecution of other offenders against company or bankruptcy law. The present 'dark figure' of undetected fraud is probably vast: this could become larger still if there were a flood of CBOs with which to deal.

(6) There is at present a probably inadvertent inequity in the administration of Criminal Bankruptcy Orders. Where such Orders are made against more than one defendant in a multiple-defendant trial, they are often made against *each* individual for the *full* sum proved to have been defrauded or stolen. In cases where unequal amounts are recovered from co-defendants, or where co-defendants obtained very different amounts from their crime, the result may be regarded as 'unfair' upon some concerned. Furthermore, the sum for

which the CBO is made may be well in excess of the amount obtained by a particular defendant, and this too may (or may not) be regarded as a defect in the present system. The Advisory Council makes no reference to this particular problem in its discussion of Criminal Bankruptcy Orders.

(7) Unless the sentences imposed on fraudsters are comparatively long, that is, well in excess of two years, the suggestion that the Official Receiver be asked to indicate the degree of co-operation to the Parole Board will be wholly meaningless.

Longer sentences?

There are some other issues of importance which are implicit in the approach of the Advisory Council to sentences of imprisonment in the future. The underlying penal philosophy of the report is that retributive and deterrent considerations can, in the main, be satisfied within the 90 per cent rule. After all, if current sentencing practice is to be taken as the relevant standard, they already are so satisfied. The Council also appears to believe that it is a reasonable aim of punishment to seek to incapacitate the offender who is considered (on what grounds?) to be likely to cause 'serious harm' to 'the public' at some undefined future date. Many people will have serious qualms about these views.

Even looking more narrowly at the *practical* implications of the Report's recommendations, we may note that in an area such as fraudulent credit trading, where crimes generally are self-consciously planned and where the probability of detection and prosecution is low, the substitution of a Criminal Bankruptcy Order for a sentence of imprisonment will provide even less of a deterrent than exists at present to a businessman contemplating long-firm fraud. For even if he is caught *and convicted*, all that is likely to happen is that the assets that he possesses or those that can be proved to have been created by the fraud will be returned to the victims. Since he will probably have spent many of those assets already, it will follow that apart from the status degradation ceremony in court, he will have escaped scot-free and will have enjoyed at least some of the proceeds of his crime. Furthermore, if, as at present, sentencers will continue not to be informed about whether or not the CBO has been activated by the Director of Public Prosecutions, and how much money the bankruptcy examiners have been able to retrieve from the criminal bankrupt, they may base their sentences upon wholly fallacious assumptions about the impact of such Orders.

The Criminal Bankruptcy Order could become a more efficient tool of penal policy if, in addition to the Advisory Council's proposals, there were to be instituted a feedback system to inform judges about the value of the Orders they make, and an élite full-time squad of Department of Trade officials who would have the responsibility of deciding which CBOs should be activated and who also would have *carte blanche* to dig around for information about where the assets have gone. Unless this is done, the judiciary would best be advised to regard CBOs merely as moderately useful supplements to the sentences they would otherwise have imposed.

It may be a desirable social objective to divert 'criminally-minded' people from robbing or burgling banks or hijacking lorries to long-firm fraud, where the sentences as well as the chances of being convicted are lower. However, the Advisory Council's attempt to provide a framework for the prophylactic detention of those whom it considers to be 'dangerous offenders' may eschew all *fresh* value judgements, but represents an ossification of contemporary dominant views about the relative and absolute *seriousness* of different offences; a charge that might be levelled also against the codification of the Court of Appeal's sentencing criteria by Thomas (1970, 1978). The Advisory Council appears to take the view that the 'white-collar criminal' does not represent a serious harm to the community and ought never to be sentenced to a term of imprisonment exceeding three years (or four if one can charge him with conspiracy to defraud). Furthermore, if there is some prospect that some of the proceeds of crime can be recovered for victims, this is regarded as sufficient to free the offender from medium-term imprisonment. (A recommendation which presumably does not apply to those equally non-violent people who covertly break into banks or practise the art of safe-blowing.) The implications of this penal philosophy for the *increased* differential treatment of offenders from the upper and lower socio-economic classes should not be overlooked: those who can afford to repay some of the money they have stolen will end up losing nothing except, perhaps, their reputations. Some readers may find this disturbing; others may be quite content. I hope, however, that if this Report is adopted, it will be after explicit consideration of the analysis I have put forward and not by the moral default implicit in what we may term the Advisory Council's 'non-decision-making process'.

Incapacitation on the outside: an appropriate penal strategy?

If we set aside the question of 'just punishment' for long-firm fraudsters, we may concern ourselves with the question of whether or not their activities can be contained in a non-custodial context. Can they be incapacitated *without* sending them to prison? This issue was addressed indirectly by the City of London magistrates in the case of *R*. v. *Altman* et al., reported in *The Guardian*, 22 April 1978:

> A City stockbroker and his company involved in a £2 million currency fraud...were ordered to pay more than £220 000 in fines and costs yesterday...
> The magistrates, in a written judgment, said they were anxious about the proper sentence, and said that although Mr Altman was a first offender who should not be imprisoned unless there was no suitable alternative, he had committed breach of trust and aided a very substantial fraud...In the event, they concluded, a very substantial monetary penalty was the right sentence.
> The magistrates protested that there was an anomaly in the laws designed to help rehabilitation of offenders. Because they had decided not to imprison Mr Altman, he would become 'rehabilitated' after only five years, and no-one would be allowed to refer to his conviction. Society would wish to regard serious white-collar fraudsmen of this type as 'second-class' citizens for a long time, they said.

Stigma may persist without the necessity of referring formally to convictions. However, the Rehabilitation of Offenders Act, 1974 does prohibit the publication in credit references of the previous convictions of a long-firm fraudster given a non-custodial sentence, provided that five years have elapsed since his conviction. (The period before rehabilitation rises to seven years in the case of prison sentences of six months or less, and ten years for those given prison sentences of between six and thirty months. Persons sentenced to longer than thirty months' imprisonment are never rehabilitated under the Act. It is important to note that for this purpose, *suspended* prison sentences are treated as if they were *actual* prison sentences). Whether this is a good or a bad thing is debatable, but it is one important consequence of the trend away from imprisonment advocated by the Advisory Council (1978), given the crucial role that trade protection societies play in the prevention of fraud.

Allied to this rehabilitation issue is the use of Interdiction Orders to forbid offenders from engaging in future commercial activities without the leave of the court. These are clearly a form of incapacitation strategy 'on the outside', instead of the normal form which occurs *inside* prison. Leigh (1977a, pp. 133–7) provides an excellent account of the use of such orders within EEC countries. As he points out, the French are somewhat liberal in their interdiction provisions, while the English are very sparing in their use of them. However, there have been two important developments in the provision for such Orders in England since his study, and I shall summarize the current position in so far as it may affect long-firm fraudsters. (It should be noted that the Department of Trade has shown great reluctance to make use of these new provisions: between 1976 and June 1981, only two people were banned from management under the Insolvency Act.)

There are four principal legislative provisions under which people may be banned (for a maximum of *five* years) from taking part in the management of a company:

(1) Section 187 of the Companies Act, 1948, which applies to bankrupts;

(2) Section 188 of the Companies Act, 1948, (discussed earlier in Chapter X), which applies to those who are convicted under the Companies Acts, but only when the trial judge makes a specific order to that effect;

(3) Section 28 of the Companies Act, 1976, which may be applied to those persons who persistently fail to submit returns of their annual accounts to the Registrar of Companies when required to do so;

(4) Section 9 of the Insolvency Act, 1976, which states (Subsection 1) that

  (a) a person who

     (i) is or has been a director of a company which has at any time gone into liquidation (whether while he was a director or subsequently) and was insolvent at that time;
     (ii) is or has been a director of another such company which has gone into liquidation within five years of the date on which the first-mentioned company went into liquidation;

  (b) a person whose conduct as director of any of these companies makes him unfit to be concerned in the management of a company;

may be banned by a winding-up court from taking part in the management of a company for no longer than five years. (These periods are increased by the Companies (No. 2) Bill, 1981.)

The maximum penalties for conviction on indictment for all of these offences are two years' imprisonment, a fine, or both. They suffer from all the ethical and predictive difficulties of all incapacitatory strategies. Moreover, under the present system for the regulation of commerce, none of the four types of Order is likely to prove very effective, for the following reasons:

(1) Orders made under Section 188 of the Companies Act, 1948 apply to a maximum of five years from the date of *sentence* rather than

from the date at which the offender is released into the community;

(2) the present level of surveillance of commerce is too low for these Orders to be supervised effectively, that is, to ensure that banned persons do not in fact engage in management. As Leigh (1977a, p. 137) notes:

> France encounters the problem of the 'man of straw' who, although interdicted, is only prosecuted where the business for which he is in truth responsible is found to have been the facade for crimes of fraud or bankruptcy. The prevalence of nominee shareholdings conduces to this result. Similar problems arise in Belgium in connection with bankruptcy offences. The problem is likely to become more acute if the suggestion . . .is adopted that we should use such devices as primary methods of control rather than the traditional devices of fine or imprisonment.

At present, bankrupts and other interdicted persons who change their names and move elsewhere are unlikely to be found out unless they go 'bust' again. Even if there were to be a central fingerprint register through which all businessmen had to pass, they would escape detection if they had the deviousness to use nominees. If such a register (of all directors) were matched up with the Criminal Records Index, it might lead to the detection of 'front men' and 'upfront organizers' who possessed criminal records, but 'background operators' would not be detected any more efficiently than they are at the moment. Indeed, although *prima facie*, the Interdiction Orders provide an easy source of 'strict liability' convictions, the prosecution still has to prove that the accused was acting in a directive capacity.

The term 'director' is defined by Section 9(7) of the Insolvency Act, 1976 as including any person in accordance with whose directions and instructions the directors of the company have been accustomed to act. It is clear, therefore, that this covers 'background operators'. However, if, as often happens, the authorities learn about a fraud only when it is well advanced, they may find it just as easy to prosecute for conspiracy to defraud as for breaches of the Insolvency Act. It is only when there are no other grounds for intervention and arrest, for example, for fraudulent trading or theft, that Interdiction Orders are particularly useful. Under such circumstances, they provide a ready-made legal justification for Department of Trade investigations (or an alternative count in a plea-bargain).

However, if there is to be a trend towards 'dangerous offender' strategies in the field of commercial crime control, the general critiques of such strategies cannot be brushed aside. Incapacitation *outside* prison may be less undesirable than incapacitation *inside* it, but the issues of justice and common sense still arise. The assumption that the 'problem of fraud' is one that is imported from 'villainous outsiders' rather than generated by 'the enemy *within*' the *corpus capitalisti* may be a convenient one, but is not necessarily warranted by the facts. Glaser (1978, p. 467) has made some highly pertinent observations about the moral panic which greets 'the invasion of legitimate commerce by organized criminals':

> It is unfortunate that almost every government commission and many writers on organised crime deplore the fact that persons who have been in illegal commerce enter legitimate businesses, as though such a move invariably results in scams [long-firm frauds] or other offences. It is easy to find instances in which such persistence in crime has occurred, and it is appropriate for policing agencies to make legal and discreet checks upon this possibility. But the fact of ethnic succession in organised crime is one proof that people do move from illicit to licit enterprises and, especially, direct their children into law-abiding vocations. It has been mainly through gradual assimilation, as organised criminals and their descendants have become successful in 'straight' businesses, that the minority groups once conspicuous in illegal selling and coercion have become less prominent in the criminal world.

(See also Chambliss, 1978, for a more detailed *critique* of the view that 'organised crime' is an alien conspiracy.)

The use of Interdiction Orders may serve to 'freeze' people diagnosed as 'villains' into an Underworld status, and thus prevent them from being able to be both affluent and respectable. We may seek to justify such a policy on the grounds of retribution or of general deterrence, just as we may feel that someone who has run two businesses that have gone 'bust' within five years does not *deserve* the right or privilege to continue in a managerial capacity. However, we must accept that by forbidding people to take part in corporate management, we may hinder their attempts either to *re*align themselves with conventional *mores* or to become thus aligned for the first time, but be unable to assess the real validity of our predictions. For people who commit frauds subsequent to their interdiction may attribute their continued criminality to the closure of options for legitimate money-making: it is easier to run a short-term 'bent' business than a long-term 'straight' one *sub rosa*. (This is not to suggest that the imposition of an Interdiction Order is a sufficient condition to impel someone into further fraud, for no-one *has* to be a businessman.)

In conclusion, it appears that although Interdiction Orders are a

useful supplement to existing measures of control, they are unlikely
to prove effective until the general policing of business is improved
considerably, except in cases where it is impracticable for the
interdicted to remain anonymous or in the background. There is no
reason to suppose that either on deterrent or retributive grounds are
Interdiction Orders (or Criminal Bankruptcy Orders) likely to be an
adequate substitute for a custodial sentence.

Deterring long-firm fraudsters: some general conclusions
I have discussed at length some of the central policy changes that
might lead to greater rates of conviction for long-firm fraudsters and
to the prevention of fraud. I shall now seek to summarise these issues
at a more general theoretical level.

The prevention of long-firm fraud has two principal dimensions:

(1) people may be prevented from putting their desires to defraud
into predatory effect;
(2) people may be deterred from *seeking* to defraud suppliers of their
goods.

These dimensions feed back into one another, for insofar as people
perceive that they will not succeed in obtaining credit unlawfully,
they may comply with the law. However, whereas the first
dimension is a direct function of the active social control exercised
by credit controllers and policing agencies, the second relates to
social control in a much wider sense. There are three main ways in
which, in this broad sense, long-firm fraud may be deterred:

(a) by socialising individuals so well that they have no *desire* to
defraud;
(b) by providing sufficient life opportunities so that people will
not be tempted by 'relative deprivation' to seek to defraud;
(c) by generating a social control system which induces them to
desist from acting upon desires to defraud if and when they
experience them.

The first two aspects have been discussed already in Chapter XI
where I concluded that individualistic morality and current levels of
social opportunity and economic prosperity provide insufficient
protection against fraudulent trading, but that most traders are kept
broadly in line by what Tawney (1920, p. 30) has described thus:
'Before the eyes of both (strong and weak), it suspends a golden
prize, which not all can attain, but for which each may strive, the
enchanting vision of infinite expansion.' I shall now discuss the third
aspect: what one might term *active* deterrence. The fear of

punishment for law-breaking can lead to virtuous sentiments, as we can see in the film where W.C. Fields refrains from robbing a sleeping cowboy after he sees the latter's gun. As he tiptoes away from danger, he exclaims that to steal thus 'would be dishonest'.

Observations about deterrence tend to be based more upon intuition than upon research and reasoned analysis. However, there is criminological support for the view that the most crucial factor in deterrence is the probability of conviction (see Chiricos & Waldo, 1970; Logan, 1972; and, for an example of deterrence in consumer fraud, Stotland *et al.*, 1980). The probability of conviction does, of course, depend on the probabilities of reporting, recording, detection, prosecution, and conviction for any given act of 'fraud'.

Both pre-planned and intermediate fraudsters know that they are breaking the criminal law, for their actions involve criminal foresight and planning. In consequence, they fulfil part of the criteria necessary for theories of deterrence to apply. Objectively, we may note that in the 1970s, the 'front men' of crude long-firm frauds which *were* reported to the police had a *high* probability of conviction, while cautious background operators and sophisticated falsifiers of asset values had fairly *low* probabilities of conviction. This situation may be the result of difficulties in formulating laws to govern their activities without banning other actions that are considered to be legitimate and of the acquittal of some of those alleged sophisticates who *are* prosecuted. However, it is likely that the main reasons for the relative immunity of fraudsters are the low rates of reporting of crime (due to low visibility and victim inertia) and the low levels of surveillance of business affairs maintained by the Department of Trade and by the police.

In order to analyse the deterrent impact of probabilities of conviction properly, however, we must take into account people's *perceptions* of risk rather than 'the reality', and there is as yet no direct evidence on these perceptions. All that we can infer is that at present levels of social control, the probability of conviction might well prove inadequate to deter a rational businessman *whose business was not prospering* from committing bankruptcy fraud.

Although it may be the principal factor influencing deterrence, the probability of conviction is not the only such factor. We must also take into account the alternatives to crime, the rewards of crime (irrespective of conviction), and the consequences of conviction in terms of the things any given individual fears and values. Discussions with former fraudsters indicate that in the absence of what they saw as profitable alternatives, the possibility of making large amounts of money fraudulently was more salient than the risk of conviction and the prospective sentences if convicted (as they estimated them). Consequently, it was the proactive police strategy of making arrests before they had made much money that led them to quit fraud. (This is sound 'avoidance learning theory'!) Furthermore, such proactive intervention has important secondary effects in making 'backers' less willing to finance large-scale frauds: the extra risk puts their financing into the category of adventure capital. Hence, although police arrests prior to the closure of the *suspected* long firm may make it harder to secure convictions and to prove dishonest intentions, such a policy may have a great deterrent impact upon potential or actual long-firm merchants.

This issue is connected also with the levels of sentencing in long-firm fraud cases. It is more important that the police or Department of Trade should detect and close down long firms before their depredations become too great than that the courts should impose heavy sentences upon those who *are* convicted. However, unless the chances of conviction *and* loss of investment become very high, existing levels of sentencing may well be inadequate to deter all save those who are particularly concerned about their social reputations. Current sentencers clearly do not act instrumentally towards a deterrent philosophy of punishment in long-firm fraud cases. Instead, they inadvertently collude with long-firm merchants by reflecting the view that long-firm fraud is not 'serious crime'.

However, it is when we consider 'slippery-slope' fraudsters that we encounter major problems for the deterrability of their actions. When discussing the social psychology of 'slippery-slope' fraud, I raised the question of whether they might be said to possess any criminal intent. One might argue, for instance, that people who know that they are insolvent at present but who hope or expect that they will not go 'bust' are not susceptible to deterrent sanctions. (A relevant issue in view of the general economic crisis which has led to massive rises in the numbers of bankruptcies and company liquidations in Britain and America.) Nevertheless, it is arguable that the present levels of 'inadvertence to crime' shown by 'slippery-slopers' are due in part to the light levels of social control in force. For example, even fraudulent trading might become the object of greater concern to businessmen if they believed that there was a serious prospect that the Department of Trade might prosecute them *before* they reached the stage of bankruptcy or liquidation. (This may be possible if the DoT implements the powers in Clause 49 of the Companies (No. 2) Bill, 1981.) Furthermore, there are some acts, such as the sale of goods below cost price, where the onus is placed upon the businessman to justify his conduct (s. 154 of the Bankruptcy Act 1914 and s. 328 of the Companies Act 1948). If there were much higher levels of proactive policing, and if more severe punishments were imposed on conviction, then traders might be persuaded to display greater awareness of the risks entailed by their actions and might be deterred from trading whilst insolvent.

However, as the annual Criminal Statistics for England & Wales, (Home Office, 1978, 1979) and Leigh's (1980) study of bankruptcy may illustrate, the courts do not treat commercial offences very severely. Indeed, in terms of imprisonment, the costs of conviction are negligible. And unless an individual is particularly attached to his self-conception as a 'law-abiding person', mere advertence to the criminality of his actions is not a *sufficient* (though it may be a *necessary*) condition for him to be deterred.

These issues are linked to substantive criminal law as well as to matters such as levels of enforcement and 'techniques of neutralisation'. For example, by decriminalising the offence of deferring payment by deception provided that one intends to repay *eventually* (Section 2 (1) (b) of the Theft Act 1978), Parliament may have actually *encouraged* such conduct: at the least, it may have confirmed its moral neutrality. Furthermore, the average 'slippery-sloper' is questioned – if at all – only after he has gone 'bust', and one may hypothesise that the knowledge that the Department of Trade or the police might investigate the running of one's business *after* one has gone 'bust' is likely to prove less of a deterrent to the 'slippery-sloper' than active demands for a justificatory account while his business is still in progress.

A high level of policing is even more necessary to deter those 'slippery-slopers' who do *not* perceive that they are doing anything abnormal, for even if they knew that certain detection and heavy sanctions would ensue from 'naughty' behaviour, they would not perceive the relevance of such sanctions to their own conduct. Consequently, deterrence would require us to bring the consequences of their actions for others and for themselves into the foreground of their consciousness: a *gestalt* theory of deterrence. In other words, the socialisation of businessmen in an atmosphere where people have been punished for paying insufficient attention to the effects of their behaviour may deter fraud – at an unconscious level – by making businessmen more thoughtful about putting the money of others in jeopardy. The present levels of the policing of commerce are conducive towards commercial sociopathy.

In an intriguing game-theoretical analysis of optimal policing strategies against burglars and 'fences', Walsh (1977, ch. 6) argues that the police ought to view theft as a stolen-property transfer system and go after the 'fences' to a far greater extent than they do at present. 'Criminal fences' play a less important role in many long-firm frauds, particularly those carried out by non-underworld figures, because long-firm goods can be sold to businessmen 'as if' they were ordinary goods. Consequently, intensive police action against 'fences', which in any case is hampered by the latter's claim to licit title upon the long-firm goods, might have its principal effects upon those long-firm fraudsters with poor legitimate contacts, though it might have secondary effects in sensitizing businessmen in general to 'ordinary' transactions. However, the optimal policing strategy against *all* types of fraudulent credit trading would appear to be more widespread and searching investigation into businesses *while they are still running*, supplemented by laws placing the onus on the businessman to justify his honest intentions, by larger and more expert prosecution departments, and by the heavier sentencing of commercial criminals.

The 'problem of fraudulent credit trading' (if it be regarded as a problem) resides not only in the undoubted fact that many 'background operators' are not brought to book for all (if indeed any) of their recorded crimes but also in the presence of a great deal of unrecorded fraud within the business community. If long firms and allied commercial frauds are to be deterred – and the present gross imbalance between the resources devoted to the control of 'crimes of the upperworld' and 'crimes of the underworld' is to be redressed – major changes must occur in social attitudes towards such crimes, particularly among those charged with law enforcement. Even if we take for granted existing definitions about what kind of commercial behaviour *ought* to be criminal, social control agencies may proceed upon the assumption that businessmen *are* a class of individuals among whom many criminals may be found. For until they do so, *all* suppliers of goods on credit are at risk from *any* debtor who chances upon hard times.

Appendices

Appendix A. Methodology of this Study

The ideal methodology section should aim to provide a natural history of the research project as well as discuss the validity and reliability of its findings. Unfortunately, the necessity to make cuts somewhere in this manuscript has led me to abandon the former and truncate the latter. More extensive analysis of these is to be found in Levi (1979, ch. 3). Although this book does not neglect broad issues of political economy and the impact these have on motivations for and social reactions to crime, its general method is that of 'appreciating' its subjects. This, however, does not solve the problem of whose behaviour one is to appreciate, and despite Becker's (1967) advocacy of a 'sociology of the underdog' – on the grounds that deviants are the section of society who most need understanding – I have sought to empathise with *all* my subjects, social controllers and controlled. In any event, it is a moot point whether it is the law enforcers or the fraudsters who are 'the controllers' here.

Albini (1971), Ianni (1972), Mack (1964), and Walsh (1977) have all put forward *rationales* against the attempt to gain the confidence of both police and 'villains', but on the sound principle that the naive discover things that the wise do not, I interviewed both groups: readers may judge for themselves how successful this has been. However, I thought it sensible to study the control of fraud before interviewing fraudsters, because it seemed unlikely that fraudsters would be forthcoming if they knew I was in regular contact with the police and credit controllers (and *vice versa*), and it is always better to know a little about one's subject before interviewing experts in deception.

I commenced by examining *all* court records from the London Old Bailey during the period 1962–1972, a period chosen because the first half was marked by the involvement of the major London gangs – the Krays and the Richardsons – in long-firm fraud, while the second would show me what had happened to the organisation and control of fraud after their imprisonment. I eliminated most of these records and files, because they did not relate to long-firm frauds, but built up a complete set of records on sentencing, prior criminal convictions, acquittals, and data on techniques and organisation of long-firm frauds. I then collated similar data for the period 1948–1961 at the Old Bailey and, to examine whether or not the Old Bailey data were idiosyncratic, I examined all court records at Manchester Crown Court for the period 1961–1971 (1972 data being unavailable at the time). This proved to be a useful exercise, since some important differences emerged which are analysed in the book.

I interviewed a large number of credit controllers, businessmen, police and other control agency officers, prosecutors, defence lawyers, and two judges. I also observed four long-firm fraud trials at the Old Bailey over a period of seven months. The interviews were open-ended and semi-structured, aimed at eliciting general information about the organisation of long-firm fraud and the problems that they felt they faced in controlling it. Because of the sensitivity of the information contained in the police files, it was impracticable to examine the control of fraud in the way Cicourel (1968) examined juvenile justice. After I wrote up the chapters on the police and the courts, I sent them to some of the agencies concerned with invitations for comment. In some minor cases, amendments have been made in response to their criticisms, but no fundamental objections have been raised by those who replied. I also invited criticisms from individuals other than those who provided the data in the first place: the 'construction sample' is different from the 'validation sample'. I believe that I have taken all reasonable steps to check the reliability of what I have written. My hope is that the absence of critical response is not an indication of any gross *lack* of insight: the danger faced by all who fail to distance themselves sufficiently from their subjects.

Interviewing criminals

My study of the Old Bailey files and numerous discussions with a variety of social control agents and businessmen had enabled me to amass a considerable amount of data regarding the techniques of fraud and the organisational connections between long-firm fraudsters and other figures from inside and outside 'the Underworld'. However, such information provides a somewhat stylised picture of the world of long-firm fraud, since it excludes both a first-hand 'appreciation' of those fraudsters who *are* 'known to the police' and also a knowledge of those 'fraudsters' *not* 'known to the police'. Polsky (1971, pp. 115–147) has justly berated criminologists for their failure to carry out ethnographic studies of criminals in their natural habitats, and has proposed some useful guidelines as to how such research may be conducted. Unfortunately, with less than 12 months of my full-time research left, and on an income of approximately £750 per annum, the prospects for studying long-firm fraudsters in their (highly expensive) natural habitats were far from propitious. Unlike those hustlers who are involved in 'street culture', long-firm fraudsters do not 'hang out' in any place that I could afford to go to. Furthermore, at the time of my research, the success of police operations against long-firm fraud had led to a dramatic drop in the numbers of big-time 'fraudsters' still at liberty. Since they were 'missing' or in prison, they were not available in their natural habitats.

Despite these ill omens, I did manage to interview some retired long-firm merchants outside prison. I had become friendly with a number of businessmen who had been trading for many years and who knew a number of successful fraudsters. I met three such fraudsters and talked to them in a very general way about crime: they were reluctant to talk about their involvement, for perfectly understandable reasons, and I did not press them unduly. In other cases, my businessman informants did not want the 'fraudsters' concerned to know that the latter had been discussed with me, and I respected their confidences. I have used some of the information that they gave me in this work, since to the best of my knowledge, my friends had no motive for misinforming me and the information had been imparted to *them* by the fraudsters in circumstances where there was no discernible reason why they should have lied. Unfortunately, however, I have been unable to verify some of the data, since the original activities were wholly covert. Only in some cases, e.g. where company registrations were involved, has it been possible to make checks. In those cases where I did not personally interview a 'fraudster' but where I have quoted what they are supposed to have done, I have mentioned this fact in the text.

My other principal source of long-firm fraudsters was the prisons. Normally, one may expect that few skilled 'professional criminals' will be in prison, and one's sample of 'criminals' will be heavily biased in favour of the incompetent. However, there were a number of major 'background operators' who were imprisoned shortly before my study, which – although unfortunate from their point of view – meant that my institutional sample included far 'better class' fraudsters than one would normally expect to find 'inside'.

From my reading of court depositions and from discussions with the police about the 'quality' of different fraudsters, I selected nine people I knew to be in prison: three 'front men' and six 'organisers'.

Home Office Prison Department helpfully agreed to my interviewing them 'in sight but out of hearing' of prison officers, provided the prisoners agreed to be interviewed and I agreed not to mention them by name in any subsequent publication. Only one prisoner refused, stating that he was upset about his sentence and did not want to talk to me.

Interviewing in prison: its value and reliability

Polsky (1971, p. 121) has offered some cogent arguments against interviewing prisoners to illuminate the world of crime. He has stated that

> data gathered from caught criminals, for reasons in addition to and quite apart from possible sampling bias, are not only very partial but partially suspect. These are data that are much too heavily retrospective; data from people who aren't really free to put you down; data often involving the kind of 'co-operativeness' in which you are told what the criminal thinks you want to hear so that you will get off his back or maybe do him some good with the judge or parole board; data from someone who is not behaving as he normally would in his normal life-situations; and, above all, data that you cannot supplement with, or interpret in the light of, your own direct observation of the criminal's natural behaviour in his natural environment.

Although his comments are sobering in the extreme, he both *under*estimates the difficulties of validating one's accounts of behaviour in a natural setting and *over*estimates the errors entailed *intrinsically* by prison interviews. For example, in my view, the most insightful work on 'professional crime' is Chambliss' (1972) study of a safebreaker, *Box Man*. Although his interviews were conducted outside prison, thus eliminating one source of 'response bias', they were based around the retrospective musings of one well-travelled and long-lived man. Similarly, Klockars's (1975) study of a 'professional fence' called Vincent provides an illuminating and interesting account of his world. Yet although Vincent was still criminally active, and was observed in his natural setting, we have no means of knowing whether others shared his view of himself or his view of the way he operated. The difficulties entailed by this kind of study are discussed further later in this appendix, but insufficient concern has been expressed regarding the difficulties created by 'self-deception' and 'other-deception' in observational field studies. Access is not a sufficient condition for validity of observation.

However, the mere observation that fieldwork also has its methodological problems does not destroy the power of Polsky's *critique* of research in institutional settings. I sought to mitigate the sources of error in a number of ways:

(1) At the beginning of each interview, I assured the fraudster that I would not reveal him as the source of my information, nor would I inform the police of anything he told me (though I did not expect him to tell me any details that might lead to his conviction). To encourage this trust, I did not use tape recorders and wrote down the absolute minimum during the interview, leaving the writing up for the moment we parted. Selectivity of recall is always a difficulty in this situation, particularly since the interviews were generally 2½ to 3 hours long, but as a partial validation of my use of it, I can cite the favourable comments of my interviewees on my ability to reproduce their statements without taking completely contemporaneous notes. I also pointed out to them that I was sure that they would have appropriate extralegal means of redress should I break my promise. To reduce response bias further, I informed them that as a mere postgraduate student, I was not in a position to help them either financially or in terms of preferential treatment for parole. In general, I sought to present myself only for what I was: a tolerably well-informed 'innocent' who was interested in the organisation of long-firm frauds and in *their* side of the story. (However, I might add that unlike Klockars (1975), I had actually spent more than three hours in the company of 'criminals' before I commenced my study.)

(2) Although most of the interviewees were in different prisons, they knew each other or *of* each other, and to some extent, I was able to check the information given by one against that given by another. This was particularly important when they spontaneously mentioned some of their joint activities or made positive and negative comments about one of their colleagues. In some cases, I was also able to check some of the data with people *outside* the prison.

Finally, there is one actual research *benefit* accruing from interviewing in institutional settings which is seldom acknowledged by fieldwork enthusiasts. Although the enforced 'settling down' process inside prison may generate great bitterness, it does present an *opportunity* for serious soul-searching which rarely arises in the world outside prison. While they are on 'the outside', most major criminals are highly action-oriented: they have too much trouble taking care of environmental threats to engage in existential contemplation. When they are in prison, however, they are less bothered by environmental threats, more thoughtful about the meaning and value of their involvement in crime, and untroubled by having to conceal current operations (apart from prison 'rackets').

Hence, the researcher has the advantage of finding the law-breaker in a more introspective frame of mind than he would normally be outside prison. Although naturally there is retrospective telescoping of facts and distortion of perceptions, *a priori*, there seems no reason to suppose that explanations of motives given when criminals are 'active' are any more reliable or valid than retrospective explanations, though direct observation of conduct does give one a better baseline against which to evaluate claims regarding motives and morality. (However, in case the reader should be encouraged by this to adopt a Benthamite view of the value of meditation in confinement, I should add that the benefits are reaped only by the researcher: there is no evidence that reflection in prison is linked to subsequent reformation.)

I became particularly friendly with one top-class fraudster, and in fact remained in regular contact with him during the years after his release. This enabled me to put into perspective the things that he and others had said while in prison. In brief, although the material presented in Chapters III, IV, and V falls short of the ideal of ethnography based on (participant?) observation on site, I would seek to justify its analysis of the motives, social and economic relations, and techniques of a broad cross-section of long-firm fraudsters. However, I make no claims to have uncovered the *totality* of motives for or routes into fraud, nor have I produced a representative study of the *distribution* of motives among *all* long-firm fraudsters. Neither of these aims is fulfillable, even in principle, for one can never know that one has a representative sample of an unknowable population.

The validation of respondents' accounts of motives and actions: some difficulties

Austin (1979, pp. 175–204) has shown that motives and intentions are integral parts of our descriptions of actions, and interactionist sociologists and social psychologists such as Harré and Secord (1972) have advocated lucidly that people should be taken seriously as commentators upon their own actions. However, there are epistemological difficulties in seeking to test the truth of people's claims about their states of mind and moral identities which make it impossible for us to know when people can *safely* be *believed* (see Levi, 1979, ch. 3). It is perfectly possible, for example, that Klockars' fence, Vincent, may genuinely regard himself as 'on balance' a good guy – despite our having been told earlier that he had manufactured sweaters from explosive cloth – but how can we tell? Moreover, the demands of 'faithfulness to the phenomenon' do not absolve us from examining his account critically: it would certainly be interesting to see what conduct would be required to make someone a 'bad guy' in his eyes! Unfortunately, pragmatic considerations may induce researchers to desist from critical questioning lest they offend their subjects, but we should at least be aware that this is a deficiency.

Henry (1978, pp. 117–122) has sought to resolve the difficulty of inferring motives in an imaginative way. In a thoughtful exposition of the 'hidden economy' of bartering and reselling pilfered goods, he juxtaposes the common motivational account that 'I did it for the money' with the observation that people rarely make much money and derive a great deal of pleasure from the social interchanges which occur in their illicit roles. Henry suggests that the social rather than the financial aspect is the 'true' motive for the transactions, and that because people in capitalist societies are trapped into a set of motivational accounts that *excludes* social reciprocity, they mistakenly believe that their motives are solely profit-oriented.

Although I have reservations about the data from which Henry draws his inferences and about the risks entailed by inferring motives from behaviour in this way, the basic idea seems to be a good one. As we shall see, the motivational accounts offered by long-firm fraudsters tend to be centred on economic factors, but some also spoke warmly of the *camaraderie* and the pleasure of 'putting one over' on suppliers by their verbal skill. It seems, then, that desire for money is not their *sole* motive, but one can never be certain.

In steering the middle-course between 'reasonable' and 'excessive' scepticism, I have tried to follow the somewhat abstract guidelines laid down by Schutz (1967a, pp. 43–45) as appropriate for the 'objective' rendering of the subjective meaning of social action. Schutz argues that a scientific account must observe the canons of logical consistency, must account for the meaning of such action to the actor, and must be consistent with the ways in which actors and their fellow men understand and interpret their conduct. Consequently, I have tried to check with subjects and others my accounts of their conduct and states of mind, and I have tried to open up my procedures as far as possible for inspection. However, in view of the inaccessibility of my original sources to readers, it seems unavoidable that some observations will have to be accepted or rejected on the basis of trust or distrust: 'indefinite triangulation' stops here! This is a general problem that we all face in evaluating the work of others, and it is somewhat disingenuous to imply that replication is a *practical* possibility in such cases, e.g. how might we be able to assess the representativeness of the cases selected by Cicourel (1968) as typical of decision-making in juvenile justice? I have tried to take all reasonable steps to check the reliability of my data: it is for the reader to decide whether or not these accord with his or her criteria of adequacy.

Appendix B. Predicting those Factors which may Influence the Sentencing of Long-Firm Fraudsters

Criminological research on sentencing, most notably that conducted by Hogarth (1971), Hood (1962, 1972) and Thomas (1970, 1978), as well as my interviews with lawyers and with judges, gave good reason to suppose that the factors set out below and in my discussion of 'the tariff' in Chapter X would be important influences on sentence. Other factors, such as specific plea-bargains, special personal mitigation for individual defendants, quality of defence counsel, judicial sentiments about the contributory negligence of suppliers or about the handling of the defence case (for example, attacks on police or prosecution witnesses), could not be included in a documentary study such as this, and this may explain why the variables I *could* use predicted only 37·4 per cent of variations in sentence.

Given the size of sample (215), I thought it worthwhile to attempt a statistical analysis of the ability of each of the variables and 'tariff clusters' to predict variations in sentence. Multiple regression appeared to be the most appropriate tool for this purpose, since it uses the pattern of correlations between variables to determine the relative effect of each variable, once its associations with other variables have been taken into account (see Maxwell, 1977). Multiple regression does have the potential disadvantage that those variables which are ordered first may exhaust some of the predictive power of those variables ordered later, but this occurs mainly when the variables are highly intercorrelated. In this study, intercorrelations were measured with both Pearson and rank-order methods, and the only very significant relationships were between the variables of time spent previously in prison, number of previous convictions, and number of previous fraud convictions. Even then, the maximum Pearson correlation coefficient was 0·570 – the highest found on any measure. In any case, these three variables were included together in one 'step' of the regression, so there is no reason to suppose that the results are contaminated by the ordering to any significant extent.

The results of the multiple regression analysis, along with the simple regression of each variable against sentence imposed, are set out in Table B.1 below.

TABLE B.1 Predictors of sentence variations in long-firm fraud cases: a
regression analysis

Variable	Multiple regression	Simple regression	R square change
Being a principal	·27560	·27560	·07595
Time spent in prison before	·40925	·32377	·09153
Plea	·40944	− ·01455	·00848
Age	·41875	·00447	·00766
Number of previous fraud convictions	·45556	·32678	·00348
Number of previous convictions	·45819	·26576	·00247
Size of fraud	·59974	·41856	·15310

The major unexpected consequence of these findings was that the
size of the fraud played as big a part as it did, particularly since the
qualitative analysis of the data showed little correspondence
between size of fraud and number of co-conspirators or number of
previous convictions. It is clear, however, that no single variable can
account for more than 15·31 per cent of the variations in sentence.

References

ADVISORY COUNCIL ON THE PENAL SYSTEM (1978), *Sentences of Imprisonment*. London: HMSO.

ALBINI, J. (1971), *The American Mafia: Genesis of a Legend*. New York: Appleton-Century-Crofts.

AUBERT, W. (1977), 'White-collar crime and social structure', in Geis and Meier (eds.) (1977). *White-Collar Crime* (op. cit.).

AUSTIN J. L. (1979), *Philosophical Papers*. Oxford: Oxford University Press.

BACHRACH P. and BARATZ, M. (1963), 'Decisions and nondecisions', *American Political Science Review*, **57**, 641–7.

BALDWIN, J. and McCONVILLE, S. (1977), *Negotiated Justice*. Oxford: Martin Robertson.

BALDWIN, J. and McCONVILLE, S. (1979), *Jury Trials*. Oxford: Martin Robertson.

BALL, C., CHESTER, L., and PERROTT, R. (1978), *Cops and Robbers*. London: André Deutsch.

BARRÈRE, A. and LELAND, C. (1879), *Dictionary of Slang, Jargon and Cant*, 2nd edition. London: Bell.

BECKER, H. (1963), *Outsiders*. New York: The Free Press of Glencoe (Macmillan Publishing Co., Inc.).

BECKER, H. (1967), 'Whose side are we on?', *Social Problems*, **14** (Winter), 239–47.

BEQUAI, A. (1978), *White-Collar Crime*. Lexington: Lexington Books.

BEQUAI, A. (1979), *Organised Crime*. Lexington: Lexington Books.

BEYLEVELD, D. (1978), *The effectiveness of general deterrents against crime: an annotated bibliography*. Cambridge: Cambridge Institute of Criminology (microfiche).

BEYLEVELD, D. and WILES, P. (1979), 'How to retain your soul and be a political deviant', in Downes, D. and Rock, P., (eds.), *Deviant Interpretations* (op. cit.).

BONGER, W. (1916), *Criminality and Economic Conditions*. Boston: Little, Brown.

BOTTOMS, A. E. (1977), 'Reflections on the renaissance of dangerousness', *The Howard Journal of Penology and Crime Prevention*, **16**, 70–96.

BOX, S. (1971), *Deviance, Reality, and Society*. Eastbourne: Holt, Rinehart & Winston.

BRECHT, B. (1976), *The Threepenny Novel*. Harmondsworth: Penguin.

BREED, B. (1979), *White-collar Bird*. London: John Clare.

CARLEN, P. (1976), *Magistrates' Justice*. Oxford: Martin Robertson.

CARSON, W. G. (1970), 'White-collar crime and the enforcement of factory legislation', *British Journal of Criminology*, **10**, 383–98.

CARSON, W. G. (1974), 'Symbolic and instrumental dimensions of early factory legislation', in Hood, R. G. (ed.), *Crime, Criminology, and Public Policy*. London: Heinemann.

CARSON, W. G. (1979), 'The conventionalisation of early factory crime', *International Journal for the Sociology of Law*, **7**, 37–60.

CATO CARTER, F. (1972), *The Real Business*. London: private print.

CHAMBLISS, W. (1972), *Box Man*. New York: Harper Row.

CHAMBLISS, W. (1978), *On the take*. London: Indiana university Press.

CHAMBLISS, W. and SEIDMAN, R. (1971), *Law, Order, and Power*. Reading: Addison-Wesley Publishing Co.

CHAMBLISS, W. and MANKOFF, M. (1976), *Whose Law? What Order?* New York: John Wiley & Sons.

CHIRICOS, T. and WALDO, G. P. (1970), 'Punishment and crime: an examination of some empirical evidence', *Social Problems*, **18** (Fall), 200–17.

CICOUREL, A. V. (1968), *The Social Organisation of Juvenile Justice*. New York: John Wiley & Sons.

CLINARD, M. (1952), *The Black Market: a Study of White-Collar Crime*. New York: Holt, Rinehart & Winston.

CLINARD, M. (1954), 'Review of Cressey's *Other People's Money*', *American Sociological Review*, **19**, 362.

COHEN, A. K. (1977), 'The concept of criminal organisation', *British Journal of Criminology*, **17**, 97–111.

COHEN, S. (1973), 'Property destruction: motives and meanings', in Ward, C. (ed.), *Vandalism*. London: Architectural Press.

COHEN, S. (1979), 'Guilt, justice, and tolerance', in *Downes, D. and Rock, P.* (eds.), *Deviant Interpretations*, op. cit.

COHEN, S. and TAYLOR, L. (1972), *Psychological Survival*. Harmondsworth: Penguin.

CONKLIN, J. (1977), *Illegal But Not Criminal*. Englewood Cliffs: Prentice-Hall.

COSSON, J. (1971), *Les Industriels de la Fraude Fiscale*. Paris: Éditions de Seuil.

COX, B., SHIRLEY, J. and SHORT, M. (1977), *The Fall of Scotland Yard*. Harmondsworth: Penguin.

CRESSEY, D. R. (1953), *Other People's Money*. Glencoe: Free Press.

CRESSEY, D. R. (1962), 'Role theory, differential association, and compulsive crimes' in Rose, A. (ed.), *Human Behaviour and Social Processes*. New York: Houghton & Miflin.

CRESSEY, D. R. (1965), 'The respectable criminal', in Short, J. (ed.) *Modern Criminals*. New York: Transaction-Aldine.

CRESSEY, D. R. (1969), *Theft of the Nation*. New York: Harper & Row.

CRESSEY, D. R. (1972), *Criminal Organisation*. London: Heinemann.

CRIMINAL LAW REVISION COMMITTEE (1966), *8th Report: Theft and Related Offences*. London: HMSO, Cmnd 2977.

CRIMINAL LAW REVISION COMMITTEE (1974), *Working Paper: Section 16 of the Theft Act 1968*. London: HMSO.

DAVIS, A. (1971), *If They Come in the Morning*. New York: Orbach & Chambers.

DE FRANCO, E. J. (1973), *Anatomy of a Scam*. Washington D.C.; US Department of Justice.

DITTON, J. (1977), *Part-time Crime: An Ethnography of Fiddling and Pilferage*. London: Macmillan.

DITTON, J. (1979), *Controlology: Beyond the New Criminology*. London: Macmillan.

DOWNES, D. and ROCK, P. (eds.) (1979), *Deviant Interpretations*. Oxford: Martin Robertson.

EDELHERTZ, H. (1970), *The Nature, Impact, and Prosecution of White-Collar Crime*. Washington D.C.: Government Printing Office.

EDELHERTZ, H. and ROGOVIN, C. (eds.) (1980), *A National Strategy for Containing White-Collar Crime*. Lexington: Lexington Books.

THE ENCYCLOPAEDIC DICTIONARY (1909), London: Cassells.

ERIKSON, K. (1964), 'Notes on the sociology of deviance', in Becker, H. (ed.), *The Other Side*. New York: The Free Press of Glencoe (Macmillan Publishing Co., Inc.).

EYSENCK, H. (1977), *Crime and Personality*. London: Paladin.

FINER, M. (1966), 'Company Fraud', *The Accountant*, 5 November 1966, 583–8.

FORDHAM, P. (1972), *Inside the Underworld*. London: George Allen & Unwin.

FREDUR, T. (1879), *Sketches from Shady Places*. London: privately printed.

GEIS, G. and MEIER, R. (eds.) (1977), *White-Collar Crime*. New York: Free Press.

GERTH, H. and MILLS, C. (1954), *Character and Social Structure*. London: Routledge & Kegan Paul.

GIBBONS, D. (1977), *Society, Crime, and Criminal Careers*, 3rd edn. Englewood Cliffs: Prentice Hall.

GIBBS, J. P. (1975), *Crime, Punishment, and Deterrence*. New York: Elsevier.

GLASER, D. (1978), *Crime in Our Changing Society*. New York: Holt, Rinehart & Winston.

GOFFMAN, E. (1952), 'On cooling the mark out', *Psychiatry*, **15**, no. 4, 451–63.

GOFFMAN, E. (1971), *Relations in Public*. London: Allen Lane.

GOWER, L. C. B. (1979), *Modern Company Law*, 4th edn. London: Stevens.

GUNNINGHAM, N. (1974), *Pollution, Social Interest, and the Law*. Oxford: Martin Robertson.

HOUSE OF COMMONS (1950–1), *Report of a Committee to Review Punishments in Prisons, Borstal Institutions, Approved Schools and Remand Homes, Parts I and II. Prisons and Borstal Institutions*. Cmnd 8356; Sessional Papers 1950–1, vol. XVIII.

HADDEN, T. (1967a), 'The development and administration of the English law of criminal fraud. Cambridge: PhD thesis.

HADDEN, T. (1967b), 'The origin and development of conspiracy to defraud', *American Journal of Legal History*.

HADDEN, T. (1977), *Company Law and Capitalism*, 2nd edn. London: Weidenfeld & Nicholson.

HALL, J. (1952), *Theft, Law and Society*. Indiannapolis: Bobbs-Merrill.

HALL. S., CRITCHER, C., JEFFERSON, T., CLARKE, J. and ROBERTS, B. (1978), *Policing the Crisis*. London: Macmillan.

HARRÉ, R., and SECORD, P. (1972), *The Explanation of Social Behaviour*. Oxford: Basil Blackwell.

HARTUNG, F. E. (1965), *Crime, Law, and Society*. Detroit: Wayne State University Press.

HARTUNG, F. E. (1977), 'White-collar offences in the wholesale meat industry in Detroit' in Geis, G. and Meier, R. (eds.), *White-Collar Crime*. op. cit.

HENRY, S. (1976), 'Fencing with accounts', *British Journal of Law and Society*. **3(1)**, 91–100.

HENRY, S. (1978), *The Hidden Economy*. Oxford: Martin Robertson.

HILL, B. (1955), *Boss of Britain's Underworld*. London: Naldrett Press.

HIRSCHI, T. (1970), *The Causes of Delinquency*. Berkeley: University of California Press.

HOGARTH, J. (1971), *Sentencing as a Human Process*. Toronto: University of Toronto Press.

HOLDSWORTH, W. (1925), *A History of English Law*. London: Methuen.

HOME OFFICE (1978), *Criminal Statistics for England and Wales, 1977*. London: HMSO, Cmnd 7289.

HOME OFFICE (1979), *Criminal Statistics for England and Wales, 1978*. London: HMSO, Cmnd 7670.

HOOD, R. G. (1962), *Sentencing in Magistrates' Courts*. London: Stevens.

HOOD, R. G. (1972), *Sentencing the Motoring Offender*. London: Heinemann.

HOOVER, J. E. (1962), 'Investigation of fraudulent bankruptcies by the F.B.I.', *New York Certified Public Accountant*, 1962, 187–94.

HOOVER, J. E. (1967), 'The Christmas trade no business wants', *Nation's Business*, 45–8.

HOTTEN, J. C. (1874), *The Slang Dictionary*. London: Chatto & Windus.

HOWSON, G. (1970), *Thief-Taker General: the Rise and Fall of Jonathan Wild*. London: Hutchinson.

HUGHES, E. (1945), 'Dilemmas and contradictions of status', *American Journal of Sociology*, L., (March), 353–9.

IANNI, F. (1975), *Black Mafia*. New York: Simon & Schuster.

JACKSON, R. (1967), *Occupied with Crime*. London: Harrap.

JOHNSON, S. (1773), *A Dictionary of the English Language*, 4th edn. London: Bell.

JUSTICE (1980), *Breaking the Rules*. London: Justice.

KELLENS, G. (1974), *Banqueroute et Banqueroutiers*, Coll. 'Psychologie et sciences humaines'. Bruxelles: Dessart et Mardaga.

KELLENS, G. (1977), 'Sociological and psychological aspects of economic crime', in Council of Europe, Strasbourg, *Criminological Aspects of Economic Crime*, Collected Studies in Criminological Research, vol. XV.

KITSUSE, J. (1962), 'Societal reaction to deviant behaviour: problems of theory and method', *Social Problems*, **9** (Winter), 247–56.

KITSUSE, J. and CICOUREL, A. (1963), 'A note on the uses of official statistics', *Social Problems*, **11**, 131–9.

KLAPP, O. (1969), *Collective Search for Identity*. New York: Holt, Rinehart & Winston.

KLOCKARS, C. B. (1975), *The Professional Fence*. London: Tavistock.

KOSSACK, N. E. (1964), 'New steps to frustrate fraud', *Credit and Financial Management*, June 1964, 12–45.

KOSSACK, N. E. (1965), 'Scam, the planned bankruptcy racket', *New York Certified Public Accountant*, 417–23.

KOSSACK, N. E., and DAVIDSON, S. (1966), 'Bankruptcy fraud: the unholy alliance moves in', *Credit and Financial Management*, April 1966, 20–4.

LEIGH, L. H. (1977a), 'Policy and punitive measures in respect of economic offences', in Council of Europe, Strasbourg, *Criminological Aspects of Economic Crime*.

LEIGH, L. H. (1977b), 'Some aspects of crimes in bankruptcy', paper presented at a conference on Economic Crimes. University of London.

LEIGH, L. H. (ed.) (1980), *Economic Crime in Europe*. London: Macmillan.

LEMERT, E. (1972), *Human Deviance, Social Problems, and Social Control*. New York: Prentice-Hall.

LEVI, M. (1979), The organisation and control of long-firm fraud, PhD thesis. University of Southampton:

LEVI, M. (1979a), 'Long-firm fraud, sentencing, and the Advisory Council', *The Howard Journal*, xviii, pp. 92–99.

LITHNER, K. (1978), personal communication, unpublished.

LOGAN, C. H. (1972), 'General deterrent effects of imprisonment', *Social Forces*, **51** (September), 64–73.

LUCAS, N. (1969), *Britain's Gangland*. London: W. H. Allen.

MACK, J. (1964), 'Full-time miscreants, delinquent neighbourhoods, and criminal networks', *British Journal of Sociology*, **15**, 38–53.

MACK, J. (1970), 'The able criminal', in Mack, *The Crime Industry*, (op. cit.).

MACK, J. (1975), *The Crime Industry*. London: Saxon House.

MACK, J. (1976), 'Full-time major criminals and the courts', *Modern Law Review*, **39**, 241–67.

MANNHEIM, H. (1940), *Social Aspects of Crime in England between the Wars*. London: George Allen & Unwin.

MARK, R. (1973), 'Minority Verdict'. London: BBC Publications.

MARK, R. (1978), *In the Office of Constable*. London: Collins.

MARTIN, J. P. (1962), *Offenders as Employees*. London: Macmillan.

MARTIN, J. P. and WEBSTER, D. (1971), *The Social Consequences of Conviction*. London: Heinemann.

MATZA, D. (1964), *Delinquency and Drift*. New York: John Wiley & Sons.

MATZA, D. (1969), *Becoming Deviant*. New Jersey: Prentice-Hall.

MAURER, D. (1940), *The Big Con*. New York: Bobbs–Merrill.

MAURER, D. (1964), *Whizz Mob*. New Haven: College and University Press.

MAXWELL, A. E. (1977), *Multivariate Analysis in Behavioural Research*. London: Chapman & Hall.

MAYHEW, H. (1862), *London Labour and the London Poor*. London: Griffin, Bohn.

MILLEN, E. (1972), *Specialist in Crime*. London: Harrap.

MILLS, C. WRIGHT (1940), 'Situated actions and vocabularies of motive', *American Sociological Review*, **5** (4), 904–13.

MONAHAN, J. (1975), 'The prediction of violence', in Chappell, D. and Monahan, J. (eds.), *Violence and Criminal Justice*. Lexington: Lexington Books.

MOORE, M. G. (1933), *Frauds and Swindles*. London: Gee & Co.

MORRIS, N. and HAWKINS, G. (1970), *The Honest Politician's Guide to Crime Control*. Chicago: University of Chicago Press.

MORRIS, T. (1965), 'The social toleration of crime' in Klare, H. (ed.), *Changing Concepts of Crime and its Treatment*. Oxford: Pergamon.

MORRIS, T. (1976), *Deviance and Control: the Secular Heresy*. London: Hutchinson.

McCLINTOCK, D. and GIBSON, E. (1961), *Robbery in London*. London: Macmillan.

McINTOSH, M. (1975), *The Organisation of Crime*. London: Macmillan.

McINTOSH, M. (1976), 'Thieves and fences: markets and power in professional crime', *British Journal of Criminology*, 259–66.

NETTLER, G. (1974), 'Embezzlement without problems', *British Journal of Criminology*, **14**, 70–7.

NEWMAN, D. J. (1977), 'White-collar crime: an overview and analysis' in Geis, G. and Meier, R. (eds.), *White-Collar Crime*, (op. cit.).

OGILVIE, (1882), *Oxford English Dictionary*. Oxford: Oxford University Press.

PAULUS, I. (1974), *The Search for Pure Food*. Oxford: Martin Robertson.

PAYNE, L. (1973), *The Brotherhood*. London: Michael Joseph.

PEARCE, F. (1976), *Crimes of the Powerful*. London: Pluto Press.

PEARSON, J. (1972), *The Profession of Violence*. London: Weidenfeld & Nicolson.

PEASE, K. and WOLFSON, J. (1979), 'Incapacitation Studies' in *The Howard Journal of Penology and Crime Prevention*, XVIII (3), 160–8.

PELHAM, C. (1841), *Chronicles of Crime*. London: privately printed.

PETERSILIA, J. (1977), 'Developing programs for the habitual offender', in Huff, C. Ronald (ed.), *Contemporary Corrections*. Beverley Hills: Sage.

PHELAN, J. (1953), *The Underworld*. London: Harrap.

PILIAVIN, I. and BRIAR, S. (1964), 'Police encounters with juveniles', *American Journal of Sociology*, **52**, 206–14.

PLUMMER, K. (1979), 'Misunderstanding labelling perspectives', in Downes, D. and Rock, P. (eds.), *Deviant Interpretations*, (op. cit.).

POLSKY, N. (1971), *Hustlers, Beats, and Others*. Harmondsworth: Penguin.

RADZINOWICZ, L. and HOOD, R. G. (1978), 'A dangerous direction for sentencing reform', *Criminal Law Review*, 713–24.

REISS, A. (1971), *The Police and the Public*. New Haven: Yale University Press.

REUSCHEL, R. (1895), *The Knights of Industry*. London: privately printed.

ROCK, P. (1973a), *Deviant Behaviour*. London: Hutchinson.

ROCK, P. (1973b), *Making People Pay*. London: Routledge & Kegan Paul.

RUBINGTON, E. and WEINBERG, S. (1968), *Deviance: The Interactionist Perspective*, 1st edn. New York: Macmillan.

RUSSELL, K. (1978), *Complaints against the Police*, 2nd edn. Leicester: Milltak.

SCHATTSCHNEIDER, E. (1960), *The Semi-Sovereign People*. New York: Holt, Rinehart & Winston.

SCHRAGER, L. S. and SHORT, J. F. (1980), 'How serious a crime? Perceptions of organisational and common crimes' in Geis, G. and Stotland, E. (eds.) *White-Collar Crime: Theory and Research*, Beverley Hills: Sage.

SCHUTZ, A. (1967a), in Natanson, M. (ed.), *Alfred Schutz Collected Papers*, Vol. II. The Hague: Martinus Nijhoff.

SCHUTZ, A. (1967b), in Natanson, M. (op. cit.), vol. I.

SCOTT, M. B. and LYMAN, S. M. (1970), 'Accounts, deviance, and the social order' in Douglas, J. B. (ed.), *Deviance and Respectability*. London: Basic Books.

SHANNON, H. A. (1931), 'The coming of general limited liability', *Economic History*, **2**, 267–91.

SHANNON, H. A. (1933), 'The limited companies of 1866–1883', *The Economic History Review*, vol. 4(3), 290–316.

SMIGEL, E. O. and ROSS, H. L. (1970), *Crimes against Bureaucracy*. New York: Van Nostrand Reinhold.

SMITH, J. C. (1979), *The Law of Theft*, 4th edn. London: Butterworth.

SPARKS, R. F., GENN, H. and DODD, D. (1977), *Surveying Victims*. London: Wiley.

STOTLAND, E., BRINTNALL, M., L'HEREUX, A., and ASHMORE, E. (1980), 'Do convictions deter home repair fraud?' in Geis, G. and Stotland, E. (eds.) *White-Collar Crime: Theory and Research*, Beverley Hills: Sage.

SUTHERLAND, E. H. (1937), *The Professional Thief*. Chicago: University of Chicago Press.

SUTHERLAND, E. H. (1961), *White-Collar Crime*. New York: Holt, Rinehart & Winston.

SUTHERLAND, E. H. and CRESSEY, D. R. (1974), *Principles of Criminology*, 9th edn. Philadelphia: Lippincott.

SYKES, G. and MATZA, D. (1957), 'Techniques of neutralisation: a theory of delinquency', *American Sociological Review*, **22**, December, 664–70.

TANNENBAUM, V. (1938), *Crime and the Community*. New York: McGraw-Hill.

TAWNEY, R. (1920), *The Acquisitive Society*. London: Bell.

TAYLOR, L. (1970), 'The significance and interpretation of replies to motivational questions: the case of sex offenders', *Sociology*, **6**(1), January, 23–40.

TAYLOR, L. (1979), 'Vocabularies, rhetorics, and grammar: problems in the sociology of motivation', in Downes, D. and Rock, P. (eds.), *Deviant Interpretations*, (op. cit.).

TERESA, V. (1973), *My Life in the Mafia*. St. Albans: Granada.

THOMAS, D. A. (1970), *Principles of Sentencing*, 1st edn. London: Heinemann.

THOMAS, D. A. (1978), *Principles of Sentencing*, 2nd edn. London: Heinemann.

THOMPSON, R. (1977), *The Law Relating to Bankruptcy, Liquidations, and Receiverships*, 6th edn. London: Macdonald & Evans.

THORP, A. (1954), *Calling Scotland Yard*. London: Allen Wingate.

TIEDEMANN, K. and SASSE, C. (1973), *Delinquenzprophylaxe, Kreditsicherung und Datenschutz in den Wirtschaft*. Koln: Karl Heymanns.

TOCH, H. (1972), *Violent Men*. Harmondsworth: Penguin.

TURK, A. (1969), *Criminality and the Legal Order*. Chicago: Rand, McNally & Co.

VAN DEN HAAG, E. (1975), *Punishing Criminals: Concerning a Very Old and Painful Question*. New York: Basic Books.

VAN DINE *et al.* (1977), 'The incapacitation of the dangerous offender: a statistical experiment', *Journal of Research in Crime and Delinquency*, January, 23–34.

VOLD, G. (1958), *Theoretical Criminology*. Oxford: Oxford University Press.

VON HIRSCH, A. (1972), 'Prediction of criminal conduct and preventative confinement of convicted persons', *Buffalo Law Review*, **21**, 717–58.

VON HIRSCH, A. (1976), *Doing Justice*. New York: McGraw-Hill.

WALKER, N. (1972), *Sentencing in a Rational Society*. Harmondsworth: Penguin.

WALSH, M. E. (1977), *The Fence*. Westport: Greenwood Press.

WERTHMAN, C. and PILIAVIN, I. (1967), 'Gang members and the police', in Bordua, D. J. (ed.), *The Police: Six Sociological Essays*. New York: John Wiley & Sons.

WEST, R. (1952), *The Meaning of Treason*. London: The Reprint Society.

WHITAKER, B. (1979), *The Police in Society*. London: Eyre Methuen.

WILKINS, L. (1964), *Social Deviance*. London: Tavistock.

WILKINS, L. (1965), 'New thinking in criminal statistics', *Journal of Criminal Law, Criminology, and Police Science*, **56**, 277–84.

WILLIAMS, G. (1978), *A Textbook of Criminal Law*. London: Stevens.

WILSON, J. Q. (1975), *Thinking about Crime*. New York: Basic Books.

ZANDER, M. (1974), 'Are too many professional criminals avoiding conviction?', *Modern Law Review*, **34**, 26–61.

Index